Genders and Sexualities in History

Series Editors: John Arnold, Joanna Bourke and Sean Brady

Palgrave Macmillan's series, Genders and Sexualities in History, aims to accommodate and foster new approaches to historical research in the fields of genders and sexualities. The series will promote world-class scholarship that concentrates upon the interconnected themes of genders, sexualities, religions/religiosity, civil society, class formations, politics and war.

Historical studies of gender and sexuality have often been treated as disconnected fields, while in recent years historical analyses in these two areas have synthesized, creating new departures in historiography. By linking genders and sexualities with questions of religion, civil society, politics and the contexts of war and conflict, this series will reflect recent developments in scholarship, moving away from the previously dominant and narrow histories of science, scientific thought, and legal processes. The result brings together scholarship from contemporary, modern, early modern, medieval, classical and non-Western history to provide a diachronic forum for scholarship that incorporates new approaches to genders and sexualities in history

Confronting Modernity in Fin-de-Siècle France situates the body and sexuality at the heart of what it meant to be 'French'. Profoundly sensitive to power and its deployment, the volume contributes to our understanding of the sense of national crisis that emerged during the Third Republic. Masculinity is as rigorously explored as femininity. Central themes include the gendered nature of republicanism, relations of authority between physicians (including psychiatrists) and clerics, and conflicting interpretations of bourgeois codes of honour. The effect is a reinterpretation of this period of French history that also has resonance for the history of the rest of Europe.

Titles include

Matthew Cook
QUEER DOMESTICITIES
Homosexuality and Home Life in Twentieth-Century London

Jennifer Evans
RECONSTRUCTION SITES
Spaces of Sexual Encounter in Cold War Berlin

Christopher E. Forth and Elinor Accampo (*editors*)
CONFRONTING MODERNITY IN FIN-DE-SIÈCLE FRANCE
Bodies, Minds and Gender

Dagmar Herzog (*editor*)
BRUTALITY AND DESIRE
War and Sexuality in Europe's Twentieth Century

Jessica Meyer
MEN OF WAR
Masculinity and the First World War in Britain

Jennifer D. Thibodeaux (*editor*)
NEGOTIATING CLERICAL IDENTITIES
Priests, Monks and Masculinity in the Middle Ages

Genders and Sexualities in History Series
Series Standing Order 978-0-230-55185-5 Hardback 978-0-230-55186-2 Paperback
(*outside North America only*)

You can receive future titles in this series as they are published by placing a standing
order. Please contact your bookseller or, in case of difficulty, write to us at the address
below with your name and address, the title of the series and the ISBN quoted above.

Customer Services Department, Macmillan Distribution Ltd, Houndmills,
Basingstoke, Hampshire RG21 6XS, England

Confronting Modernity in Fin-de-Siècle France

Bodies, Minds and Gender

Edited by

Christopher E. Forth
Howard Professor of Humanities & Western Civilization, University of Kansas

Elinor Accampo
Professor of History, University of Southern California

palgrave
macmillan

First published 2010 by
PALGRAVE MACMILLAN

Palgrave Macmillan in the UK is an imprint of Macmillan Publishers Limited,
registered in England, company number 785998, of Houndmills, Basingstoke,
Hampshire RG21 6XS.

Palgrave Macmillan in the US is a division of St Martin's Press LLC,
175 Fifth Avenue, New York, NY 10010.

Palgrave Macmillan is the global academic imprint of the above companies
and has companies and representatives throughout the world.

Palgrave® and Macmillan® are registered trademarks in the United States,
the United Kingdom, Europe and other countries.

ISBN 978–0–230–22099–7   hardback

This book is printed on paper suitable for recycling and made from fully
managed and sustained forest sources. Logging, pulping and manufacturing
processes are expected to conform to the environmental regulations of the
country of origin.

A catalogue record for this book is available from the British Library.

A catalog record for this book is available from the Library of Congress.

10 9 8 7 6 5 4 3 2 1
19 18 17 16 15 14 13 12 11 10

Printed and bound in Great Britain by
CPI Antony Rowe, Chippenham and Eastbourne

This book is dedicated to Robert A. Nye
Scholar, Teacher, Friend

Contents

Acknowledgements

This volume is the work of a number of confidants, conspirators and accomplices, and it was only a matter of time before the guilty ones were named. Michael Wilson helped hatch the original plan, Mark Micale offered some useful tips on how to pull it off, and Mary Jo Nye was our inside agent from the beginning. However it was Ed Berenson who first proposed showcasing these chapters as conference papers. This is how many contributors ended up presenting their work in two special sessions organized for the 23rd Annual Meeting of the Society for French Historical Studies, held in Houston, Texas (15–17 March 2007). We accuse Sarah Fishman and the other SFHS organizers of very generously accommodating our unconventional proposal, and Angus McLaren of offering constructive comments on one of the panels. Of course it wouldn't have been possible without a rogue's gallery of hardened contributors who were in on it from the start and who patiently put up with numerous delays and editorial queries. The spotlight must also be turned on Michael Strang and Ruth Ireland at Palgrave for supporting the project and shepherding it to completion, and the anonymous readers whose comments improved the whole. By the time Barbara Slater finished her excellent copyediting we were in the clear.

The guiltiest party, however, remains Robert A. Nye. Without his mentoring, friendship, example, and inspiration none of us would have bothered.

"A Tribute to Robert A. Nye"

$$\frac{I + II}{(7E) \quad (8A)}$$

Notes on Contributors

Elinor Accampo is Professor of History at the University of Southern California. She is author of *Blessed Motherhood, Bitter Fruit: Nelly Roussel and the Politics of Female Pain in Third Republic France* (2006); co-editor with Rachel Fuchs and Mary Lynn Stewart of *Gender and the Politics of Social Reform in France* (1995); and author of *Industrialization, Family Life, and Class Relations* (1989).

James Smith Allen is Professor of History at Southern Illinois University Carbondale. His books include *Popular French Romanticism: Authors, Readers, and Books in the 19th Century* (1981), *In the Public Eye: a History of Reading in Modern France, 1800–1940* (1991), '*In the Solitude of My Soul': The Diary of Geneviève Bréton, 1867–1871* (1993), and *Poignant Relations: Three Modern French Women* (2000). He has just completed a book-length reflection on the intersection between personal and historical memory, entitled *A Privileged Past: Recollections of a World Apart in Six Acts*. His book on women in modern French civic culture, *Sisters of Another Sort: Freemason Women and Modern French Civic Life, 1725–1940*, is nearly finished.

Venita Datta is Professor of French at Wellesley College. She is the author of *Birth of a National Icon: the Literary Avant-Garde and the Origins of the Intellectual in France* (1999) and is currently preparing a book manuscript entitled *Legends, Heroes and Superwomen: Gender, Politics and National Identity in Fin-de-Siècle France*. Her recent articles include ' "L'appel au soldat": Visions of the Napoleonic Legend in Popular Culture of the Belle Epoque,' *French Historical Studies* (2005), 'Sur les boulevards: les représentations de Jeanne d'Arc dans le théâtre populaire,' *CLIO, Histoire, Femmes et Société* (2006), and 'Superwomen or Slaves? Women Writers, Male Critics and Nietzsche in Belle-Époque France,' *Historical Reflections/Réflexions historiques* (Fall 2007).

Christopher E. Forth is the Howard Professor of Humanities & Western Civilization at the University of Kansas. His books include *The Dreyfus Affair and the Crisis of French Manhood* (2004), *Masculinity in the Modern West: Gender, Civilization and the Body* (2008), and the co-edited volumes *Cultures of the Abdomen: Diet, Digestion and Fat in the Modern World* (2005) and *French Masculinities: History, Culture and Politics* (2007).

Rachel G. Fuchs is Distinguished Foundation Professor of History at Arizona State University where she has been since 1983. She has published extensively on various aspects of women's and family history in modern France. Her books include *Abandoned Children: Foundlings and Child Welfare in Nineteenth-Century France* (1984), *Poor and Pregnant in Paris: Strategies for Survival in the Nineteenth Century* (1992), *Gender and the Politics of Social Reform in France, 1870–1914* (with Elinor Accampo and Mary Lynn Stewart, 1995), *Gender and Poverty in Nineteenth-Century Europe* (2005), and *Contested Paternity: Constructing Families in Modern France* (2008). Fuchs earned a PhD from Indiana University and has held fellowships from the National Endowment for the Humanities and the Camargo Foundation. In 2005 she received the Distinguished Faculty Award from the College of Liberal Arts and Sciences at Arizona State University.

Ruth Harris is Fellow and Tutor at New College, Oxford. She is the author of numerous articles and books on the history of the human sciences and religion in modern France, notably *Murders and Madness: Medicine, Law, and Society in the Fin de Siècle* (1989) and *Lourdes: Body and Spirit in the Secular Age* (1999). She has almost finished a large history of the Dreyfus Affair in which she examines the emotional and spiritual reasons behind the passionate engagement of both Dreyfusards and their opponents in this *cause célèbre*.

Steven C. Hause is Senior Scholar in the Humanities and Co-Director of European Studies at Washington University in St Louis and Professor Emeritus and Thomas Jefferson Fellow at the University of Missouri – St Louis. He is the President of the Society for French Historical Studies (2008–09) and has previously served as President of the Western Society for French History (1987–88). He is the author or co-author of several books including *Women's Suffrage and Social Politics in the French Third Republic* (1984), *Hubertine Auclert: the French Suffragette* (1987), *Feminisms of the Belle Époque* (1995), *Hubertine Auclert: pionnière du féminisme* (2007) and three textbooks. His essays on women's rights have appeared in the *American Historical Review* (1981), *Catholic Historical Review* (1981), *Behind the Lines* (1986), and *Le Siècle des féminismes* (2006). Essays from his current research, on the role of the French Protestant community in shaping the Third Republic, have appeared in *French Historical Studies* (1989), *The Columbia History of Twentieth-Century French Thought* (2005), and *Religious Differences in France* (2006).

Andrea Mansker is Assistant Professor of History at the University of the South in Tennessee. She has published articles on feminism, sexuality and honor in fin-de-siècle France. She is currently completing a manuscript which considers how republican women and feminists prior to the Great War appropriated the masculine honor code to formulate 'modern' demands for legal, political, and sexual justice.

Karen Offen is a historian and independent scholar, affiliated as a Senior Scholar with the Michelle R. Clayman Institute for Gender Research, Stanford University. She publishes on the history of modern Europe, especially France and its global influence; Western thought and politics with reference to family, gender, and the relative status of women; historiography; women's history; national, regional, and global histories of feminism; and comparative history. She has co-edited three volumes of interpretative documentary texts: *Victorian Women: a Documentary Account of Women's Lives in Nineteenth-Century England, France, and the United States* (1981), and the two-volume *Women, the Family, and Freedom: the Debate in Documents, 1750–1950* (1983). Her monograph, *Paul de Cassagnac and the Authoritarian Tradition in Nineteenth-Century France*, appeared in 1991. She has also co-edited the 1991 volume, *Writing Women's History: International Perspectives* (with Ruth Roach Pierson and Jane Rendall), on behalf of the International Federation for Research in Women's History. Karen's latest book is *European Feminisms, 1700–1950: a Political History* (2000). She is currently completing a book on the 'woman question' debate in modern France and an edited volume, *Globalizing Feminisms before 1945*.

Matt T. Reed is an independent historian based in London. He is also Director of Analysis and Partnerships with the Aga Khan Development Network. Prior to joining AKDN, he held positions at the Keck Graduate Institute of Applied Life Sciences, the John D. and Catherine T. MacArthur Foundation, and the Salzburg Seminar. He is currently preparing a book manuscript entitled, 'Making the Case: the Evolution of the Psychiatric Case Study in Nineteenth-Century France.' His articles include, ' "La Manie d'écrire": Psychology, Auto-Observation, and Case History,' *Journal of the History of the Behavioral Sciences*, 25(3) (Summer 2004): 265–84, and 'Historicizing Inversion; or, How to Make a Homosexual,' *History of the Human Sciences*, 14(4) (November 2001): 1–30.

Charles Sowerwine is Professorial Fellow in History at the University of Melbourne. He entered the area of women's history with his 1973 PhD thesis, revised as *Sisters or Citizens? Women and Socialism in France since 1876* (1982). His 1982 *Journal of Modern History* article, 'Workers and Women in France before 1914: the Debate over the Couriau Affair,' received the Koren Prize from the Society for French Historical Studies. With Claude Maignien he wrote a biography of the pioneering socialist feminist, Dr Madeleine Pelletier (1992), the first woman psychiatry intern in France. His general history, *France since 1870: Culture, Politics, and Society* (Palgrave, 2001; 2nd edition, 2009), sought to mainstream gender history. He is currently working with Susan Foley on 'Passion and Politics: Léon Gambetta, Léonie Léon, and the Making of the Third Republic' (forthcoming from Palgrave, 2009).

Elizabeth A. Williams is Professor of History at Oklahoma State University. She is the author, most recently, of *A Cultural History of Medical Vitalism in Enlightenment Montpellier* (2003) and is currently working on a comparative history of women and psychiatry in modern France and Britain.

Michael L. Wilson is Associate Professor of History and Humanities at the University of Texas at Dallas. He has published articles on bohemianism, visual culture, and the history of sexuality.

Introduction: Confronting Modernity in Fin-de-Siècle France

Elinor Accampo and Christopher E. Forth

As Marshall Berman so eloquently stated in *All that is Solid Melts into Air* (1982), paradox and contradiction define the modern experience. His definition still stands as one of the most useful for understanding the late nineteenth century as well as our own:

> Modern environments and experiences cut across all boundaries of geography and ethnicity, of class and nationality, of religion and ideology: in this sense, modernity can be said to unite all mankind. But it is a paradoxical unity, a unity of disunity: it pours us all into a maelstrom of perpetual disintegration and renewal, of struggle and contradiction, of ambiguity and anguish.[1]

Although today we live amidst continuing changes and challenges generated by modern life, from a twenty-first century perspective it is nonetheless difficult to appreciate the subjective sensory experience of those who inhabited the nineteenth-century transformations wrought by industrialization, migration, imperial conquest, the rapid growth of cities, and the changes in everyday sensory stimuli. These phenomena, among numerous others, included the increased speed and frequency of train travel and rapid transit systems (both under and above ground) that transformed the social, psychological, and geographical space of human encounters. Phenomena from the rise of the mass press and the literacy to consume it to the multiple wonders of electricity transformed perceptions of reality, particularly in the instantaneous spread of words and of images. The press had the power not just to represent 'reality,' but to create its own, and to empower groups that had previously been voiceless – workers, feminists, bohemian artists, anarchists, and others who had the potential to, and often did, upset the social order. The rise of popular culture and mass consumption, and the visual bombardment of advertising cards and posters that accompanied it, threatened elite hegemony in all matters of taste and class distinctions. The acceleration of communications through the telegraph and telephone, in addition to print culture, photographs, and world exhibitions, not only gave access to the exotic, but reinforced fears about difference, global competition, and national identity.[2]

It is no wonder the diagnosis of 'neurasthenia,' the nervous disorder among bourgeois men resulting from the stresses of modern urban life, became epidemic in this period.[3] The 'unity of disunity' to which Berman refers blurred the very boundaries upon which identities were built: social class, sex, gender, race, nationality, and even what constituted the 'normal.' It is no wonder as well that bourgeois male elites embraced developments in science, medicine, economics, and political thought as intrinsically progressive phenomena that would allow them to impose order on the 'maelstrom' of the body politic, women, proletarians, sexual deviants, or the insane. Through such measures, they erroneously believed, order would also be conferred upon themselves.

Late nineteenth-century France experienced more than its share of the paradoxes and social ills associated with modernity. From its inception in 1792, the French experiment with a democratic republic – born of violent revolution against Church, monarchy, and aristocracy – was fraught with contradictions between the universalism of human rights and the practical need to deny certain categories of people the rights of citizenship. The first long-term success at this experiment – the Third Republic (1870–1940) – exhibited one of these contradictions by persistently refusing throughout its existence to grant women the vote, even when every other major Western nation which had not yet done so extended the franchise in the wake of the First World War. The early Third Republic (1870–1914) has long attracted the interest of historians, in particular because of its struggles with the status of women, but more generally too because of its tumultuous nature, and the fact that it represented a crossroads in the process of modernization between fin-de-siècle ambivalence about change and the brave new world of the 1920s. Emerging from the ashes of the Franco-Prussian War and the civil war of the Paris Commune, the early Third Republic suffered constant threats from the nationalist resurgence of the Boulanger Affair, the rise of militant trade unions, anarchist bombings of the 1890s, virulent anti-Semitism, and the explosive politics of the Dreyfus Affair (1894–1906). In many respects the experiences of this period explain how and why France, and other European nations, took the paths they did in the twentieth century.

Historians now recognize that France's weakened geopolitical status, partly as a result of the defeat of 1870, spawned deep fears about the mental and physical state of French citizens that were exacerbated by a precipitous decline in national birth rates. Politicians, health professionals, and social critics became obsessed with sexual and reproductive disorders, venereal disease, mental illness, alcoholism, emerging feminist movements, and other violations of the social and gender order that seemed symptomatic of the Republic itself and its broader engagement with modernity. For the French, then, modernity was a complex and double-sided phenomenon that propelled the nation towards the future while threatening to overturn many of its oldest traditions and newest achievements.

The real complexity of this tumultuous period has only become evident in recent decades, partly as a result of new developments in social and historical theory and historians' efforts to use these tools in novel ways. Many of these innovations came from France itself, notably among those intellectuals who came of age during the 1950s and 1960s and who are often described as 'postmodernist' or 'post-structuralist.' Of all the post-structuralist theorists who have risen to prominence in French and Anglophone scholarship since that time, Michel Foucault has had the most marked and durable impact on historians of France, particularly among those seeking to think beyond the methodologies offered by conventional social and political history. To historians accustomed to examining the emerging capitalist, political, legal, and social institutions of the nineteenth century as ways of understanding social conflict, Foucault offered an alternative model of power that emphasized the more fluid role played by discourses and techniques of constraint rather than the juridical power 'possessed' by specific individuals and institutions. As Foucault demonstrated, the post-revolutionary French world gave rise to 'disciplines' in new sciences such as criminology, penology, and psychiatry, and in the increasingly scientific field of medicine. In the absence of a monarchy, and with the waning power of the Church, the 'experts' in these professions assumed the discursive authority to distinguish truth from falsehood, particularly in their power to define the 'normal' and the 'pathological' or deviant.[4] These discourses and disciplines played a special role in the recently consolidated Third Republic, which grounded its secularist worldview in bodies of knowledge purporting to offer the light of 'truth' rather than the obfuscations of religious tradition or popular custom. Nevertheless, as Foucault reminds us, 'truth is a thing of this world' and necessarily bound up in knowledge regimes seeking to impose particular perspectives of social reality.[5]

An attention to the power of language to shape and alter our understandings of the social world has played a critical role in sensitizing scholars to how metaphors of, for instance, dirt, taste in food, or diagnoses of disease and weakness are often closely bound up with ideas about gender, class, race, and representations of the body politic. Acknowledging and unraveling the interarticulation of cultural categories, French historians have built upon Foucault's innovations to open up and pursue new paths of research and interpretation. The groundbreaking work of Georges Vigarello and Alain Corbin provided an early indication of the productive uses to which these ideas could be put. Inspired by Foucauldian analyses as well as the sociological theory of Norbert Elias, Vigarello's inquiry into the history of French notions of posture, cleanliness, and filth through the twentieth century revealed the complex ways in which the apparently 'natural' facts about the body are shaped, perceived, and experienced through culture over time.[6]

Related to this work are Corbin's well-known historical studies of prostitution, odor, church bells, and sea-bathing, which have been particularly
influential in 'somatizing' our views of class, gender, sexuality, and the
images of the nation.[7] The multifaceted and influential body of scholarship
that Vigarello and Corbin have developed since these books, culminating
in their three-volume joint venture with Jean-Jacques Courteline, *Histoire du
corps* (2005), attests to the continuing importance of viewing the body as
profoundly implicated in political institutions and social representations.[8]
Although works like these address a wider time-frame than the Third Republic, they have provided important methodological insights into how gender,
sexuality, and the body were bound up with representations of the nation
during the fin de siècle.

Describing, in a Foucauldian vein, the ways in which formal bodies
of knowledge construct (rather than simply 'discover') their subject matter represents an important dimension of this new direction in historical
scholarship. Studies of psychological knowledge figured prominently in new
histories produced during the 1980s, especially the works on crowd psychology by Robert Nye and Susanna Barrows and the articles written by
Jan Goldstein on anti-Semitism and hysteria.[9] This association between the
discourses of the human sciences and representations of the body politic
was further reinforced in Robert Nye's *Crime, Madness, & Politics in Modern
France: the Medical Concept of National Decline* (1984) and Daniel Pick's *Faces
of Degeneration: a European Disorder, c. 1848–c. 1918* (1989).[10] Both of these
works offered new ways of interpreting how the French and (in Pick's case)
Europeans more broadly, expressed a sense of pessimism and anxiety over
perceived racial, cultural, and national decline, a perspective that clearly
influenced decisions of political and social policy. Nye's work in particular
offered new models for analyzing social and cultural norms and conceptions
of the 'abnormal' constructed by criminology and anthropology. Particularly relevant to a rethinking of this period are Nye's contextualization of
the medical concepts of deviance and degeneration, and the use of medical
models of cultural crisis as a way to explain – and offer apparent cures for –
the widespread concerns about national decline that obsessed the French by
1900.

While the scholarship described above was hardly blind to issues of women,
gender, and sexuality, it was Joan Wallach Scott's highly influential discussion of gender as 'a useful category of historical analysis' that most
effectively demonstrated how post-structuralist methodologies could be fruitfully applied to the theory and practice of gender history. By outlining how
gender is 'a constitutive element of social relationships based on perceived
differences between the sexes, and ... a primary way of signifying relationships of power,'[11] Scott not only critiqued the social histories of the 1960s
through the 1980s that either completely ignored or focused entirely on
women, but she corrected the gender-blindness of Foucault's model of power

to account for the subtle and overt ways in which ideas about the masculine and the feminine operate in social discourses. This examination of the ways in which power is deployed through the categories of gender – and, by extension, those of class, race, and other vectors of difference – fostered greater sensitivity to the subtleties of language in politics and society during the Third Republic. Gender and other ways of perceiving difference became not merely 'useful' categories for historical analysis, but virtually indispensable ways of approaching the complexity of politics and society during this period.

A cross-fertilization between new developments in gender history and a growing attention to organicist models of the nation bore fruit fairly quickly, especially in studies that took women or sexual orientation as their focus. In notable works like Ruth Harris's *Murders and Madness: Medicine, Law, and Society in the Fin de Siècle* (1989), Mary Louise Roberts's *Civilization without Sexes: Restructuring Gender in Postwar France, 1917–1927* (1994), and Ann-Louise Shapiro's *Breaking the Codes: Female Criminality in Fin-de-Siècle Paris* (1996), the 'deviant' gender performances of certain women were shown to have been readily medicalized and deemed pathological by a spectrum of medical and state authorities during the Third Republic.[12] But other scholarship has also shown that women – especially journalists, literary figures, some feminists, and even some murderesses in this period – could successfully undertake unconventional behaviors if they cast themselves in proper 'performative' roles by manipulating cultural codes to their own ends.[13] Historians of sexuality have also profited by examining the ways in which images of sexual orientation were forged out of medical discourses of pathology. Just as women who moved outside of their assigned gender roles could be depicted as social and political menaces, so too did those people (male or female) whose sexual proclivities did not conform to the heterosexual standard that was so integral to dominant conceptions of the body politic.[14]

Scott's persuasive demonstration of gender as a useful analytical category has not only had a huge impact on historians of women and feminism, but it has also helped open the way to a rigorous analysis of men and masculinities as inextricably tied to representations of women and femininity, particularly for the period of the Third Republic in which unstable concepts of gender fueled a sense of national crisis. Whereas Annelise Maugue provided an early, largely literary analysis of a 'crisis of masculinity' during this period,[15] Robert Nye's *Masculinity and Male Codes of Honor* was the first work to examine how deeply medical and social views of male sexuality, masculinity, and gendered codes of behavior influenced the bourgeois society upon which the Third Republic was based.[16] Emerging as one of the most widely-cited historical studies of masculinity, and exercising a scholarly influence well beyond French history, *Masculinity and Male Codes of Honor* has facilitated new inquiries into how gender both signifies and facilitates relationships of power. Thanks to Nye's pioneering scholarship, a number of important works

published since or now under way further explore these themes and contribute to a major reinterpretation of the early Third Republic. These works
highlight the way in which conceptions and practices of gender and of masculinity undergirded a host of policies ranging from the formulation of civil
and political rights to public health and empire-building. Today the critical
study of men and masculinities is clearly on the agenda of gendered inquiries
in the Third Republic as well as other periods of French history, both in France
and overseas. André Rauch's two surveys of French manhood attest to this
growing willingness to examine critically the history of masculinities, as do
three recently published edited volumes exploring French masculinities from
the early modern era to the present.[17]

One consequence of these new approaches to the Third Republic was the
generation of novel perspectives on the Dreyfus Affair, the most divisive
'event' of the period that had for decades been the preserve of conventional
political and social historians. Building upon these recent developments in
gender scholarship, but also drawing upon French sociologies of intellectual groups, new scholarship on the Dreyfus Affair has sought to overcome
the implicit 'Dreyfusism' of historical work that, by understandably sym-
pathizing with the humanitarian and apparent philo-Semitic perspective of
Dreyfus's supporters, has nevertheless tended to collapse differences within
the pro-Dreyfus camp as well as to overlook similarities between Dreyfusards
and anti-Dreyfusards. Hence much new scholarship on the affair demonstrates just how deeply embedded this political event was in the cluster of
gendered, corporeal, and racial concerns of the fin de siècle. Several scholars have offered provocative new interpretations of the self-images of – and
tensions between – the warring camps of pro- and anti-Dreyfus intellectuals
during and after the affair, drawing attention to points of convergence rather
than the sharp ideological distinctions observed by most scholars.[18] Most
fully developed in Datta's *Birth of a National Icon: the Literary Avant-Garde and
the Origins of the Intellectual in France* (1999) and in Christopher E. Forth's *The
Dreyfus Affair and the Crisis of French Manhood* (2004), this scholarship shows
how, by consistently invoking anxieties about disease, effeminacy, and madness, the most vocal participants in the Dreyfus Affair reveal how fully they
experienced the gendered discourse of national decline described by Nye. The
Dreyfus Affair was thus thoroughly implicated in anxieties about diminished
manhood that were one consequence of the modernity the French at once
relished and abhorred.

In addition, these new perspectives on the Dreyfus Affair have shed critical
light on contemporary perceptions of Jews and women. Despite important
new perspectives on Jewishness and anti-Semitism produced by scholars such
as Sander Gilman, Daniel Boyarin, and others associated with the 'New Jewish
Cultural Studies,' histories of French anti-Semitism have typically focused on
'the Jew' more as a religious and social category than as a figure of discourse
crafted partly from medicalized anxieties about degeneration, effeminacy,

and modernity.[19] By bringing insights from this scholarship to bear on the Dreyfus Affair, Datta and Forth each offer reconsiderations of the vexed status of Jewishness during this time, revealing the shared anti-Semitism of both sides of the Dreyfus controversy. Similar innovations have been made in regard to the role played by women during the Affair. Most evident in Willa Silverman's important biography of the anti-Semitic writer Gyp and Mary Louise Roberts's reconsideration of the feminist newspaper *La Fronde*, the complex intervention of women in the gendered and racialized tensions of the Affair has been amply and persuasively examined.[20] Despite the pervasive misgivings about manhood and modernity generated during this crisis, the Dreyfus Affair was hardly just the business of men.   *feminism*

The above-mentioned works on women, gender, and masculinity have also been inspired by the considerable scholarship on French feminism produced since the 1970s, which has also remained connected to the historiographical developments described above. Three contributors to this volume – Charles Sowerwine, Steven Hause, and Karen Offen – are among the pioneers in the history of women and feminism. Each in his or her own way has addressed not only the paradox of why France lagged in granting women the vote, but has also examined its corollary: why, in a nation with a tradition of advancing human rights, did the French women's movement remain the starving stepsister to the more vibrant and visible movements in other countries, particularly the US and Britain? Charles Sowerwine's *Sisters or Citizens? Women and Socialism in France Since 1876* (1982) queried not only why the French women's movement of the nineteenth century was comparatively weak, but why women socialists failed to represent working-class women. His answers point to the same complexities scholars continue to explore today, especially the fear that giving women the vote would re-empower the Catholic clergy and the contradictory position in which that left socialist women: their ideological loyalties rested first with working-class emancipation. In 1984, Steven Hause, writing with Anne Kenney, continued to expose the interstices of culture and politics that shaped the path of French feminism with *Women's Suffrage and Social Politics in the French Third Republic*, in which they not only explained why the Radicals denied the vote for women in 1922 (fear of clerical influence in a wholly new context), but provided detail about what, in contrast to movements in other countries, kept the French women's movement so divided.[21]

That same year, Karen Offen brought to the center stage of French feminist history a fact with which demographers had long grappled: France was unique during the nineteenth century in its precipitously falling birth rate.[22] She was the first historian of women to demonstrate the political and cultural links that French men made between depopulation, nationalism, and feminism at the fin de siècle. Not only did she highlight the importance that weak birth rates had for the thinking of policymakers (thus vividly confirming the period's organicist anxieties about national decline), but she explained how and why the mainstream movement for French women's rights focused on motherhood as a claim to citizenship. Offen's analysis deepened and broadened the context within which feminist politics had to be understood and clearly demonstrated just how inseparable the 'Woman Question' and the 'social question' really were. But she also brought attention to the fact that the issue of depopulation rendered the attitudes of legislators and other public officials toward women arguably more complex and more ambiguous than in other countries. Indeed, the prospect of population decline had important implications for the value the state accorded to children and motherhood. Rachel Fuch's *Poor and Pregnant in Paris: Strategies for Survival in the Nineteenth Century* (1992) documented not only poor women's sometimes ingenious strategies for daily survival, but the deep stakes the state had in the survival of their children. The meeting of the two gave birth to the early stages of the French welfare state. Indeed it was motherhood, rather than individual female emancipation, that became a basis upon which women's *social* (if not political) rights advanced, even though the rights women achieved in the name of motherhood may have further weakened the French women's movement by making it seem less necessary.[23]

But with regard to the question of women's full citizenship – that is, the acquisition of full political rights – Joan Wallach Scott's *Only Paradoxes to Offer: French Feminists and the Rights of Man* (1996) offered another postmodern answer – and challenge – to the history of French feminism, and indeed to human rights movements in general. If the goal of feminism was to eliminate sexual difference in politics, she pointed out, how could it then make its claims on behalf of 'women,' a category defined as different from men? By acting on behalf of women as a category, feminism implicitly reinstated the sexual difference it sought to dismantle. Such was the paradox – the need both to accept and refuse 'difference' – inherent to feminism as a political movement. She argued that this paradox had been produced by republican ideologies that were themselves contradictory, especially in their changing definitions of the 'individual' and 'his' relationship to citizenship. Produced by, and dependent upon the language of liberal individualism, feminism is also a symptom of liberalism's internal contradictions at various stages of its evolution. The four feminists Scott analyzed from the French Revolution through the Third Republic represented, in her terms, 'discursive sites' whose cases illustrated the unstable meanings of language. The 'paradox' she identifies is not a pessimistic one, for beyond an 'unresolvable proposition that is true and false at the same time,' paradox is 'an opinion that challenges prevailing orthodoxy ... [and] that is contrary to received tradition.'[24] So even if republicans changed definitions of citizenship in response to feminists' demands, the continued challenge to orthodoxy in the form of paradox became (and can become in all cases) a subversive, destabilizing power that reinvented itself with every new stage of republican politics. Scott's book spawned a number of discussions, some of which we will see in this volume, about whether French republican ideology excluded women, and whether female emancipation was based on liberal individualism and the vote. The campaign for rights based on motherhood suggests it was not, at least among some feminists.

* * *

The paradoxes confronting French feminists and republicans were inherently rooted in the broader experience of what it meant to be 'modern' at the end of the nineteenth century. What we sometimes loosely refer to as 'modernity,' then, was for the French a rich and complex problem that could be approached from a number of different angles, many of which are implicit in the chapters that follow. *Confronting Modernity in Fin-de-Siècle France* grows out of the historiographical debates – and the works that they have inspired – whose outlines we have briefly sketched here. It demonstrates how the various theoretical and methodological strands discussed above have come together in different ways in the study of the fin de siècle.

Part I, 'Gender, Citizenship, and Republicanism,' reopens the debate about whether republicanism itself excluded women from the body politic or whether exclusion resulted from the attitudes of anti-feminist men. Charles Sowerwine's essay, providing a broad overview, argues that women were denied the vote for so long in France because republicanism was 'gendered male' from its inception in 1792. Karen Offen develops a different argument: that republicanism itself was not anti-feminist, but individual republican men were, and thus the so-called 'Woman Question' is more appropriately understood as a 'Man Problem' during the Third Republic. By approaching this volume's central problematic from different directions, these chapters provide essential background to the more tightly focused sections that follow.

Part II, 'Bodies, Minds, and Spirit' probes the sometimes complementary and at other times tense relationship that medicine and religious morality had in constructions of identity during the Third Republic, thus approaching the issues of politics and gender from a new combination of perspectives. As republican medicine and psychiatry became increasingly professionalized during this period they not only usurped social roles hitherto filled by the clergy, but represented themselves as performing a 'masculine' service that was at odds with the 'feminine' spirituality of both the Church and its mostly female adherents. The effects of this development were manifold, from the labeling of various individuals and groups as 'degenerate' and the diagnosis of female appetites as inherently pathological, to the growth of outright occultist movements that appropriated medical knowledge to promote their own programs for gender order. Matt Reed's chapter sets the tone of this section by providing a broad account of how the concept of degeneration was employed to make sense of the 'normal' subject of republican politics, one whose reason and free will needed to be in evidence. The chapter by Elizabeth Williams develops this nexus of psychiatry and politics in a novel direction by examining the influence that developing gastronomy had on medical and psychiatric diagnostics, and in particular the manner in which it asserted gender differences in taste and consequential real or perceived eating disorders among women. James Smith Allen's chapter analyzes yet another response to the modernist moral dilemmas, one that countered prevailing bourgeois republican culture. Papus, a physician and apologist for the occult, was greatly influenced by the contemporary concerns about fertility and shifting gender roles. He and his many women followers sought a spiritual alternative to Catholicism and the growing materialism of the fin de siècle. Papus's work, his personal comportment, and his largely female following offer another complex example of how French women and men negotiated shifting gender roles in the context of growing tensions between secularism and religion.

Part III, 'Morality, Honor, and Masculinity,' shows how the urban world generated a dizzying array of mental and physical temptations and conflicts between social classes, men and women, and within bourgeois identity itself. Bourgeois male codes of honor often played a role in regulating contested relationships, but also often created the paradoxes and contradictions that provoked contestation. Chapters by Rachel Fuchs and Andrea Mansker address the importance of 'honor' to men and women as well as the body politic during this time. Fuchs explores how male honor – and women's appropriation of it – influenced legislation and court cases regarding the status of children born out of wedlock. Mansker's chapter provides another context in which women appropriated male honor but also directly challenged it by publicly shaming men for their sexual behavior and attacking their own sense of masculinity. For the Protestant reformers examined in Steven Hause's chapter, urban modernity was fraught with sensual vice and stimulation, not least as a result of the proliferation of cabarets, prostitution, pornography, homosexuality, alcohol, and tobacco in 'modern Babylons' such as Paris. As Michael Wilson shows in his chapter, bohemian males self-consciously constructed 'masculine' identities by active rejection of normative masculinity and bourgeois morality, providing a fascinating example of how this marginal group negotiated their artistic needs against the predominant culture of parliamentary politics. All four of these chapters demonstrate the malleability of gender identities during this time, and their capacity to be appropriated and reworked in politically or legally useful ways.

In many respects the Dreyfus Affair may be viewed as the culmination of the gendered anxieties about modernity that mounted in France after 1789.[25] Part IV brings together many of the foregoing themes to offer new perspectives on the Dreyfus Affair, a series of events that not only left an indelible mark on France and on the individual lives of countless people, but which came close to destroying the Third Republic. Venita Datta's chapter examines the recent effort to rescue Dreyfus from his anti-hero status, held even among his supporters who were nonetheless influenced by the pervasive anti-Semitism. She explores the Dreyfusard concept of heroism, one that was imbedded in the values of the masculinist culture of the Third Republic. Ruth Harris's chapter focuses on two women active on each side of the political divide during the Affair – *salonnières* who were the center of male political, literary, and artistic networks and who had enormous influence on the male protagonists. Her analysis reveals the importance of subjective experience to the public and political aspects of these events.

This volume stands as testimony to important changes in historical understandings of the early Third Republic, shifts that are traceable to theoretical and methodological developments that have been under way since the 1980s. The various topics addressed demonstrate the myriad of ways in which women and men, as individuals and in groups, negotiated the contradictory expectations of the modern republican self and the insecurities inherent to mass democracy, where boundaries between male and female, the normal and abnormal, elites and popular classes, moral and immoral, good citizen or bad citizen, nationalist or traitor, were blurred.

Notes

1. Marshal Berman, *All that is Solid Melts into Air: the Experience of Modernity* (New York: Simon and Schuster, 1982), p. 15.
2. Examples of works that address these issues include: Stephen Kern, *The Culture of Time and Space 1880–1918* (Cambridge, MA: Harvard University Press, 1983); Wolfgang Schivelbusch, *The Railway Journey* (Berkeley: University of California Press, 1977); Eugen Weber, *France: Fin de Siècle* (Cambridge, MA: Belknap Press, 1986); Christophe Prochasson, *Les Années électriques, 1880–1910* (Paris: Éditions la Découverte, 1991); Vanessa R. Schwartz, *Spectacular Realities: Early Mass Culture in Fin-de-Siècle Paris* (Berkeley: University of California Press, 1998); Dominique Kalifa and Alain Vaillant, 'Pour une histoire culturelle et littéraire de la presse française au XIXe siècle,' *Le Temps des médias. Revue d'histoire*, 2 (2004): 197–214; Greg Shaya, 'The *Flâneur*, the *Badaud*, and the Making of a Mass Public in France, circa 1860–1910,' *American Historical Review*, 109(1) (February 2004): 41–77; and Dean de la Motte and Jeannene M. Przyblski (eds), *Making the New: Modernity and the Mass Press in Nineteenth Century France* (Amherst, MA: University of Massachusetts Press, 1999). Willa Silverman's *The New Bibliopolis: French Book Collectors and the Culture of Print, 1880–1914* (Toronto: University of Toronto Press, 2008) offers an excellent example of how modernity threatened elite identity: in addition to recoiling from the democratization of taste in general, book collectors faced the disappearance of what they most cherished – old books and the traditional modes of book production. The unstoppable use of new technologies for cheap, mass production threatened one of the most important markers of their identity and status.
3. Edward Shorter, *From Paralysis to Fatigue: a History of Psychosomatic Illness in the Modern Era* (New York: Free Press, 1993), p. 221; Christopher E. Forth, 'Neurasthenia and Manhood in Fin-de-Siècle France,' in *Cultures of Neurasthenia from Beard to the First World War*, Marijke Gijswijt-Hofstra and Roy Porter (eds) (Amsterdam: Rodopi, 2001), pp. 329–61.

4. Among Michel Foucault's most influential works are *Discipline and Punish: the Birth of the Prison*, trans. Alan Sheridan (New York: Pantheon, 1977) and *The History of Sexuality*, vol. 1, trans. Robert Hurley (New York: Vintage, 1980). Foucault, of course, contributed heavily to the 'cultural turn' in historiography pioneered by Hayden White and deeply influenced by theorists such as Clifford Geertz, Roland Barthes, Jacques Derrida, Pierre Bourdieu, and many others. For a helpful overview and analysis of this subject, see Victoria E. Bonnell and Lynn Hunt (eds), *Beyond the Cultural Turn* (Berkeley: University of California Press, 1999), pp. 1–32.

5. Michel Foucault, 'Truth and Power,' in *Power/Knowledge: Selected Interviews and Other Writings, 1972–1977*, Collin Gordon (ed.) (New York: Pantheon, 1980), p. 131.

6. Georges Vigarello, *Le Corps redressé: Histoire d'un pouvoir pédagogique* (1978; reprint, Paris: Armand Colin, 2001); *Le propre et le sale, l'hygiène du corps depuis le Moyen Age* (Paris: Seuil, 1985). Also worth mentioning are some pioneering historical anthropological investigations: Françoise Loux, *Le jeune enfant et son corps dans la médecine traditionnelle* (Paris: Flammarion, 1978); Françoise Loux and Philippe Richard, *Sagesses du corps: La Santé et la Maladie dans les proverbes français* (Paris: Maisonneuve et Larose, 1978); and Marie-Christine Pouchelle, *Corps et chirurgie à l'apogée du Moyen Age* (Paris: Flammarion, 1983).

7. Alain Corbin, *Les Filles de noce. Misère sexuelle et prostitution (XIXe siècle)* (Paris: Flammarion, 1978); *Le Miasme et la Jonquille. L'odorat et l'imaginaire social, XVIIIe–XIXe siècles* (Paris: Flammarion, 1982); *Le Territoire du vide. L'Occident et le désir du rivage, 1750–1840* (Paris: Flammarion, 1988).

8. Alain Corbin, Jean-Jacques Courtine, and Georges Vigarello (eds), *Histoire du corps* (Paris: Seuil, 2005–06), 3 vols.

9. Robert A. Nye, *The Origins of Crowd Psychology: Gustave Le Bon and the Crisis of Mass Democracy in the Third Republic* (London: Sage, 1975); Susanna Barrows, *Distorting Mirrors: Visions of the Crowd in Late Nineteenth-Century France* (New Haven: Yale University Press, 1981); Jan Goldstein, 'The Hysteria Diagnosis and the Politics of Anti-clericalism in Late Nineteenth-Century France,' *Journal of Modern History*, 54(2) (June 1982): 209–39; 'The Wandering Jew and the Problem of Psychiatric Anti-Semitism in Fin-de-Siècle France,' *Journal of Contemporary History*, 20(4) (October 1985): 521–52. See also Goldstein, *Console and Classify: the French Psychiatric Profession in the Nineteenth Century* (New York: Cambridge University Press, 1987), and Ian R. Dowbiggin, *Inheriting Madness: Professionalization and Psychiatric Knowledge in Nineteenth-Century France* (Berkeley: University of California Press, 1991).

10. Robert A. Nye, *Crime, Madness and Politics in Modern France* (Princeton: Princeton University Press, 1984); Daniel Pick, *Faces of Degeneration: a European Disorder, c. 1848–c.1918* (Cambridge: Cambridge University Press, 1989).

11. Joan Wallach Scott, 'Gender: a Useful Category of Historical Analysis,' in *Gender and the Politics of History* (New York: Columbia University Press, 1989), p. 42.

12. Ruth Harris, *Murders and Madness: Medicine, Law, and Society in the Fin de Siècle* (Oxford: Clarendon Press, 1989); Mary Louise Roberts, *Civilization without Sexes: Restructuring Gender in Postwar France, 1917–1927* (Chicago: University of Chicago Press, 1994); and Ann-Louise Shapiro. *Breaking the Codes: Female Criminality in Fin-de-Siècle Paris* (Stanford: Stanford University Press, 1996). See also Jean Pedersen, *Legislating the French Family: Feminism, Theater, and Republican Politics, 1870–1920* (New Brunswick, NJ: Rutgers University Press, 2003).

13. Edward Berenson, *The Trial of Madame Caillaux* (Berkeley: University of California Press, 1992); Jo Burr Margadant, *The New Biography: Performing Femininity in*

Nineteenth-Century France (Berkeley: University of California Press, 2000); James Smith Allen, *Poignant Relations: Three Modern French Women* (Baltimore: Johns Hopkins University Press, 2000); Mary Louise Roberts, *Disruptive Acts: the New Woman in Fin-de-Siècle France* (Chicago: University of Chicago Press, 2002); Elinor Accampo, *Blessed Motherhood, Bitter Fruit: Nelly Roussel and the Politics of Female Pain in Third Republic France* (Baltimore: Johns Hopkins University Press, 2006). Also relevant to the status of 'deviant' women – and the increased respectability that actual actresses achieved during the Third Republic – is Lenard Berlanstein's *Daughters of Eve: a Cultural History of French Theater Women from the Old Regime to the Fin de Siècle* (Cambridge, MA: Harvard University Press, 2001). In fascinating ways, women also appropriated the language of republicanism, male honor, and legal codes for their own benefit. See Whitney Walton, *Eve's Proud Descendents: Four Women Writers and Republican Politics in Nineteenth Century France* (Stanford: Stanford University Press, 2000); Andrea Mansker, ' "Mademoiselle Aria Ly Wants Blood!" The Debate over Female Honor in Belle Epoque France,' *French Historical Studies*, 29 (Fall 2006): 621–47; and Rachel G. Fuchs, *Contested Paternity: Constructing Families in Modern France* (Baltimore: Johns Hopkins University Press, 2008).

14. Jeffrey Merrick and Bryant T. Ragan (eds), *Homosexuality in Modern France* (New York: Oxford University Press, 1996); Vernon A. Rosario, *The Erotic Imagination: French Histories of Perversity* (New York: Oxford University Press, 1997); Carolyn J. Dean, *The Frail Social Body: Pornography, Homosexuality, and Other Fantasies in Interwar France* (Berkeley: University of California Press, 2000).

15. Annelise Maugue, *L'Identité masculine en crise au tournant du siècle, 1871–1914* (Paris: Rivages, 1987).

16. Robert A. Nye, *Masculinity and Male Codes of Honor in Modern France* (Oxford: Oxford University Press, 1993).

17. André Rauch, *Le premier sexe: mutations et crise de l'identité masculine* (Paris: Hachette Littératures, 2000); Rauch, *L'identité masculine à l'ombre des femmes: de la Grande Guerre à la Gay Pride* (Paris: Hachette Littératures, 2004); Régis Revenin (ed.), *Hommes et masculinités de 1789 à nos jours* (Paris: Éditions Autrement, 2007); Christopher E. Forth and Bertrand Taithe (eds), *French Masculinities: History, Culture and Politics* (Basingstoke: Palgrave, 2007); Todd W. Reeser and Lewis C. Seifert (eds), *Entre Hommes: French and Francophone Masculinities in Culture and Theory* (Newark, DE: University of Delaware Press, 2008).

18. Christophe Charle, *Naissance des 'intellectuels,' 1880–1900* (Paris: Minuit, 1990); John Cerullo, 'The Intellectuals and the Imagination of Heroism During the Dreyfus Affair,' *Proceedings of the Western Society for French History*, 25 (Fall 1997): 185–95; 'Religion and the Psychology of Dreyfusard Intellectualism,' *Historical Reflections/Réflexions historiques*, 24 (Spring 1998): 93–114; Venita Datta, *Birth of a National Icon: the Literary Avant-Garde and the Emergence of the Modern Intellectual* (Albany: State University of New York Press, 1999); Christopher E. Forth, *The Dreyfus Affair and the Crisis of French Manhood* (Baltimore: Johns Hopkins University Press, 2004).

19. Few historians of France have examined the deep cultural connections between anti-Semitism and this wider matrix of physical, moral, and gendered anxieties. Notable exceptions include Pierre Birnbaum, *Anti-Semitism in France: a Political History from Léon Blum to the Present*, trans. Miriam Kochan (Oxford: Blackwell, 1992) and Jan Goldstein, 'The Wandering Jew and Psychiatric Anti-Semitism.' Sander Gilman's many important works on the medicalization of Jewishness include *The Jew's Body* (New York: Routledge, 1991) and *Franz Kafka, the Jewish Patient*

(New York: Routledge, 1995). See also Jonathan Boyarin and Daniel Boyarin (eds), *Jews and Other Differences: the New Jewish Cultural Studies* (Minneapolis: University of Minnesota Press, 1997); Daniel Boyarin, *Unheroic Conduct: the Rise of Heterosexuality and the Invention of the Jewish Man* (Berkeley: University of California Press, 1997).

20. Willa Z. Silverman, *The Notorious Life of Gyp: Right-Wing Anarchist in Fin-de-Siècle France* (New York: Oxford University Press, 1995); Roberts, *Disruptive Acts.*

21. One of the first scholarly publications on French feminism was edited by Karen Offen, *Third Republic/Troisième République*, a special double issue, 2(3–4) (1977) on 'Aspects of the Woman Question during the Third Republic,' to which she, Patrick Bidelman, Linda Clark, Charles Sowerwine, Marilyn Boxer, Persis Hunt, and Steve Hause contributed articles. This publication was followed by Sowerwine, *Sisters or Citizens? Women and Socialism in France Since 1876* (Cambridge: Cambridge University Press, 1982); Bidleman, *Pariahs Stand Up! The Founding of the Liberal Feminist Movement in France 1859–1889* (Westport, CT: Greenwood Press, 1982); Hause, with Anne Kenney, *Women's Suffrage and Social Politics in the French Third Republic* (Princeton: Princeton University Press, 1984); and Claire Moses, *French Feminism in the Nineteenth Century* (Albany: SUNY Press, 1984). Scholars on either side of the Atlantic initially worked independently of each other. The first modern history of French feminism appearing in France was that of Maité Albistur and Daniel Armogathe, *Histoire du féminisme français*, 2 vols (Paris: des Femmes, 1978).

22. Karen Offen, 'Depopulation, Nationalism, and Feminism in Fin-de-Siècle France,' *American Historical Review*, 89(3) (1984): 648–76. Angus McLaren also established the important influence depopulation had on social policy in *Sexuality and Social Order: the Debate over the Fertility of Women and Workers in France, 1770–1920* (New York: Holmes and Meier, 1983).

23. Rachel Fuchs, *Poor and Pregnant in Paris: Strategies for Survival in the Nineteenth Century* (New Brunswick, NJ: Rutgers University Press, 1992). For an expanded discussion of the attitudes and actions of policymakers vis-à-vis women in the early development of the welfare state, see Mary Lynn Stewart, *Women Workers and the French State: Labor Protection and Social Patriarchy, 1879–1919* (Montreal: McGill University Press, 1989); Elinor A. Accampo, Rachel G. Fuchs, and Mary Lynn Stewart, *Gender and the Politics of Social Reform in France, 1870–1914* (Baltimore: Johns Hopkins University Press, 1995); Linda Clark, *The Rise of Professional Women in France: Gender and Public Administration since 1830* (Cambridge: Cambridge University Press, 2000). Anne Cova's *Maternité et droits des femmes en France (XIXe–XXe siècles)* (Paris: Anthropos, 1997) follows in great detail the way in which feminists based their demands on maternal rights and protection. Accampo's *Blessed Motherhood, Bitter Fruit*, originally inspired by the issues raised in Offen's article, investigates the contested relationship between birth control and feminism, and reproductive rights more generally in the face of pronatalism during this period.

24. Joan Wallach Scott, *Only Paradoxes to Offer: French Feminists and the Rights of Man* (Cambridge, MA: Harvard University Press, 1996), p. 4.

25. Forth, *Dreyfus Affair*, pp. 5–9.

Part I
Gender, Citizenship, and Republicanism

Introduction to Part I

Among the most salient modernizing forces of nineteenth-century France were the contested concept of citizenship and the issue of precisely who had rights to civil freedoms and protections, social justice, and political power. This book begins with two chapters that advance the discussion of the meaning of citizenship in France's long struggle with the republican experiment, and particularly its relationship with female emancipation. At its inception in 1792, French republicanism did indeed imply equality and liberty for all human beings. With the granting of universal manhood suffrage, France became the most democratic country in the world. Political distinctions were no longer based on wealth or on lineage through birth. Women, whose civil and social rights largely depended on their marital status, were categorically excluded from political rights on the basis of biological sex. Many historians contend that the equality ushered in by the revolution made sex a more important marker of distinction and difference as other sources of distinction (such as noble birth) became legally and politically untenable. As followers of Rousseau and other Enlightenment thinkers, many revolutionaries justified the exclusion of women on their conception of 'natural law.' Anaxagoras Chaumette, for example, pointed to nature when he argued that women were meant to confine themselves to domestic chores because they, not men, had been given breasts. And indeed, motherhood assumed a distinct importance in the new democratic context: women now had the civic responsibility of nurturing and raising the good citizens required of a successful republic. Although few demanded the vote for women in the Revolution of 1789, more did so in the Revolution of 1848 and during the Second Republic (1848–1852), the Paris Commune of 1871, and in the feminist movement of the fin de siècle.

In the first chapter of this section, Charles Sowerwine provides a very compelling overview of this history as well as the historiography addressing the issue of women's political exclusion. He argues that legislators systematically denied women the vote because French republicanism was 'gendered male' and continued to be until 1944. But was it French republicanism itself, or anti-feminist men who denied women the vote?

Karen Offen's chapter argues the latter position. She points out that even though the Third Republic failed to grant women the vote, many republican men supported women's suffrage. Moreover, even without the vote, women exercised considerable power both in the home and in civic life. Indeed, beginning with the First French Republic, republican rhetoric and the legal and civil changes it wrought opened new ways for women to appropriate power even without the vote – and it was this power and influence that in fact fueled the anti-feminism excluding women from the body politic.

These chapters not only provide two very different perspectives about gender and citizenship, but together they raise a number of important questions: what were the ideological tenets of French republicanism over the course of the first four republics, and were they consistent in the manner in which they excluded women? Did women need the vote to exercise influence – and indeed did the influence that they already exercised make the vote less central to French feminism? What can the interplay between republican ideology, feminism, and gender relations tell us about the experience of modernity in France? Finally, what can the French experience suggest about countries with strong patriarchal traditions that are trying to establish modern democratic republics?

1

Revising the Sexual Contract: Women's Citizenship and Republicanism in France, 1789–1944[1]

Charles Sowerwine

France pioneered universal suffrage on a national basis. The Constitution of 1791 set up propertied male suffrage. The uprising which brought the proclamation of the First Republic in 1792 suppressed the property qualification, leaving quasi-universal male suffrage. The Second Republic formally proclaimed universal male suffrage in 1848, but it was not until 1944 that France introduced female suffrage. It was introduced in New Zealand in 1893, in Finland, Norway, and Denmark over the next quarter century, and in many nations in the aftermath of World War I: Canada, the USSR, Germany, Poland, Holland, the US, Turkey, and the UK.[2]

For half a century, French feminists fulminated against what they saw as the French lag. They expected that the homeland of the 'Rights of Man and the Citizen' would take the lead in granting women the suffrage, especially once committed republicans took over the government in the 1870s. But the Third Republic (1870–1940) failed to introduce female suffrage. It was not until the Liberation, under a new regime, that women obtained the suffrage and then it was not republicans but Gaullists and communists who took the lead in granting it.

Like feminists at the time, historians today view this as the French lag. Karen Offen calls it 'the astonishing backwardness of a nation whose leaders portrayed it as the vanguard of civilization.' Offen argues that contingent political circumstances explain 'this long delay,' particularly 'the intransigent resistance of the Radical [republican]s in the Senate,' fed by 'social conservatism,' fear of women's support for social reform (alcohol and prostitution), and fear of women's support for the Church.[3]

These issues played a role, but they do not suffice to explain the profound resistance to women's suffrage. Similar political circumstances obtained in the countries which granted women the vote before World War II. As the pre-eminent historian of the suffrage argues, 'the power of the prejudices about women's nature does not suffice to explain the nearly absurd character that the idea of opening the right of suffrage to women had during the Revolution' and, this chapter will argue, through the nineteenth and well into the twentieth century. Why was France so far ahead in granting citizenship to men and so far behind in granting it to women? Why did republicans preach equality but deny it to women?[4]

It was not a question of hypocrisy. Republicans believed sincerely in equality, but when they translated their discourse of equality into reality, they viewed the actual citizen as embodied male. Some republicans, of course, transcended this vision, but the vast majority did not. Republicans disappointed expectations of women's political rights because citizenship was gendered male: it was men who were to enjoy 'the Rights of Man.'

Republicans were not more hostile to women's rights than conservatives, but conservatives did not preach equality. Republicans did and thus, as Offen notes, feminism 'confronted them squarely on the ...very principles to which they subscribed. But the various republican factions, including the Radicals, resisted.'[5] Their resistance was the major barrier to women's obtaining the suffrage. This chapter argues that their resistance resulted from the way citizenship was embodied male as it was constructed.

The chapter first explores the origins of women's exclusion in the very process of constructing citizenship. It then turns to the historiographical debates surrounding that exclusion. The core of the chapter demonstrates that the tension between the exclusion of women and the egalitarian discourse of the Revolution played out across the nineteenth century and increased republicans' difficulties in the face of women's demands for rights. It then analyzes the passage of women's suffrage in 1944, led by non-republican elements. It concludes with some observations about the implications of its argument for the question of women's suffrage beyond France.

Constructing citizenship: excluding women in the eighteenth century

Women's exclusion, like the discourse of equality, originated in the eighteenth century. Enlightenment thinkers discursively created what Robert Nye calls 'gendered public and private spheres:' women were destined for the affective, 'private realm;' men were free 'to roam over both.' Citizenship was constructed as innately masculine.[6]

The exclusion of women was long assumed to be at odds with the Enlightenment vision, a result of prejudice, 'accidental' to Enlightenment thought (in the philosophical sense of not inherent in it). The bicentenary of the French Revolution saw the emergence of studies by Carole Pateman, Joan Landes, and others, which challenged that assumption. They demonstrated that the exclusion of women was not accidental to but inherent in the discursive construction of the citizen, which proceeded by embodying the citizen as public man in opposition to private woman, constructing a masculine universal by creating a feminine 'other.'[7]

Enlightenment theorists (and *a fortiori* the men of 1642 in England and 1789 in France) had to think their way to citizenship from a culture in which citizenship and public sphere were inconceivable. Power in the *ancien régime* was understood in paternal terms; the path to citizenship thus led from paternity to fraternity. Carole Pateman showed that the social contract idea on which Locke and Rousseau built modern political theory derived from their confrontation with theorists of the monarchy, for whom the state was a family of which the king was the father, and for whom civil society was constituted by accepting this patriarchal authority. The new democratic order sought legitimacy by shifting the paternal model of power from the kingdom to the home: if men, as heads of households, were kings in their own domains, then they could represent their households to the outside world, even against the king/father. A society discursively constructed as a family – all are children of the king – gave way to one constructed as a band of brothers – a fraternity of male citizens. It was no accident that 'fraternity' played such a major role in eighteenth-century and revolutionary discourse. The subordinate political position of women in the new society was a logical consequence of the discursive construction of citizenship as masculine.[8]

Lynn Hunt went beyond Pateman's sometimes static textual analysis, analyzing the dynamic by which these changes played out before and during the French Revolution, and Joan Scott showed how they played out during the nineteenth century. While these thinkers differed in many respects, they all built on the then recent heritage of second-wave feminism; we will therefore call their view the original feminist interpretation. They all shared a sense that Enlightenment discourse operated on two levels: on the one hand, a discourse of Reason inherent in and accessible to all human beings, which assumed erasure of sexual difference; on the other hand, a gendered ideal of the active male defined in opposition to the passive female, which assumed sexual difference.[9]

The tension generated by these two levels of discourse played out as men and women engaged in the construction of formal political democracy and of the broader public sphere which made it possible at the same time as they struggled over the issues of inclusion in and exclusion from that democracy and public sphere. Throughout, there were women and men who looked to the egalitarian implications of Enlightenment discourse and made use of this discourse to call for women's inclusion in the polity. But their call was undermined by the second level of Enlightenment discourse, which subordinated women to men, offering women an affective role in place of equality. The prevailing common sense was that women were destined for activities that derived from their presumed role in the private realm, giving and nurturing life, while men were also destined for public life, not only nurturing their children but also shaping the polity. Citizenship emerged and long remained discursively gendered male.

Rousseau

It was Rousseau who most forcefully articulated the categories private woman and public man[10] and it was Rousseau to whose writings people turned most frequently as the French Revolution constructed the institutions of citizenship and representation.[11] As Dorinda Outram suggests, Rousseau's discourse 'denied women full status as individuals, at precisely the time that men were increasingly defining themselves as autonomous individual actors.'[12] As the democratic mood intensified, so did the assumption that public activity – what would soon be called citizenship in the broad sense – was intrinsically male, defined by and in opposition to private activity, which was intrinsically female. This mood reached every level of social activity. Lenard Berlanstein tells us that, during 1789, members of the *Comédie française* proposed to exclude female actors from the partnership (*société*) governing the institution. The proposal failed only because the female actors voted against it.[13]

That proposal was articulated in the Rousseauist language of male virtue, in which republican virtue was innately masculine and masculinity was characterized by such virtue. Robert Darnton quotes a minor tax official who wrote to Rousseau: 'At the age of twenty-eight, I am a father of four children, and I will follow your lessons in order to form them into men – not the kind of men you see everywhere around you, but the kind that we see in you alone.' By 'men,' Rousseau, like his readers, meant males rather than generic human beings. 'When they [women] take on the masculine and firm assurance of the man and turn it into effrontery,' wrote Rousseau in the *Second Discourse*, 'they abase themselves by this odious imitation and dishonor both their sex and ours.'[14]

Rousseau and later republican thinkers did not exclude women from the Republic in a wholly negative fashion; rather they assigned them a higher role in the family, a role which they believed compensated for their exclusion from active public life: 'It is for you [women] to maintain always, by your amiable and innocent dominion and by your insinuating wit, love of laws in the State and concord among the citizens.'[15] Whatever women gained from this higher role, it deprived them of legitimacy in the political public sphere. As we shall see, that private role extended beyond the family to many roles perceived as nurturing, such as teaching (at least at lower levels), charity work, and the Church. But all such areas were also open to men, while women were excluded from formal political processes. To influence the direction of their polity, women were constrained to work through men because men alone enjoyed citizenship.

The Revolution opened up enormous political energies, among women as among men. 'The militant woman,' Dominique Godineau reminds us, 'wished to be a citizen.' In this she was responding to the inclusionary and egalitarian level of Enlightenment discourse in a revolutionary climate, in which everything seemed possible. But the militant woman lost the struggle to be a citizen.[16]

The first article of the 1789 *Declaration of the Rights of Man and the Citizen* stipulated that 'men are born and remain free and equal in rights.' Feminists at the time understood that this meant men. Olympe de Gouges responded in 1791 with a *Declaration of the Rights of Woman and the Female Citizen*: 'woman is born free and remains the equal of man in rights.' But no one spoke in favor of women's participation when, in 1789, the constituent assembly discussed modes of election. The Constitution of 1791 designated propertied men as 'active citizens,' unpropertied men and all women as 'passive citizens,' with civil rights but without political rights.[17] In 1793, 'the Convention cracked down on popular clubs and societies.' Jack Censer and Lynn Hunt continue, 'First to be suppressed were women's political clubs.' De Gouges went to the scaffold later that year.[18]

'The Jacobins,' Karen Offen notes, 'rigorously insisted on the hierarchical model of the nation as a collection of male-headed families, in which women and children were subordinate, and … reconsigned women to the private (and, in their minds, subordinate) sphere of the household.' As Lenard Berlanstein puts it, 'it was not the case that the revolutionaries opened political possibilities for women only to reverse themselves later because groups of females proved to be too potent a political force.' Most republicans found women's public activity a threat to the male-headed family. They could not conceive of women as citizens. Reconsigned to the household sphere, women lost the right even to form clubs or petition the government, not because they were too radical but because they were women. The Civil Code of 1804 set women's legal subordination to fathers and husbands for the rest of the century.[19]

Challenges to the original feminist interpretation

Some recent studies – by Denise Davidson, Suzanne Desan, Carla Hesse, and Rebecca Rogers – have made claims or have been claimed to revise this interpretation.[20] They focus on specific areas of human activity or culture during the revolutionary and post-revolutionary period (Rogers on the nineteenth century) and demonstrate that women were more active in those areas than some may have thought. All these works contribute to our understanding of the ways women made use of the egalitarian discourse of the Revolution to demand equality, but the claim that they revise the original feminist interpretation does not stand up to scrutiny.

Peter McPhee argues that, after Desan's book, 'standard feminist interpretations of the Revolution – by Joan Landes, Karen Offen, Madelyn Gutwirth, among others – are no longer tenable.'[21] Rogers suggests that 'most interpretations see the Revolutionary period as ushering in a misogynistic nineteenth century, where women were increasingly confined to their roles of mother and wife. This vision of the years between 1789 and the fall of Napoleon in 1815 has recently come under criticism.'[22]

Much of the claim for revision depends on red herrings. No one, for instance, calls the nineteenth century 'misogynistic:' *misogyny* is the hatred of women by men and such an argument would be not only ahistorical but also inaccurate: to the extent one can generalize about such matters, nineteenth-century men adored women. The point is rather that their model of sexual difference made it difficult for them to conceive of women's taking roles beyond their presumed affective vocation. Similarly, no one claims that women were 'confined' to such roles. What is certain, however, is that the culture strongly encouraged such roles and discouraged or excluded women from public activity.

That exclusion was, to be sure, contested during the Revolution and indeed throughout the nineteenth century, usually in terms derived from the egalitarian level of Enlightenment and republican discourse, but few now deny that during the nineteenth century it triumphed despite that contestation. Rogers herself points out that, even 'during the Empire, political, economic, and scientific discourses contributed to essentializing the differences between the sexes so that women were in effect banished from public life.' Rogers's study makes a valuable contribution to understanding the gendering of education. But, far from revising the original feminist interpretation, her account reminds us of the continuing barriers to women's participation above the lower rungs of the academic hierarchy and their continuing marginalization from secondary and higher education.[23]

Davidson shows that women participated in civic festivals, on boulevards, at theaters, in salons and *cercles*; she then questions the concept of 'separate spheres.' Of course women went to the theater. That in no way undermines the argument that they were presumed to have an affective vocation focused on home and family (a presumption to which exceptions could occasionally be made). 'Women,' Davidson herself says, 'were consciously negotiating increasingly well-defined behavioral norms for the genders and the classes.'[24] Women could to an extent engage with public life, especially during the early period of the Revolution, but the manner of their engagement reflected their negotiation of these norms, which evolved toward domesticity rather than toward participation in politics.

Desan studies the evolving conceptualization of the family and divorce and suggests that women's domestic vocation was contested during the Revolution, but agrees that 'everyone imagined distinct and complementary roles for men and women within the Republic and ...believed that marriage, heterosexual love, and gender complementarity [could] underpin patriotism.'[25] That is precisely the point of the original feminist interpretation: republican belief in complementarity underpinned the whole culture, including its restriction of women's political rights.

Carla Hesse studied women's literary production and found that women's share increased, from 2 per cent in 1784 to 4 per cent in 1820. That hardly constitutes equal access to the public sphere. Hesse, moreover, concedes that, in the nineteenth century, 'the modern public sphere was … opened to women on differential terms … the husband replaced the sovereign as the arbiter of the fate of their ideas.'[26] The term 'modern public sphere' occults the issue. Women had access to the *literary* public sphere, though 'on differential terms,' but although they sought access to the political public sphere – particularly during the Revolution – they were firmly pushed back.

The claim that these studies revise the original feminist interpretation hinges in large measure on confusion about two key concepts: 'separate spheres' and the 'public sphere.'

'Separate spheres' is the common English phrase for the concept signaled figuratively in French as *la femme au foyer* (literally 'woman at the hearth'), women's particular vocation for nurturing, symbolized by the hearth (*foyer*). This concept goes under many names: angel of the home, domestic life, nurturing, private realm, or sphere. Whatever the nomenclature, the concept points not to a physical space but to an affective vocation for women; that vocation was, to be sure, largely focused on the domestic realm, but it would be absurd to imagine bourgeois women as confined to the home. Servants tended the actual fire; the lady of the house was responsible for its symbolic, affective warmth.[27]

'Public sphere' is a concept developed by Jürgen Habermas and is central to most formulations of women's exclusion. Habermas distinguished the *politische Öffentlichkeit* (political public sphere) from the *literarische Öffentlichkeit* (literary public sphere); neither term referred to physical space, but to a virtual community 'made up of private people gathered together as a public and articulating the needs of society with the state,' a bridge between civil society and the state, 'the opening space for public activism (press, association, public opinion, etc.)'[28]

While the political public sphere is much broader than formal political processes, Habermas's definition does include the political arena; the public sphere is the totality of activity to develop and influence public opinion and affect the direction of the polity. Participation in the public sphere without the vote cannot compensate for the lack of standing that results from not being a citizen. The positions to which men alone had access, as voters and as office-holders, gave them much greater standing than women in public opinion. The public roles open to women were those which involved nurturing, roles such as tutors of the young (from governess to occasionally running schools, as Rebecca Rogers has shown), charity work (as Susan Foley has shown) and of course the Church, which (as both Rogers and Caroline Ford have shown) provided a forum for women's independent advancement. These roles, however valued by society, could not and did not give women the standing men enjoyed in the political public sphere.[29]

No one denies the significance of these roles. The point is that they justified ruling out or at best severely curtailing women's public activity. The more women performed functions perceived as consonant with their nurturing vocation, the more they conformed to the very norms which justified their exclusion from the public sphere. Conversely, non-nurturing public functions were coded male and the same exclusionary logic meant that women who undertook such functions were thought thereby to have disqualified themselves as women. Michelet's disciple Jules Simon, a leading republican politician of the 1870s and 1880s, argued in his masterpiece, *L'Ouvrière* (The Woman Worker), 'the woman who becomes a worker is no longer a woman;' women workers left the 'hidden, sheltered, modest life, surrounded by warm affection, that is so necessary to their happiness and ours.' However positive one finds Simon's vision of woman's role, it contained women within a limited scope while men were not restricted.[30]

The claim that these studies revise the original feminist interpretation also hinges on the assumption that contestation and/or enlargement of women's activities during the Revolution affects our view of the nineteenth-century gender dynamic. The effervescence of the revolutionary situation, in the early 1790s as in 1848 and 1871, allowed women scope for political action, especially since the revolutionary forces preached equality. But there is no doubt that the broad tendency of the revolutionary dynamic was to channel women toward what was understood as their affective vocation and to exclude them from political life.

Margaret Darrow demonstrated how this dynamic operated, even with French noblewomen, the group least open to domesticity before the Revolution: '[they] actively adopted, and adapted, domestic ideology as part of a response to the changing social and political realities of the Revolution and the Restoration.'[31] This is still more true of the nineteenth century and of the various middling classes who thought of themselves as the bourgeoisie. Once the revolutionary turbulence came to an end, so did many of the openings for women.

The studies emphasizing female agency in the public sphere do not challenge the cultural dynamic by which man was constructed discursively as destined for public life and woman as destined for private life. Nor do they challenge what Mary Louise Roberts calls 'the absolute centrality of this view of womanhood to the bourgeois democratic society that rose up in the wake of the 1789 Revolution.'[32] They do remind us that this view was achieved despite contestation, through an ongoing cultural struggle in which the modes of exclusion were constantly reconfigured, in large part through elaboration of a model which destined women for other callings.

They should remind us too, as Hunt pointed out in a major 1995 article, that the Revolution was not all bad for women. On the contrary. Even the status of 'passive citizen' granted by the Constitution of 1791 made an enormous and positive difference to women. In particular, the revolutionary regime of equal inheritance, confirmed by Napoleon, gave women a much stronger bargaining position within the family. And the Revolution gave women new avenues of freedom by opening up divorce, and the taste remained long after divorce was eliminated by the Restoration.[33]

Even on the terrain of political equality, the Revolution offered the first chance for women to claim equality through its egalitarian discourse. 'What was new' in the French Revolution, Hunt reminds us, 'was not the predictable governmental reaction and repression but rather the surprisingly open political space,' in which women could demand political rights, and 'the articulation of a concept of universal rights, which, in the French case, and apparently only in the French case, led ineluctably to a reconsideration of everyone's rights, including those of women,' an articulation which justified women's demand for political rights.[34]

We need to grasp that the dynamic at the origins of the new mode of thought was twofold. It should not be a question of being for or against the Revolution and certainly not of condemning the Revolution as a misogynist plot, as Landes and Gutwirth occasionally verge on doing.[35] Nor should it be a question of blaming the revolutionaries for not having achieved a twenty-first century understanding of equality; they and their forebears deserve praise for their unique achievement in moving humanity away from the paternal and patriarchal model of power, however imperfectly. The Revolution's universal concept of equality could not simply emerge fully fledged like Botticelli's Venus. Equality had to be constructed painfully, on the basis of the existing cultural materials, and this was accomplished through a gendering process.

The cultural work necessary to construct the citizen and the universal ideal of equality was gendered and it helped bring into being the new gender order of the nineteenth century, in which women were thought to have a special affective vocation. Women obtained significant benefits but were denied political equality even as it was introduced, in the name of their destiny for affective or domestic life (in a 'separate sphere'). That destiny remained in tension with the universal assumption of equality. Both were at the heart of Enlightenment discourse, which explicitly prescribed a universal ideal of the citizen and thus assumed erasure of sexual difference, but simultaneously gendered citizenship male so that it became almost impossible to imagine women as citizens.

Women were thus offered contradictory prescriptions: on the one hand, the universal ideal of equality; on the other, the gendered ideal of domesticity, offering a nurturing vocation in private life to complement male activity in public life. Both these contradictory prescriptions were played out during the Revolution and its aftermath. 'In the age of democratic revolutions,' Joan Scott suggests, '"women" came into being as political outsiders through the discourse of sexual difference.' The early twentieth-century socialist and feminist, Madeleine Pelletier, claimed that it was during the first Revolution that feminism 'learned how to enunciate all its claims for rights.' Scott comments, 'The legitimacy of those claims and their satisfaction depended on the

recognition that the Revolution's proclamation of the rights of all was incon-
sistent with its refusals of citizenship to women. But what for feminists was
a self-evident contradiction was not obvious as such to the legislators who
repeatedly denied them the vote on the grounds of their difference from
men.' The dominant tendency of ascendant republicanism was to work to
exclude women from the political public sphere, at informal levels as well as
in politics proper, while the universal claim of equality on which it was built
led women to demand equality. The nineteenth-century gender order would
thus prove inherently unstable.[36]

Gender and republicans/republicanism in the nineteenth century

The tension between the two levels of Enlightenment discourse, egalitarian
and gendered, played out through the nineteenth century. On the one hand,
building on the egalitarian discourse of the Revolution, women sought to
participate in the public sphere and to demand rights and equality. On the
other hand, the construction of gender resulting from the Revolution was
embedded in a biomedical model which, in Robert Nye's words, 'made the
sexes "naturally" suited for their respective social and familial roles.' The
result was 'a system ... which excluded women, *by their nature* [italics original]
from participation in politics.'[37]

An older model of biological sex, in which 'men and women were
arrayed ... along an axis whose *telos* was male,' was replaced by what Thomas
Laqueur has called a new 'anatomy and physiology of incommensurability,'
in which women became 'the other sex,' inherently different from men.[38]
The new model normalized the assumption of difference needed to justify
women's subordination in a culture premised on equality.[39] It became the
common sense of the nineteenth century and over-determined responses to
women's demands for the suffrage, negating women's pretensions to equality.

We see this dynamic played out as women struggled throughout the nineteenth century to gain the suffrage, but were unable to reverse the dynamic
of exclusion. With the Bourbon Restoration (1814–1830) and the consequent
eclipse of republicanism, some elite women temporarily regained access to
power as the premise of universal male suffrage was displaced by the revived
patriarchal model of the monarchy. As Susan Foley has shown, for example, 'the wives of "Ultra" politicians played crucial supportive roles.' Céleste
de Montjustin, married to a minister in the ultraconservative Villèle government in the 1820s, acted as her husband's campaign manager. Women's
indirect exercise of political power was, however, again reduced during the
Orleans or July Monarchy (1830–48). With the Second Empire (1852–70),
some avenues opened to women. 'Restrictions on opposition campaigning
forced candidates to rely largely on family members, particularly their wives,
for assistance ... On occasion women cast the ballots on their husbands'

behalf and they were even involved in vote-counting, which sometimes occurred in the mayor's kitchen.'[40]

In the 1870s, with the installation of the Third Republic, the basis for all subsequent republican regimes, universal male suffrage became the foundation of government. The accompanying renewal of egalitarian discourse in turn facilitated the emergence of what we now call first-wave feminism, with significant support from a very small number of male republicans.

In 1872, Léon Richer and Maria Deraismes organized a banquet of 150 supporters of women's emancipation. The keynote speaker was Victor Schoelcher, who had signed the 1848 decree abolishing slavery. The highlight of the evening was a letter from Victor Hugo. Women, he argued, were virtual slaves: 'There are citizens, THERE ARE NOT CITIZENESSES. This is a violent fact; it must cease.' The group was quickly silenced. The Minister of the Interior prohibited their meetings: they were 'only a pretext for the assembly of numerous women who are too emancipated.' Richer and Deraismes cancelled a feminist congress planned for 1873 and changed the name of their group to eliminate the word 'droit [right]:' from L'Association pour le Droit des femmes (Association for Women's Right) it became L'Association pour l'amélioration du sort de la femme (Association for the Improvement of Women's Condition).[41]

In the debates over the Constitution of 1875, no one raised women's suffrage, as some had in 1848 and many had in the 1790s.[42] Conservatives were still talking the language of de Maistre and Bonald. *Le Figaro*, well to the right then as now, railed at '[the supposed demand for] the suppression of paternal authority ... [which] would be the dissolution of the family:' 'of the two spouses, one must govern as absolute master [*il faut que l'un gouverne en maître absolu*].'[43]

That conservatives opposed women's rights and, *a fortiori*, women's suffrage is not surprising. What is surprising, at least from the perspective that women's exclusion was accidental to republicanism, is that no voice was raised in its favor from the ranks of the 'Radical republicans,' who would effectively establish the Republic. Rather than enfranchise women, the republicans renewed emphasis on the complementarity of men and women, premised on women's presumed aptitude for domesticity, a presumption in turn buttressed by the biomedical model of sexual and vocational difference.

Medical discourse helped to root this model in common sense, accentuating the exclusion of women at the same time as republican thought increased its hegemony. The medical profession reinforced the biomedical model, which fitted perfectly in their materialist and anticlerical worldviews. This tendency was strongest during the Third Republic. Jack D. Ellis has shown that doctors were the second largest single professional group in the Chamber of Deputies between 1870 and 1914.[44]

Georges Clemenceau, that most republican of politicians and himself a doctor, deployed such arguments in extensive notes for a refutation of

John Stuart Mill's *The Subjection of Women*, begun in 1869. He planned six of seven sections around physiology. Women were biologically different from men; if given the vote, therefore, 'they would find themselves in the position of the negroes [*sic*] in America, whose circumstances ruined their admission to the political body.'[45] He never published the refutation, but he articulated such views throughout his long career.

Eugène Pelletan, father of Camille (the Third Republic Radical republican), wrote in 1869 that woman's place was 'at home, directing, administering the house and above all constantly forming those young souls which Providence has confided to her, making them one day citizens worthy of their country. Thus, to define marriage ... I would call it a constitutional government. The husband minister of foreign affairs, the wife minister of the interior, and all household questions decided by the council of ministers.'[46] Pelletan's metaphor is more conciliatory than the paternal metaphors that dominated conservative thinking, but it obviously represents a public/private dichotomy.

The exclusion of women from the political public sphere reinforced their domestic destiny while perpetuating the notion that the Republic needed wives and mothers, that is, women in their private, domestic roles. This was one of the most frequent forms of the model of complementarity. Juliette Adam's husband was, like Adam herself, close to Léon Gambetta, the greatest republican of the day and leader of the Radical republicans. Adam confided to her his concern that these republican leaders did not have women to support them:

> But do you know what worries me, Juliette? That in the tide of our young friends, I don't see any women following them: Gambetta, Challemel, Spuller, Ranc [leading republican politicians], have no wives ... Cafés may maintain the spirit of opposition, but once the Republic is founded, I look in vain for the hearths [*foyers*] which will preserve it.[47]

Ludovic Halévy (the librettist of *Carmen*) similarly complained that Gambetta and his entourage were 'all boys ... without home or hearth [*feu*], without wife or children.'[48] Women as wives, associated with the hearth, were essential to marking manhood and thus, as Judith Surkis has shown so effectively, to citizenship. As Pateman argued for the eighteenth century, the justification for male citizenship in the nineteenth century remained men's representing their women and families.[49]

This discourse of republican fraternity was markedly different from the discourse of Bonald and de Maistre, the discourse of conservative paternalism, but it excluded women just as effectively. By giving women a positive republican destiny outside active citizenship, this discourse made it easier to justify their exclusion. Women didn't need citizenship: they had the higher role of preserving the Republic in the home, the cradle of male citizenship.

Thus even a politically active and involved woman like Adam – famous for her response to Proudhon's misogyny[50] – remained unaware of her exclusion, accepting instead informal political participation, initially through her salon, then as Gambetta's confidant, and later as Déroulède's backer. Similarly, Gambetta's mistress, Léonie Léon, whom he styled his political confidant and with whom he exchanged political views daily for ten years, never once envisaged the possibility of herself participating directly in political activity, although she found politics 'this fascinating preoccupation ... in which I would like to have lived exclusively.'[51]

The belief in women's higher calling, built on the biomedical model, was so profoundly rooted in nineteenth-century French society that even some feminists accepted it. Ernest Legouvé argued for 'equality in difference:' 'the 'virile' republican principles of liberty and equality must ... be complemented by the feminine virtue of fraternity.' Legouvé's notion that republican principles were 'virile' brings us back to the arguments of Pateman, Landes, and Hunt. Legouvé did not consider 'political rights for women.' Instead, he proposed significant civil rights for women as women, especially within marriage. That is essentially what the 1791 Constitution aimed to do by making women 'passive citizens.' It is not equality. 'Equality in difference' is, like 'separate but equal,' inherently unequal.[52]

Equality is at the core of citizenship and thus of status in the polity. 'Political equality,' Pierre Rosanvallon argues, 'marks the definitive entry of individuals into the world ... It affirms a kind of equivalence of position [*qualité*] between men [*sic*].' Equality is confirmed by the right to vote and the right to vote in turn confirms and reinforces equality: 'Universal [male] suffrage,' Rosanvallon continues, 'is a kind of sacrament of the equality between men.'[53] If one does not have the right to vote, one does not count in the same way as those who do. Without the suffrage and without citizenship – the two were indissolubly linked – women were not perceived or accepted as fully-fledged individuals in the world and they did not have the same weight as men in public discussion. It is no use arguing, as Legouvé did, that other channels were open to them. The channels that counted, the channels through which one could participate effectively in shaping the future of the polity, were fully open only to citizens, to those whose equivalence of position and status was consecrated by the suffrage.

Until women were citizens, with the right to vote and hold office, even their participation in 'public activism' – the informal aspects of the political public sphere – was less legitimate, less weighty, than men's. A few women were tolerated, but their position was always weaker than that of men. Women could and did use all the avenues open to them in informal public life: journalism, publication, teaching, and lecturing were not rigidly barred to them, but they struggled to make an impact. As non-citizens, they could not speak in the café, the *cercle*, the club, or the Masonic Lodge (or, at best, they could not speak with the same authority as men).[54] Without equality, without citizenship, without the suffrage, it was always harder for women to be taken seriously in public discussion than for men.

Instead of equality, republicans offered women complementary rights, usually as wives and mothers. The republican discourse of complementarity left open nurturing roles, but only indirect participation in politics, such as salon hostess (*salonnière*) and occult influence (*égérie*), of which Juliette Adam and Léonie Léon were perfect exemplars. Such roles could not compensate for women's exclusion from the suffrage. Far from giving women a position of influence, the salon 'accentuated,' in Berlanstein's words, women's exclusion from the public sphere: 'it brought men together, [and] empowered them [in part against women].'[55] Women played host to men and excluded other women. Steven Kale has shown that, when the salon was recreated in postrevolutionary France, it ceased to be a site of female influence. Instead, 'politics and *mondanité* became separated, and women were left to preside over a sociability of leisure that was increasingly marginal to public life.'[56] To be sure, as Anne Martin-Fugier has shown, *salonnières* played critical roles after 1870, helping the new republican political elite.[57] But they were not actors; instead they were tutors, teaching provincial republicans the social graces.

Playing the role of *égérie*, 'a woman considered as the counselor, the inspiration of a political or literary man,' while it may have compensated a few women like Léon, confirmed women's exclusion from formal politics: an *égérie* was a woman who, 'in the shadows and in the corridors of power,' influenced male politicians.[58] The *philosophes'* campaign against noblewomen had long presented the *égérie* as the mistress asking the great man for favors.[59] Republicans reaffirmed the word's negative connotations when women overstepped the bounds. In 1879, Léon Gambetta broke with Juliette Adam. She had scrubbed him up and brought him into fashionable society, making possible his key role in the founding of the Third Republic. But when she rejected his policy of understanding with Germany and moved to authoritarian patriotism, one of his colleagues wrote – with Gambetta's blessing – an article which thundered against her: 'the role of harmful [*néfastes*] *égéries* is over for our Republic, and may it be so for the peace of states and the happiness of peoples.'[60]

Complementarity was one pillar of reconfigured, republican exclusion. The other was anticlericalism. After 1848, Pius IX (pope 1848–78) turned against republicanism. The Church became a bastion of anti-republicanism in France. As republicans came to power in the last quarter of the century, they reconfigured the exclusion of women, linking women to the Church, which increasingly appeared to be a threat to the Republic. Women had been driven to the Church as one of the few avenues of public expression appropriate to their vocation and welcoming to them, but their association with the Church was then invoked by republicans to justify denying them the suffrage.

To the extent that women did attend church in greater numbers than men, this was clearly a result of the different duties prescribed for each sex: independence, autonomy, and rationality were identified, as Judith Surkis points out, as traits 'of masculinity itself;'[61] dependence, affectivity, and morality were identified as the essence of femininity in line with the biomedical model. The Church was to reinforce these traits: religion was usually a major part of women's upbringing.

Thus the republican model of complementarity was built on and in turn fed a fear that women's attachment to the Church would lead them to vote against the Republic. The republicans' anticlericalism, as Susan Foley points out, never led them to envisage restricting the suffrage of priests or of the religious orders they expelled with such vigor between the 1880s and 1905. It was inconceivable to exclude males from the suffrage, even enemy males, because they were men. Their sex sufficed to justify their enjoying the franchise, despite their anti-republican views.[62] *Clerical influence*

Even Léon Richer feared clerical influence on women. In 1877, his major book, *La femme libre* (The Free Woman), devoted 'an entire chapter ... to explaining why feminists should not seek the vote,' asking, in effect, for them to silence debate. 'Among nine million women ... only several thousand would vote freely; the rest would take their orders from the confessional.'[63] So even the leading male supporter of women's rights shifted his fundamental position toward that of the republicans by the time they came to power.

Richer's associate Maria Deraismes also became reticent about the suffrage. It has been argued that she was acting for tactical reasons, but both Steven Hause and this author concluded that she shared with Richer a deep anxiety about women's subjection to the confessor.[64] In 1878, after the republicans had taken full control of government, she and Richer organized a women's congress in conjunction with the Universal Exposition, but they prohibited discussion of the suffrage. The young feminist Hubertine Auclert reacted strongly: unable to gain a foothold among mainstream feminists, she sought and gained support from the socialists at the Congress of Marseilles in 1879.[65] This incident demonstrates the depth of silence which surrounded women's suffrage as the republicans triumphed. The socialists were a tiny sect well outside legitimate politics until the 1890s. For Auclert to go to the socialists demonstrated that she had no recourse among the republicans.

Anticlericalism reinforced republicans' opposition to women's suffrage. A fundamental text of republicanism and a major basis of republican fear of women's support for the Church was Jules Michelet's celebrated essay, *Du prêtre, de la femme et de la famille* (Priest, Woman and Family). It remained popular well into the twentieth century.[66] 'Our [*sic*] wives and our daughters,' Michelet argued, 'are raised, governed, *by our enemies ... Enemies of the modern world view* [italics in the original].' The priest was 'the husband's rival [literally 'the envious one'] and his secret enemy.' Having learned a woman's sexual secrets through confession, Michelet argued, the priest had power over men: 'Humiliation, to obtain nothing of that which was yours except by authorization and by indulgence, to be pursued in the most intimate intimacy [*sic*]

michelet

by an invisible witness who rules you [the husband; the book was addressed to men] and apportions your part, to meet in the street a man who knows better than you your secret weaknesses.'[67]

Michelet's preoccupation with male sexual inadequacy points to the link between mainstream anticlericalism and male domination. Here, the 'Woman Question' was indeed the 'Man Problem.' Michelet's discourse remained dominant in republican circles: Clemenceau had planned to use Michelet in his refutation of Mill; in 1928, still opposing female suffrage, he remarked, 'woman is led by the priest.'[68] The struggle between rational, republican husband and religious, reactionary wife became a staple of republican literature.

To win this struggle, some republicans supported women's education, if not their rights. Jules Ferry enacted education for women in the 1880s, a huge advance, but on the grounds that 'women must belong either to Science or to the Church;' too many republicans, he thought, failed to take into account 'the secret and persistent support she [woman] brings to [monarcho-clericalism].'[69] Ferry and other republicans shared the concern that women ought not to be exposed to too much learning and thus deliberately avoided a program for the baccalaureate. Women had to fill this gap through extensive private tutoring to obtain the baccalaureate and thus qualify for higher education. Only in 1924 was a baccalaureate stream established for women's schools, by the conservative Education Minister Leon Bérard, who as Chairman of the Senate Committee on Women's Suffrage was largely responsible for its defeat in 1922![70]

Before World War I, in a Chamber composed largely of republicans, there were never enough supporters even to get women's suffrage onto the floor for debate. Catholics and socialists did more for women's suffrage than republicans. The socialists, once united as the SFIO (Section Française de l'Internationale Ouvrière) in 1905, reaffirmed their commitment to women's suffrage at the 1906 Congress of Limoges, pushed by Madeleine Pelletier. The socialists and later the communists were the only parties to endorse women's suffrage during the whole of the Third Republic. No republican party did so.[71]

It was the Catholic deputy Paul Dussaussoy who, in 1906, introduced the only proposal for women's suffrage that got near to being debated, a modest proposal to give women the vote in local elections only. The republican Ferdinand Buisson produced a favorable report, but discussion was delayed until 1913 and then adjourned indefinitely. Few republicans saw the contradiction between equality and women's affective role that was self-evident to feminists.

Feminism and the vote beyond republicanism

Women's demands for autonomy and for citizenship reached new heights before World War I, just as contestation of the Republic, in the Boulanger and especially the Dreyfus Affair, renewed fears of decadence and anxieties about the male body, as Robert Nye and Chris Forth have shown. Feminism gained traction and the 'New Woman' emerged at the same time as the republican project went on the defensive: both, as Mary Louise Roberts argues were part of the challenge to the norms of liberal bourgeois culture at the turn of the century.[72]

The word 'feminist' entered public discourse with the founding of a federation of 'feminist' groups in 1892.[73] After the death of Deraismes in 1894, the Ligue française pour le droit des femmes (French League for Women's Rights) became the main focus of feminist activity. In the late 1890s, new leaders brought the Ligue around to wholehearted support for the suffrage. These groups provided the framework for an explosion of feminist activity at the end of the century.

While many republican women were feminists, basing their feminism on the universalist message of republican discourse, reshaping or even ignoring the concomitant message of domesticity, activism after 1900 was also significant among women who were not republicans. The Ligue des femmes françaises (French Women's League) was founded in 1901 as a women's counterpart to the anti-Dreyfusard Ligue de la patrie française (Ligue of the French Fatherland). The following year, other conservatives founded the Ligue patriotique des françaises (French Women's Patriotic League), which emphasized family and religion rather than royalism. By 1914, the League had 545,000 members, making it the largest women's organization in France. In 1919, the umbrella organization of Catholic women's groups endorsed the principle of women's suffrage and formed a Catholic suffrage group. They claimed to represent 'over one million women,' as against 100,000 for the Conseil national des femmes françaises (National Council of Frenchwomen), still the major feminist coalition. Such support from Catholics did not help the cause in the eyes of republicans fearful of clerical influence; it fanned their fears that women voters would reverse the Republic's secular orientation.[74]

The Chamber finally voted women's suffrage, on 20 May 1919, by the astonishing margin of 329 for, 95 against. But behind the vote lay mixed motives. The original gender basis of citizenship had eroded: it was now less acceptable to argue that women were inherently inferior. But it was more acceptable and more common to argue that, if women were granted the suffrage, they would vote with the anti-democratic parties supported by the Church and thus overturn the Republic. (This argument carried weight at a time when many remembered the Boulanger, Panama and Dreyfus Affairs.[75]) This anticlerical argument effectively reconfigured the older argument that women were inferior. In this form, it now carried great weight with republican men and indeed with republican women: 'to give the right to vote to women in France would be to give the priest in each village the ballots of all the women,' wrote one provincial feminist militant.[76] The Senate, reflecting these sentiments, delayed consideration and finally rejected women's suffrage, on 21 November 1922, by a vote of 156 to 134. The majority was dominated by rural republicans.

On the very day the Senate rejected women's suffrage, Victor Margueritte's novel, *La Garçonne* (The Bachelor girl), appeared in bookstores. The novel was enormously successful: it sold a record 300,000 copies by the end of 1922 and caused an enormous scandal, leading to Margueritte's ouster from the Légion d'honneur. The word *garçonne* became common to describe a girl who behaved in boyish ways, referring both to boyish appearance and to independent life. The *garçonne* reflected the definitive emergence of the 'New Woman' and the collapse of the old gender order and the biomedical model, as the Great War had finally buried the hopes associated with the Enlightenment and as republicanism went on the defensive.

Women's suffrage was enacted only in 1944, on the ruins of the Third Republic and, one could argue, of the Enlightenment project. At the Algiers Assembly (the 'Assemblée consultative provisoire'), republicans continued to oppose women's suffrage; it succeeded thanks to Gaullists and communists, arguably those least implicated in traditional republicanism. The president of the committee discussing the question – Paul Giacobbi, a leading Radical republican – asked, 'Do you think it would be wise during such a troubled period ... to throw us into the adventure that women's suffrage would constitute?' The committee did offer to grant women the right to vote in the first municipal elections, but proposed that a minimum of 80 per cent of the male electors participate for the vote to be legal. This was an opposition to women's suffrage that dared not say its name.[77]

Other participants understood this. According to Raymond Aubrac, who was present, the discussion was 'acrimonious: the delegates of Radical orientation voted against, fearing the influence of the Church.' The socialist Louis Vallon, a confidant of de Gaulle, argued that the Radical republicans' hesitations were a throwback to the bad old days: 'I hear in this debate the traditions of the old French Parliament in their most detestable form. Many times, the Parliament voted women's suffrage with near unanimity, but each time it was arranged behind the scenes, by procedural arguments, to prevent it. These small-minded maneuvers have to end (Applause).'[78] It was a communist, Fernand Grenier, who proposed an amendment: 'Women will vote and be eligible on the same conditions as men.' The committee unanimously rejected this. The Assembly, however, passed it, thanks to communist and Gaullist votes. Thus it was that women finally obtained the vote in France despite persistent republican opposition.[79]

The French lag?

The exclusion of women was inherent in the process of constructing citizenship in modern France. Constantly fought and reconfigured, it reached its

apogee not in the 1790s but in the 1880s, with the triumph of the Republic. The exclusionary dynamic, central to the construction of citizenship and
the public sphere in the eighteenth century, remained central to republicanism into the twentieth century. In these later forms it manifested itself
in the discourse of complementarity and the fear of clerical influence on
women.

The French case has implications for understanding the nature of citizenship in all liberal democracies. All liberal democracies trace their roots to
the three great revolutions of the seventeenth and eighteenth centuries. Of
these, only France established a Republic from within a strong divine right
monarchy without external aid, indeed against most of Europe, and, as Hunt
points out, only France articulated 'a concept of universal rights, which ...
led ineluctably to a reconsideration of everyone's rights, including those of
women.'[80]

If the exclusion of women was inherent in the republican project, then
the quarter century between women's obtaining the vote in America and
Britain and their obtaining it in France may well indicate a French advance.
Contrary to the implicit teleology in the idea of a 'French lag' in the suffrage, it may well be that, if the exclusion of women from the political public
sphere was more deeply rooted in France than elsewhere, it was not because
republicanism failed but because republicanism had deeper roots in France
than elsewhere. If women were excluded for longer where republicanism was
strongest, then we could expect that they would have been included sooner
where republicanism was weakest. There is some evidence to suggest this is
so. Patricia Grimshaw pioneered work about the origins of women's suffrage,
work since taken up by Louise Newman.[81] Grimshaw began with a key fact
often overlooked: the places where women obtained the vote before 1900
were all frontier lands – New Zealand, two Australian states (South Australia
and Western Australia) and four American states (Colorado, Idaho, Utah, and
Wyoming).[82] These were not the vanguards of republican universalism; they
were settler states involved in struggles for law and order and for the land
they were taking from indigenous peoples. Women's suffrage was granted for
many motives, including the creation of a coalition against frontier lawless-
ness and against the indigenous peoples whom white settlers had displaced,
but it was not granted because of the power of the republican tradition and it
was not granted first in the heartland of republicanism or in one of the great
cities associated with the birth of republicanism.

On the contrary, republicans fought against women's suffrage to the bitter end and delayed it until 1944. Then it was only implemented by parties
outside the republican mainstream. Around the world, women's suffrage was
achieved not as the fruit of republicanism but as the result of pressures that
were anything but republican. The republican project, having constructed
citizenship on a gendered base, never transcended its origins in the exclusion of women. Republicanism never on its own resolved the contradiction

that had given it birth, between public man and private woman, though it did forge the hammer of equality which others would use to smash the chains of inequality.

Constantly reconstructed during the nineteenth century and well into the twentieth, women's exclusion was only overcome when republicanism went on the defensive and other forces came into play. Women obtained the vote only after citizenship had been fully constructed and had become the uncontested foundation of the modern polity, thereby fulfilling and exhausting the republican project.

Notes

1. The author thanks the Australian Research Council for support, Alice Garner for research, Susan Foley (*formerly* Grogan), Steve Hause, Joy Damousi, Elinor Accampo, and Chris Forth for reading drafts.

2. Pierre Rosanvallon, *Le Sacre du citoyen: Histoire du suffrage universel en France* (Paris: Gallimard, 1992), pp. 96–101, 105–12.

3. Karen Offen, 'Women, Citizenship and Suffrage with a French Twist, 1789–1993,' in Melanie Nolan and Caroline Daley (eds), *Suffrage and Beyond: International Feminist Perspectives* (Auckland, NZ: Auckland University Press, 1994), p. 151.

4. Rosanvallon, *Le Sacre*, p. 176.

5. Offen, 'Women,' pp. 156, 161–3.

6. Robert Nye, *Masculinity and Male Codes of Honor in Modern France* (New York: Oxford University Press, 1993), pp. 47, 54.

7. Carole Pateman, *The Sexual Contract* (Stanford: Stanford University Press, 1988); Joan Landes, *Women and the Public Sphere in the Age of the French Revolution* (Ithaca: Cornell University Press, 1988); Madelyn Gutwirth, *The Twilight of the Goddesses: Women and Representation in the French Revolutionary Era* (New Brunswick, NJ: Rutgers University Press, 1992).

8. Pateman, *Sexual Contract*, chs 3 and 4; Lynn Hunt, *The Family Romance of the French Revolution* (Berkeley: University of California Press, 1992), pp. 17–88; Judith Surkis, *Sexing the Citizen: Morality and Masculinity in France, 1870–1920* (Ithaca: Cornell University Press, 2006), p. 6.

9. Hunt, *Family Romance*; Joan Scott, *Only Paradoxes to Offer: French Feminists and the Rights of Man* (Cambridge, MA: Harvard University Press, 1996), esp. pp. 3–11; Joan Landes, *Visualizing the Nation* (Ithaca: Cornell University Press, 2001).

10. Nicole Fermon, *Domesticating Passions: Rousseau, Woman, and Nation* (Hanover, NH: University Press of New England, 1997); Dena Goodman, *The Republic of Letters* (Ithaca: Cornell University Press, 1994).

11. Carla Hesse, 'Revolutionary Rousseaus: the Story of his Editions after 1789,' in Marie-Christine Skuncke and Robert Darnton (eds), *Media and Political Culture in the Eighteenth Century* (Stockholm: Kungl. Vitterhets, 2005), pp. 105–28.

12. Dorinda Outram, *The Enlightenment* (2nd edn; Cambridge: Cambridge University Press, 2005), p. 81.

13. Lenard Berlanstein, *Daughters of Eve: a Cultural History of French Theater Women from the Old Regime to the Fin de Siècle* (Cambridge, MA: Harvard University Press, 2001), pp. 74–6.

14. Robert Darnton, 'Readers Respond to Rousseau: the Fabrication of Romantic Sensibility,' in *The Great Cat Massacre and Other Episodes in French Cultural History* (New York: Basic Books, 1984), p. 24; Rousseau, *Émile*, quoted in Landes, *Women*, p. 85.

15. Rousseau, *Discourse on Inequality* [1754], quoted ibid., pp. 68–9.

16. Dominique Godineau, *The Women of Paris and their French Revolution*, trans. K. Streip (Berkeley: University of California Press, 1998), p. 108.

17. Compare Pierre Rosanvallon, *La Démocratie inachevée: Histoire de la souveraineté du peuple en France* (Paris: Gallimard, 2000), p. 169.

18. Jack Censer and Lynn Hunt, *Liberty, Equality, Fraternity: Exploring the French Revolution* (University Park: Pennsylvania State University Press, 2001), pp. 100–1.

19. Karen Offen, 'Ernest Legouvé and the Doctrine of "Equality in Difference" for Women: a Case Study of Male Feminism in Nineteenth-Century French Thought,' *Journal of Modern History*, 58(2) (June 1986): 461; Berlanstein, *Daughters*, p. 76; Dorinda Outram, *The Body and the French Revolution: Sex, Class and Political Culture* (New Haven: Yale University Press, 1989), pp. 72–87. Rachel Fuchs, *Contested Paternity: Constructing Families in Modern France* (Baltimore: Johns Hopkins University Press, 2008), demonstrates how the Civil Code's precepts entered culture and society.

20. Denise Davidson, *France after Revolution: Urban Life, Gender, and the New Social Order* (Cambridge, MA: Harvard University Press, 2007); Suzanne Desan, *The Family on Trial in Revolutionary France* (Berkeley: University of California Press, 2004); Carla Hesse, *The Other Enlightenment: How French Women Became Modern* (Princeton: Princeton University Press, 2001); Rebecca Rogers, *From the Salon to the Schoolroom: Educating Bourgeois Girls in Nineteenth-Century France* (University Park: Pennsylvania State University Press, 2005).

21. *H-France Review*, Vol. 5 (September 2005), No. 98, http://www.h-france.net/vol5 reviews/mcphee5.html (accessed 11 September 2008).

22. Rogers, *From the Salon*, p. 17.

23. Ibid., pp. 21, 130–1, 135–59.

24. Davidson, *France after Revolution*, pp. 3–5.

25. Desan, *Family*, p. 11; compare pp. 20–4.

26. Hesse, *Other Enlightenment*, pp. 8–9.

27. Compare Michelle Perrot (ed.), *From the Fires of Revolution to the Great War* (Cambridge, MA: Belknap Press of Harvard University Press, 1991); Bonnie Smith, *Ladies of the Leisure Class: the Bourgeoises of Northern France in the Nineteenth Century* (Princeton: Princeton University Press, 1981).

28. Jürgen Habermas, *The Structural Transformation of the Public Sphere: an Inquiry into a Category of Bourgeois Society* (Cambridge, MA: MIT Press, 1991), pp. xvi, 30, 176.

29. Rogers, *From the Salon*; Susan K. Grogan (now Foley), 'Women, Philanthropy and the State: the Société de Charité maternelle in Avignon, 1802–1917,' *French History*, 14(3) (2000): 295–321; Caroline C. Ford, *Divided Houses: Religion and Gender in Modern France* (Ithaca, NY: Cornell University Press, 2005).

30. Joan Wallach Scott, ' "L'Ouvrière! Mot impie, sordide ..." ": Women Workers in the Discourse of French Political Economy, 1840–1861,' in *Gender and the Politics of History* (New York: Columbia University Press, 1988), p. 155.

31. Margaret Darrow, 'French Noblewomen and the New Domesticity, 1750–1850,' *Feminist Studies*, 5(1) (Spring 1979): 57.

32. Mary Louise Roberts, *Disruptive Acts: the New Woman in Fin-de-Siècle France* (Chicago: University of Chicago Press, 2002), p. 4.

33. Lynn Hunt, 'Forgetting and Remembering: the French Revolution Then and Now,' *American Historical Review*, 100 (4 October 1995): 1119–35; Margaret Darrow, *Revolution in the House: Family, Class, and Inheritance in Southern France, 1775–1825* (Princeton, NJ: Princeton University Press, 1989); Jennifer Heuer, *The Family and the Nation: Gender and Citizenship in Revolutionary France, 1789–1830* (Ithaca: Cornell University Press, 2005); Desan, *Family*.

34. Hunt, 'Forgetting and Remembering,' 1131–2.

35. Compare, for example, Gutwirth, *Twilight*, pp. 383–5.

36. Scott, *Only Paradoxes*, pp. 3, 11. Compare Charles Sowerwine, *Sisters or Citizens? Women and Socialism in France since 1876* (Cambridge: Cambridge University Press, 1982), ch. 5.

37. Nye, *Masculinity*, pp. 47, 54.

38. Thomas Laqueur, *Making Sex: Body and Gender from the Greeks to Freud* (Cambridge, MA: Harvard University Press, 1990), p. 6.

39. Outram, *Enlightenment*, pp. 86–7.

40. Susan K. Foley (*formerly Grogan*), *Women in France since 1789: the Meanings of Difference* (New York: Palgrave, 2004), pp. 109, 130.

41. Patrick Bidelman, *Pariahs Stand Up! The Founding of the Liberal Feminist Movement in France, 1858–1889* (Westport, CT: Greenwood Press, 1982), pp. 97, 83; *L'Avenir des femmes*, 7–8 July 1872; Steven Hause, *Hubertine Auclert: the French Suffragette* (New Haven: Yale University Press, 1987), p. 19; Laurence Klejman and Florence Rochefort, *L'Egalité en Marche: Le féminisme sous la Troisième République* (Paris: Presses de la Fondation Nationale des Sciences Politiques/Editions des femmes, 1989), p. 52.

42. Charles Sowerwine, *France since 1870: Culture, Society and the Making of the Republic* (2nd edn; Basingstoke: Palgrave, 2009), p. 29.

43. Albert Wolff, *Le Figaro*, 14 June 1872.

44. Jack D. Ellis, *The Physician-Legislators of France: Medicine and Politics in the Early Third Republic, 1870–1914* (Cambridge: Cambridge University Press, 1990), pp. 4, 11, 100.

45. David Watson, 'Clemenceau and Mill,' *The Mill Newsletter*, 6(1) (1970): 13–19, esp. 16–17.

46. Eugène Pelletan, *La Femme au XIXe siècle* (Paris: Pagnerre, 1869), p. 29; compare Judith Stone, 'The Republican Brotherhood: Gender and Ideology,' in Elinor Accampo, Rachel Fuchs, and Mary Lynn Stewart (eds), *Gender and the Politics of Social Reform in France, 1870–1914* (Baltimore: Johns Hopkins University Press, 1995), p. 29.

47. Juliette Adam, *Nos Amitiés politiques avant l'abandon de la revanche* (Paris: A. Lemerre, 1908), p. 31.

48. Daniel Halévy, *Trois diners avec Gambetta*, ed. Ludovic Halévy (Paris: B. Grasset, 1929), p. 61.

49. Surkis, *Sexing*.

50. Juliette Adam [Juliette Lamber], *Idées Anti-proudhoniennes sur l'amour, la femme et le mariage* (1st edn; Paris: A. Taride, 1858).

51. Susan Foley, ' "Your Letter is Divine, Irresistible, Infernally Seductive": Léon Gambetta, Léonie Léon, and Nineteenth-Century Epistolary Culture,' *French Historical Studies*, 30(2) (Spring 2007): 239. Compare Susan Foley and Charles Sowerwine, *Passion and Politics: Léon Gambetta, Léonie Léon, and the Making of the Third Republic*, forthcoming Palgrave, 2009.

52. Offen, 'Ernest Legouvé and the Doctrine of "Equality in Difference" for Women,' pp. 453, 461, 469.

53. Rosanvallon, *Le Sacre du citoyen*, pp. 15–17; C.B. Macpherson, *The Political Theory of Possessive Individualism: Hobbes to Locke* (London: Oxford University Press, 1962).

54. Maurice Agulhon, *Le Cercle dans la France bourgeoise: 1810–1848, étude d'une mutation de sociabilité* (Paris: A. Colin, 1977); Evelyne Lejeune-Resnick, *Femmes et associations, 1830–1880: Vraies démocrates ou dames patronesses?* (Paris: Publisud, 1991); Eliane Brault, *La Franc-maçonnerie et l'émancipation des femmes* (Paris: Dervy, 1953).

55. Berlanstein, *Daughters*, p. 4.

56. Steven D. Kale, 'Women, Salons, and the State in the Aftermath of the French Revolution,' *Journal of Women's History*, 13(4) (2002): 54, 80; *French Salons: High Society and Political Sociability from the Old Regime to the Revolution of 1848* (Baltimore: Johns Hopkins University Press, 2004).

57. Anne Martin-Fugier, *Les Salons de la IIIe République: Art, littérature, politique* (Paris: Perrin, 2003); Foley, *Women*, p. 134.

58. Marie-Thérèse Guichard, *Les Égéries de la République* (Paris: Payot, 1991), p. 9.

59. Hunt, *Family Romance*.

60. *Le Voltaire*, 10 December 1879, quoted in Guichard, *Les Égéries de la République*, p. 45.

61. Surkis, *Sexing*, p. 2.

62. Foley, *Women in France*. p. 151.

63. Hause, *Hubertine Auclert*, p. 41. Compare Léon Richer, *La Femme libre* (Paris: E. Dentu, 1877); *Le Livre des femmes* (Paris: Librairie de la Bibliothèque démocratique, 1872), in which there is little question of the suffrage.

64. Charles Sowerwine, 'The Organization of French Socialist Women, 1880–1914,' *Historical Reflections/Réflexions historiques*, 3 (1976): 3–24; Steven C. Hause, 'The Limits of Suffragist Behavior: Legalism and Militancy in France, 1876–1922,' *American Historical Review*, 86 (1981): 781–806.

65. Hause, *Hubertine Auclert*, pp. 42–67; Sowerwine, *Sisters or Citizens?* pp. 23–8

66. Jules Michelet, *Du Prêtre, de la femme et de la famille* (1843; 3rd edn; Paris: Hachette, Paulin, 1845).

67. Michelet, *Le Prêtre, la femme et la famille* (new edition; Paris: Calmann-Lévy, 1890), pp. 2, 208–9.

68. David Watson, 'Clemenceau and Mill,' pp. 16–17.

69. Bidelman, *Pariahs Stand Up!* p. 17.

70. Sowerwine, *France*, p. 121.

71. Sowerwine, *Sisters or Citizens?* pp. 108–10, 114–15.

72. Christopher E. Forth, *The Dreyfus Affair and the Crisis of French Manhood* (Baltimore: Johns Hopkins University Press, 2004); Nye, *Masculinity*; Roberts, *Disruptive Acts*, pp. 7, 5.

73. Karen Offen, 'On the French Origin of the Words Feminism and Feminist,' *Feminist Issues*, 8(2) (1988): 47.

74. Steven Hause and Anne Kenney, 'The Development of the Catholic Women's Suffrage Movement in France, 1896–1922,' *Catholic Historical Review*, 67(1) (1981): 11–30; compare Steven Hause and Anne Kenney, *Women's Suffrage and Social Politics in the French Third Republic* (Princeton: Princeton University Press, 1984).

75. Sowerwine, 'The Organization of French Socialist Women, 1880–1914;' Hause, 'The Limits of Suffragist Behavior.'

76. Hause and Kenney, *Women's Suffrage,* p. 60; Christine Bard, *Les Femmes dans la société française au 20e siècle* (Paris: Colin, 2001), pp. 84–7.
77. William Guéraiche, 'Les Femmes politiques de 1944 à 1947,' *Clio: Histoire, Femmes et Sociétés,* 1 (1995): 165–86, esp. 169, 170, and n. 7; compare Christine Bard, *Les Filles de Marianne: histoire de féminismes, 1914–1940* (Paris: Fayard, 1995), pp. 448–9.
78. Guéraiche, 'Les Femmes politiques,' 170-2, 175; letter to author from Raymond Aubrac, 2 October 1998; Sowerwine, *France,* p. 212.
79. William Guéraiche, *Les Femmes et la République: Essai sur la répartition du pouvoir de 1943 à 1979* (Paris: Atelier, 1999), pp. 265, 268, 271.
80. Hunt, 'Forgetting,' p. 1132.
81. Louise Newman, *White Women's Rights: the Racial Origins of Feminism in the United States* (New York: Oxford University Press, 1999).
82. Patricia Grimshaw, 'Women's Suffrage in New Zealand Revisited: Writing from the Margins,' in Nolan and Daley (eds), *Suffrage and Beyond,* pp. 38–40.

2
Is the 'Woman Question' Really the 'Man Problem'?

Karen Offen

Can the so-called 'Woman Question' (*la question des femmes*) that has repeatedly erupted in print through the centuries in France be better understood as the 'Man Problem'?[1] Although the terminology only dates back to the 1830s, along with the 'Social Question' (*la question sociale*) and 'Socialism,' the debate over what women should be and do is much older, and until recent times the overwhelming majority of debaters were men. Only from the early fifteenth century did a few women raise their voices, usually to protest what men were saying on this subject, but from the eighteenth century on, in the wake of mounting literacy and the advent of civil society, their voices multiplied and they began to challenge masculine dominance with vigor, calling for women's rights, equality of the sexes, and full inclusion in the shaping of French society.[2] In fact, the so-called 'sexual contract' that Carole Pateman has identified as existing prior to and undergirding the 'social contract' was under attack and beginning to crumble.[3]

Throughout the nineteenth century, amidst numerous changes in political regimes, this feminist critique grew louder and more significant. In response, a number of articulate French men (whom we would now call antifeminist) made exceptional, well-publicized efforts to assert and justify male authority, which they viewed as a key component of masculine honor. The most vehement spokesmen worried obsessively about controlling women, about retaining them in subservient domesticity; they often demeaned and disparaged women even as they acknowledged women's singular power and influence over men. Even with the combined forces of law, prescription, custom, religion, institutions, organized knowledge – and, not least, physical strength – behind them, such men seemed to feel increasingly insecure in their 'right' to rule over women. The volume and shrillness of this masculine antifeminism suggests, in retrospect, that such men could no longer assume male supremacy; they had to assert it and justify it – and print became their medium of choice. Consequently, the literature of antifeminism has until very recently taken up a disproportionate amount of shelf space compared to that of feminism.

43

Neither feminism nor antifeminism was in short supply in the French aristocratic society of the Old Regime monarchies, the immediate source of the cult of masculine bourgeois honor about which Robert A. Nye has written so convincingly.[4] For example, early in the reign of Louis XIV, the antifeminist messages embedded in Molière's well-known plays (among other sources) were widely propagated in opposition to feminist arguments that the institution of marriage was, for wives, analogous to slavery.[5] Feminist criticism did not disappear during the eighteenth century, but focused on women's inadequate education; it was 'culture,' not 'nature,' women insisted, that underlay women's inequality; in other words, they claimed that women's 'inferiority' was culturally constructed.[6] This critique sharpened and grew louder during the revolutionary upheavals, thanks to a new and powerful vocabulary that included terms such as liberty, equality, justice, and citizenship – each of which carried great resonance with regard to ending the subordination of women. With the revolution, a number of women publicly demanded full and equal citizenship, and even called for the end of male privilege. Their audacity provoked an immense, immoderate backlash.

Especially after the French Revolution many non-noble men, both bourgeois and proletarian, took advantage of earlier antifeminist arguments and elaborated them at length, generally pointing to the ill effects of women's exorbitant power and influence during the Old Regime. If the more extreme among them were asserting masculine brotherhood in the face of women's claims to citizenship, it was a concrete – by no means 'abstract' – brotherhood, embodied in husbands and heads of households rather than one that encompassed all male individuals. They believed that the male-headed family must be preserved at all cost and that women's influence must be channeled – or broken! The monarchy was gone, and a republic substituted in its place, but the change in label had little significance when it came to reinforcing and defending male authority.

Even though optimists such as Charles Therémin thought that women's status should improve under a republic, medical men in particular (with a few notable exceptions) used their scientific credibility to counter contemporary perceptions of women's power and influence, and their cultural importance, by attempting to 'prove' women's physical ('biological') and mental inferiority.[7] They elaborated what I am calling a 'biotheology.' Philosopher-physicians such as the misogynistic J.-J. Virey insisted that the differences between women and men (and, consequently, their sociopolitical roles) were irrevocably grounded in physiology, with an emphasis on childbearing for women; that they were not simply a consequence of their differing educations as many reformers, both women and men, had been claiming prior to the Revolution. 'The word "femme" [woman, wife, in French] comes from [the Latin word] *foemina*, which comes from *foetare*, *foetus* [to give birth, offspring], because woman's natural purpose is to give birth.'[8] And only that. Opponents of women's emancipation would relentlessly deduce social roles – and 'prove' the necessity of women's subordination by insisting on the superiority of male physiological traits. Thus were male muscular strength and relative female 'weakness' constantly reinvested with political significance. That some women were not unaware of this deliberate effort to reinforce sexual hierarchy by positioning women as the 'weaker sex' is attested to by Constance de Theis (later the princesse de Salm) in a bittersweet verse published in 1797:[9]

> Let the anatomist, blinded by his science,
> Artfully calculate the power of a muscle,
> Infer, without appeal, 'twixt the more and the less,
> That his wife owes him eternal respect.

Throughout the early nineteenth century, medical men continued to elaborate their theories on sexual difference. Following the revolutions of 1848 and the failure of the Second Republic, secular critics eagerly consumed, regurgitated, and embellished these theories, emphasizing women's inferiority to men and the necessity of subordinating them. Pierre-Joseph Proudhon (who was far more antifeminist, even misogynist, than Jules Michelet) is perhaps the most notorious, while scholarly theorists such as Jules Michelet and Auguste Comte, who respected women more, placed them on a pedestal, in effect daring them to venture off.[10] During the Second Empire neo-conservative men such as Paul Bernard and Frédéric Le Play even produced justificatory historical defenses of 'patriarchy.'[11] At the same time, however, several women (notably Clémence Royer and Jenny P. d'Héricourt, and subsequently Juliette Lambert LaMessine Adam, Maria Deraismes, and André Léo) challenged such arguments, kicking off what I have called elsewhere the 'knowledge wars.'[12] Along with Henriette Wild, who championed women's history, these women proclaimed the need for female forms of knowledge and understanding – and woman-centered content – to counterbalance the prevailing and biased forms of knowledge, particularly medical knowledge, produced by men. As the century rolled on and the Third Republic gained traction, increasing numbers of progressively-minded women and men spoke out on behalf of women's rights. The fervent republican Maria Deraismes put it bluntly in 1882, 'One must recognize that in France masculine supremacy is the last aristocracy.'[13]

In 1885, the suffragist Hubertine Auclert proposed a 'women's electoral program' in twelve articles which demanded women's full inclusion in the French nation. It proposed a series of measures designed to promote the equality of the sexes, including the vote, and to replace what she called the 'Minotaur State' by the 'Motherly State' (*État mère de famille*), which would assure 'security and work to able-bodied French citizens, assistance to children, old people, the sick and the infirm.' In conclusion, she insisted that 'the human equality it [this program] proposes is the goal of a Republic; for Republic and justice should be synonymous.'[14] In Auclert's view – and she was not alone – women had everything to gain under a republic.

By the 1890s many advocates of women's equality and rights were calling themselves 'feminists' – and opposing 'masculinisme,' by which they meant the presumption of male privilege and male rule, with 'féminisme,' by which they meant both improving the status of women, and, more subtly, challenging male authority. Antifeminist men, however, were not ready to admit a partnership of equals; in their view of the world, if men were not in charge, women would be 'on top.' They adhered to the 'topsy-turvy' theory of social organization.[15]

Scholars have not been inattentive to this resurgence of 'masculinisme' in France or to efforts made to reconfigure it in positive directions. In her studies of novels by late nineteenth-century male writers, Annelise Maugue has discerned evidence of a growing 'crisis of masculinity;' Christine Bard has edited an entire conference volume on the subject of mounting antifeminism in France.[16] Robert Nye has superbly explored this 'crisis' with reference to discourses about 'degeneration' and 'male codes of honor,' while Christopher Forth has elaborated on its particular significance during the Dreyfus Affair.[17] Judith Surkis has investigated the deliberate efforts made toward 'sexing the citizen,' by examining prescriptive efforts by Third Republic intellectuals and educators to advocate a new anti-authoritarian masculinity, and especially, a revised masculine heterosexuality suitable to undergird republican citizenship.[18] This chapter, conversely, addresses the implications of the new challenges to 'masculinisme' during the Third Republic, as the prevailing post-revolutionary assertions of male privilege and honor based on notions of male superiority came under attack by pro-feminist and republican proponents of a more democratic culture, a culture in which women and men would complement one another. It offers several short case studies, including a look at one 'new man,' a republican who was entirely devoted to female emancipation, and at one republican feminist's effort to challenge men's assumptions about their sexual needs by advocating abolition of government-regulated prostitution and the need for a single, higher standard of morality for both sexes.

In the face of this 'masculinity crisis,' feminists of the French fin de siècle (both female and male) exuded optimism, rather than dwelling on degeneration and decadence. With the stabilization of the Third Republic, in fact, they insisted that a new day was surely dawning for women's emancipation.[19] And indeed, French women – like women elsewhere in Europe and North America – were making great strides, educationally, economically, and professionally, if not yet legally. Invoking the very principles of liberty, equality, and fraternity consecrated by the new republican government, Third Republic feminists demanded major changes to the country's legal, sociopolitical, and economic structures, not least in the institution of marriage. Already in 1889 one feminist congress obtained official sponsorship from the Third Republic's government, and, in 1900, two congresses won support from the republic's Solidarist ministers. Women and women's emancipation seemed fashionable; the republicans who organized the Paris international exposition of 1900 crowned 'La Parisienne' as the queen of the new century.[20] Admittedly, 'La Parisienne' seemed the antithesis of the caricature of the 'Femme nouvelle' (cigar-smoking, cycling) but she certainly symbolized the importance of well-bred, fashionable women and their influence in French culture under the Republic.[21] The question of woman provided a prominent theme among male artists around the turn of the century.

I return to my original question. Was the much-discussed 'Woman Question' in fact by, about, and for women? Or did this debate really reflect a 'Man Problem,' a growing problem of stabilizing particularly fragile male identities, of bolstering the egos of men who only understood masculinity as based on domination of women, children, and underlings? Was it about re-drawing rhetorical as well as physical lines of separation to cordon off a troubling, invasive female 'other,' as today's cultural theorists might put it?

Here I want to approach this question from an entirely different angle, by asking what made other men – whom we will call the French republican 'male-feminists' – supportive of women's emancipation? How does one explain the fact that not all French men, especially not all of those who were committed republicans, stood on the side of male dominance and patriarchy? Why, for example, were the pro-feminist works of the progressive writer, educator, dramaturge, and academician Ernest Legouvé (who addressed the 'Woman Question' in supportive terms both before and after the revolutions of 1848) so widely circulated in France and translated throughout Europe?[22]

Charles Sowerwine insists that the Third Republic was unrepentantly 'gendered' male from the outset. His argument, however, ignores the considerable support for women's emancipation, including their admission to the vote, from highly visible republican men, both of the preceding and ensuing generations.[23] Why did European observers such as the German women's rights activist Käthe Schirmacher (who lived in France during the 1890s) claim that, during the first decade of the twentieth century, French feminist demands found greater support from pro-feminist men in government and intellectual circles than seemed available to women in any other European country? 'Thanks to the republican and socialist movements, which for thirty years have controlled France, the woman's rights movement is for political reasons supported by the men to a degree not noticeable in any other country. The republican majority in the Chamber of Deputies, the republican press, and republican literature effectively promote the woman's rights movement.'[24]

Male feminism was, in fact, a 'genre' that developed substantially during the Third Republic, encompassing significant political and intellectual figures such as Victor Schoelcher, Auguste Vacquerie, Jules Ferry, Jules Favre,

Léon Richer, René Viviani, Léon Blum, Paul and Victor Margueritte, Ferdinand Buisson, Léopold Lacour – the list could go on and on. Indeed, the growth of male feminism under the Third Republic in particular provides an important and overlooked counterpoint to the claims made in support of the fundamental misogyny of 'the republic.' This is not to say that, for many men, usually of more conservative political persuasions, the crisis of masculinity and the affront to male honor was not real, but it reminds us that other currents, more favorable to women's advancement, also existed within the world of French men. Even though the feminist journalist Harlor observed in 1900 that 'Male antifeminism is usually so profound, even among the elite, that it is ... ingenuous: the most distinguished spirits eliminate quite naïvely from their human and national preoccupations [both] feminine humanity and the female nation,'[25] in fact, as Schirmacher substantiated, support for moderate feminist claims was making considerable headway among progressive republican men.

In what follows I will offer some intertwined observations, drawn from my ongoing research on the 'Woman Question,' that may provide new ways of approaching and contextualizing constructions of 'masculinity' and the changing meanings of 'male honor' with reference to women's rights and roles in republican France. I will highlight three interrelated points: (1) that women and men both acknowledged women's power and influence over men in French society; (2) that, thanks to mechanization, the disparity between the physical strength of men and women became less of a determining issue; and (3) that once the republican government restored freedom of the press, the world of print and publicity dramatically amplified the pro-feminist arguments of both women and men, including those that critiqued men's warlike propensities and their sexual habits. Claims for women's rights that might have seemed outrageous in earlier times began to receive a hearing among those who took seriously the principles that the republic supposedly stood for, including the principle that a true democracy – a true democratic republic – should encompass everyone – and that 'everyone' included women.

The public acknowledgement of (and male ambivalence about) women's power and influence is one of the most distinctive characteristics of French approaches to the 'Woman Question' and it cannot be considered apart from the five-hundred-year long obsession with gendering formal political authority as male.[26] It is important, though, that we not confuse discussions of women's lack of legal or political authority in France with assessments of their power and influence. All too often authors of French history textbooks, or synthetic studies of women's history, have insisted on the near-total legal subordination of nineteenth-century French women by the Napoleonic Code, but overlook entirely their still enormous societal importance.[27] It is certainly true that French wives were subordinated in the law; but it is also true that single adult women had been legally emancipated in the 1790s and remained emancipated throughout the nineteenth century. And even as wives, women's power and influence was never treated lightly.

In fact, contemporaries paid extraordinary tribute to women's power and influence. This tribute has been discussed much too little, especially by earlier feminist scholars who, perhaps understandably, were so put off by the notion of 'Woman' as man's 'Muse' that they refused to grapple with its psychic and cultural significance for men and women alike. We all know about the Goncourt brothers' back-handed tribute to the nefarious influence of women in the Old Regime, but we have neglected to consider the contextual implications of their restatement of this view in the 1860s, under the Second Empire, from the perspective of contemporary male attempts to check and channel women's influence. To be sure, this power and influence was grounded in sexual attraction, in sensual influence, the attraction of opposites – but that was not all. The Goncourts also paid tribute to innate female intelligence. Couple these insights with recognition by men that the importance of male physical strength was diminishing, and we come to a more penetrating understanding of the crisis of masculinity. I will have more to say about that connection below.

Scholars have probed the earlier views of Auguste Comte and Jules Michelet on 'Woman,' which placed her on a pedestal, along with the views of their immediate predecessors among the more radical utopian socialists (analyzed by Naomi Andrews), not to mention the later, obsessive problem of the 'femme fatale' (discussed by Bram Dijkstra and others).[28] But a new factor becomes visible in comparative insights, such as those of the nostalgic Orientalist, Gerard de Nerval, translator of Goethe's *Faust* and himself a seeker of the 'Eternal Feminine.' In his *Voyage en Orient* (1851) Nerval wrote:[29]

> Yes, let us be young in Europe as long as we can, but go to spend our old age in the Orient, the country of men worthy of the name, the land of the patriarchs. In Europe, where our institutions have suppressed physical strength, woman has become too powerful. With all that power of seduction, of ruse, of perseverance and persuasion with which heaven has endowed her, the woman of our own countries has become socially the equal of man, and this was more than was necessary to ensure that he should inevitably and eternally become her victim.

In Nerval's vision, the Orient embodies a last refuge for masculine domination, as against the effeminized West. We think of 1851 in terms of the repression of the 1848 revolutions, and particularly the silencing of politically-active Parisian women, but there is more going on.

Emerging from these and other works by male authors is a multifaceted insight into the causes of women's influence, which in no way treats women as negligible or suppressed beings. In these men's eyes, women were empowered not only by their sexuality but also by their novel form of intelligence, their kin networks, and their associations with other women. Taken together, these insights provide us with a searing portrait of male psychological insecurity in the face of unleashed female power. Michelet, to take one example, thought that the only way to contain and channel the power of women was for men to marry much younger women, to isolate them from their family networks, not to mention their female friends, and to undertake their training as men's companions. For this men needed a handbook, which Michelet offered with his guide *Woman/La Femme*: 'Woman cannot live without man,' he insisted. 'Woman, constantly cultivated by man and enriched by his thought, soon believes; and some morning she finds herself superior to him.'[30] Or, like their Jacobin predecessors, they might have recourse to repeating the public/private strictures insisted on by Jean-Jacques Rousseau in the fifth book of *Emile*, without acknowledging one of Rousseau's less-known statements: 'When the time comes that women are no longer concerned with men's well-being, men will no longer be good for anything at all.'[31]

Another way of looking at this issue is from the perspective of women's awareness of and use of their own power and influence. Intriguingly, French feminist writers throughout the nineteenth-century also insisted on its importance – and the necessity of directing it to constructive use through better education and action in civil society. In the prospectus for her publication, the 'Women's Counselor,' in 1833, Eugénie Niboyét insisted on the power of women's influence, despite their de facto political powerlessness; Jeanne Deroin made a similar point in 1849.[32] So did the feminist novelist and essayist André Léo (Léodile Champseix) in 1869, when she wrote that women's 'influence, though difficult to pin down in ordinary times, nevertheless exists. The heart of the matter is to know whether this influence should be instinctive or cultivated ... whether it should be exercised in broad daylight or in the shadows.' And in Hubertine Auclert's pro-suffrage newspaper, *La Citoyenne*, the masthead subheading declared that 'Woman is one of the *forces vives* of France that has been neglected for too long.'[33] These women were basing their claims for women's rights and emancipation squarely on the power and influence that they already exercised; it was simply a question of bringing French laws into harmony with French *moeurs*.

After 1880, however, an important change occurred: women's influence had to be aligned with the principles of the new republican regime. Diana Holmes and Carrie Tarr have underscored a point that many of us have been making for years when they note that 'the Republic provided the ideological bases for contestation of its own practices.'[34] The groundwork had already been set for this by the feminist rearticulation of republican principles in the 1830s and 1840s, as Whitney Walton has so beautifully demonstrated.[35] *Pace* the recent claims of scholars who insist on the exclusionary aspects of the 'universal,' many nineteenth-century French progressives never viewed the theoretical foundations of 'republic' or 'democracy' as by definition excluding women.[36]

Practice, of course, could unfold in arbitrary ways, as when, in 1848, the provisional government stipulated that 'Every Frenchman [*Français*] of mature age [*en age viril*] has political citizenship.' Note that in the French, 'Français' could include men and women, but the qualification '*en age viril*' – virility – made it clear that political citizenship applied only to men. A group of women promptly petitioned the new government, insisting on the complementarity of the sexes, and the fact that if the 'revolution has been made for all,' women were assuredly 'half of everyone,' that 'there could not be two liberties, two equalities, two fraternities,' that 'the people' is 'composed of two sexes...'[37] This was no 'universal' suffrage: it was universal *manhood* suffrage.

Such laws of exclusion could also be changed, and for decades feminists repeatedly insisted on legal revision in the status of wives. In 1889, the leaders of two international women's congresses meeting in Paris during the expositions laid out a stunning agenda for revision of the formalities that governed relationships between French women and men, including the granting of women's suffrage. They followed up on all these claims during the 1890s and into the twentieth century. Sympathetic men agreed, in principle, even though they found many practical reasons for not pushing through the reforms.

My second point concerns the changing perceptions of the importance of physical strength as a condition of continuing masculine dominance and masculine political authority. 'Physical force in defense of one's honor,' Elinor Accampo has pointed out, following Robert Nye, 'lay at the heart of masculine identity.'[38] But physical strength in itself seemed to be in jeopardy. Gerald de Nerval's 1851 observation, quoted above, includes a particularly telling phrase: '... where our institutions have suppressed physical strength, woman has become too powerful.' This statement takes on greater significance when juxtaposed with Jeanne Deroin's 1848 proclamation in *La Voix des femmes*: 'The reign of brute force has ended; that of morality and intelligence has just begun.'[39] The Goncourt brothers also echoed Deroin in their observation that the power of women in France derived from their instinctive intelligence, their uncanny insight into human nature that allowed them to develop strategic skill at managing men. Some might call this 'cunning' or 'ruse,' but there is more to it than that; around this same time women such as Jenny P. d'Héricourt were openly challenging male forms of knowledge. Given these powerful testimonies, one cannot conclude that mere legal and economic dominance sufficed to keep women subordinate, especially as men's brute strength itself became subject to challenge as a foundational principle of the right to rule. This challenge subsequently manifested itself in women's new claims for citizenship based on their physical service to the nation through maternity and social service, paralleling men's physical contribution through military service.

y third point concerns feminist responses to male antifeminism and the ex oration and amplification of new and penetrating arguments. Even as late nineteenth-century antifeminists sought new justifications for male dominance, feminists in republican France (and elsewhere in Europe) began to openly critique militarism, war, and demonstrations of physical strength and unnecessary killing in the interest of dominance. They even began to challenge male sexual habits and practices, calling for a single standard of morality for both sexes.[40] They sought conciliation, partnership, and a balance of power between the sexes.

This only made the antifeminists, who thought only in terms of domination/subordination, shriller in their opposition. By 1900, threats came from prolific writers such as Theodore Joran to the effect that if women were to aspire to be men's equals, they would be treated roughly, like men; men's chivalric treatment of women would quickly disappear if they aspired to equality (or as Virginia Woolf put it some years later, if they did not remain content to reflect men at twice their normal size). Other antifeminist men (mostly conservative Catholics and irredentist nationalists) alleged that 'feminism' was un-French, a foreign import[41] – a claim that historians of French feminism have rejected as completely false. Indeed, French feminists from Maria Deraismes and Hubertine Auclert to Ghénia Avril de Sainte-Croix (via Theodore Stanton's long essay, 'France,' in his 1884 book *The Woman Question in Europe*) repeatedly rested their case for women's emancipation on the fundamental principles of the Revolution and the Third Republic.[42]

By restoring freedom of the press and freedom of association, the Third Republic dramatically amplified these feminist voices, female and male. From the late 1880s until the outbreak of war in 1914, feminist women and men, virtually all of whom supported the republic, ceaselessly talked back to the supporters of patriarchal arrangements and male dominion. No longer did French men have a monopoly on or control over either the printed or publicly spoken word. No longer were French women suffering 'often silently and invisibly,' to quote Robert Nye, 'in the thrall of patriarchal culture.'[43] Mary Louise Roberts has provocatively pointed to the ways in which a small number of highly visible 'New Women' were 'performing' femininity, even acquiring tremendous cultural influence.[44] Jean Elisabeth Pedersen has ably examined various discourses about the family among male parliamentarians and playwrights.[45] Cecilia Beach has carefully studied the works of feminist playwrights.[46]

What were feminist women – and men – saying about masculinity and femininity, and about the cultural construction of gender as such? How did they speak about physical prowess, military valor, and the cult of honor? These individuals were 'performing' feminism by pointing to and condemning various aspects of male rule and male privilege. They began campaigning earnestly for the vote in 1909 so they could have a say in their society's so-called democratic decision-making processes. Their male allies took these women's arguments to the parliament, published them in the press, and advocated them in the meetings and publications of the Ligue des Droits de l'Homme.[47]

The parallel careers of two feminists – a man and a woman – illustrate the character of challenges to male dominance under the sign of 'La Parisienne' in 1900. Léopold Lacour (1854–1939) launched his literary career with the *Nouvelle Revue*, 'the republican review' that challenged the older, more austere *Revue des deux mondes*. The *Nouvelle Revue* was directed by none other than the remarkable Juliette Adam, who as a very young woman had squared off forcefully against Proudhon and other antifeminists in the 1850s before becoming a *salonnière*, a distinguished journalist and publisher, and, not incidentally, the patron of Léon Gambetta. Lacour referred to her as 'a famous woman, a literary amazon.'[48] In the 1890s Lacour became one of the most prominent male-feminist public speakers and authors, with his two works, *Humanisme Intégral: le duel des sexes; la cité future* (1897) and *Trois Femmes de la Révolution* (1900). He also staunchly defended co-education of the sexes, and championed the complete 'association, [of] the collaboration of the feminine soul and the masculine soul, of the masculine and feminine minds [esprit].'[49] In his conclusion to *Humanisme Intégral* he took a direct swipe at the notion of 'honor' as it was construed through the workings of the militarized state and its 'symbols of a so-called honor which in reality only trumpets the antique and bloody right of Force.'[50] Clearly, the physical force imperative did not reside at the heart of Lacour's identity, or of his honor. Rather he was among those 'new men' who supported – and helped to shape and promulgate – the feminist rethinking of the relations between the sexes in accordance with the 'republican' principles of liberty and equality. Indeed, it was Lacour who, with the feminist journalist Savioz (Ghénia Avril de Sainte-Croix, born Glaisette and known before 1900 as Mlle de Sainte-Croix), his near exact age mate (1855–1939), organized in 1897 a huge banquet honoring the aging and highly original *savante* Clémence Royer, the translator of Darwin and seeker after new forms of female knowledge, whom everyone by then had acknowledged as a female 'genius.'

French feminists of both sexes in the belle époque did think that the 'Woman Question' was largely a 'Man Problem,' or in any case a problem of outmoded institutions that privileged men. They were determined to bring the institutions and laws of the Third Republic into harmony with its stated principles. As the deputy and future prime minister René Viviani pointed out at the 1900 International Women's Rights Congress: 'The legislators make the laws for those who make [elect] the legislators.'[51] That is, if only men can vote, they will make laws that favor men. In addition to demanding the vote, in one of the few European regimes that had enfranchised all adult males, French feminists had other, very specific suggestions as to how the 'Man Problem' could be resolved and they were not shy about stating them. For one thing, the prevailing code of 'honor' around male sexual behavior

Avril de Ste-croix

and expectations – the so-called 'double standard' – had to be reshaped and de-institutionalized. Nelly Roussel braved public opinion by calling on women to take responsibility for their reproductive behavior – to engage in sexual relations and bear children only if and when *they* pleased. She insisted that women must not provide cannon-fodder for the male war machinery.[52]

The journalist Savioz took an equally controversial tack, calling for a single standard of responsible sexual behavior for both sexes. She had been shocked by the horrors of government-licensed brothels, providing convenient venues for sexual release for men at the expense of poor women, and promoting an increasingly international traffic in women – and underage girls. Fundamentally she was challenging as 'un-republican' the dominant (bourgeois) male assumption that men had an implicit right to satisfy their sexual urges whenever and wherever they pleased, with government assistance (to ensure men's health through the licensing and inspection of the prostituted women). The honor of good republican men, she argued, should not rest on the chastity of 'their' women, while placing other poor women literally outside the law, fair game for sexual exploitation. According to Savioz, responsible sexual behavior on the part of both sexes would lift the entire standard of morality and sexual behavior for republican society. Henceforth men had to be held accountable and the *police des moeurs* and licensed brothels abolished.[53] Under the Third Republic, feminists of both sexes argued, there must be equal rights and justice for everyone. In speaking thus, they exemplified both courage and personal bravery – the chief virtues of 'honor' that had been associated with masculinity.[54]

The speech Avril de Sainte-Croix gave at the 1900 Women's Rights Congress in Paris, summarized above, exemplifies her approach. Subsequently published and widely-circulated as a pamphlet entitled *Une morale pour les deux sexes* Savioz critiqued the double standard as, from antiquity to the present day, 'the most certain source of misery, immorality and oppression for women.'[55] She did not directly blame men for this situation, though she did insist on their 'sexual appetites;' rather, she blamed the state (which, of course, under the Third Republic as earlier under the monarchies was run exclusively by men). But government-regulated brothels and the police licensing system of prostitutes had to be eliminated. She did blame men who, posing as moralists, assured everyone that the institution should be maintained 'for the safety of honest women, the safety of the family,' and she implicated those who, like Senator René Berenger, supported it 'quand même,' by which she meant despite all objections to the contrary. Quoting her Swiss counterpart Emma Pieczynska (from the neighboring Swiss republic that had also enfranchised men in 1848 yet continued to exclude women until 1971), Savioz insisted that 'honest' women's voices must be heard on this subject – that their silence implied consent. She particularly targeted the French *police des moeurs* not only for suppressing women's liberty but also for suppressing men's responsibility, for blaming women who sold their bodies for sex but not the men who paid. The state, she argued, thereby violated its own principles, both liberty and equality – and, besides, stood in violation of Articles 1, 5, 6, and 7 of the Declaration of the Rights of Man.[56]

Even as Avril de Sainte-Croix applauded the men who in many countries were already partisans of a single standard and opposed state-regulated prostitution, she called on privileged women to stand together in solidarity with their less privileged, more desperate sisters, to struggle on their behalf, to abolish 'all exceptional measures concerning women in matters of morals.' The attendees, among whom were many men, voted *unanimously* for this resolution. Nowhere was the subject of male honor raised as such, but Sainte-Croix clearly implied that supporting regulated prostitution and a double moral standard amounted, in effect, to dishonorable behavior on the part of men. The honorable thing to do would be to support the single standard and gender equality before the law. Since women did not yet have the vote, she asserted (like Viviani) that politicians only accorded these injustices 'a relative importance.' No woman could ignore this outrage; women had to fight back:[57]

> We do not want a woman, whoever she is, to be subjected to laws of exception. Like man, she is a human being with a right to her integral autonomy, and we protest against every kind of regulation that, under the pretext of safeguarding the health of men, or even the family, sanctions and consolidates the principle of a double morality for the two sexes.

The arguments that Avril de Sainte-Croix used to undermine male sexual privilege were based squarely on a concept of women's human rights. And, as it turns out, only a conception of human rights that encompasses women's rights, one that is truly 'universal,' seems capable of trumping the old system of patriarchal masculine honor and reconfiguring it to include such things as rational control and curbing of physical force and sexual drives, partnership in marriage, and responsible paternity.[58] The Third Republic's leaders may have proved slow to move on any issue that threatened to further destabilize male authority in a context of threats of war, depopulation, and class conflict, especially the dismantling of that authority in marriage and women's suffrage – but move they ultimately did, albeit with considerable reluctance.[59] We can appreciate these delays better if we pause to contemplate the magnitude of the changes in gender relations that feminists were then demanding – *in the name of republican principles.*

The efforts of feminists, male and female alike, to address these issues began to exert traction during the Third Republic, but their work continues today under the Fifth Republic.[60] There is still some way to go before the 'Woman Question' ceases to be the 'Man Problem' as well, as a cursory reading of any newspaper today (in France or elsewhere) will attest. Indeed, male fear of women's emancipation and the perceived loss of male privilege continue to fuel antifeminist backlash in many areas of the world today – irrespective of the name of the regime in power.

Looking historically at issues such as male honor in relation to feminist efforts to dismantle patriarchal institutions, while acknowledging the extent and threat of women's influence, helps to deepen and broaden our understanding of the fundamental importance of gender issues to politics.

So, in conclusion, the answer to the question I posed in my title must be 'yes.' Women's issues do not exist in a vacuum. The 'Woman Question' is simultaneously the 'Man Problem' – each is a strand of the intertwined complex that we call the sociopolitical relationship of the sexes (or 'gender,' for short). Despite the existence in France of a great number of male antifeminists in the late nineteenth and early twentieth centuries (and since), we must also point to the growing number of republican men who, like Léopold Lacour, did not feel their masculinity threatened by women's power and influence, and who welcomed women's emancipation and full citizenship, along with the possibility of heterosexual companionship on an equal footing.

But the battle is far from won. Notions of masculinity bound up with male dominance and codes of honor, generally at the expense of women's freedom, continue to shape the sociopolitical relations of the sexes, if less in France than formerly, then clearly in other parts of our contemporary world. If indeed a 'sexual contract' still lies behind the 'social contract,' it has little to do with the label given to the regime in power, or for that matter, with 'liberalism' or 'socialism.' Notions about male honor and authority seem, historically, to transcend regimes.

Implementation of sexual equality or equity has everything to do with the hopes and fears of those who hold power and with the surrounding social, cultural, economic, and educational context. As long as men who define their masculinity in terms of masculine dominance and privilege monopolize political decision-making, it will remain difficult to find acceptance for the principle that women's rights are human rights. Male feminists are still in rather short supply. The hope and promise of democracies – and republics – is that the principles of liberty, equality, and justice promoted, however sporadically, by the French and their republics can provide guideposts in the ongoing worldwide struggle to end women's subordination.

Notes

1. My question rephrases an assertion made in 1893 by the German feminist Helene Lange in an editorial: see Lange, 'Was wir wollen,' *Die Frau*, 1(1) (October 1893): 2; '...die Frauenfrage auch eine Männerfrage ist.'
2. See Karen Offen, *European Feminisms 1700–1950: a Political History* (Stanford: Stanford University Press, 2000), and the documents in *Women, the Family, and Freedom: the Debate in Documents, 1750–1950*, ed. Susan Groag Bell and Karen

Offen, 2 vols (Stanford: Stanford University Press, 1983), for further insight into this debate.

3. See Carole Pateman, *The Sexual Contract* (Stanford: Stanford University Press, 1988).
4. Robert A. Nye, *Masculinity and Male Codes of Honor in Modern France* (New York: Oxford University Press, 1993).
5. See Karen Offen, 'How (and Why) the Analogy of Marriage with Slavery Provided the Springboard for Women's Rights Demands in France, 1640–1848,' in *Women's Rights and Transatlantic Antislavery in the Era of Emancipation*, ed. Kathryn Kish Sklar and James Brewer Stewart (New Haven: Yale University Press, 2007), pp. 57–81.
6. See Offen, 'Le gender est-il une invention américaine?' *Clio: Histoire, Femmes et Sociétés*, 24 (2006): 291–304.
7. See Le citoyen [Charles] Therémin, *De la Condition des femmes dans les républiques* (Paris: Chez Laran, an VII [1799]) especially p. 11. Therémin viewed women and men as morally equal and physically complementary; he nevertheless stipulated that the husband should serve as political representative of the republican family.
8. 'Femme vient de *foemina* qui vient de *foetare, foetus*, parce que sa destination naturelle est d'engendrer.' See in particular Virey's encyclopedia articles: 'Femme,' *Dictionnaire des sciences médicales* (53 vols, 1812–1822), vol. 14 (1815), pp. 503–72; and 'Femelle,' 'Femme,' 'Féminin,' *Nouveau Dictionnaire d'Histoire naturelle* (36 vols, 1816–1819), vol. 11 (1817), pp. 332–9. For a discussion of Virey's views, see Yvonne Knibiehler, 'Les Médecins et la "nature féminine" au temps du Code Civil,' *Annales: Economies, Sociétés, Civilisations*, 31(4) (July–August 1976): 824–45; Jean-Pierre Peter, 'Entre femmes et médecins à la fin du XVIIIe siècle,' *Ethnologie française*, 6(3–4) (1976): 341–8; Yvonne Knibiehler and Catherine Fouquet, *La Femme et les médecins: analyse historique* (Paris: Hachette, 1983); and Geneviève Fraisse, 'Le Genre humaine et la femme chez J.-J. Virey, ou Une certaine harmonie d'inégalités correspondantes,' in *Julien-Joseph Virey, naturaliste et anthropologue*, ed. Claude Bénichou and Claude Blanckaert (Paris: J. Vrin 1988), pp. 183–206.
9. 'Laissons l'anatomiste, aveugle en sa science,/D'une fibre avec art calculer la puissance./Et du plus ou du moins inférer sans appel./Que sa femme lui doit un respect éternel.' Constance-Marie de Salm-Dyck, *Épître aux femmes* (1797), as republished in *Oeuvres complètes de Madame la princesse Constance de Salm*, 4 vols, I (Paris, 1842), p. 13. Translated from the French by Dorothy Backer in *The Defiant Muse: French Feminist Poems from the Middle Ages to the Present: a Bilingual Reader*, ed. Domna Stanton (New York: The Feminist Press, 1986), quotes, p. 115. On Constance de Salm, see Elizabeth Colwill, 'Laws of Nature/Rights of Genius: the *Drame* of Constance de Salm,' in *Going Public: Women and Publishing in Early Modern France*, ed. Elizabeth C. Goldsmith and Dena Goodman (Ithaca: Cornell University Press, 1995), pp. 224–42.
10. On Michelet, Proudhon, and Comte, see my analysis in *European Feminisms*, chapters 4 and 5. See also Mary Pickering, *Auguste Comte: an Intellectual Biography*, Vol. 1 (Cambridge: Cambridge University Press, 1993). On the story that lies behind Comte's mounting adulation of 'Woman,' see Pickering's account of his relationship with Clotilde de Vaux: 'Clotilde de Vaux and the Search for Identity,' in *The New Biography*, ed. Jo Burr Margadant (Berkeley: University of California Press, 2000), pp. 137–70.
11. As, for example, Paul Bernard's prize-winning study, *Histoire de l'autorité paternelle en France* (Montdidier: Radenez, 1863), and Frédéric Le Play's *La Reforme sociale en France*, 2 vols (Paris: Plon, 1864).

12. Karen Offen, '"Woman Has to Set her Stamp on Science, Philosophy, Justice, and Politics": A Look at Gender Politics in the "Knowledge Wars" of the European Past,' in *Geschlecht und Wissen – Genre et Savoir – Gender and Knowledge: Beiträge der 10. Schweizerischen Historikerinnentagung 2002*, Catherine Bosshart-Pfluger, Dominique Grisard, and Christina Späti (eds) (Zurich: Chronos, 2004), pp. 379–93. See also Offen, *European Feminisms*, ch. 5.

13. Maria Deraismes, speech at the Masonic Banquet in Le Pecq, 14 January 1882, in *Oeuvres complètes de Maria Deraismes*, vol. 2 (Paris: Alcan, 1895), p. 283.

14. Hubertine Auclert, 'Programme électoral des femmes,' *La Citoyenne*, no. 99 (August 1885), p. 1. All translations provided here are mine, unless otherwise indicated.

15. The term 'topsy-turvy' with reference to inverting the sexual order has centuries-old roots in European popular culture; see the still valuable discussion in Natalie Zemon Davis, 'Women on Top,' in her book, *Society and Culture in Early Modern France: Eight Essays* (Stanford: Stanford University Press, 1975), pp. 124–51.

16. Annelise Maugue, *L'Identité masculine en crise au tournant du siècle* (Marseille: Rivages/Histoire, 1987) and Christine Bard (ed.), *Un Siècle d'antiféminisme* (Paris: Fayard, 1999), which also contains an essay by Maugue, 'Littérature antiféministe et angoisse masculine au tournant du siècle,' pp. 69–83.

17. Nye, *Masculinity and Male Codes of Honor*. See also Christopher E. Forth, *The Dreyfus Affair and the Crisis of French Manhood* (Baltimore: Johns Hopkins University Press, 2004), see especially Chapter 4, 'Adventures of the Naked Truth: Women and the Dreyfusard Imagination.' See also Edward Berenson's penetrating examination of the sexual politics of the years around 1914, in *The Trial of Madame Caillaux* (Berkeley: University of California Press, 1992).

18. Judith Surkis, *Sexing the Citizen: Morality and Masculinity in France 1870–1920* (Ithaca: Cornell University Press, 2006); see my review essay of this book on *H-France Forum*, 2(1) (Winter 2007), no. 3; http://www.h-france.net/forum/forumvol2/OffenOnSurkis1.html (accessed 17 June 2009). See also Ruth Harris, *Murders and Madness: Medicine, Law, and Society in the Fin de Siècle* (Oxford: Clarendon Press, 1989).

19. The poster announcing the publication of the women's daily newspaper, *La Fronde*, in late 1897, exemplified this optimism. In her revisionist study of women's contributions to European intellectual history, Ann Taylor Allen also underscores the optimism of turn-of-the-century feminist intellectuals in France and other European countries; see her article, 'Feminism, Social Science, and the Meanings of Modernity: the Debate on the Origin of the Family in Europe and the United States, 1860–1914,' *American Historical Review*, 104(4) (October 1999): 1085–113.

20. The fifteen-foot high sculpture of 'La Parisienne,' by Paul Moreau-Vauthier, stood atop the Porte Binet entrance to the 1900 Paris Exposition. The image was widely reproduced in the contemporary press.

21. See Debora L. Silverman, 'The "New Woman," Feminism, and the Decorative Arts in Fin-de-Siècle France,' in *Eroticism and the Body Politic*, ed. Lynn Hunt (Baltimore: Johns Hopkins University Press, 1991), pp. 144–63.

22. Karen Offen, 'Ernest Legouvé and the Doctrine of "Equality in Difference" for Women: a Case Study of Male Feminism in Nineteenth-Century French Thought,' *Journal of Modern History*, 58(2) (June 1986): 452–84.

23. In addition to Sowerwine's chapter in this volume, see his ' "La politique, cet élément dans lequel j'aurais voulu vivre": l'exclusion des femmes est-elle inhérente au républicanisme de la Troisième République?' *Clio: Histoire, Femmes et Sociétés*, 24 (2006): 171–94, and 'The Sexual Contract(s) of the Third Republic,' in *French*

History and Civilization: Papers from the George Rude Seminar, ed. Ian Coller, Helen Davies, and Julie Kalman, Vol. 1 (Melbourne: The George Rude Society, 2005), pp. 245–53. Available online at http://h-france.net/rude/rudepapers.html (accessed 17 June 2009). Sowerwine grounds his interpretation of republican hostility to women in the theoretical analyses of Joan B. Landes, Carole Pateman, and Michel Foucault, but does not take into account the abundant evidence of a more conciliatory approach to women's rights dating from the late Second Empire or from the Third Republic after 1880. He draws instead on evidence from the 1870s, during the immediate backlash against women's activism in the Paris Commune, which was also accompanied by extreme forms of masculine violence. Of course it is essential to note the extent of Frenchwomen's activity in 'civil society' throughout the nineteenth century, and especially during the Third Republic – even though they did not have the vote or the right to hold elective office. Yet Sowerwine seems to mistake Habermas's 'Offentlichkeit' (so poorly translated in English as the 'public sphere') for the political arena, when in fact the term indicates the opening space for public activism (press, association, public opinion, and so on) that lies between government and household. For a different perspective on this issue, see Karen Offen, 'Feminists Campaign in "Public Space:" Civil Society, Gender Justice, and the History of European Feminisms,' in *Civil Society, Public Space, and Gender Justice*, Gunilla Budde, Karen Hagemann, and Sonya Michel (eds) (New York: Berghahn, 2008), pp. 97–116.

24. Käthe Schirmacher, *The Modern Woman's Rights Movement: a Historical Survey*, trans. from the second German edition (1909) by Carl Conrad Eckhardt (New York: Macmillan, 1912; reprinted New York: Kraus Reprint Co., 1971), p. 181.

25. Harlor, 'The Education of Women's Will,' originally in *La Revue Socialiste* (April 1900), as translated in Jennifer Waelti Walters and Steven C. Hause (eds), *Feminisms of the Belle Epoque* (Lincoln: University of Nebraska Press, 1994), pp. 74–84; quote p. 75.

26. Discussed at length in Chapters 1 and 2 of Offen, 'The Woman Question in Modern France' (unpublished manuscript). See also Sarah Hanley, 'The Salic Law,' in *Political and Historical Encyclopedia of Women*, ed. Christine Fauré (New York and London: Routledge, 2003); Éliane Viennot, *La France, les femmes et le pouvoir: L'invention de la loi salique (Ve–XVIe siecle)* (Paris: Perrin, 2006). See also Margaret L. King and Albert Rabil Jr, 'Introduction to the Series' *The Other Voice in Early Modern Europe*, in *Against Marriage* by the Duchess de Montpensier (Chicago: University of Chicago Press, 2002), on what they call 'the problem of power,' by which they really mean 'authority,' xxiii–xxiv: 'Women were excluded from power: the whole cultural tradition insisted on it. Only men were citizens, only men bore arms, only men could be chiefs or lords or kings. There were exceptions, which did not disprove the rule, when wives or widows or mothers took the place of men, awaiting their return or the maturation of a male heir. A woman who attempted to rule in her own right was perceived as an anomaly, a monster, at once a deformed woman and an insufficient male, sexually confused and, consequently, unsafe.'

27. See, for instance, two recent syntheses: James F. McMillan, *France and Women, 1789–1914* (London and New York: Routledge, 2000) and Susan K. Foley (formerly Susan Grogan), *Women in France since 1789: the Meanings of Difference* (Basingstoke: Palgrave, 2004).

28. See Naomi J. Andrews, *Socialism's Muse: Gender in the Intellectual Landscape of French Romantic Socialism* (Lanham, MD: Lexington Books, 2006). See also Bram Dijkstra, *Idols of Perversity: Fantasies of Feminine Evil in Fin-de-Siècle Culture*

(New York: Oxford University Press, 1986), and most recently, Elizabeth K. Menon, *Evil by Design: the Creation and Marketing of the Femme Fatale* (Urbana: University of Illinois Press, 2006).

29. Gerard de Nerval, *Voyage en Orient* (Paris: Charpentier, 1851); as translated in *The Women of Cairo: Scenes of Life in the Orient*, vol. 2 (New York: Harcourt, Brace and Company, 1930), p. 36. The context for these remarks seems to be the author's recent purchase of a young slave girl, presumably to serve his every need.

30. Jules Michelet, *Woman (La Femme)*, trans. J. W. Palmer, MD (New York, 1873; originally published in Paris, 1860). As excerpted in Bell and Offen, *Women, the Family, and Freedom: the Debate in Documents*, vol. 1, pp. 339–42; quotes, pp. 339, 341.

31. As translated in Bell and Offen, *Women, the Family, and Freedom*, vol. 1, p. 45.

32. Eugénie Niboyet, 'Prospectus,' *Le Conseiller des femmes* (1 October 1833), p. 2; Jeanne Deroin, 'Mission de la femme,' *L'Opinion des femmes*, 28 January 1849 (doc. 77 in Bell and Offen, *Women, the Family, and Freedom*, vol. 1, p. 261).

33. André Léo, *La Femme et les moeurs: liberté ou monarchie* (Paris, 1869), p. 7. *La Citoyenne*, various issues of the late 1880s. See the authoritative list of Auclert's articles in Steven C. Hause, *Hubertine Auclert: the French Suffragette* (New Haven: Yale University Press), Appendix 1, pp. 221–36.

34. Diana Holmes and Carrie Tarr (eds), *A Belle Epoque? Women in French Society and Culture 1890–1914* (New York and Oxford: Berghahn, 2006), editors' introduction, p. 12.

35. See Whitney Walton, *Eve's Proud Descendants: Four Women Writers and Republican Politics in Nineteenth-Century France* (Stanford: Stanford University Press, 2000), and Whitney Walton, 'Republican Women and Republican Families in the Personal Narratives of George Sand, Marie d'Agoult, and Hortense Allart,' in Margadant, ed., *The New Biography*, pp. 99–136.

36. See note 23 above. Also Joan W. Scott, *Only Paradoxes to Offer: French Feminists and the Rights of Man* (Cambridge, MA: Harvard University Press, 1996). The real issue here is the 'gender' of democracy. See Christine Fauré, *Democracy without Women: Feminism and the Rise of Liberal Individualism in France* (Bloomington: Indiana University Press, 1991; originally published in French, 1985), and various essays in Fauré's *Political and Historical Encyclopedia of Women* (cited above). For source-based clarification on what the term 'republic' and its associated terms 'democracy,' 'nation,' 'people,' and so on actually signified to male political figures during the long nineteenth century, see Claude Nicolet, *L'Idee républicaine en France: Essai d'histoire critique* (Paris: Gallimard, 1982).

37. See Offen, 'Women and the Question of "Universal" Suffrage in 1848: a Transatlantic Comparison of Suffragist Rhetoric,' *NWSA Journal*, 11(1) (Spring 1999): 150–77; quotes p. 151.

38. See Elinor Accampo's splendid biography of Nelly Roussel, *Blessed Motherhood, Bitter Fruit: Nelly Roussel and the Politics of Female Pain in Third Republic France* (Baltimore: Johns Hopkins University Press, 2006), p. 66.

39. Jeanne Deroin, 'Aux Citoyens Français!' *La Voix des Femmes*, 7 (27 March 1848); as trans. in Bell and Offen, *Women, the Family, and Freedom*, vol. 1, doc. 70.

40. See Andrea Mansker in Chapter 8 of this book.

41. I discussed this point at some length and with examples in 'Depopulation, Nationalism, and Feminism in Fin-de-Siècle France,' *American Historical Review*, 89(3) (June 1984): 648–76; see especially pp. 662–3.

42. See Offen, 'Women's Memory, Women's History, Women's Political Action: the French Revolution in Retrospect, 1789–1889–1989,' *Journal of Women's History*,

1(3) (Winter 1989–90): 211–30. Ghénia Avril de Sainte-Croix, *Le Féminisme* (Paris: Giard et Brière, 1907) boldly states this case.

43. See Nye, *Masculinity and Male Codes of Honor*, p. 11.

44. See Mary Louise Roberts, *Disruptive Acts: the New Woman in Fin-de-Siècle France* (Chicago: University of Chicago Press, 2002).

45. Roberts, *Disruptive Acts*; also Jean Elisabeth Pedersen, *Legislating the French Family: Feminism, Theater, and Republican Politics, 1870–1920* (New Brunswick: Rutgers University Press, 2003).

46. Cecilia Beach, *Staging Politics and Gender: French Women's Drama, 1880–1923* (Basingstoke: Palgrave, 2005).

47. See Wendy Ellen Perry, 'Remembering Dreyfus: the Ligue des Droits de l'Homme and the Making of the Modern French Human Rights Movement,' PhD dissertation, UNC-Chapel Hill, 1998, and Anne-Martine Fabre, 'La Ligue des droits de l'homme et les femmes au début du 20ème siècle,' *Materiaux pour l'histoire de notre temps*, 72 (2003): 31–5, based on her DEA d'histoire contemporaine, 'La Ligue des Droits de l'Homme et les femmes: des origines à 1914,' under Pierre Milza, Institut d'Etudes Politiques, 1987–88. Other studies of the Ligue and the 'Woman Question' focus on the period following 1914 and especially following World War I.

48. Quotes from Léopold Lacour, *Une Longue Vie: Histoire d'un homme*, vol. 1 (Paris: Éditions Malfère, 1938), pp. 262–3. On Lacour, see Harlor, *Léopold Lacour: Biographie critique* (Paris: E. Sansot, s.d. [c. 1920]).

49. Léopold Lacour, *Une Longue Vie: Histoire d'un homme*, vol. 2 (Paris: Éditions du Dauphin, 1958), p. 160. This second volume appeared twenty years later than the first.

50. *Une Longue Vie*, vol. 2, p. 161. The full phrase is: 'La patrie, alors, ne gêne pas plus ce dernier sentiment que ne peut le gêner l'amour de la compagne et de l'enfant. Du moins, les conflits qui se produisent entre tel ou tel de ces penchants de l'âme ne sont-ils imputables, précisément, qu'a la grossièreté farouche de l'encore actuelle idée de patrie, dans la presque totalité des intelligences, qu'à l'exigeante barbarie des Etats en lutte, avec leurs casernes, leur diplomatie de ruse et de proie, leurs frontières hérissées de forts et de douanes, leurs drapeaux de vanité, symboles d'un soi-disant honneur qui ne claironne, en réalité, que l'antique droit sanglant de la Force.'

51. See Offen, 'Women, Citizenship, and Suffrage in the French Context, 1789–1993,' *Suffrage and Beyond: International Feminist Perspectives*, ed. Melanie Nolan and Caroline Daley (Auckland: Auckland University Press; co-published with New York University Press and Pluto Press, London, 1994), pp. 151–70, see esp. p. 158.

52. See Elinor Accampo's publications on Nelly Roussel, especially *Blessed Motherhood, Bitter Fruit*.

53. On the European continent, the critique of the double standard and the accompanying campaign for a single, and higher standard of sexual morality took wing in the early 1880s, with Bjørnstjerne Bjørnson's 1883 play, *A Gauntlet [En Hanske]*, which made the case for premarital chastity for men. Bertha von Suttner upped the stakes by critiquing the way in which men treated women solely as sex objects and promoted, through militarism, the values of death above the values of life. See her *Das Maschinenzeitalter* (1889). Key excerpts in translation appear in Bell and Offen, *Women, the Family, and Freedom*, vol. 2 (docs. 11 and 12). In England and subsequently on the continent, the campaign of Josephine Butler and her colleagues against state-regulated prostitution likewise raised the issue of the moral

double standard. See the April 2008 special issue of *Women's History Review*, ed. Anne Summers, on Butler's international campaigns. Ghénia Avril de Sainte-Croix was frequently referred to in print as 'the Josephine Butler of France.'

54. See Nye, *Masculinity*, p. 224, and the essays in Part III of this book.
55. 'Rapport de Mme Savioz de Sainte-Croix,' *Congrès International de la Condition et des Droits des Femmes* (Proceedings) (Paris: Imprimerie des Arts et Manufactures, 1901), pp. 97–111; quotation on p. 107; republished as *Une Morale pour les deux sexes* (Paris: Imprimerie Paul Dupont, 1900).
56. 'Rapport,' pp. 100–9.
57. 'Rapport,' p. 110.
58. See the publications on the paternity issue by Rachel G. Fuchs, 'Seduction, Paternity, and the Law in Fin-de-Siècle France,' *Journal of Modern History*, 72(24) (December 2000): 944–89, and her recent book, *Contested Paternity: Constructing Families in Modern France* (Baltimore: Johns Hopkins University Press, 2008). See also the essays by Mansker and Fuchs in this volume.
59. The first major changes in the Civil Code laws concerning marital authority came only in 1938. Feminist criticism of Article 231 and many other articles that subordinated wives dated from the 1830s.
60. See the conclusion to my article, 'Les Femmes, la citoyenneté et le droit de vote en France, 1789–1993,' in *Féminismes et identités nationales: Les Processus d'intégration des femmes au politique*, ed. Yolande Cohen and Françoise Thébaud (Lyon: Programme Rhône-Alpes de Recherche en Sciences Humaines, 1998), pp. 47–70. See also Siân Reynolds, 'Rights and the Republic: the Inter-War Years as Antechamber to Democracy,' in Reynolds, *France between the Wars: Gender and Politics* (London: Routledge, 1996), pp. 204–26.

Part II
Bodies, Minds, and Spirit

Introduction to Part II

As the chapters in Part I demonstrate, the meanings of liberty and equality in the context of modern democracy were far from stable during France's early Third Republic. The formation of good citizens, however, faced far greater challenges than contested notions of citizenship, for the subjective experience of 'selfhood' was in flux. In the second half of the nineteenth century an array of modern sensory stimuli challenged the bodies, minds, and spiritual well-being of French men and women, and offered different ways of being. Train travel – its sensory experience as well as the horizons it opened – and a bustling urban street life inundated with colorful advertising promised entertaining escapes, brought together the sexes and disparate social classes, and offered new ways to imagine one's self. The new consumerism especially offered to women alternate modes of self-fashioning. Their greater access to education and various forms of employment contributed to the image of the 'New Woman' who threatened to overturn rules about gender by manifesting independence from the conjugal and maternal obligations that had acquired heightened significance in the modern era. The status of the Church further contributed to the spiritual confusion in this era of increasing anxiety. Disaffection with both Catholicism and secular materialism during this acutely anti-clerical period of the Third Republic opened the way to occult movements offering alternate paths to self-realization.

The modernity that gave individuals the subjective power to fashion themselves also created its opposite in the pervasive perception of degeneration, and the need to define what was normal, discover the abnormal, and to cure the sick and 'mad.' As Matt Reed's chapter shows, psychiatry came of age during the last third of the nineteenth century at a time when modern stimuli were thought to be the causes of new mental illnesses such as neurasthenia and new manifestations of old illnesses (notably hysteria). It is no coincidence that a train is the site of sexual exposure in one of the cases he describes: the train was this period's symbol of the paradoxes of modernity, capable of astounding speed that abolished distance while producing for passengers a mechanical agitation widely believed to cause sexual arousal as well as 'railroad spine' and traumatic neurosis. But the overriding concern among psychiatrists during this period, hereditary degeneration, Reed argues, completely reversed the manner in which psychiatry treated 'singular subjectivity.'

Elizabeth Williams's chapter examines another response to modernization through the intersection of medicine, gastronomy, and gender. As the medical profession diagnosed anorexia as a female disease and a form of 'hysteria,' gastronomy, a 'model of discipline, control, and moderation,' represented what women purportedly could not be. The medical profession and gastronomic experts converged in viewing the ability to eat and to taste as a marker of difference between male and female, and as a way for men to assert their will over women. Indeed food was not the only realm in which male elite 'taste-makers' sought to defend themselves against the ravages of mass production and consumption and the incursions of women who blurred gender lines. James Smith Allen's chapter demonstrates another version of the same process. The occultist Papus used science, medicine, mysticism, and male codes of honor to fashion himself into a highly influential leader whose cult met the spiritual needs of a large following, among which were many women. Occultism offered men an escape from the routine hegemony of bourgeois culture without the scrutiny of the medical and psychiatric professions; it also afforded them another means to dominate women and reassert their superiority.

Each chapter in this section recounts a response to the disintegration of traditional hierarchies and the need to establish discipline and control in the modern context of entitlement to rights, including that of shaping one's identity. All three highlight the role that expertise – particularly scientific and medical expertise – played in recreating hierarchies. A strong undercurrent of misogyny drove much of that expertise and assured that men would stay on top. Nonetheless, as the chapters in Part III will show, masculinity remained unstable, religion sought to regulate it, and women succeeded in appropriating its codes for their own ends.

3

From *aliéné* to *dégénéré*: Moral Agency and the Psychiatric Imagination in Nineteenth-Century France

Matt T. Reed

At the end of the eighteenth century, Philippe Pinel inaugurated psychiatric science, properly so-called, through a crucial theoretical gesture. By insisting on the methodical observation of patients, Pinel revealed the periodicity of mental disturbance – discrete, alternating episodes of delirium and lucidity.[1] Where doctors once spoke of the mentally deranged as *insensé* – insensible – Pinel insisted that such individuals were in fact *aliéné* – alienated – and that within them remained a '*reste de raison,*' a 'shred of reason,' from which they were temporarily separated.

According to Marcel Gauchet and Gladys Swain, the history of psychiatry can be told as a history of its waxing and waning appreciation of these shreds, which they call 'subjective singularity.' '[T]he entire movement of psychiatric knowledge reduces itself in the last resort to a continually deepening inscription of the object in subjective singularity ...' It is, they write, a persistent search for 'that which confers personal consistence to alienation ...'[2]

My work is generally concerned with the way this pursuit of 'subjective singularity' has been expressed in and through the psychiatric case study as a scientific technique and a genre of writing about the self. At the end of the eighteenth century, observations in mental medicine were characterized by the nosological method, featuring histories of the malady in the patient.[3] The *disease* was the object of the record, not the individual. During the nineteenth century, the genre underwent a subtle, but crucial, transformation: it became less a story about the progression of the disease than it was a history of the patient's life. Or rather, it was at least as much a story about the individual – life, habits, relatives – as it was a story about the progression of the malady itself.[4]

As it changed, the psychiatric case also became a genre of ethical inquiry, in which patients were subjected to, and constituted by, the moral judgments and anxieties of doctors and the bourgeois society they represented. By the late 1870s, one can see the case in something close to its modern form, a medico-moral narrative of the patient's life that sought to account for present conduct by connecting it to elements in his or her past. The history of the case study, then, is relevant to understanding the relationship between psycho-medical discourses and the people they purport to describe. Understanding its evolution can tell us something important about the construction of modern selves, which feature identities elaborated through the excavation of individual experience.[5]

Although Pinel started psychiatry down its path of individualization, I argue in this chapter that the appreciation of 'subjective singularity' was not simply an amplification of the notion that the mentally disturbed were *aliéné*. Indeed, I claim quite the opposite: psychiatry's study of individuals in all their *particularity* came to the fore through its study of them in their pathological, degenerate *peculiarity*.

As Michel Foucault observed, by the end of the nineteenth century, that which was understood as most individual about a person was also that which was seen to be most pathological: '[In our civilization] when one wishes to individualize the healthy, normal and law-abiding adult, it is always by asking him how much of the child he has in him, what secret madness lies within him, what fundamental crime he has dreamt of committing.'[6] Tending to these secrets of the soul, these kernels of identity, is a hallmark of modern selfhood. In describing or denying, in resisting or revealing, in acknowledging or cultivating these intimate regions, we acquire and inhabit our identities. How did this happen?

One crucial way this aspect of our selves came to flourish was through the identification and elaboration of what might be called 'degenerate human kinds' during the second half of the nineteenth century.[7] A passage in 1895 from the prolific French sexologist, Dr Laupts, helps demonstrate this notion. Writing of Valentin Magnan's theory of hereditary degeneration, he cautioned:

> The public is possessed by this news with an avidity that almost constitutes a new anomaly; there is no reader who is not preoccupied from a personal point of view; there is no one who, from now on, does not protect himself from a 'phobia,' from a 'philia' or from a 'mania' of some sort, which some caress, maintain, and develop like a precious mark of originality. Partly made of the need to imitate and of vanity, it is fair to recognize that many are worried and that the obsession with disequilibrium will end by overtaking some of these good spirits: in good faith, they persuade themselves that they are 'degenerates' or 'abnormal.'[8]

As Laupts's last phrase suggests, the figure facilitating the drive to catalogue 'subjective singularity' was not only Pinel's *aliéné*; it was also the *dégénéré* of Benedict Augustin Morel and Valentin Magnan, a figure whose hidden, pathological foundation was revealed through an analysis of experience, habits, and tastes – not just relatives. In principle, hereditary degeneration was limited to those with family histories of anti-social behavior, alcoholism, criminality, or mental illness, for example. As the concept of hereditary degeneration spread from the clinic to the culture, however, it caused people to ask new questions about themselves, to describe their acts in new ways, to see their pasts in new light. This had consequences. Laupts alluded to some: curiosity and anxiety, shame and celebration, a new concern with signs of one's 'precious originality.' When modern individuals ask, 'Who am I?', we frequently answer by speaking about who we desire and our most secret longings. And then we ask: 'Am I normal?' The degenerate helped introduce this question into modern self-consciousness.

'Degenerate human kinds' is an unusual phrase. I coin it deliberately. Why? There is a vast literature on what Charles Taylor calls the 'sources' of the self. Much of it, like Taylor's, concerns the philosophy of selfhood and traces the intellectual roots of the modern idea that we each have a core, a self, that is characterized by interiority; that is distinctive to us as individuals; that is free – capable of choice or agency; and that is natural – an expression of nature or order.[9] More recently, following Foucault's lead, many scholars have been equally concerned with 'technologies' of selfhood – discourses, practices, and institutions that have produced, or anchored, our sense of our selves in different times and places.[10] Where Taylor speaks of 'sources' or 'roots,' this archeological work is more likely to think about the 'techniques,' 'vectors,' or 'epistemologies' that have facilitated the elaboration of selves during different historical periods.

Foucault identified several paradigmatic figures in the pantheon of modern identity – the criminal, the madman, the hysteric, the pervert. Each accompanied the rise of specific bio-political discourses in the nineteenth century and were embedded in systems of knowledge that perpetually produced the subjects they described.[11] John Forrester suggests that such figures or types, which were elaborated in and through case studies, functioned as 'well-understood exemplars.'[12] They helped define the limits of normal and abnormal behavior, and their profiles served as templates against which others could be compared and judged.

I argue for adding another figure to Foucault's list: the degenerate. In the nineteenth century, all of Foucault's exemplary types were considered first and foremost as hereditary degenerates.[13] For each, it was assumed as a matter of course that their background would reveal a pathological stain expanding progressively across generations and throughout their life, leaving a trace in their actions and attitudes. It was simply a matter of looking deeply enough into their personal and familial past. In this sense, the degenerate should be understood as an enabling figure of sorts, a vector for modern identities.

This is why I have chosen to follow Ian Hacking's lead in writing here about the emergence and importance of 'degenerate human kinds' at the end of the nineteenth century. Hacking has written provocatively about the notion of 'world-making by kind-making,' what he also refers to as 'looping effects,' 'dynamic nominalism' or 'making up people.' Simply put, this is the tendency of people to react to the ways that they are described and grouped. Hacking thinks this is terribly important to the way we become people with particular identities at a given historical moment. As he puts it:

> I have from time to time spoken of the looping effect of human kinds – that is, the interactions between people, on the one hand, and ways of classifying people and their behavior on the other. Being seen to be a certain kind of person, or to do a certain kind of act, may affect someone. A new or modified mode of classification may systematically affect the people who are so classified, or the people themselves may rebel against the knowers, the classifiers, the science that classifies them. Such interactions may lead to changes in the people who are classified, and hence in what is known about them. That is what I call a feedback effect. Now I am adding a further parameter. *Inventing or molding a new kind, a new classification, of people or of behavior may create new ways to be a person, new choices to make, for good or evil. There are new descriptions, and hence new actions under a description. It is not that people change, substantively, but that as a point of logic new opportunities for action are open to them.*[14]

Hereditary degeneration became a culturally powerful description in the late nineteenth century. The identification of degenerate human kinds put new pressure on individuals to examine themselves – to scan every aspect of their conduct in the present and the past – for the slightest signs of a pathological instinct or appetite.

This chapter demonstrates the crucial place of the *dégénéré* in the psychiatric imagination under the Third Republic and its role in the creation of modern selfhood. I begin by discussing the rise of degenerative heredity as a theory of mental illness and the important place it came to have in French politics and culture. Then I turn to two exemplary cases. The cases show how the theory of degenerative heredity and its application in the clinic entailed an intense examination of an individual's character and comportment for signs of pathological taint. The doctrine itself suggested the existence of a new kind of person – the hereditary degenerate – set apart from 'normal' people by the inability to resist dangerous compulsions. However, as the theory became ubiquitous – explaining everything and therefore nothing – doctors were driven deeper and deeper into the details of the patient's life, looking for signs of incubating mental illness. In the end, as Laupts wrote, virtually everyone became 'preoccupied from a personal point of view.' It is in this sense that this distant relative, the degenerate, played a role in making up our modern selves.

From subjects to citizens: politics, psychiatry, and social hygiene

The point of departure for this volume of essays is the French experiment with democracy during the Third Republic, which featured a mix of radical political optimism, reactionary conservatism, and cultural dislocation inherited from the various republics and regimes that preceded it. The opening chapters by Charles Sowerwine and Karen Offen suggest that the desire to maintain order – or, perhaps more accurately, the fear of losing control – was not only a political impulse in nineteenth-century France, it had deep cultural resonance as well. The systematic creation of gendered private and public spheres before the Revolution and the systemic exclusion of women from political power afterwards are perhaps the most obvious examples of the contradictions inherent to the Revolution. Throughout the nineteenth century, successive post-revolutionary governments sought to re-establish social order by excluding various groups from full civic participation – women, the working classes, the mentally ill, and others.

In this context, the question of 'selves' took on great significance. Jan Goldstein has argued that:

[C]orporate structures were widely perceived in eighteenth-century France as integral to the regular and predictable functioning of persons. Thus the specter of a society without corporations effectively problematized the self for contemporaries: it posed the question of whether, in the absence of a corporate matrix, a person's own inherent resources were adequate to ensure that person's stability or whether, buffeted by an overactive imagination, the person would be thrown ominously off-kilter.[15]

As a science of the self, the development of French mental medicine was connected to the radical interrogation of personhood implied by the emergence of modern democratic thought.[16] Put simply, individuals mattered in new ways after the French Revolution. No longer monarchical subjects, they were democratic *citizens*, sovereign actors in the political and social spheres.[17] In contrast to the way monarchical subjects were born, however, democratic citizens needed to be made. The therapeutic possibilities introduced by Philippe Pinel and other theorists of mental medicine – the presumption that doctors and patients can act on selves – should be understood in relation to the ideas of self-governance, 'perfectibility,' and individuality opened by the Revolution, as well as to the anxieties these provoked.[18]

The energy expended by the state in creating such citizen-selves in France has been well-documented.[19] The project of molding these citizens was by no means limited to the political realm. Virtually every area of public and professional life was engaged, but especially medicine, which would come to play a critical role in French society as a force for 'social hygiene.'[20] Throughout the nineteenth century, French doctors – particularly those practicing the new specialty of mental medicine – saw themselves as important stewards of political and cultural health. Quite consciously, alienists created a professional identity aligned with state authority by taking on medico-legal responsibilities in the courts and lobbying for the creation of a state-sponsored asylum system. Over the course of the century, they expanded their social prestige through these obligations and wielded extraordinary powers to diagnose and confine patients.[21] The influence of mental medicine reached its apex under the Third Republic, what Jan Goldstein has called its 'multifaceted professional apotheosis,' when it consolidated its institutional and interpretive authority.[22]

Alienism proved a capable ally in the post-revolutionary effort to mold citizens – to forge selves – capable of self-governance. Under the Third Republic, the issue seemed to take on new urgency. As Robert A. Nye has written, '[T]he common denominators of this new alliance were property, order, and democracy ... Republican campaigners endlessly stressed the defense of order, social conservatism, and a thorough disapproval of the class antagonisms that had led to the Commune of 1871.'[23] Formed in the wake of a humiliating military defeat in the Franco-Prussian war and following the social chaos of the Commune, the new government was conceived with an acute consciousness of existential threats from within and without. As the Republic was establishing itself, troubling statistics showing precipitous declines in French natality seemed to link these two dangers by suggesting how vulnerable France was vis-à-vis the growing populations of its neighbors and strategic competitors – especially across the Rhine, where the German birth rate outpaced France by almost six to one during the period from 1872 to 1911.

How could France possibly hope to regain its geopolitical status, contemporaries wondered, if it was weak at its very core, enfeebled by its inability to reproduce itself, and at risk of even greater domestic and international impotence? Thus, as the Third Republic embarked on its version of the democratic experiment, it did so with deep reservations about the health of French society and profound questions about the capacity of its citizens to meet the country's challenges.

In confronting these anxieties, leaders in the new government turned to doctors for guidance. Nye writes:

> Of particular concern to the French were the health and well-being of [its] population ... [R]apidly falling birth rates and a host of social pathologies ... appeared to call into question both the quantity and the quality of the French population ... The thoroughly secular outlook of the new Republican leadership was unusually compatible with a scientific and medical mode of social analysis; under the spur of the internal and external events of the era, a medical model of cultural crisis developed that exercised a linguistic and conceptual imperialism over all other ways of

viewing the nation's plight ... Through this model, the French perceived and labeled social deviance, and through this model they sought the means to cure it.[24]

Degenerative heredity and the etiological method

The medical model of cultural crisis that Nye identifies was provided by the theory of hereditary degeneration, which held that mental pathologies of various kinds – from epilepsy to alcoholism, from hysteria to general paralysis – were part of a general syndrome passed by generation and worsening over time. The concept of degeneration gave doctors a way of connecting individual patients to the aggregate effects of mental illness on society at large. At the center of medical efforts to regulate French society – and therefore, selves – in the Third Republic, the theory of hereditary degeneration had been articulated almost twenty years earlier by Bénédict-Augustin Morel's *Traité des dégénérescences physiques, intellectuelles et morales de l'espèce humain*, published in 1857.[25] Morel's treatise was French psychiatry's foundational text for more than a half a century.

The evolution of the species and the laws of heredity had been subjects of scientific investigation since the early nineteenth century. These concepts were generally understood by later theorists in terms outlined by the thought of Jean-Baptiste Lamarck. For Lamarck, the present was a testament to the successes of the adaptations of previous generations. Indeed, Lamarck saw heredity as a progressive, *active* force that adapted directly to environments in the face of natural adversity. For Morel and other theorists of degeneration, however, heredity was not foolproof: internal dangers to organic life still existed. Maladaptive organisms did not always die off; some managed to survive conditions that did not suit them. Alternately, an organism might acquire and transmit behaviors that were *harmful* to it and to the rest of the species.

The notion that heredity played a role in the transmission of mental illness had been long acknowledged in the alienist community, beginning with Pinel and his celebrated student, Jean-Étienne Dominique Esquirol.[26] What distinguished Morel's theory was his claim that degenerative heredity was a progressive syndrome encompassing a range of illnesses previously believed to be unrelated. He wrote:

> From the slightest eccentricity in the acts, from the simplest anomaly in the laws of moral sensibility, designated under the names moral insanity [or] reasoning mania to ... the states called more or less improperly imbecility, idiocy, [or] cretinism, there exist diverse degrees of the same affection.[27]

Whereas doctors like Esquirol had approached mania, melancholy, and monomania as distinct syndromes, Morel viewed them as variations of a

single, more profound disturbance. In Morel's articulation of hereditary theory, it was the profundity of an alteration that was passed on, not the exact
manifestation. So, for example, an alcoholic father could produce a daughter
who was a hysteric, who could in turn produce a son who was deaf, and so
on. The disease was progressive both as it developed in the individual and as
it was passed on through generations.[28]

As much a methodological approach as an explanatory theory, hereditary degeneration focused attention on an individual's familial past and on
the course of his or her life. The theory did this in two ways: by replacing nosological classification with etiological analysis; and by understanding
a variety of actions – from mere eccentricity to outright catalepsy – as
degrees of illness to be evaluated along a continuum. As the theory grew
in prominence and practice, it made reading an individual's history fundamental to the art of being an *aliéniste*. For professionals of mental medicine
in the 1860s and 1870s, this implied a wholesale revision of psychiatric
methodology.

Morel's work relied on a technique of investigation called the 'etiological'
or 'pathogenic' method. The Pinellian tradition classified diseases according to a categorization of *symptoms*. The etiological method emphasized a
search for the *causes* or *origins* of the malady in an individual's hereditary
make-up, which were then closely followed as they evolved throughout the
patient's life. As Jules Falret remarked, Morel's etiological method, '[has] the
goal of returning to the primary origin of mental maladies, of following
their successive evolution, their transformations and their terminations.'[29]
Historical interpretation was at the heart of Morel's method. It was not simply that degenerative heredity allowed different kinds of stories to be told
using information already gathered in clinical observation; it also entailed a
wholly different way of investigating and emplotting mental illnesses. Morel
himself insisted upon this point. His contribution was not simply theoretical, he argued, it was practical, rooted in practices of observation and
diagnosis:

> A classification is not a thing of fantasy; it is a *method*. Who could deny that
> one can make progress in science through classifications that are neither
> etiological nor pathogenic? Nonetheless, can we not go one step further
> by employing a method that, in drawing out the origin and the transfor-
> mation of the malady better, indicates more for prognosis and treatment,
> or even for the legal analysis of the acts of *aliénés*? This is precisely what
> I have attempted.[30]

Etiological investigation was not merely a form of genealogy; it was an
interpretation of actions in the past and present. Morel insisted throughout
his career that even the slightest eccentricities could be signs of hereditary

muddled!

insanity. Because the condition was progressive, each instance had grave potential. The implication was that almost every act could be read as a sign or symptom of the incubating or 'larval' illness. Morel wrote:

> We are and remain persuaded that what these honorable doctors call *predisposition* is *already* the initial and confirmed stage of the periodic state of insanity proper to *héréditaires* and during which these 'candidates' for insanity, as the experts call them, commit acts of the highest unreason, sometimes under the influence of a passional element or from an apparently trivial cause, sometimes without any appreciable motive. It is quite sad to say, but it must be said in the interest of suffering humanity; they act in an instinctive and impulsive manner.[31]

This expansive view – that even quirks of character or alterations of mood could be symptoms of mental alienation in its early stages – drew on long-established practices in mental medicine. During the 1840s, for instance, a diagnosis of monomania often relied heavily on similar details to show retrospective indications of a mental irritation that later developed into a full-blown malady.[32] Degenerative heredity took this further, however, as Dr E. Dumesnil wrote in 1867: 'Reasoning insanity is merely a symptom of the principle forms of mental alienation: it is a delirium of acts [*délire des actes*] and wicked tendencies in contrast to reasonable words and writings.'[33] Strange acts, abrupt changes in mood, and general oddity could all be read as signs of hereditary *folie*. They did not need to be accompanied by other affective or intellectual symptoms. The very eccentricity of an act or behavior was often believed to be sufficient evidence of a festering mental disturbance.

Mental liberty and voluntary extravagance: the case of young X...

A case presented in 1868 by Dr Gabriel Doutrebente is instructive of the way cases were used to search a person's past for signs of peculiar or 'abnormal' behavior. When paired with evidence of hereditary antecedents – relatives or ancestors who also behaved in ways the doctors judged suspect or had been diagnosed with a mental disorder – such signs confirmed the potential for further degeneration and eventually insanity.

Doutrebente began: 'Young X ..., age twenty-one, is the best, characteristic type that one can find of this class of individuals whom it is difficult to regard as *aliénés*, but who, nevertheless, are incapable of controlling themselves [*se diriger*] and of living in the world. He is a striking and awful example of the fatal influence of hereditary vice.'[34]

Young X... came from a wealthy family; he was well-educated and well-traveled, having trained in the commercial centers of Europe in order to run the family business. Upon his return to France, he began to act 'deplorably' and to 'commit unnamable extravagances.' After his father's death, he was put in charge of the company, but he was uninterested in it and was asked to resign after one year.

During this period, his family life was also irregular, Doutrebente wrote: X... often quarreled with his mother, 'even in public,' as well as with his siblings. 'He never knew how to regulate or dominate his lavish instincts.' On several occasions, X... spent money for days without ever realizing the magnitude of his expenditures. A year after his dismissal from the company, he abruptly moved to Paris. In Paris, he changed apartments once a month, at one point moving every eight days – '[I]n order to know Paris better,' he said, '... but in reality,' the doctor noted, 'it was to escape detection by the police who, at the insistence of his mother, had watched him ceaselessly during his diverse movements.' Doutrebente alluded to a life of debauchery and mentioned a venereal infection, but offered no details, preferring, he explained, to focus on the young man's behavior after returning home, 'now that he was sick and was afraid of his illness.'[35]

Doutrebente now saw X... regularly and 'could study, at leisure, this bizarre product of a consanguinity tainted by morbid heredity.' By the standards of his contemporaries, young X... 's bloodline was certainly polluted. His parents had children together before they were married, Doutrebente pointed out, implying the family's moral weakness. X....'s father died following an 'epileptoid stroke,' and apparently had often fallen into fits of anger during which he bit, tore, and broke everything in his path. X...'s mother suffered from crossed eyes (strabismus) and deafness. His maternal grandfather was 'a true *aliéné*,' Doutrebente remarked: 'bizarre, eccentric, who his fellow citizens had nicknamed "*bête noire*", in allusion to his hairstyle, which consisted of an immense black mane.' His uncle, on whom young X... had modeled his life, was also 'a bizarre character; he lived alone and did nothing.' Young X... 's cousin had been 'attacked by kleptomania since childhood' and, according to the mother, had died in America after fleeing the tribunals in France. He did not steal out of financial hardship, Doutrebente assured his readers in spite of having never examined him. Rather, 'it was a need, an instinctive impulsion, an obvious symptom of a pathological state that would have soon spread and generalized itself.'[36] Finally, X...'s three siblings also showed signs of hereditary illness. These ranged from strabismus, epilepsy, and involuntary tics to precocious feats.

This was the hereditary context in which young X...'s behavior was interpreted. Doutrebente noted the young man's hypochondria, which he attributed to 'venereal accidents' during X...'s life of excess in Paris. X... suffered from a 'perversion of sentiments,' the doctor wrote, a lack of filial piety. Despite the fact that X... 's education made him easily employable, he avoided seeking an occupation:

> [H]e was afraid of becoming bored and moreover did not want to tie himself to anything. A situation determined in advance seemed to him an absurdity; he could not do the same thing two times in a row; he always needed something new. He passed his time looking for novelty, a new way to eat, to sit, to travel, to speak, etc., etc.

Family life was impossible for young X..., Doutrebente opined, because he would change addresses – even change countries – every day if permitted. While he was in Paris, X... woke for dinner and did not go to sleep until five o'clock the next morning. He found a way to eat only one meal a day, the doctor underlined incredulously, and once went several days without eating at all, 'in order to feel something new and to study the effects of starvation on himself.'[37]

Doutrebente concluded the case by explaining that he and his colleagues had often tried to convince X... that 'his manner of being and acting' bordered on madness. X... resisted, arguing that he conducted his life voluntarily and was perfectly conscious of his actions. For Doutrebente and his fellow *aliénistes* however, this was not a legitimate response: the acts *themselves* were the evidence. 'Many people would agree with him; fewer of those, however, who understand that the pathological lesion bears principally on liberty of action, and that these *allegedly voluntary extravagances* are nothing other than instinctive reactions.'[38] For the doctors, X... 's ability to reason with them, his explanations for his behavior, were beside the point: the very fact that he acted in these ways – and thought himself justified in doing so – was for them proof that he was mentally disturbed. His hereditary make-up and his history of eccentricity confirmed the diagnosis.

Doutrebente's observation of X... helped him win the coveted Prix Esquirol of 1868. There was nothing extraordinary about the case, in the sense that it did not break new theoretical or methodological ground. Doutrebente's contribution was in his exemplary application of the etiological method and his 'demonstration' of the way hereditary degeneration could be revealed through behaviors that, to the untrained eye, might not seem connected or remarkable. When linked through the case and framed in their hereditary context, however, the pathology stood out for those who knew how to look. Thus, the 'genealogical study' was extravagantly praised for its clarity by Auguste Motet in his report to the Société Médico-Psychologique, which awarded the prize. For Motet, the path of hereditary degeneration and the diverse symptoms that resulted from its transmission '[were] not only described and observed, but demonstrated by indisputable facts.' Special praise was reserved for Doutrebente's 'perceptive' investigation of an individual patient. Motet held it up as a model of clinical writing: 'We have read the whole work, which one has the right to call a clinical demonstration, bearing especially on the distinctive characters of predisposed individuals.'[39]

Doutrebente's case was praised by contemporaries for setting X… 's actions in their hereditary context. We can understand them for their historical significance. X… 's behavior was read as pathological in a society where bourgeois values were ascendant. X… 's rejection of these conventions was profoundly disturbing for his family and the doctors who treated him. Without defining it explicitly, the case posits a standard for 'normal' behavior against which X… was judged. From the transgressions that captured the doctor's attention, we can infer some of them: order, thrift, moderation, industry, respect for tradition, sociability.

In a post-revolutionary environment, X… 's actions were perceived as threatening, as an affront to the bourgeois norms of family, personal industry and responsibility, and wider sociability, all of which were intended to anchor French society in the nineteenth century. In a hereditary context, his unconventional behavior was believed to be pathological – understood as literally dangerous to himself and to society at large.

Delirious acts

We are now in a better position to understand how the theory of degenerative heredity provided what Nye calls a 'medical model of cultural crisis.' The power of heredity theory after 1850 and the popularity of degeneration as a scientific, medical, and cultural metaphor at the fin de siècle must be understood as part of a more general preoccupation with progress and social change in nineteenth-century France. As Daniel Pick has argued, these worries had a particular resonance in France after 1848, when degenerative heredity was first fully theorized.

> The theory of *dégénérescence* was bound up with the problematic of the Revolution's repetition, the sad lineage of 1789, through its intoxication, criminality, imbecility and eventual self-extinction. Morel's treatise, with its procession of themes – alcoholism, cretinism, crime, pollution, insanity, and sterility – spoke to, and displaced, deep concerns about the genealogy of history. In the aftermath of 1848, the problems of history were displaced into the problem of inheritance.[40]

The ideas of degeneration and national progress provided a vocabulary through which broader social anxieties could be expressed. Indeed, in an 1857 review of Bénédict-Augustin Morel's foundational text, *Traité des dégénérescences physiques, intellectuelles et morales de l'espèce humaine*, the doctor and *aliéniste* Philippe Bouchez noted that the theory of hereditary degeneration was quite consciously a philosophy of history, engaged with questions of national progress and cultural perfectibility:

> In my opinion, it is to the philosophy of history that we owe the rigorous definition and, consequently, the status of the question of the degeneration of the human species ... *[O]ne has a clear perception of the degeneration of the individual and of the human species only by acquiring an idea of their progress. The idea of perfectibility defines that of degradation by its very opposition.*[41]

This passage highlights how French doctors viewed individual pathologies in historico-cultural terms, using individual cases to make wider cultural generalizations and bringing broader national concerns to bear in their diagnostic judgments about particular patients. Thus, while the dangers of heredity and degeneration had emerged as theoretical problems around 1850 with the publication of Morel's work, after 1870 they became the central focus of mental medicine, dominating both the practical and theoretical landscapes. During the years following the Franco-Prussian War and the Paris Commune, degenerative heredity became *the* language through which concerns about individual and cultural health were expressed.[42] Born in a context of demographic and geopolitical instability, the Third Republic was characterized by doubts about national health. Communards and criminals, alcoholics and perverts, hysterics and syphilitics – deviants of all kinds – were featured prominently in the press and its *fait divers*. They were visible reminders of France's perceived fragility. French elites latched on to degeneration as a way to explain the existence of these dangerous 'others.'

It is perhaps little wonder that the leaders of the Third Republic were eager to project an image of bourgeois rationality, strength, and reassuring moderation. Alienists were natural partners in their efforts to improve national health and combat perceived threats to it.[43] As Nye has argued: 'Degeneration was the perfect expression of a hygienic medicine whose primary concern was the health and moral well-being of a whole population.'[44] Accordingly, questions of responsibility and free will became a central preoccupation for mental medicine during the Third Republic. As doctors emphasized at every turn, *héréditaires* could seem quite normal to the untrained observer, but they were characterized by a fundamental deficit of 'mental freedom' (*liberté morale*). As Dr Girard de Cailleux argued:

> It is not uncommon to find people in the world who seem to reason soundly, but whose life and acts are in discord with reason, in whom there is a passive consciousness of the chain of ideas that motivate them and the acts they commit. What makes up the delirious act, then, is the absence or inadequacy of mental liberty [*liberté morale*] to stop them from happening.[45]

Medical tracts of the period were rife with arguments about the degree to which degenerates of all kinds could be said to be responsible for their actions. Morel's etiological method was perfectly suited to such concerns. It required an intimate engagement with the details of a patient's life, while the very process of narrativizing and describing these conditions created an environment in which moral and ethical judgments were constantly made under the aegis of scientific detachment and medical neutrality.

Valentin Magnan was emblematic of this new approach during the Third Republic, the single most important writer on degenerative heredity at the fin de siècle. Building on Morel's theories, during this period, Magnan defined degeneration as a weakening of the cerebral centers of psychological resistance and intelligence through hereditary taints and the accumulated effects of certain vices.[46] For Magnan, the individual was physically changed by degeneration. It was:

> a pathological state of the organism which, in relation to its most immediate progenitors, is constitutionally weakened in its psycho-physical resistance and only realizes in part the biological conditions of the hereditary struggle for life. That weakening, which is revealed in permanent stigmata, is essentially progressive, with only intervening regeneration; when this is lacking, it leads more or less rapidly to the extinction of the species.[47]

One of Magnan's innovations was to interpret Morel's progressive syndrome through the lens of free will. Magnan's version of the theory focused on the weakening of 'psycho-physical' faculties, which impaired their ability to regulate instincts and impulsive behavior. Degenerates were, quite simply, less able to control themselves than other people. Whatever the specific trigger of a patient's impulsive action – a thunderclap, the recognition of a face, an object encountered by chance – 'they are but a drop of water causing the glass to overflow; behind the immediate, often banal, cause there is always a distant cause, the predisposition; the subject was ripe for the hatching [*l'éclosion*] of such accidents.' Despite their awareness of and even disgust for their own actions, *dégénérés* were destined to remain 'enslaved by [their] peculiarities.'[48]

For Magnan, the purpose of medical observation was to uncover what he called the 'psychic stigmata' that indicated the existence of a hereditary mental syndrome. These 'cerebral anomalies' were made evident to the doctor through a detailed immersion in the patient's life history. Studying the patient's past would reveal 'the instincts, the appetites, the pathological sentiments that, due to the weaknesses of the will, push toward the most extravagant, and sometimes the most dangerous, acts.'[49]

Note the shift from Morel, who emphasized that eccentricities and quirks of character could provide early warning signs (or retrospective confirmation) of mental derangement. Magnan extended this beyond an individual's behavior to stress the importance of instincts, appetites, and feelings – internal pulsations driving degenerates to pathological excess and against which they were powerless.

Impulsives

Magnan's work demonstrates the degree to which psychiatric medicine as practiced under the sign of degeneration became as much a history of an individual as it was the history of an illness. Indeed, in a subtle and paradoxical way, even as psychiatry made heredity the theoretical foundation of its thought, it was individuals that increasingly came into focus – their lives and habits, but also their feelings, drives, and desires.

An observation from Auguste Motet illustrates the way psychiatry began to excavate its patients' instincts and impulses during this period. Describing a case of *outrage public à la pudeur* (violating public decency) in 1886, Motet began:

> Heredity ... is sometimes easily recognized by indelible stigmata and sometimes hidden, revealed only by signs that are perceptible to doctors used to conducting such delicate investigations. It can be difficult to admit that a man can conduct himself correctly in the world, demonstrate an active intelligence, sometimes even remarkable aptitudes, and still be for those who live with him the most eccentric, the most violent, the most disagreeable, the most depraved of men. Nevertheless, nothing is more true... [50]

Writing on behalf of several colleagues, Motet presented the case of M. B... to show how hidden signs of hereditary pathology could be revealed through an attentive investigation of the patient's past, and to demonstrate how these interior impulsions thoroughly compromised the patient's will.

M. B... was arrested at the age of thirty-six, after confessing to the crime of having exposed his genitals for some ten minutes, alone, while traveling second-class in an otherwise empty train car. The circumstances of his arrest are unclear. He does not seem to have been seen exposing himself – there is no mention of witnesses or an incident of this sort. B... may have approached the authorities on his own – the doctors suggest elsewhere that he worried about his actions and tried to resist them. In any event, initially to the police, then to the doctors, B... reported that this was not the first time he had walked alone through a train car with his penis exposed in the open air, 'forgetting everything in order to give in to his instinctive temptation.' Although B... did not excuse his conduct, he said that he was 'incapable of resisting; when the genital temptation was aroused, everything disappeared for him, and, by either word or deed, the impulsion led to acts of an often excessive brutality.' [51]

As was standard interpretative practice, Motet and his colleagues made much of B...'s heredity, which the doctors found tainted. Without citing details, they reported that although both the father and mother were intelligent, they were also 'neuropaths to the highest degree.'[52] The father was a melancholic hypochondriac, the doctors judged, and B... 's paternal grandmother was assumed to have had similar problems. B... had been an excellent student who excelled in the sciences, but his early life was otherwise unremarkable from a medical point of view. However, Motet noted four incidents when B... had suffered blows to the head. The first occurred at age 15, while raising himself from the sink. In 1873, at age 24, he fell from a horse. The following year, he jumped from a second-storey window on a dare. Finally, in 1884, at the age of thirty-five, he fell from another horse, injuring his head and shoulder. On each occasion, B... had lost consciousness; twice he had been hospitalized. Following the first accident, B... began to suffer from vertigo and fainting. Always a heavy drinker, he experienced several associated health problems, including increased dizziness.

For Motet, B... 's hereditary make-up, combined with the cranial accidents, was enough to explain the cause of his impulsive behavior: the repeated blows to the head had damaged his already weakened faculties of resistance. 'No more is required to explain the nervous accidents to which M. B... remained subject.' This was not the entire story, however, as Motet explained,

> Until now, we have only occupied ourselves with the physical state of M. B... Before studying the deviations, the intellectual and moral perversions that M. B... presents to such a high degree, we must now establish his pathological underside. Our task is easier: we have determined the cause, we have now only to trace its effects and to complete through these long-known details the cerebral biography of a man who, for us, was disturbed [*un malade*] from an early date.[53]

One would have thought that the recitation of head traumas and related accidents would have qualified as this 'cerebral biography,' but for Motet those events are merely occasioning causes. Instead, he emphasized the 'pathological underside,' the already existing chords of heredity that were struck in B... upon each impact.

First and foremost was B... 's pathological inheritance, passed on by his hypochondriac father and neuropathic mother. Building upon these tainted foundations, Motet commented, B... had also been a masturbator during childhood and adolescence. In the nineteenth century, masturbation was assumed to weaken a person's will and to make them more psychologically 'impressionable,' more open to pathological influences.[54] In hereditary degenerates, Magnan always stressed, masturbation aggravated their conditions and undermined their already feeble capacities of 'psycho-physical resistance.'[55]

Although B... had been precocious, the doctors judged that his genital urges as a young adult were not yet pathological. They were, however, preceded by modifications of his character, which emerged in force after his fall from a horse in 1873, at age twenty-four. From that date, Motet wrote, B... was in a state of continual excitation. Already a masturbator, 'he became an *onanist*, which he aggravated through alcoholic excess.' The obscenity of his language was 'without equal.' His audacity with women was 'beyond imagination.' Married at twenty-six, he continued to masturbate. In 1879, he spent a season at Vichy for stomach pains. His doctors there counseled him to stop masturbating, which he promised to do. Despite his efforts, he could not control himself: 'He was worried about his condition, but he could not resist the genital irritations that tormented him. When alone, he masturbated with frenzy.' Often required to travel for business, he would masturbate on the trip: 'He admits that, more times than one would think, while alone in a train compartment, he has gotten an erection and walked around with his penis out while the train was moving, forgetting everything in order to accede to his instinctive solicitation.'[56]

The doctors reported that they were aware of many other examples of B... 's extravagant conduct. They wrote of an incident when B... went to a train station, unbuttoned his pants, and urinated through the bars of the ticket window: 'He was not drunk. They knew what he wanted, what he was capable of; no one said anything to him.' Only a few months before his arrest, B... crossed a prominent citizen of his city on the street and remarked, 'I've seen your daughter and masturbated while thinking of her.' Such a man, Motet wrote, 'a man of thirty-six years who masturbates and boasts of it is an abnormal creature [*un être anormal*]'. Motet's diagnosis was categorical: B... suffered from a 'cerebro-spinal lesion ... consecutive to a trauma, exaggerated in its effects by a hereditary, neuropathic predisposition.'[57]

Motet insisted that he was not investigating B...'s 'personality,' but rather his 'evident *singularity*,' his profoundly altered state.[58] Motet's aim was to divine the 'pathological underside, hereditary or acquired, that nurtures peculiarities of character or the perversion of feelings, and substitutes instinctive practices and irresistible impulses for rational and free decisions.' Individuals like B... were powerless against their pathological impulses, incapable of resisting them:

When the genital erethism is produced, when a gust of heat rises to the face, it is the result of spinal irritation and the impulsion explodes, irresistibly, brutally. The man, the patient, is no longer in control; he surrenders. He is no more able to defend himself against it than he is able to suspend vertigo. And when we have said that these patients behaved in fits – in these complex, instantaneous, unpredictable pathological states – this means they are suddenly transformed by unpremeditated, unconscious acts, by unexpected impulses.[59]

Against the recommendation of Motet and his colleagues, B... was convicted of 'violating public decency' and sentenced to one month in prison.[60] Although Motet strongly condemned B... 's behavior, the doctor insisted that B... 's condition meant that he could not be held responsible for his actions. As a degenerate, B... was physically incapable of controlling himself, the doctors determined. In line with common practice, their judgments should be understood as an implicit argument for indefinite internment in an asylum, rather than temporary imprisonment.

B... is an example of what I referred to in the introduction as a 'degenerate human kind,' referred to by both experts and the public as *dégénérés* or *héréditaires*. During the Third Republic, hereditary degeneration provided a generalized vocabulary for thinking about social deviance that was used by doctors, politicians, journalists, and many others. Alcoholics, criminals, hysterics, syphilitics, epileptics, and perverts of all sorts were identified and implicated. Especially as it was elaborated by Magnan, the theory suggested that pathological individuals were not always recognizable to the untrained eye, that they could even carry themselves correctly in everyday life without suspicion, but that such people harbored insidious instincts and dangerous impulses that could explode into action under the right circumstances. Because of the theory's tautological aspects – degeneration produced pathological impulses, which produced abnormal behaviors, which were evidence of degeneration in its 'larval' stages – its psychiatric logic was applied well beyond the clinic to virtually everyone. Hacking's concept of 'world-making by kind-making' is apt. As the passage from Dr Laupts suggested: 'there is no reader who is not preoccupied from a personal point of view; there is no one who, from now on, does not protect himself from a "phobia," from a "philia," or from a "mania" of some sort... '[61]

Conclusion

We are now in a better position to understand how the theory of degenerate heredity crystallized a new way of thinking about what it meant to be insane, entailing a fundamental redefinition of alienation during the early years of the Third Republic. At the dawn of the century, Philippe Pinel's signature contribution to the study of mental disturbances had been to demonstrate that *insensés* were in point of fact merely *aliénés*, that there existed within them a 'shred of reason' (*reste de raison*) and, hence, of humanity. For Pinel, the tragedy of the *'insensés'* lay in their alienation from reason, in their partial separation from themselves and society. In line with the post-revolutionary effort to mold citizens, Pinel's nascent specialty held out the hope that such subjects could be reformed, recuperated, and reintegrated.

With the rise of Morel's theory of hereditary degeneration, however, the *malade-aliéné* was gradually replaced in the medical imagination by something we might call the *malade-dégénéré*. No longer someone who suffered to me this is about the abandonment of the rational individual of liberal ideology

the indignity of an illness, this person *was* the illness; in heredity and history, the degenerate was at once symptom and pathogen. A statement from 1897 marks the distance from Pinel: 'One speaks to us of *aliénés* as one speaks of them in novels; one gives them sentiments, ideas, aspirations that, for my part, I have never found among them. They are *inconscients* who must be watched.'[62]

As France took up its democratic experiment anew under the Third Republic, with fresh memories of national humiliation and internal disruption, its elites took a similarly skeptical view of the 'others' it worried were in its midst. Dangers to the Republic lay hidden beneath the surface of society, rooted in the organic life through degenerative heredity. For the health of the country, they argued, it was important to find and neutralize these human pathogens. Thus, the central concern of psychiatrists in the last third of the century was to show how seemingly reasonable persons could in fact be *aliéné*, how there existed within them '*reservoirs de déraison*,' one might say. This was nothing less than a complete inversion of psychiatry's founding impulses.

The heuristic reversal implied in the shift from *malade-aliéné* to *malade-dégénéré* helps explain the important legacy that the theory of degenerative heredity left to the modern world. Through its personalization of social and political anxiety, marks of pathology – eccentricities, peculiarities, perversions – came to form the secret center of modern selves, our 'precious marks of originality,' as Laupts put it. They have become signs of that which is individual in us, of that which distinguishes us into different human kinds. Today they form the core of our identities. It is a legacy that continues to give each of us pause as we contemplate our desires, our pasts, and our selves.

Notes

1. See Marcel Gauchet and Gladys Swain, *La pratique de l'esprit humain: L'institution asilaire et la révolution démocratique* (Paris: Gallimard, 1980); recently published in an abridged translation as, *Madness and Democracy: the Modern Psychiatric Universe*, trans. Catherine Porter (Princeton, NJ: Princeton University Press, 1999).
2. Marcel Gauchet and Gladys Swain, 'Du traitement de la manie aux passions: la folie et l'union de l'âme et du corps,' in *Des Passions considérées comme causes, symptômes et moyens curatifs de l'aliénation mentale, par E. Esquirol (1805)* (Paris: Librairie des deux-mondes, 1980), p. xxi.
3. See Sergio Moravia, 'Philosophie et médecine en France à la fin du 18ème siècle,' *Studies on Voltaire and the Eighteenth Century*, 89 (1972): 1089–151; Dora B. Weiner, *The Citizen-Patient in Revolutionary and Imperial Paris* (Baltimore and London: Johns Hopkins University Press, 1993); and Guenter B. Risse, 'Medicine in the Age of Enlightenment,' in *Medicine in Society: Historical Essays*, Andrew Wear (ed.) (Cambridge: Cambridge University Press, 1992), pp. 149–95.
4. John Forrester, 'If *p*, then what? Thinking in cases,' *History of the Human Sciences*, 9(3) (1996): 1–25.
5. Matt Reed, 'Making the Case: the Evolution of the Case Study in Nineteenth-Century Psychiatry,' PhD dissertation, Claremont Graduate University, 2002. Also

see Ian Hacking, 'Making up People,' in T.C. Heller, M. Sosna, and D.E. Wellbery (eds), *Reconstructing Individualism: Autonomy, Individuality, and the Self in Western Thought* (Stanford, CA: Stanford University Press, 1986), pp. 222–36; idem., *Rewriting the Soul: Multiple Personality and the Sciences of Memory* (Princeton, NJ: Princeton University Press, 1995); and Matt Reed, 'Historicizing Inversion: How to Make a Homosexual,' *History of the Human Sciences*, 14(4) (2001): 1–30.

6. Foucault, *Discipline and Punish: the Birth of the Prison*, trans. Alan Sheridan (New York: Vintage, 1979), p. 193.

7. See, for instance, Ian Hacking, 'World-Making by Kind-Making: Child Abuse for Example,' in M. Douglas and D. Hull (eds), *How Classification Works: Nelson Goodman among the Social Sciences* (Edinburgh: Edinburgh University Press, 1992), pp. 180–238.

8. Dr Laupts, 'Une perversion de l'instinct. L'amour morbide; sa nature et son traitement,' *Annales médico-psychologiques*, 1 (1895): 174–82.

9. The secondary literature in this philosophical vein is immense, spanning the Greeks to Freud. A few recent texts serve as a useful *tour d'horizon*; see, for example, Charles Taylor, *Sources of the Self: the Making of the Modern Identity* (Cambridge, MA: Harvard University Press, 1992); Jerrold Siegel, *The Idea of the Self: Thought and Experience in Western Europe since the Seventeenth Century* (Cambridge: Cambridge University Press, 2005); and Jan Goldstein, *The Post-Revolutionary Self: Politics and Psyche in France, 1750–1850* (Cambridge, MA: Harvard University Press, 2005).

10. See Michel Foucault, *Discipline and Punish*; idem., *The History of Sexuality, Volume I: an Introduction*, trans. Robert Hurley (New York: Vintage Books, 1978); Hacking, *Rewriting the Soul*; and Arnold Davidson, *The Emergence of Sexuality: Historical Epistemology and the Formation of Concepts* (Cambridge, MA: Harvard University Press, 2004).

11. These figures also correspond roughly to one or more of the characteristics of modern selves as suggested by Taylor: interiority, freedom, individualism (distinctiveness), and embeddedness in nature. A number of works illuminate the cultural history and significance of these exemplars, each of which was also in its own way a vector for key aspects of modern identities. On the criminal, see Foucault, *Discipline and Punish*. On the madman, see Foucault, *Madness and Civilization: a History of Insanity in the Age of Reason*, trans. Richard Howard (New York: Vintage Books, 1965) and Gauchet and Swain, *La pratique de l'esprit humain*. On the hysteric, see Foucault, *The History of Sexuality, Volume I*; Mark Micale, *Approaching Hysteria: Disease and its Interpretations* (Princeton, NJ: Princeton University Press, 1994); and Elaine Showalter, *Sexual Anarchy: Gender and Culture at the fin de siècle* (New York: Viking, 1990). On the pervert, see Robert A. Nye, *Masculinity and Male Codes of Honor in Modern France* (Oxford: Oxford University Press, 1993) and Vernon Rosario, *The Erotic Imagination: French Histories of Perversity* (New York: Oxford University Press, 1997).

12. Forrester, 'If *p*, then what?' p. 10.

13. Robert A. Nye's work has exhaustively demonstrated the role of degenerative heredity in nineteenth-century France and the important role it played in the discovery of the perversions at the fin de siècle. See his *Crime, Madness and Politics in Modern France: the Medical Concept of National Decline* (Princeton, NJ: Princeton University Press, 1984) and *Masculinity and Male Codes of Honor*. See also Daniel Pick, *Faces of Degeneration: a European Disorder, c. 1848–c. 1918* (Cambridge: Cambridge University Press, 1989) and Laura Otis, *Organic Memory: History and the*

Body in the Late Nineteenth and Early Twentieth Centuries (Lincoln, NE: University of Nebraska Press, 1994).

14. Ian Hacking, *Rewriting the Soul*, p. 239; my emphasis.
15. Goldstein, *The Post-Revolutionary Self*, p. 9.
16. See Gauchet and Swain, *La pratique de l'esprit humain*; Gladys Swain, *Le Sujet de la Folie*, 2nd edn (Paris: Calmann-Lévy, 1997 [1977]) and *Dialogue avec l'insensé* (Paris: Gallimard, 1994).
17. See, for example, Lynn Hunt, *The Family Romance of the French Revolution* (Berkeley: University of California Press, 1994) and Dorinda Outram, *The Body and the French Revolution: Sex, Class and Political Culture* (New Haven: Yale University Press, 1989).
18. Gauchet and Swain, *Madness and Democracy*.
19. See, for example, Pierre Nora, *Les Lieux des memoire: La République* (Paris: Gallimard, 1984) and Joan Landes, *Women and the Public Sphere in the Age of the French Revolution* (Ithaca: Cornell University Press, 1988).
20. See Weiner, *The Citizen-Patient* and W. F. Bynum, *Science and the Practice of Medicine in the Nineteenth Century* (Cambridge and New York: Cambridge University Press, 1994).
21. For example, see Foucault, *Discipline and Punish*; Robert Castel, *The Regulation of Madness: the Origins of Incarceration in France*, trans. W. D. Halls (Berkeley: University of California Press, 1988); and Jan Goldstein, *Console and Classify: the French Psychiatric Profession in the Nineteenth Century* (Cambridge and New York: Cambridge University Press, 1987).
22. Goldstein, *Console and Classify*, p. 339.
23. Nye, *Crime, Madness and Politics*, p. 50
24. Nye, *Crime, Madness and Politics*, pp. xii–xiii.
25. Bénédict-Augustin Morel, *Traité des dégénérescences physiques, intellectuelles et morales de l'espèce humain* (Paris: Victor Masson, 1857).
26. For instance, see Prosper Lucas, *Traité philosophique et physiologique de l'hérédité naturelle dans les états de santé et de maladie du système nerveux* (Paris: J.-B. Baillière, 1847); Jacques Moreau de Tours, *La Psychologie morbide dans ses rapports avec la philosophie de l'histoire ou de l'influence des névropathies sur le dynamisme intellectuel* (Paris: Masson, 1859); P.A. Piorry, *De l'hérédité dans les maladies* (Paris: Bury, 1840).
27. Bénédict-Augustin Morel, *Traité des maladies mentales* (Paris: Victor Masson, 1860), p. iii.
28. This allowed Morel to sidestep the problems of traditional classification, which were based on the observation and categorization of symptoms. It posed no problem to Morel if, in a single patient, melancholia shaded into mania and was accompanied by various kinds of monomania, derangement of ideas, or eccentricities. (See Jules Falret, 'Discussion sur les classifications de la folie,' *Annales médico-psychologiques*, 7 (1861): 145–77.) Likewise, Morel avoided the mimetic problem faced by previous proponents of hereditary mental disorders: the transmission of an identical malady was no longer a necessary condition for establishing a hereditary link.
29. Falret, 'Discussion sur les classifications de la folie', 164.
30. Ibid, 177; my emphasis. Morel's response to Falret (pp. 171–7) is in Falret, 'Discussion sur les classifications de la folie'.
31. Bénédict-Augustin Morel, 'Consultation médico-légale sur l'état mental de Jeanson,' *Annales d'hygiène publique et de médecine légale*, 32 (1869): 153–210. My emphasis.
32. See Goldstein, *Console and Classify* and Castel, *The Regulation of Madness*.

_____ . Dumesnil, 'De la folie raisonnante et de l'importance du délire des actes pour le diagnostic et la médecine légale, par le docteur A. Brierre de Boismont,' *Annales médico-psychologiques*, 10 (1867): 574–82.

34. Gabriel Doutrebente, 'Étude géneologique sur les aliénés héréditaires,' *Annales médico-psychologiques*, 2 (1869): 197–237; 369–94.
35. Doutrebente, 'Étude géneologique,' p. 373.
36. Ibid.
37. Ibid, p. 374. As Elizabeth Williams's chapter in this volume suggests, taking a meal was a critical form of French sociability, at least for men. Gastronomy was seen as a 'model of discipline, control, and moderation' – civic virtues in the bourgeois republic. In renouncing his meals, X... was seen as renouncing his culture.
38. Ibid. Emphasis in original.
39. Auguste Motet, 'Rapport sur le prix Esquirol pour l'année 1868,' *Annales médico-psychologiques*, 2 (1869): 148–54.
40. Pick, *Faces of Degeneration*, p. 59.
41. Philippe Bouchez, 'Rapport fait à la Société médico-psychologique sur le *Traité des dégénérescences physiques, intellectuelles et morales de l'espèce humaine et des causes qui les produisent*, par le docteur B.-A. Morel,' *Annales médico-psychologiques*, 3 (1857): 455–67; my emphasis.
42. Nye, *Crime, Madness and Politics*; also see Pick, *Faces of Degeneration*, pp. 97–105.
43. On the 'fit' between the profession and the regime, see Goldstein, *Console and Classify*, pp. 361–9; and Nye, *Crime, Madness and Politics*, pp. 49–97.
44. Nye, *Crime, Madness and Politics*, p. 45.
45. Henri Girard de Cailleux, 'Discussion sur les aliénés avec conscience de leur état,' *Annales médico-psychologiques*, 3 (1870): 466–86.
46. A number of cultural historians have addressed the attention paid to each of these groups in late nineteenth-century France. See Susanna Barrows, *Distorting Mirrors: Visions of the Crowd in Late Nineteenth-Century France* (New Haven: Yale University Press, 1981); Emily Apter, *Feminizing the Fetish: Psychoanalysis and Narrative Obsession in Turn-of-the-Century France* (Ithaca: Cornell University Press, 1991); and Jeffrey Merrick and Bryant T. Ragan, Jr (eds), *Homosexuality in Modern France*, (Oxford: Oxford University Press, 1996).
47. Valentin Magnan and Paul-Maurice LeGrain, *Les Dégénérés* (Paris: Reuff, 1895), p. 79; as quoted in Nye, *Crime, Madness and Modern Politics*, p. 124.
48. Valentin Magnan and Jean-Martin Charcot, 'De l'onomatomanie,' *Archives de neurologie*, 10 (1885): 157–68.
49. Valentin Magnan, 'De l'Enfance des criminels dans ses rapports avec la prédisposition naturelle au crime,' *Archives de l'Anthropologie criminelle*, 4 (1889): 549–615.
50. Auguste Motet, 'Outrage public à la pudeur. Condamnation. – Appel. – Confirmation,' *Annales d'hygiène publique et de médecine légale*, 15 (1886): 202–13.
51. Ibid., pp. 205, 210.
52. Ibid., p. 206.
53. Ibid., pp. 207, 209.
54. Rosario, *The Erotic Imagination* and Thomas W. Laqueur, *Solitary Sex: a Cultural History of Masturbation* (New York: Zone Books, 2004).
55. See Magnan and LeGrain, *Les dégénérés*.
56. Motet, 'Outrage public,' pp. 206–7, 210.
57. Ibid., pp. 210–11.
58. Ibid., p. 203. My emphasis.

59. Ibid., pp. 203, 211.
60. Under the Third Republic, public decency laws were a common way to regulate private behaviors and were regularly used to police sexual activities of many kinds – sodomy, prostitution, genital exposure, even adultery. See Nye, *Masculinity and Male Codes of Honor*; Merrick and Ragan, *Homosexuality in Modern France*; and Jeffrey Merrick and Michael Sibalis, *Homosexuality in French History and Culture* (Binghamton, NY: Harrington Park Press, 2001).
61. Dr Laupts, 'Une perversion de l'instinct.'
62. Jules Christian, 'Des asiles d'aliénés à portes ouvertes,' *Annales médico-psychologiques*, 6 (1897): 446–65.

4
Gastronomy and the Diagnosis of Anorexia in Fin-de-Siècle France

Elizabeth A. Williams

> Everything which is eaten is the food of power. [1960]
>
> (Elias Canetti, *Crowds and Power*[1])

Students of European cultural history have long characterized the late nineteenth century and the years leading up to the Great War as a period of pronounced public and private anxieties. In the late 1950s the American historian H. Stuart Hughes chronicled the 'social disorder, economic crisis, and institutional malfunctioning' that helped to effect an 'intellectual revolution' against the era's 'self-satisfied cult of material progress' and the optimistic positivism on which it rested. No historian has done more than Robert A. Nye to extend this insight to France, the nation that had long enjoyed cultural dominance over its neighbors but that, with the currents of the fin de siècle, entered a period of broad-spectrum cultural anxieties. Nye traced the pessimism and fearfulness of the era to the wrenching shock of France's defeat in the Franco-Prussian War of 1870–71, and meticulously traced French fears of national degeneration and decline. Chief among Nye's contributions is his demonstration of the leading role played by physicians and biological scientists in diagnosing the nation's cultural pathologies with the help of what he called a 'medical model of cultural crisis.'[2] Prominent among the physicians and life scientists who turned their sights on France's cultural maladies were the diagnosticians of mental pathology, the 'alienists,' who, from the moment when 'mental medicine' first emerged amid the turmoil of the French Revolution, had claimed special understanding of intellectual, emotional, and behavioral aberration. In the fin de siècle, practitioners of mental medicine, by the 1890s increasingly known by the loftier cognomen 'psychiatrists,' asserted that great numbers of French citizens were beset by amorphous, jointly physical-moral ills rooted in deep-seated pathological tendencies and predispositions. The maladies of criminals and neuropaths, weaklings and lunatics exerted noxious influence throughout French society, sapping the political, cultural, and biological strength of the nation.

90

In recent years historians have come to recognize the extent to which French cultural anxieties of the fin de siècle were fixed on disruptions of gender roles, producing an era of veritable gender panic.[3] By the end of the century powerful currents of change – industrial capitalism, science and technology, the dynamic of France's commitment to universal human rights – had combined to undermine traditional thinking about differences in the basic nature of males and females and to unsettle the everyday lived experience of demarcated gender roles. The position of cultural elites – scientists, physicians, *hommes de lettres* – amid this gender panic was fraught. While some intellectuals and artists promoted the emergence of the 'New Woman,' pursuing critiques of the legal, theological, and philosophical underpinnings of patriarchy, others vociferously reasserted the appropriateness of prohibitions against public-roles for women, honing new rhetorical and conceptual tools to stem the feminist tide.[4]

Amid controversies over gender, medical men assumed an especially authoritative position. From the late eighteenth century forward, French physicians had striven to restate in modern scientific terms ancient teachings about women's fragility, instability, and unsuitability for public activity.[5] Fin-de-siècle physicians eagerly joined debates set off by the emergence of the 'New Woman,' among which those over women's access to higher education and the professions were of special concern. Thanks to the efforts of a small coterie of reformers and activists, French medical schools were among the first in Europe to admit women and to open the possibility of women practicing as formally certified physicians, but the backlash against the entry of women to the medical profession was sometimes ferocious.[6] It was in the context of such angry controversies that fin-de-siècle physicians, experts in the emergent fields of psychiatry and neurology but general practitioners as well, pursued their investigations of mental and emotional disorders, often linking them to upsets in gender definitions and roles. As Matthew Reed observes in his chapter in this volume, much psychiatric thinking of the late nineteenth century focused on the concept of 'degeneracy': hereditary 'taints' that were passed in family lines and that ultimately produced diseased physical-moral types. The diffuse pathologies besetting 'degenerates' were manifested in frightful maladies and behavioral aberrations, including criminality, sexual debauchery or inversion, epilepsy, phobias, alcoholism, and many others.[7] Noting that much psychiatric inquiry of the earlier nineteenth century, inspired by the work of the French 'father of psychiatry' Philippe Pinel, had sought merely to describe and classify illnesses, Reed traces the emergence of an intensified interest in the causes of disease, with the patient's biography regarded as the key to identifying pathogenic influences.

The descriptive and classifying bent of French medicine never gave way entirely, however, and during the fin de siècle students of mental and emotional disease sought to isolate, describe, and label conditions that had previously gone unrecognized. Among the most consequential results of their efforts was the move, from around 1870, to identify and explore conditions that may be viewed as precursors to modern eating disorders. In the last decades of the century and up to 1914, physicians evinced an ever-growing interest in the general link between gastric and psychic pathologies, and they began to concentrate for the first time on conditions – obesity, diabetes, gastropathy, 'nervous vomiting,' bulimia, and especially anorexia – that had previously been regarded as symptoms rather than independent disease entities. This interest was encouraged in part by changing conceptions of the connections between the central nervous system that governed conscious, voluntary bodily activities and the autonomic ('vegetative') system responsible for the involuntary functions of the viscera (gut, liver, heart). But, as I seek to show in this chapter, enhanced attention to psycho-gastric disorder also responded to the cultural anxieties, especially the gender panic, that characterized the age. This chapter explores the move made by medical men of the fin de siècle to establish for the first time a distinct disease entity characterized by repugnance for or refusal of food and labeled as some kind of 'anorexia.' It seeks to relate the mapping of this new disease to developments in the discourse of gastronomy, one of the great sites of cultural power in modern France.[8] Gastronomic discourse was intensely masculine, dismissive of women, on occasion even frankly misogynistic. In consequence of long-standing connections between medicine and the culinary arts, gastronomy was readily adapted to the ends of those physicians who, in constructing the anorexia diagnosis, asserted in new terms the weakness, fragility, and instability of women. To explore this connection, I will align some elements of medical and gastronomic discourse and then offer some suggestions about how their shared assumptions about gender helped to establish anorexia as a peculiarly female affliction.

The 'anorexia' diagnosis in French medicine

Of Greek derivation, the term 'anorexia' was used for centuries in Western medicine to indicate the manifestation of a symptom common in many states of ill health: the loss of appetite. By extension, it was often used to designate the refusal of food, and the general bodily consequences of such refusal, whether that refusal was motivated by distaste for food or, when hunger and appetite were present, other reasons – the inability to swallow, the experience of pain after eating, or psychological distress.[9]

Medical interest in the phenomenon of food refusal was heightened, if not intellectually refined, by the medicalization of institutions that housed the insane, a process that, in France, got seriously under way during the French Revolution. By 1809, so we are told in Philippe Pinel's famed treatise on mental alienation, French physicians were resorting to use of a feeding apparatus to force-feed patients who threatened to expire from inanition.[10] Much talk, none of it very astute, ensued throughout the century about forced-feeding – the best instruments to use, how to position the patient and the operative, and so on. The nature of anorexia also drew attention, the first meaningful attempts at definition and classification being made amid intensifying medical discussion of gastric woes generally. This interest was pronounced during the heyday of 'Broussaisism,' the medical philosophy of the iconoclast F.-J.-V. Broussais, who viewed the stomach as the organ of greatest anatomical and physiological importance, and thus any gastric 'irritation' as a central cause of disease. Up to the 1860s anorexia was seen as a sometimes life-threatening symptom of an underlying pathology, whose cause was either gastric ('gastralgia,' 'dyspepsia') or psychic (especially disturbances of affect such as melancholia).[11]

Beginning in the 1860s the discourse of anorexia took an important turn, simultaneously in French and British medicine. First in an 1860 work by the alienist L.-V. Marcé, and then more consequentially in an article published in 1873 by the neurologist Charles Lasègue, anorexia began to be explored as a distinct syndrome observed in females, either exclusively, as some physicians asserted, or nearly so, as others said. Marcé associated anorexia with hypochondria, while Lasègue linked it to the other of the two great neuroses, hysteria, coining the term *'anorexie hystérique.'* At the same time, the British physician William Withey Gull, who served as consulting physician to Guy's Hospital and enjoyed a wide practice among members of London's social elites, offered a similar description of anorexia as a distinct clinical entity; it was he who coined the term 'anorexia nervosa.' All of these physicians described anorexia as a condition afflicting young girls of high, or at least comfortable social station, who were either in the throes of puberty or just past it. For reasons seldom explored, these girls were determined to achieve extraordinary states of thinness and thus were locked in prolonged battles with their families, and particularly their mothers, who wanted them to eat.[12]

Historical investigations of food refusal, especially those produced by modern clinicians, sometimes suggest that a more or less unbroken history of 'anorexia nervosa' has unfolded from the 1870s to the present.[13] Yet the historical record from the publication of Marcé's first article in 1860 into the early twentieth century indicates, at least in French medicine, a radically unstable terminology that reflected continuing debates over the classification and conceptualization of the phenomenon. Below is a list of the labels employed in some of the works on the subject that appeared in these years:

- Une forme de délire hypochondriaque (Marcé 1860)
- Anorexie hystérique (Lasègue 1873)
- Anorexie nerveuse primitive (Charcot 1887)
- Anorexie hystérique (sitiergie hystérique) (Sollier 1891)
- Délire de maigreur (Brissaud and Souques, 1894)
- Anorexie mentale (Sollier 1895)

- Anorexie primitive (Gilles de la Tourette, 1895)
- Anorexie dyscénesthésique (Ballet 1907)
- Anorexie nerveuse (Comby 1908)
- Anorexie des nourrissons (Comby 1908)
- Anorexie des adolescents (Bérillon 1909–10)
- Psychopathies gastriques (Sollier 1910)[14]

Although some of these offerings prefigured the modern clinical portrait of anorexia nervosa, physicians were far from agreement in these years on the essentials of the disease.[15] Much debate focused on the connection of anorexia to hysteria. In contrast to Gull and some French physicians who favored Gull's view, Lasègue never used the term 'anorexia nervosa,' preferring instead, 'hysterical anorexia,' and thus positioning the syndrome within the general category of what the neurologist Jean-Martin Charcot and his followers called '*la grande névrose.*' Disagreement was also evident in respect to the age of those afflicted with anorexia: while most authors agreed that the disease was ordinarily observed in young women, some reported seeing anorexia in women as old as fifty-four.[16] And at least one authority, the pediatrician Jules Comby, diagnosed anorexia in baby girls, linking the condition to excessive summer heat and arguing that this infant malady was 'closely related to *anorexie nerveuse.*'[17] Moreover, a key symptom in the modern diagnosis of anorexia nervosa – 'weight phobia' – appeared in some of these French discussions but not others.[18]

What *was* a constant in the French medical literature – indeed, the only diagnostic constant for the first half century – was the claim that the disease was a female disorder, either exclusively so or in all but rare instances.[19] While food refusal was sometimes observed in males, the instances reported were generally linked either to 'sitophobia' (the eating behavior of psychotics caused by phobias or hallucinations surrounding food), or to conditions such as obsessions and *idées fixes* in which the 'content' – fixation on food and eating – was incidental.[20] Especially notable in this regard was the position of those investigators and physicians associated with the school surrounding Charcot. One of the most contentious steps taken by Charcot and his associates in establishing their position within French neurology and psychiatry was their extension of the label 'hysteria' to men, in the face of opposition from theorists and practitioners in France and elsewhere who insisted on essential differences between male 'traumatic neurosis' and female hysteria.[21] Thus the Charcot school was not only prepared, but eager to reverse longstanding gender claims in respect to '*la grande névrose.*' But on the subject of anorexia their position was clear: this was a female disease that was only rarely, if ever, seen in males. The statement opening a case-report offered in 1895 by Maurice Debove, an early associate and admirer of Charcot, was typical: 'I wish first to draw your attention to the sex of our subject, for virtually all the pronounced cases of anorexia nervosa have been observed in women.'[22]

Only around 1910, after decades of categorical assertions, did this view begin, hesitantly, to shift. At that point Paul Sollier, who enjoyed renown chiefly as a clinician (he operated a sanatorium in Boulogne-sur-Seine to which Charcot sent private patients), began to extend the anorexia diagnosis to males. After two decades of treating patients who refused food, Sollier reversed his long-held earlier view that anorexia was strictly a female disorder and began diagnosing it in men who suffered from what he described as functional 'inhibition,' a breakdown of some phase of the digestive process.[23] Sollier's move presaged the change of emphasis that was to come in the interwar years, when many investigators abandoned the study of anorexia as a psychic disease afflicting females and began to conceptualize it as one of a range of hormonal and gastric organic illnesses that resulted in marked weight-loss in both sexes.[24] But from the 1860s to the 1920s anorexia was well established as a female disorder. The explanation for this is complex, but one of its elements is revealed in the discourse of gastronomy as it developed in this same period, especially in regard to what *gastronomes* had to say about the roles of men and women in appreciating and consuming food.

Gastronomy and gender

While physicians claimed authority on all matters concerning ingestion and digestion, they faced a powerful challenge from the *gastronome*, who judged foods and styles of eating according to standards of pleasure and social refinement rather than health and disease.[25] And just as medical men who styled themselves experts on eating discerned essential differences in the tendencies of females and males, so gastronomy upheld clear dicta on the connection between eating and gender, the fundamental truth being that only men knew how to eat. In its stark assertion of gendered differences, French gastronomic discourse incorporated what some social theorists, especially those of misogynistic temper, have asserted as universal truths about men, women, and eating. Striking in this connection is the observation of Elias Canetti that eating, which is obviously about nutrition and staying alive, is also about exercising power. Canetti was acutely interested in the different powers exerted by men and women in relation to eating practices. As Canetti writes of the male: 'The man who can eat more than anyone else lies back satisfied and heavy with food; he is a champion. There are peoples who take such a champion eater for their chief. His full belly seems to them a guarantee that they themselves will never go hungry for long.' Characterizing the eating-power of woman, Canetti positions her in the frame of the family: first as wife – 'In a *family* the husband contributes food and the wife prepares it for him. The fact that he habitually eats what she has prepared constitutes the strongest link between them' – and then as mother – 'A mother is one who gives her own body to be eaten. She first nourishes the child in her womb and then gives it her milk ... Her passion is to give food, to watch the child eating and profiting by the food it eats.'[26]

Canetti doubtless believed that he captured a universal human truth in asserting that the male is the being that consumes food and the female is the one who prepares and offers it up. Viewed from some distance, however, he seems, rather, to have unearthed a deep structure of thinking about the differing relations of men and women to food and to power; one that determined what a European man took as givens on this subject, whether writing in 1960, when *Crowds and Power* was published, or in 1860, when the historical actors examined here were making their diagnoses.[27] That gastronomy was a masculine preserve is suggested by the following mix of titles, aphorisms, and *bons mots* culled from the literature. One is the title of a famous essay by the figure often credited with launching gastronomy, A.-B.-L. Grimod de la Reynière: *Discourse of a True Gourmand: the Superiority of Good Eating over Women.*[28] Emile Zola also affirmed such a view in his novel *Pot Bouille*: 'All the gourmets, all the wise men agree: "No women, for women do not know how to eat; they never do justice to truffles and they ruin one's digestion." '[29] Similarly, a 'celebrated formula' among Parisian gastronomes held that the Boulevard des Italiens, famed for its great restaurants, was the 'clitoris of Paris.'[30] Lastly, a description included in the *Guide des Plaisirs de Paris* (1900) of a restaurant founded around 1850, on the Boulevard de Strasbourg, offered this witticism: 'At Maire's establishment, a singularity: it is a very gay, very high-spirited restaurant even though husbands come to dine there in private compartments with their honored wives.'[31]

As these statements indicate, the maleness of gastronomy went unquestioned by its devotees. This feature of gastronomic discourse also seems to be one of those rare facts of French history on which virtually all scholars agree. Priscilla Parkhurst Ferguson observes, for example:

> The gastronome was invariably male. Beyond the fact that men held the purse strings and haute cuisine was a very expensive pursuit, the public culinary sphere was inhospitable to women: chefs as well as gastronomes were male. The host whose duties Grimod de la Reynière spelled out with such care could only be male ... [A]s with other urban spaces ... its inherent promiscuity gave the restaurant an uncertain moral status that effectively excluded upper- and middle-class women.[32]

Ferguson explains that economic and social factors made gastronomy a male domain. But she also reveals a 'moral positioning of gastronomy' in the Larousse dictionary of 1866–79. '*Gastrolatrie*' and '*gastromanie*' were associated with excess, dangerously close to old-fashioned and disgusting gluttony. But '*gastronomie*' was 'a model of discipline, control, and moderation.'[33] If this is true, it is easy to see why gastronomy excluded women, who, so it was asserted in every authoritative discourse, were wanting in discipline, control, and moderation. Philosophers and theologians, lawyers and physicians all agreed that young girls and women were marked by defects of will, being sometimes headstrong and willful, sometimes indecisive and lacking in will-power.[34] Thus the discrimination and self-control required for gastronomic finesse were said to lie beyond female capacities.

To argue that gastronomy was a male domain is not to say that women were altogether banished from the world of the restaurant or of *haute cuisine*. While gastronomic discourse ordinarily emphasized the unparalleled skill of the male chef and the pleasures of all-male company – freedom of language, absence of wives, admixture of gambling – some authorities did credit the capacities of the *cuisinière*, the refined manners of the female diner, and, especially, the blended titillations of food and female allure.[35] In important respects French gastronomic culture validates Canetti's truism that, through the ages, women have sought and enjoyed power by preparing and providing food. Eugène Briffault, author of the July Monarchy compendium *Paris à table*, was one gastronomic commentator much impressed by the kitchens of fashionable aristocratic women, but especially by the female cooks they employed to prepare culinary delights, the *cordons bleus* of Paris:

> The dinners of which we speak are those given in houses enjoying wealth and involved in business. Offered once a week to guests whose number must never be less than five nor more than twelve, these meals are prepared by a female chef [*cuisinière*]. Those who affect disdain for the feminine sex in matters of cooking fail to recognize the degree of superiority attained by these women, known by tradition as the *cordons bleus*. It would be impossible to exceed these women in the care, taste, or intelligence devoted to the choice and preparation of dishes. A good Parisian *cuisinière* to whom one leaves a proper freedom of action wields a talent that can compete with that of illustrious [male] chefs ... Put in charge of her a hostess who directs without harassing, who guides and enlightens without tormenting, and from this happy alliance you will see presented exquisite meals that once enjoyed are never forgotten.[36]

Some authors also admired the elegant women whose exquisite manners had, at least historically, contributed to the high level of *politesse* exhibited at dinners attended by both sexes.[37] Most commonly expressed, however, was admiration for the women whose charms enhanced the already luxurious sensual experience of the restaurant. The gastronomic literature is replete with comments on women whose presence as handmaidens of the restaurant ('the beauty who shucks the oysters,' 'the lovely Mme Brébant at the register') ('la belle écaillère,' 'la belle Mme Brébant en face de la caisse') gave added pleasure to male diners/oglers.[38] Sometimes the rhetorical linkage of delicious food and alluring women became extravagant indeed, as when Briffault compared the 'delectable foods of choice' that in Paris 'become inviolable and sacred' to 'the beautiful slaves reserved to the sultan in his harem.'[39] Yet aside from occasional praise for women as preparers of food, and appreciative statements about their refined manners or erotic enticements, gastronomy was an affair of men. The celebrated chefs were men, the gastronomic critics were men, and, most significant, the great eaters were men. By contrast women, 'banned from the noble haunts of gastronomy ... can have little opinion regarding food.'[40]

Anorexia and gastronomy

Given the ancient link between cooking and dietetics, it should perhaps be unsurprising that medicine and gastronomy reached compatible conclusions in regard to gender and eating. Medical tradition had throughout the centuries impelled physicians to take into account the judgments of culinary masters on food. Recent scholarship on dietetics among the Ancients tells us that no less a figure than Galen believed the good physician must be a good cook, and that he himself was one.[41] And although some French physicians had long since dispensed with the authority of the Ancients, the continuing prestige of classical medicine was perhaps nowhere more evident than in matters gastric.[42] One recent line of inquiry pertinent to the emergence of the anorexia diagnosis in the fin de siècle is the effort historians have made to pinpoint when medical and culinary/gastronomic discourses began pulling apart. Unlike the maleness of gastronomy, this matter does not command agreement. Jean-Louis Flandrin argues, for example, that cooking gradually 'liberated' itself from medicine across the two centuries between 1600 and 1800, citing as proofs such facts as the transformed view of sugar; long regarded as medicinal, it came to be used, altogether un-medically, as a substance good for 'harmonizing flavors.'[43] Emma Spary, on the other hand, argues that in France there was a veritable war between the dietitian and the *gourmand* from the late eighteenth century, when everyone fretted over health, to the later Empire, when foods came to function once again as a source of pleasure and as a convenient marker of social distinction.[44] Historians of food do seem to agree, however, that some kind of reconciliation was achieved in the nineteenth century between gastronomy and medical science, especially those elements of medicine informed by advances in chemistry. Ferguson argues that from Brillat-Savarin forward (his famous *Physiologie du goût* was published in 1825), science was essential to the gastronome's understanding of textures and flavors, providing him with 'the reasoned knowledge,' as Brillat put it, 'of everything that concerns man and nourishment.'[45] Indeed, it seems evident that the connection to science was another reason gastronomy excluded women.

This historical literature, with its stress on the new prestige of chemistry, generally neglects the relation between gastronomy and a more traditionally-minded medicine, the kind practiced by physicians who denied that laboratory findings could ever say much of use about matters so idiosyncratic as appetite, ingestion, and digestion. Such was the case of the prolific medical author Manuel Leven, who described the case of a patient whose health steadily worsened under the guidance of 'chemical medicine, which ignores the nervous system and fails to recognize the fundamental laws of health.'[46] Old-fashioned clinicians of Leven's sort were much more important in the diagnosis and treatment of troubled eating than were the chemical sophisticates who enjoyed honor among gourmands. All through the nineteenth century and well into the twentieth, these doctors continued to inveigh against gastronomy and to offer a range of severe diets in place of the gourmand's table pleasures.[47] Such strictures were especially severe in regard to women, who (according to one early nineteenth-century compendium) were said to risk hysteric convulsions and other nervous disorders if they indulged in mushrooms, crayfish, mussels, chocolate, vanilla, cinnamon, strawberries, raspberries, spicy foods, and wines, 'especially those of the Midi.'[48] Yet men too were routinely counseled against eating the 'anti-hygienic' dishes beloved of gourmands. An especially stringent critic of *gourmandise* was the physician Lucien Pron, who couched his dietetic recommendations within an elaborate model of cerebro-nervous organization. Pron held that overindulgence was known to result in a range of disturbed mental states, including delirium, loss of consciousness, paroxysms, and even complete loss of reason. Decrying the abuse to which the stomach was too often subjected, Pron lamented that 'this poor servant' was forced to endure repeated assaults in the form of 'aperitifs, pseudo-digestive liqueurs, and anti-hygienic meals composed largely of the meat-dishes favored by refined cuisine.'[49]

Thus traditionalists within the medical profession remained hostile to the blandishments of *gastronomes* throughout the nineteenth century, and in the anxious climate of the fin de siècle their warnings became increasingly shrill. The essential point here is that, even if the chemically sophisticated physician functioned as a partner of the gourmand while the traditionally-minded clinician took him as an enemy, both kinds of physicians engaged with gastronomy and were, at the least, mindful of its assertions. In essential ways, then, gastronomy and medicine continued to be linked, despite what Flandrin and others have described as a process by which gastronomy 'liberated' itself from the joyless strictures of medicine. What this inescapable partnering with medicine meant for gastronomy is a subject beyond the bounds of this chapter. What it meant for medical diagnostics, however, is evident: it was impossible for a physician to consider matters of appetite, eating, and digestion without having the claims of gastronomy somewhere in mind. It is difficult to gauge the relative intensity of the medical-gastronomical nexus that, although weakened, persisted into the twentieth century. The uncertainty of historians on this subject, alluded to earlier, bears witness to conflicting evidence. Some indicators suggest a linear process by which physicians and *gastronomes* mutually disengaged, while other evidence indicates

reversible shifts, with cataclysms such as the Commune or the German occupation constituting moments when the nature of hunger and appetite were
of particularly acute interest.[50]

Thanks to a range of socio-cultural trends, the fin de siècle appears to have
been a moment when French physicians felt themselves strongly compelled
to reckon with the thinking of *gastronomes*. The 'democratization' of gastronomy at the end of the century gave the 'art of eating' ever greater range as
a social signifier, and while some gastronomic authorities decried what they
perceived as a decline in standards, other professionals seized the opportunities provided by elegant dining to mark their distance from outsiders or
social inferiors.[51] The pursuit of social advantage specific to medical men
is illuminated by Robert A. Nye's investigation of the intensifying struggle
physicians waged to gain victory on 'fields of honor,' not least among them
rituals of sociability.[52] Despite the gloomy counsel of physicians like Pron,
medical men were prominent in the great banquets of the era that, among
other things, signified the advancing social status of the medical profession,
and their own '*dîners médicaux*,' Pierre Darmon observes, 'constitute[d] privileged moments of [the physician's] social life.'[53] Such occasions, it should be
observed, also functioned as one of the prime social-professional sites from
which aspiring female physicians were for the most part excluded.[54] One
exception to this pattern illuminates the rule: the inclusion of women such
as Clémence Royer in the 'Freethinker's Dinner' of anthropologists was one
indicator of the unusual openness to women of this intellectual coterie in
which physicians were prominent.[55]

If it is correct to say that physicians paid close attention to gastronomy
in the fin de siècle, it remains to determine with greater precision the ways
in which gastronomy conditioned them to think about women and food.
Despite some variation, it may be suggested that, overall, gastronomy had
the following propositions to offer about women:

- that the pleasures of women and the pleasures of the table stood in an
  apposite relation, both of them being on offer to the male, either in
  tandem, or in opposition (the latter caught by Grimod de la Reynière's
  famous title, *Discourse of a True Gourmand: the Superiority of Good Eating
  over Women*);
- that women were excluded from the pleasures of the table not because men
  hoarded these pleasures but because women lacked the requisite capacities,
  not only taste and appetite but judgment, will, and self-control, all of
  which, as Ferguson indicates, were required elements of the gastronome's
  finesse;
- that women, insofar as they held a place in the world of haute cuisine, functioned (if not strictly as adornments) as providers rather than
  consumers of food;

- that women as providers of food ordinarily constituted the pole of the domestic and the quotidian (the '*pot-au-feu conjugal,*' as one authority expressed it) in opposition to which the gastronome and the restaurant of the boulevards – the 'clitoris of Paris' – assumed their cultural significance.[56]

Given this spectrum of possibilities, it was perhaps inevitable that when the refusal of food first came to constitute a distinct disease entity, as opposed to a symptomatic condition characteristic of many diseases and observed in both females and males, it was girls and women who were perceived as its obvious victims. This claim is borne out in a number of ways in the medical literature, both by what physicians included in their descriptions of anorexics and – in some ways more importantly – what they excluded. The literature of anorexia contains telling references to gastronomy as, for example, the assertion made by the physician Edgar Bérillon that anorexic girls of the middle class exhibited a familial ethic of stinginess that judged gastronomy 'an art involving too much expense.'[57] Examining patients' phobias surrounding weight gain, Pierre Janet commented at some length on reproaches they lodged against themselves 'relative to gourmandise.'[58] In a piece concerned with the nature of the appetites, published eight years after his examination of 'hysterical anorexia,' Lasègue contrasted the anorexic's loss of appetite to 'those individuals who, the meal ended, continue voluptuously to savor the foods they have consumed.'[59] As late as 1945, the physician Lucien Cornil, dean of the Paris Faculty of Medicine, in exploring the underlying problems of appetite experienced by anorexic girls and women, established the terms of the discussion not only by drawing on medical investigations of hunger, taste, and appetite but also by citing – at the outset – Brillat-Savarin's gastronomical dictum that 'animals feed; man eats; only the thinking man knows how to eat.'[60]

What physicians did not say is striking too: one of the most remarkable features of this whole literature is that, aside from the discussions of sitophobia in psychotics, physicians seldom asked why, of the many options for bodily acting out, anorexic girls and women chose not to *eat*.[61] It might be argued that this was merely one instance of a more general feature of the mental medicine of nineteenth-century France that Gregory Zilboorg captured when he characterized it as 'psychiatry without psychology.'[62] A striking instance is on view in a work on nutritional function in hysterics by the celebrated neurologist and disciple of Charcot, Georges Gilles de la Tourette, and a lesser-known colleague, H. Cathelinau. Describing the tests they had performed on the vomitus of a nineteen-year-old patient admitted to their clinic in 1888, they expressed regret at the fact that their work had been interrupted when the young woman 'was called back to her home by judicial officials in connection with a trial for rape in which she had been the victim.'[63] Single-mindedly focused on describing the woman's illness, these clinicians ignored the psychic trauma that doubtless engendered it. The physicians who labored to describe and classify anorexia were often equally single-minded. Offering long descriptions of patients' bodily condition and behavior in the course of disease – weight changes; accompanying symptoms of weakness, immobility, dry skin, fetid breath; amounts and types of food and drink consumed or refused – they commented only glancingly on why patients declined to eat, offering in lieu of sustained explorations of etiology only dismissive references to *coquetterie* or vague allusions to emotional distress.[64]

The question of why French physicians attended so little to the causes of anorexia has no simple answer. Physicians formed their views on the basis of direct clinical observation but they also brought to their work unspoken assumptions about what constituted good method and reasoning in medicine as well as a wealth of cultural assumptions. In regard to anorexia one of these assumptions was that women and men differed fundamentally in the nature of their appetites and in practices surrounding food and eating. Well before the emergence of anorexia as a distinct disease, physicians had commented on women's tendency to lack of appetite ('*inappétence*'), a cultural truth established not just by their own observations but by the insights of the gastronomes who catalogued the deficiencies that rendered girls and women incapable of genuinely appreciating food. Some physicians took such claims to real extremes, as was the case of one investigator who claimed that hysterical anorectics not only did not desire food but that their bodies did not process and assimilate food in the normal fashion.[65] Although practicing clinicians seldom lingered over problems of causation, by the end of the century physiological researchers into digestion and nutrition had begun to devise models to explain the nervous substrate and character of appetite. One approach was offered by the physiologist Jules-Bernard Luys, who postulated that while appetite was originally instinctive (the baby instinctually taking the breast), its subsequent development was dependent on 'sensorial memories.' 'It was these memories that made possible those acquired capacities [*acquis*] that little by little transformed the taking in of food into gastronomy.'[66] By this means appetite was lodged within the 'higher cortical centers,' precisely the psychic domain, so both medicine and gastronomy attested, in which females were deficient.

Anorexic girls and women suffered ills markedly different from males whose eating or digestion, if disturbed, was exemplified by those neurasthenics who suffered not from anorexia but from 'gastropathy,' a condition characterized by a range of stomach troubles. Male gastropathy and female anorexia differed in crucial ways, with anorexia invariably the more threatening. The symptoms of gastropathy – bloating, pain, gas, constipation, in some cases aversion to selected foods – were troublesome and occasionally disabling, but rarely fatal.[67] As the label indicates, gastropathy, though sometimes accompanied by severe psychic symptoms such as hallucinations, agitation, or anxiety, was seated primarily in the stomach, often appeared in transitory episodes, and frequently responded to relatively straightforward cures. These differing diagnostic viewpoints encouraged men, more readily than women, to regard psycho-gastric symptoms as temporary ills with a discernible physical cause rather than signs of profound psychic disturbance. A curious story told of Lasègue, whose 1873 article on anorexia was highly influential, makes this point well. The story, which was repeated in a medical thesis of 1886, was that in his youth Lasègue was scheduled to go to the Lycée Louis-le-Grand to sit for a highly competitive examination but that he made the mistake of eating some chocolate, suffered acute psychic and physical distress, and had to withdraw. Later, his eating error recognized and his health recovered, he sat for the examination, performed brilliantly, and went on to become highly successful.[68] Thus even solid medical men could be temporarily disabled by psycho-gastric ills, whereas the anorexic girls and women they treated suffered distress that was often intractable and, in the worst cases, fatal.

Conclusion

The story told here is largely a French one, and it might well be asked how this account connects with the rest of the Western world, where, at least in respect to anorexia, similar developments unfolded more or less concurrently.[69] While this history is not unique to France, the French case does provide us with insights into the history of anorexia that other national traditions do not, thanks to the strength of French gastronomic discourse and the ways in which it reveals the assumptions about men, women, and eating that Canetti proffered as universals. The French cultural traditions examined here suggest that deep structures of thinking about gender and appetite lay beneath the diagnosis of anorexia as a female disease rather than a symptom of ailments suffered by both sexes. No one knew in the 1860s and 1870s, and no one knows now, just what anorexia is. Debate continues to this day over whether it is a disease, a syndrome, a disorder, or a symptom, and whether it is at base organic, mental, nervous, or psychosomatic. If we adopt the perspective argued by some historians of psychosomatic illness, we may fruitfully think of anorexia as one of a range of illness 'options' available to individuals who are impelled, for whatever reason, to express in bodily manifestation some underlying trauma or suffering.

A persuasive case has been made by Edward Shorter that psychosomatic ills are peculiarly influenced by culture and, that, historically, they have emerged in different settings in response to complex interchanges between patients and practitioners whose thinking and actions have, in turn, been influenced by larger cultural dispositions lying outside the control of individuals.[70] It is only some such cultural understanding of diseases like anorexia that allows us to make any sense of the baffling range of psychosomatic disorders evident throughout history and, especially, their peculiar patterns of appearance and disappearance, concentration and dispersal. Viewed in this way, one of the central questions requiring historical analysis is how such disease 'options' come into existence. Much discussion has focused on the relative power exercised by medical men and the anorexic patients they treated. An argument developed by feminist historians holds that young girls and women – affected by changing trends in family life, fashion ideals, and standards of femininity – 'opted' for anorexia as a way to gain control over an environment in which few other means for establishing personal autonomy were available. Choosing anorexia has been seen as a way in which girls and women have exercised 'agency,' with victims of the disease in effect saying 'I cannot help suffering, and this is the way I choose to suffer.'[71]

While insights may be gained from regarding anorexia as a female 'choice,' I argue here that, at least at its point of origin, anorexia may more profitably be viewed as an illness option developed by medical men in a historical context in which asserting male over female will was of singular importance. Focusing on distressed eating as the most elemental feature of anorexia, this study seeks to illuminate the deep structures that undergirded eating culture in one of the privileged settings – fin-de-siècle French medicine – in which anorexia first appeared as a clinical entity. So viewed, French attitudes, practices, and discourses surrounding eating – thrown into dramatic relief in the world of gastronomy – bear out the anthropological assertions made by Canetti that it is men who eat and women who prepare and present food to be eaten. Guided by a powerful if unacknowledged misogyny, Canetti laid bare some cruel realities of eating practices found around the world: men eat first, men eat the best, men eat the most, even to the point that women and children are forced to a state of inanition.[72] In important ways the elegant 'art of eating' developed within French gastronomy was only a variation on these seemingly universal themes, the most important of which, in this setting, was that men alone deserved to eat well because men alone knew how to eat. The whole gastronomic enterprise in this sense was a male initiative – an elaborate and massive exercise of masculine will – to reserve the best of eating for themselves.

The literature of anorexia reveals a similarly elaborate exercise of masculine will, one that, far from being hidden or dissimulated, also celebrated male finesse. The focus of this chapter has been on the causes and symptoms of anorexia, but what was prescribed as therapeutics in the face of the 'new' phenomenon of anorexia is perhaps the most illuminating dimension of its emergence as a clinical entity. Along with the constant that the disease was exclusively female or nearly so, there was a therapeutic constant: that the only way to cure anorexia was to isolate the patient from family and friends and subject her to the directives of the physician. Should this step not be taken, physicians urged, the patient risked not only aggravated or chronic suffering (the fate of recalcitrant male neurasthenics) but death itself. Marcé sounded this theme at the very beginning of the modern discourse of anorexia, when he established what was believed as the only efficacious treatment of the disease:

> This hypochondriacal delirium cannot be successfully combated so long as the subjects remain in the family milieu ... [T]he stubborn resistance they put up, the stomach sufferings they enumerate amid incessant lamentations, arouse emotions too strong for the physician to act in complete freedom and to establish the required moral ascendancy.[73]

This necessity for the physician to substitute his will for that of the patient was repeatedly stated in ensuing decades, and it was agreed that anorexia, while always dangerous, was fatal only when the patient was left free to exercise her own will and shielded from that of the (male) physician, the one person who could save her. The death narratives in the anorexia literature frequently occasioned sentimental flourishes, as when Debove lamented the passing of a young girl whose provincial family refused to leave her in his care and who died quietly after a last walk in the garden: 'she faded out like a lamp whose oil has been consumed.'[74] More often, the note sounded was one of implacability: 'If one does not intervene, death can ensue ... It is only by a kind of intimidation that one can halt the progress [of the disease] and this intimidation cannot succeed unless the patient is isolated.'[75]

The problem of how and why eating behavior became a peculiarly charged site for such a battle of wills is complex. I have suggested elsewhere that an important part of the explanation has to do with the advance of neurological science in the fin de siècle, and the establishment of new claims by medicine to understand the links between higher-order mental faculties and the operations of the 'vegetative' (autonomic) nervous system.[76] This study offers another line of approach focused on gendered differences in eating, especially as thrown into relief by the French discourse of gastronomy. Anorexia, viewed from this perspective, became a disease precisely at the moment when women first made a bid to invade professional and occupational domains reserved for men (including the practice of medicine) and thereby to free themselves of their ancient dependency on men for income, food – the very stuff of life. It might be suggested that, in this fashion, anorexia replaced hysteria as the leading all-female disease among psychiatric and nervous ills just at the moment that hysteria, thanks to dynamics of its own, expanded to include males. Hysteria had rendered girls and women helpless and contorted; anorexia deprived them of the most basic requirement of life itself. That deep cultural structures such as those surrounding food and eating were tapped by professional men on the defensive in the fin de siècle, a moment of high gender panic, should not surprise us. Among other benefits of pursuing this line of thinking about anorexia is the encouragement it gives us to ask, now that anorexia has finally jumped gender in significant ways, which of these deep structures have been assailed in recent years, and how and why.[77]

Notes

1. Elias Canetti, *Crowds and Power*, trans. Carol Stewart (New York: Continuum, 1978 [1960]), p. 219.

2. H. Stuart Hughes, *Consciousness and Society: the Reorientation of European Social Thought, 1890–1930* (New York: Vintage, 1958), p. 41; Robert A. Nye, *Crime, Madness, and Politics in Modern France: the Medical Concept of National Decline* (Princeton: Princeton University Press, 1984).

3. Robert A. Nye, *Masculinity and Male Codes of Honor in Modern France* (New York: Oxford University Press, 1993).

4. Michelle Perrot, 'The New Eve and the Old Adam: Changes in French Women's Condition at the Turn of the Century,' in *Behind the Lines: Gender and the Two World Wars*, ed. Margaret Randolph Higonnet and Jane Jenson (New Haven: Yale University Press, 1987), pp. 51–60; on the misogyny of the influential occultist and medical popularizer 'Papus' (Gérard Encausse), see Chapter 5 of this volume by James Smith Allen.

5. Vitalist physicians of the University of Medicine of Montpellier, especially the late Enlightenment theoretician of women's nature Pierre Roussel, took the lead; see Pierre Roussel, *Système physique et moral de la femme* (Paris: Vincent, 1775); on Roussel and the Montpellier school, see Elizabeth A. Williams, *A Cultural History of Medical Vitalism in Enlightenment Montpellier* (Aldershot: Ashgate, 2003), pp. 238–47.

6. Thomas Neville Bonner, *To the Ends of the Earth: Women's Search for Medical Education* (Cambridge, MA: Harvard University Press, 1992).

7. See Matthew Reed, Chapter 3 in this volume.

8. For a characterization of gastronomy as 'France's most enduring empire,' see Albert Sonnenfeld, 'Foreword,' in Jean Robert Pitte, *French Gastronomy: the History and Geography of a Passion* (New York: Columbia University Press, 2002), p. ix.

9. Brenda Parry-Jones, 'Historical Terminology of Eating Disorders,' *Psychological Medicine*, 21 (1991): 21–8.

10. Philippe Pinel, *Traité médico-philosophique sur l'aliénation mentale*, 2nd edn (Paris: Brosson, 1809), pp. 296–7.

11. Elizabeth A. Williams, 'Neuroses of the Stomach: Eating, Gender, and Psychopathology in French Medicine, 1800–1870,' *Isis*, 98 (2007): 54–79.

12. L.-V. Marcé, 'Note sur une forme de délire hypochondriaque consécutive aux dyspepsies et caractérisée principalement par le refus d'aliments,' *Annales médico-psychologiques*, 3(6) (1860): 15–28; Charles Lasègue, 'De l'anorexie hystérique,' *Archives générales de médecine*, 6th series, 21 (1873): 385–403; William Withey Gull, 'Anorexia nervosa (Apepsia Hysterica, Anorexia Hysterica),' *Transactions of the Clinical Society of London*, 7 (1874): 22–8.

13. Tilmann Habermas, 'The Role of Psychiatric and Medical Traditions in the Discovery and Description of Anorexia Nervosa in France, Germany, and Italy, 1873–1918,' *Journal of Nervous and Mental Disease*, 179(6) (1991): 360–5; Habermas proposes that the disease itself has remained constant since the late nineteenth century and that seeming disparities in its prevalence should be attributed to

'differences in national currents in medical thinking'; for an opposing view that draws attention to the 'great confusion and disagreement about the nomenclature and associated views on cause and therapy' in early French investigations, see Walter Vandereycken and Ron Van Deth, *From Fasting Saints to Anorexic Girls: the History of Self-Starvation* (New York: New York University Press, 1994), p. 170.

14. Marcé, 'Note sur une forme de délire hypochondriaque'; Lasègue, 'Anorexie hystérique'; J.-M. Charcot, *Leçons du mardi à la Salpêtrière. Policliniques, 1887–1888* (Paris: Progrès médical, 1887), pp. 354–6; Paul Sollier, 'Anorexie hystérique (sitiergie hystérique): Formes pathogéniques – Traitement moral,' *Revue de médecine*, 11 (1891): 625–50; idem., 'L'anorexie mentale,' *Journal de médecine de Bordeaux*, 25 (1895): 429–32; E. Brissaud and A. Souques, ' "Délire de maigreur" chez une hystérique,' *Nouvelle iconographie de la Salpêtrière*, 7 (1894): 327–37; Georges Gilles de la Tourette, *Traité clinique et thérapeutique de l'hystérie*, vol. 3, *Hystérie paroxystique* (Paris: E. Plon, Nourrit, 1895), pp. 282–95; Edgar Bérillon, 'L'anorexie des adolescents,' *Revue de l'hypnotisme et de la psychologie physiologique*, 24 (1909–10): 46–9; Gilbert Ballet's use of the term 'anorexie dyscénésthésique' in an article in *La médecine moderne* (6 November 1907) is cited in Jules Comby, 'Anorexie nerveuse,' *Archives de médecine des enfants*, 11 (1908): 562–66 at 564 (Comby's term 'anorexie des nourrissons' appears at 566); Sollier's use of the term 'psychopathies gastriques' is in 'Les anorexies nerveuses,' *Journal de neurologie*, 15 (1910): 201–10.

15. The modern diagnosis rests on: (1) refusal to maintain body weight; (2) fear of gaining weight or becoming fat; (3) disturbance of body-image; and (4) amenorrhea; see Ulrike Schmidt, 'Eating Disorders,' in *Women and Mental Health*, ed. Dora Kohen (London: Routledge, 2000), pp. 174–97, at p. 176.

16. The case of a woman of fifty-four was cited in Victor-Henri Hutinel, 'L'anorexie mentale,' *Journal des praticiens* (5 June 1909): 358–60.

17. Comby, 'Anorexie nerveuse,' p. 566.

18. Fear of excessive weight is mentioned, for example, in Brissaud and Souques, ' "Délire de maigreur" ', and in Sollier, 'Les anorexies nerveuses,' but not in Maurice Debove, 'L'anorexie,' *Le Progrès medical*, 3(2) (1895): 241–2, or Georges Gasne, 'Un cas d'anorexie hystérique,' *Nouvelle iconographie de la Salpêtrière*, 13(1) (1900): 51–6.

19. Explicit statements about the disease afflicting girls and women exclusively or nearly so are made in Marcé, 'Note sur une forme de délire hypochondriaque,' p. 15; Sollier, 'Anorexie hystérique,' p. 627; Bérillon, 'L'anorexie des adolescents,' p. 47; Comby, 'Anorexie nerveuse,' p. 562; Hutinel, 'L'anorexie mentale,' p. 358. A typical statement is that of the neurologist Max Wallet: 'L'anorexie hystérique est une affection qui ne s'observe que chez les jeunes filles, en général de quinze à vingt ans; je ne l'ai du moins jamais rencontrée chez un garçon'; Wallet, 'Deux cas d'anorexie hystérique,' *Nouvelle iconographie de la Salpêtrière*, 5 (1892): 276–8; in other sources no explicit statement is made, but all the observations presented are female; see Lasègue, 'De l'anorexie hystérique' (eight cases); Brissaud and A. Souques, ' "Délire de maigreur" ' (two cases); Gasne, 'Un cas d'anorexie hystérique' (one main case, two others cited).

20. On sitophobia, see Gabriel Dromard, 'Considérations pathogéniques sur le mutisme et la sitiophobie des déments précoces,' *Annales médico-psychologiques*, 9(2) (1905): 374–92; obsessive behavior was a special concern of Pierre Janet, who discussed anorexia in connection with obsessions characterized by shame at the body ('honte du corps'); see Pierre Janet, *Les obsessions et la psychasthénie*, 2 vols (Paris: Félix Alcan, 1903), 1, pp. 33–50.

21. On this struggle, see Mark S. Micale, 'Charcot and the Idea of Hysteria in the Male: Gender, Mental Science, and Medical Diagnosis in Late Nineteenth-Century France,' *Medical History*, 34(4) (1990): 363–411; idem., 'Hysteria Male/Hysteria Female: Reflections on Comparative Gender Construction in Nineteenth-Century France and Britain,' in Marina Benjamin (ed.), *Science and Sensibility: Gender and Scientific Enquiry, 1780–1945* (Oxford: Blackwell, 1991), pp. 200–39.

22. Debove, 'L'anorexie'; Debove's report included information about two other female cases, both of them fatal.

23. Paul Sollier, 'Les anorexies nerveuses,' *Journal de neurologie*, 15 (1910): 201–10; Sollier's two male cases, both seen in overworked professionals (one a lawyer and one a physician), represented an adaptation of new terminology to gastric ills once thought especially to afflict '*hommes de lettres*'; see on this theme, Anne C. Vila, 'The *Philosophe*'s Stomach: Hedonism, Hypochondria, and the Intellectual in Enlightenment France,' in *Cultures of the Abdomen: Diet, Digestion, and Fat in the Modern World*, ed. Christopher E. Forth and Ana Carden-Coyne (New York: Palgrave, 2005), pp. 89–104.

24. For an overview, see Lucien Cornil, *Les maigreurs: Etude clinique et physio-pathologique* (Paris: Masson, 1945).

25. For an extensive bibliography of sources on gastronomy, see Priscilla Parkhurst Ferguson, *Accounting for Taste: the Triumph of French Cuisine* (Chicago: University of Chicago Press, 2004).

26. Canetti, *Crowds and Power*, p. 221, emphasis in the original.

27. For a discussion of Canetti's anthropological method that emphasizes not structuralist but evolutionary and symbolic antecedents, see Ritchie Robertson, 'Canetti as Anthropologist,' in *Critical Essays on Elias Canetti*, ed. David Darby (New York: G. K. Hall, 2000), pp. 158–70.

28. Alexandre-Balthazar-Laurent Grimod de la Reynière. *Almanach des Gourmands servant de guide dans les moyens de faire excellente chère par un vieil amateur*, 8 vols (Paris: Valmer, 1984 [1803–12]); cited in Priscilla Parkhurst Ferguson, 'A Cultural Field in the Making: Gastronomy in Nineteenth-Century France,' in *French Food on the Table, on the Page, and in French Culture*, ed. Lawrence R. Schehr and Allen S. Weiss (New York: Routledge, 2001), pp. 5–50, at p. 44, n. 6.

29. Cited in Jean-Paul Aron, *The Art of Eating in France: Manners and Menus in the Nineteenth Century*, trans. Nina Rootes (New York: Harper and Row, 1973), p. 62.

30. Cited in Robert Courtine, *La vie parisienne: Cafés et restaurants des Boulevards, 1814–1914* (Paris: Perrin, 1984), p. 12.

31. Cited in ibid., p. 28.

32. Ferguson, 'Cultural Field,' p. 44, n. 6.

33. Ibid., p. 15.

34. On the influential formulations of the philosopher Victor Cousin, who excluded adolescent girls from the 'training' of the will promoted in the lycées, see Jan E. Goldstein, 'Mutations of the Self in Old Regime and Postrevolutionary France: From *Ame* to *Moi* to *Le Moi*,' in *Biographies of Scientific Objects*, ed. Lorraine Daston (Chicago: University of Chicago Press, 2000), pp. 86–116, esp. 111 n. 63, 114.

35. Courtine, *La vie parisienne*, pp. 26, 28, 55; Aron, *Art of Eating*, pp. 219–23.

36. Eugène Briffault, *Paris à table* (Paris: J. Hetzel, 1846), pp. 21, 53–4.

37. Pitte, *French Gastronomy*, pp. 87–8.

38. Courtine, *La vie parisienne*, pp. 16, 54.

39. Briffault, *Paris à table*, p. 11.

40. Aron, *The Art of Eating*, p. 220.

41. M. Plastira-Valkanou, 'Medicine and Fine Cuisine in Plato's *Gorgias*,' *L'Antiquité classique*, 67 (1998): 195–201.
42. See, for example, Lucien Pron, *Influence de l'estomac et du régime alimentaire sur l'état mental et les fonctions psychiques* (Paris: Rousset, 1901), a work that extols insights into the brain-stomach connection drawn by Ancient philosophers and physicians.
43. Jean-Louis Flandrin, 'From Dietetics to Gastronomy: the Liberation of the Gourmet,' in *Food: a Culinary History*, ed. Jean-Louis Flandrin and Massimo Montanari, English edn A. Sonnenfeld, trans. C. Botsford et al. (New York: Columbia University Press, 1999), pp. 418–32, at 424.
44. Emma Spary, 'Making a Science of Taste: the Revolution, the Learned Life and the Invention of "Gastronomie,"' in *Consumers and Luxury: Consumer Culture in Europe, 1650–1850*, ed. Maxine Berg and Helen Clifford (Manchester: Manchester University Press, 1999), pp. 170–82.
45. Ferguson, 'Cultural Field,' pp. 23–4.
46. Manuel Leven, *La névrose: Etude clinique et thérapeutique* (Paris: G. Masson, 1887); see also A.-F. Chomel, *Des dyspepsies* (Paris: Victor Masson, 1857).
47. On the general practitioners who argued the benefits of clinical over laboratory medicine, see Williams, 'Neuroses of the Stomach.'
48. Jean-Baptiste Louyer-Villermay, 'Hystérie,' in *Dictionnaire des sciences médicales*, 60 vols, ed. N.-P. Adelon et al. (Paris: C.L.F. Panckoucke, 1812–22), 23, pp. 226–72, at p. 232.
49. Pron, *Influence de l'estomac*, pp. 31, 37–40, 46; on eating habits as the source of diverse ills, see also Leven, *La névrose*, pp. 4, 17, 22, 26–31, 43–4, 77–8.
50. On gastronomic and medical reactions to the hunger of 1870–71, see Courtine, *La vie parisienne*, pp. 59–75; for a bibliography of works on appetite, hunger, and diet generated by the German occupation of 1940–44, see Cornil, *Les maigreurs*, pp. 84–8.
51. On the democratization of gastronomy in the late nineteenth century, see Aron, *The Art of Eating*, pp. 71–9; on political uses of banquets during the Third Republic, see the essays by Olivier Ihl and Jocelyne George in *Les usages politiques des fêtes aux XIXe et XXe siècles*, ed. Alain Corbin et al. (Paris: Publications de la Sorbonne, 1994).
52. Robert A. Nye, 'Honor Codes and Medical Ethics in Modern France,' *Bulletin of the History of Medicine*, 69 (1995): 99–111; idem., 'Medicine and Science as Masculine "Fields of Honor,"' *Osiris*, 12 (1997): 60–79.
53. Pierre Darmon, *La vie quotidienne du médecin parisienne en 1900* (Paris: Hachette, 1988), p. 88.
54. Nye, 'Honor Codes,' pp. 109–10; idem., 'Medicine and Science,' pp. 75–76; the intensely male world of neurological and psychiatric medicine is discussed in Toby Gelfand, 'Sigmund-sur-Seine: Fathers and Brothers in Charcot's Paris,' in *Freud and the History of Psychoanalysis*, ed. T. Gelfand and John Kerr (Hillsdale, NJ: Analytic Press, 1992), p. 50.
55. The 'Freethinker's Dinner' is discussed in Jennifer Michael Hecht, *The End of the Soul: Scientific Modernity, Atheism, and Anthropology in France* (New York: Columbia University Press, 2003), pp. 86–90.
56. See the sources on gastronomy cited above; the remark about conjugal meals is in Briffault, *Paris à table*, p. 49.
57. Bérillon, 'L'anorexie des adolescents,' p. 48.
58. Janet, *Les obsessions*, 1, pp. 38, 40.

59. Charles Lasègue, 'De l'appétit en général et de l'appétit digestif en particulier,' *Gazette des hôpitaux civils et militaires*, 54(2) (1881): 10–11.

60. Cornil, *Les maigreurs*, p. 134.

61. Janet might be regarded as an obvious exception given his exploration of body-shame (*'honte du corps'*), but, as noted earlier, his chief concern was not with the etiology of anorexia nervosa but of obsessions and phobias manifested in diverse bodily practices; Janet summed up one case by saying that 'le refus d'aliments n'était qu'une manifestation toute partielle' of the patient's underlying obsessive pathology; see Janet, *Les obsessions*, 1, pp. 33–50 (the quotation is at 1, p. 40).

62. Gregory Zilboorg, *A History of Medical Psychology* (reprinted, New York: W. W. Norton, 1967), p. 398.

63. Georges Gilles de la Tourette and H. Cathelinau, *La nutrition dans l'hystérie* (Paris: Aux Bureaux du *Progrès medical*, 1890), p. 92.

64. For comment on a patient of sixteen who had 'arrived at 'l'âge par excellence de la coquetterie,' see Brissaud and Souques, 'Délire de maigrir,' p. 336; Debove, by contrast, traced instances of the disease to 'quelque chagrin' such as that of a woman who had lost her son; see Debove, 'L'anorexie,' p. 241. The theme of coquetry had already been sounded in the 1850s by the physician turned man-about-town L. Véron, who attributed it to the influence of Lamartine; L. Véron, *Mémoires d'un bourgeois de Paris*, 6 vols (Paris: Gabriel de Gonet, 1853), 1, pp. 210–11; for an argument that in France anorexic behavior was first documented in works of fiction rather than medicine, see Patricia A. McEachern, *Deprivation and Power: the Emergence of Anorexia Nervosa in Nineteenth-Century Literature* (Westport, CN: Greenwood Press, 1998).

65. On women's tendency to lack of appetite, see Emile Desportes, 'Du refus de manger chez les aliénés,' thesis, Faculté de Médecine de Paris, 1864, p. 10; Constantin Empereur, *Essai sur la nutrition dans l'hystérie* (Paris: Coccoz, 1876), cited in Gilles de la Tourette and Cathelinau, *La nutrition dans l'hystérie*, pp. 2–3.

66. Jules-Bernard Luys, *Le cerveau et ses fonctions* (Paris: Germer Baillière, 1876); cited in F. Gallouin and J. Le Magnen, 'Evolution historique des concepts de faim, satiété et appétits,' *Reproduction, Nutrition, Développement*, 27 (1987): 109–28; the quotation appears at p. 123.

67. J. Dejerine and E. Gauckler, 'La ré-education des faux gastropathes,' *La presse médicale* (8 April 1908): 225–7. A chronic illness, gastropathy was fatal only if conducive to a graver condition such as tuberculosis; on *'psychopathies gastriques'* originating in *idées fixes*, phobias, or 'functional inhibitions,' see Sollier, 'Les anorexies nerveuses.'

68. Cited from a thesis by a student named Soula in Pron, *Influence*, p. 173.

69. On anorexia in late nineteenth-century medical literature outside France and Britain, see Vandereycken and Van Deth, *From Fasting Saints to Anorexic Girls*, pp. 172–80.

70. Edward Shorter, *From the Mind into the Body: the Cultural Origins of Psychosomatic Symptoms* (New York: Free Press, 1994).

71. Brumberg, *Fasting Girls*; McEachern, *Deprivation and Power*; for an approach that links anorexia to literary creativity, see Marie Perrin, *Renée Vivien, Le corps exsangue: De l'anorexie mentale à la création littéraire* (Paris: L'Harmattan, 2003).

72. On gender and famine, see Sharman Apt Russell, *Hunger: an Unnatural History* (New York: Basic Books, 2005), pp. 137–56.

73. Marcé, 'Note sur une forme de délire hypochondriaque,' pp. 17–18.

74. Debove, 'L'anorexie,' p. 242.

75. Charles Féré and F. Levillain, 'Apepsie hystérique (Gull), Anorexie hystérique (Lasègue), Anorexie nerveuse (Gull, Charcot),' *Le progrès médical* (1883): 127–8. Sometimes the physician's exercise of will had to be abetted by the father's exercise of will over the mother: When Gasne insisted on isolating a patient, 'the father encountered such resistance on the part of his wife that he had to submit,' but as the patient worsened 'the father finished by vanquishing the resistance of the mother ... and the young girl, once isolated, was cured with miraculous rapidity'; Gasne, 'Un cas d'anorexie hystérique,' p. 56.

76. Williams, 'Neuroses of the Stomach.'

77. On the rising incidence of anorexia in boys and men in the West, see the Preface to the new edition of Brumberg's 1988 study: *Fasting Girls: the History of Anorexia Nervosa* (revised edn, New York: Vintage Books, 2000), p. xvi.

5
Papus the Misogynist: Honor, Gender, and the Occult in Fin-de-Siècle France

James Smith Allen

In Part II of this volume, Matt Reed and Elizabeth Williams analyzed certain new constructions of the self in the fin de siècle, constructions in large part framed by middle-class professionals in the rapidly developing field of psychiatry. The concept of neurasthenia, broadly applied to seemingly inexplicable behaviors, suggests the period's contorted relationship between modern medicine and traditional authorities, especially in longstanding institutions like the Roman Catholic Church, whose belief systems were often in conflict with modern science. The body, everyone's most precious property, had become a contested site as scientists challenged pervasive notions of human reason and individual will, which defensive bastions of social, political, and cultural power attempted to maintain.

In Reed's essay, for example, the shift in medicine from studying the patient to studying his or her disease undermined liberal assumptions of human agency, while it reinforced the new roles of university-trained experts. Despite their focus on an empirical reality outside of the self, case studies of mental illness came to inform the self's innermost individuality. Similar reversals in fin-de-siècle attitudes towards food appeared thanks to the 'medicalization' of gastronomy. Women's eating disorders, Williams argues, 'fed' the efforts of physicians to control alimentary consumption, thereby contributing to the hegemony of male authority in the health professions. In both instances – degeneracy and anorexia – modernity manifested ambivalent trends in France.

In the present chapter, I explore another manifestation of this striking ambivalence in the fin de siècle when scientific approaches to studying minds and bodies were appropriated not to train physicians or to combat pathologies, but to further traditionalist beliefs and practices. In the late nineteenth century, science also came to the defense of men's honor and established gender hierarchies in the context of occult associational life. The scientific method, or some facsimile of it, was applied to the spirit world by a flamboyant misogynist, Gérard Encausse, alias Papus, a prodigious advocate of mysticism in the many secret societies he either joined or founded.

112

His co-spiritists invariably included women, who were fascinated by his use of the scientific method to explain paranormal phenomena. How this entrepreneur of pseudo-science embodied the manifold conflicts of modernity and its discontents is most clearly evident in a dramatic incident – a duel between two confirmed occultists – which occurred early in Papus's remarkable career. It is a story well worth telling in some detail.

The duel

The tale begins just before dawn on Monday 10 April 1893, as a horse-drawn fiacre careened dangerously towards the Pré Catalan in the Bois de Boulogne on the east side of Paris. It was still dark, and the streets were wet from a light drizzle. While the vehicle swayed in its reckless trajectory, its sole passenger looked nervously at the passing cityscape. He was Jules Bois, a devoté of the renegade occultist, the defrocked abbé Joseph Boullan. In 1891 this self-proclaimed doctor of magic, and many others like him, had suffered the selective satire of Joris-Karl Huysmans's novel *La-Bàs*. 'The majority of these doctrines is insane,' Huysmans wrote in terms that had scandalized Paris's growing circle of occultists, including Jules Bois who had been Huysmans's friend.[1]

On this April morning, however, the nervous Bois was concerned with more than mere insult to his spiritual master. He was on his way to defend Boullan's memory on the field of honor. His opponent was not the novelist Huysmans, but Bois's fellow occultist, Gérard Encausse, better known by his pseudonym, Papus. Bois had accused Papus of defending the spell cast by his own spiritual guide, Stanislas de Guaïta, which had led to Boullan's death the previous January.[2] Or so Bois believed: '... even if I – I who am an adept in magic – must brave murderous rage, I must have the truth. I require clear explanations.'[3] And he demanded satisfaction from Papus as well as from Guaïta. Pistols in hand, Bois had already faced down Guaïta (both had escaped this encounter unscathed). Now the offended occultist had to face an expert swordsman.

As luck would have it, Bois arrived late for the engagement with Papus. His fiacre skidded off the road leading to the Pré Catalan and overturned in a ditch. It took him and his driver nearly an hour to recover from the mishap, unhitch the horse, right the carriage, re-hitch the horse, and continue on their way to the dueling spot. Bois was sure the accident had been another example of an evil *envoûtement*, cast this time by Papus. Already nervous about the impending fight – it was obvious the two adversaries were unevenly matched – the shaken Bois arrived badly distracted. His loyal seconds, Bernard Lazarre and Gilbert-Augustin Thierry, tried their best to calm him; they succeeded well enough to steer him towards Papus, sword in hand. Meanwhile, 'some elegant women in riding dress' gathered to watch the armed men.[4]

The action did not last more than a minute before Papus wounded Bois in the right forearm. Bois's seconds reviewed the minor wound and released their man for another round with Papus, who had taken the precaution of wearing a heavily lined, protective jacket. It took less than another minute for Bois to be wounded again in the same spot, at which point both pairs of seconds called on the principals to cease, though there was some question as to whether Bois had drawn blood, too. All the same, the duel was officially over. According to Papus's son, Philippe, who wrote light-heartedly many years later, 'As a result, Papus and ... Bois became, as you can imagine, the best friends in the world.'[5]

This amusing anecdote of two occultists dueling in the Bois de Boulogne before an admiring audience of idle women on horseback merits more than a smirk. In light of Robert Nye's work on French bourgeois male honor in modern France, the combative world of Parisian spiritualists has historical implications. One such theme is no less than the conflicted French response to a more open society as traditional hierarchies faltered in the late nineteenth century. The clash between these important developments, that is, of middle-class professional codes, on the one hand, and of a modernizing social and intellectual context, on the other, is striking in its relevance to the special province of these marginal Parisian intellectuals and their conservative notions of gender relations. The occultists tried, almost desperately, to make respectable the sweeping counter-currents of their ideas, their organizational practices, and their public presence in a changing social world. Their briefly successful efforts, as they relate to this wider issue, deserve a closer examination.[6]

In this chapter I argue that the occult's codes of bourgeois honor, like the medical and gastronomical discourses Matt Reed and Elizabeth Williams examine earlier, reinforced rather than merely imbricated gender hierarchies and a pervasive misogyny in fin-de-siècle France. Papus and his neo-Martinist followers demonstrate well the French professional opposition to the 'New Woman' phenomenon at the end of the nineteenth century. Men's discursive practices became virtually hysterical in their response to independent-minded figures in the women's movement.[7] Mysticism, like reactionary Catholicism, provided one more language in which to objectify women in order to deflect their threat to male institutional privilege. This chapter explores the recent historiographical reconsideration of the lively intellectual life in the early Third Republic when the occult's engagement with science was especially revealing.[8]

The scholarly significance of this exploration appears in the shifting notions of what it meant to be a man and a woman in fin-de-siècle France. From the perspective of the duel, it seems obvious: this time-honored ritual defined men in ways that few other public acts could, though a few women, such as Arria Ly and Astié de Valsayre, also took up arms in the defense of their own honor.[9] 'After 1880,' writes Judith Stone, such an 'aggressively masculine lifestyle ... was heightened by the mounting sense of crisis which surrounded the gender identity of many bourgeois men,' who felt besieged by independent women, not just feminists. 'For some [men] this [crisis] led to a growing incomprehension and reduced sympathy for the woman question, for others to a deep antipathy and misogyny.'[10]

From the perspective of the occult, however, the fraught relationship between biological destiny and constructed public identity was obscured by heterodoxy's penchant for secrecy. Nonetheless, the gendered norms of secret societies tended to be markedly rigid, a tendency which explains the determined efforts of Hélène Blavatsky and Madeleine Pelletier, for example, to resist by demanding strict equality between the sexes in their associations. It was this latter tendency that Papus and his circle countered in the expansion of their own audiences for pseudo-scientific studies of the paranormal. Papus sought to legitimize the occult by appropriating the authority of laboratory science in his societies, which included many women – they constituted a large portion of his audience – who remained in subordinate roles. By co-optation, Papus and other occultist leaders, attempted to minimize the threat posed by the 'New Woman', a threat which many of their followers represented in civic and professional life.

The gendered formation of a physician-occultist

According to Philippe Encausse, Papus (1865–1916) was nothing less than 'the Balzac of occultism.'[11] Like the great novelist before him, Papus attempted to establish his publicly recognized credentials by ardently pursuing ideas at the margins of nineteenth-century positivism. Although Balzac merely dabbled in mysticism for amorous and creative purposes, levitating tables and speaking to the dead while he crafted literary conventions derived from the close observation of reality, Papus actually endeavored to make this lingering fashion a respectable calling, subjecting psychic phenomena to scientific scrutiny while he consciously called into question the very empirical principles that this scrutiny assumed.[12] The result was a private, esoteric knowledge that only men could master, a practice in effect not very different from the institutionalized science in the French universities.[13] It was yet another variation on the theme of powerful social and intellectual forces at work in the denigration of the female at the end of the century. Another portion of the rising professional middle class thus became obsessed with this apparent threat to the 'natural' order of society.

Papus was born in 1865 in northwestern Spain, the first issue of an asymmetrical marriage between an illiterate Spanish mother and a technically educated French father. As an inventive and practical chemist, the elder Encausse, Louis, attempted to make the family fortune by commercializing the cutaneous absorption of medication. Well before the development of medicinal patches, the idea was to bathe the patient in a bathtub-like device filled with various healing potions, which the elder Encausse moved to Paris to promote in 1868. In time the younger Encausse would join his father in this promotion. Such para-medical interests, including the supposed pharmacological benefits to women of extracts derived from hamster semen, clearly became something of a family tradition.

In 1884, at age 19, the son took up the formal study of medicine, fully in keeping with his father's commercial activities. But Papus never actually finished his *baccalauréat* before he enrolled in the Faculté de Médecine, where he worked with the distinguished anatomist Mathias Duval and the hypno-alienist Jules-Bernard Luys. At the same time, however, he developed a serious interest in the occult, one far removed from both of his parents' inclinations. Papus sincerely believed that the purpose of pre-modern and modern science was one and the same: 'nothing is separate in nature,' he affirmed in his first book, *Hypothèses* (1884), which was published in the same year as he began his medical studies, 'every natural thing is re-united by some transition with other natural things.'[14] For the rest of his life, as both physician and occultist, Papus would explore this sweeping analogy by whatever means happened to interest him, scientific or otherwise, with consequences for gender relations as he understood them.

Despite his formal instruction, it is not clear which discipline commanded Papus's first allegiance, medicine or mysticism. He seems to have divided his time more or less evenly between them for the next ten years. While following the normal course of medical study in lecture halls, laboratories, and hospital rounds, Papus joined various theosophic circles, Mme Hélène Blavatsky's in particular, and read voraciously, including obscure works by Antoine Fabre d'Olivet, Joséphin Péladan, Stanislas de Guaïta, and Joseph Saint-Yves d'Alveydre.[15] He reputedly adopted his Latinate pseudonym, representing the spirit of medicine, from the loose translation of Apollonius of Tyana's *Nuctameron* (*c*. AD 100) in Eliphas Lévi's *Dogme et rituel de la haute magie* (1856).[16] Thus during his early, formative years, Papus was as immersed in the esoteric knowledge of Allan Kardec, whose audience included many women, as he was in the scientific method of Claude Bernard, whose work was addressed almost exclusively to men.

In one of his few autobiographical reflections, Papus explained away the apparent contradiction of his activities. In his article, 'Comment je deviens mystique' published in 1895, a year after he was granted his medical degree, Papus located the convergence of two traditions in a timeless philosophical concept, the analogy: 'this marvelous *analogic method, so little* known to modern philosophers ... permits all knowledge to re-connect in one common synthesis.'[17] However discredited by empirical science, Papus argued, analogy made science possible – scientists just did not admit it. Only by making this method a self-conscious one, he believed, could scholars and intellectuals overcome the false materialism that otherwise undermined the scope and power of modern empiricism itself. The result would be of use to men and women alike.

Papus published at least three of his most widely circulated books while he was still a medical student: *Traité élémentaire de science occulte* (1888), which saw no fewer than nine editions by 1926; *Clef absolue des sciences occultes: le tarot des bohémiens* (1889), which appeared in two more editions by 1926; and *La Kabbale* (1892), whose fourth edition appeared in 1949. These titles were derivative of a few select sources and hastily written, as was Papus's habit for all 104 works he published and the eleven periodicals he edited.[18] Aware of the marketable potential of his ideas, he became a prolific *vulgarisateur* by recycling published material of his own. Many of his subsequent publications cut-and-pasted whole passages from these three early works and from the work of others, a habit he shared with Madame Blavatsky.[19] But his focus remained the same: the study of the occult was ultimately 'the precision of the Word in all domains, the Occult is the real Invisible behind the apparent and analogous Visible.'[20] The result was a much more mixed readership than he initially anticipated from his medical training.

Papus's genius, however, was not for publication but for association. After breaking openly with Blavatsky's Société Théosophique in 1888, he joined Péladan and Guaïta's Ordre Kabbalistique de la Rose-Croix. An important offshoot of this society was the Groupe Indépendant d'Etudes Esotériques, which he established the next year. Then in 1891, with the help of Augustin Chaboseau, Papus created his own organization, the Ordre Martiniste, whose activities provided a source of income for the rest of his life. He would edit and profit from the neo-Martinists' monthly review, *L'Initiation* (1888–1912), published by bookseller and close friend, Lucian Chamuel, in one form or another for more than twenty-four years. Papus was well served by creating still more societies, whose membership lists he borrowed for paid subscriptions and for conference invitations. The lists are as long and as heterogeneous as the organizations themselves were ephemeral.[21]

Papus continued to join more secretive groups, as well, very often for the same mixed motives of professional interest (personal control) and venal opportunity (with female followers). Besides the Theosophes, he was initiated into the arcane mysteries of the Hermetic Brotherhood of Light (1888), the Hermetic Order of the Golden Dawn (1895), the Eglise Gnostique de France (1890), the Fraternitas Thesauri Lucis (1897), the Swedenborgians (1908), and various Masonic obediences, such as the Memphis-Misraïm (1910). He was very rarely an attentive initiate, however, circulating from one secret society to the next for his own purposes of promoting the occult as he taught it and of looking for receptive audiences for his own derivative syncreticism. Despite their apparent exclusivity, all of these associations were remarkably open to a larger public, as many occultist traditions tended to blur in both practice and publication. Mysticism, then and now, is a hazy phenomenon; the tendency is for numerous self-appointed adepts to appear and for doctrinal dissension to develop among them, as often as not in mixed company.

Papus's organizational and doctrinal control was frequently challenged, especially among members of the Kabbalistique de la Rose-Croix and the

Eglise Gnostique.[22] Keeping some form of respectable order was critical to the credibility of the ideas of these organizations, for members and non-members alike, but unity in the occultist camp grew increasingly difficult as heterodoxy became fashionable among both men and women in the two decades before World War I. As Martinist lodges appeared in many other countries outside France, the order's hierarchy found itself incapable of supervising all the initiations, conferences, and publications. In Brussels, for instance, the rituals were modified; and rival occultist lodges, such as Max Théon's Philosophie Cosmique, appeared. The head of the Martinists in the US was dismissed, and in his place Papus appointed Margaret Peeke of Sandusky, Ohio, 'professor of the occult ... an international celebrity in the occult sciences' and member of the Bahai faith, much to Papus's dismay. The order and its message were complicated, in part, by their very success in a changing public context.[23]

The ambivalent effect of a mixed audience

In 1894 Papus briefly turned his attention from the occult (and duels) to defending his doctoral thesis, 'L'Anatomie philosophique et ses divisions,' augmented by an essay on the methodical classification of anatomic sciences. Its grounding in empirical science was far from clear. Instead, Papus elaborated upon a particular mind-body analogy that he claimed to have discovered in Christien Ostrowski's French translation of Johann Malfatti de Monteregio's *Studien über Anarchie und Hierarchie* (1845), when in fact it was first developed in Plato's *Republic*, a much-read text in the nineteenth century well beyond the professional circles Papus thought he was addressing.[24] Setting aside any qualms about the empirical basis of the work, the jury approved the dissertation.

For Papus, like Malfatti and Plato before him, anatomic and philosophic knowledge was circumscribed by three all-important categories: the head represented the psyche and the intellect, the chest represented physiology and the emotions, and the gut represented material life and the senses. In this tripartite scheme, the human form embodied all medicine, whose convenient classifications helped explain the systemic relationships of anatomy. Accepted by the jury chaired by Mathias Duval, who had developed his own philosophic schemes based on evolutionary theory, Papus's work marked a culmination of his Procrustean synthesis of science and the occult.[25] For the rest of his life, he would use his professional credentials in medicine to legitimate his interest in the para-scientific to a growing public of men and women enthusiasts.

The clearest explication of Papus's efforts to synthesize material and spiritual manners of knowing appears years later in the program of the monthly journal that he edited on behalf of the Ordre Martiniste: 'The materialist Doctrines have survived,' he stated categorically, because experimental science had inexorably led scientists to spiritualism. The medium for this transition had been hypnotism and mental telepathy, despite science's subsequent denial of its own empirical practices. The journal *L'Initiation*, Papus continued, 'is the principal organ of this spiritualist renaissance to which these efforts tend.' In the domain of science proper, the tendency was to follow Papus's lead in applying the analogical method to experimental inquiry. In the domain of religion, the effort was to derive from 'the discovery of *the same esotericism* hidden at the heart of all cults' a more solid foundation to morality. And in the domain of philosophy, the quest was to leave behind the pure metaphysics of academics and the pure materialist methods of positivists 'in order to unify into one unique Synthesis Science and Faith, the Visible and the Occult, the Physical and the Metaphysical.'[26] The reunion of ancient and modern knowledge resulted in one glorious erudition available to all neo-Martinist initiates.

In David Allen Harvey's thorough study of neo-Martinist thought, Papus represents the deeply ambivalent discourse of occult resistance to the Enlightenment in fin-de-siècle France. 'Martinists,' Harvey writes, 'sought to restore wholeness to a deeply fractured post-revolutionary French society, and return France to the central providential role that, they believed, it was meant to fulfill.'[27] The leading lights of this movement, like Papus, consciously attempted to broaden the frontiers of human knowledge beyond the merely empirical and rational manners of knowing embraced by mainstream intellectuals, especially the professional middle class exemplified by male physicians (as opposed to their female patients). Ultimately, a new social and political order, they thought, would prevail, returning France to a saner, pre-revolutionary world. Modern society, it seemed, was 'on a fundamentally wrong path': 'man had been happier ... under a distant, divinely inspired order, in which science and religion were united and men [*sic*] lived in harmony and peace.'[28] Unfortunately, such a vision resembled the radical right's 'integrist' prescription for France, with its traditional, hierarchical gender relations, which took on a life of its own well before the disintegration of the Third Republic in the interwar period.[29]

Papus began work on his contribution to this ambitious intellectual project by opening his first clinic, on the rue Rodin, in 1892, even before he completed his formal medical studies. Then in 1895 he was appointed attending physician to the reservist health service of the Fifth Army Corps. The position paid well enough for Papus to marry, which he did that same year to Mathilde Inard, a widow with two young children, from a prominent Alsatian family. Now financially secure, Papus relocated his practice and occultist activities to Passy in the socially respectable 16th arrondissement. Two years later, at the height of the occultist vogue in Paris, Papus began regular Monday evening consultations at the Hôpital Saint-Jacques, founded the Société Homéopathique de France, and offered courses in the Ecole Française d'Homéopathie, thanks to a sympathetic medical colleague, Pierre Jousset. Papus also lent his professional prestige to various purportedly medicinal products, such as his sister Louise's 'savon amaigrissant,' which he endorsed as a remedy for obesity (and diabetes) in his women patients and occultist adepts. The Encausse family's proclivity for commercial ventures came to include Papus's clinic for electro-homeopathy, based on his 'medical' interest in magnetism and hypnotism, assured by 'the celebrated name of Dr. Papus ... a certain guarantee of the value of this modern institute.'[30] So read one advertisement in his *L'Initiation*.

Around 1900 Papus began exploring the ways in which psychic phenomena could be studied scientifically, at least as he understood the experimental method. *L'Initiation* ran a number of articles that claimed to authenticate the mystical experiences of his female friends and male colleagues. There were frequent reports on the authenticity of mental telepathy, a fin-de-siècle fascination of many occultists.[31] As his Groupe Indépendant d'Etudes Esoteriques grew, offering courses and granting certificates, its adherents specialized in areas of occultist practice such as hypnotism, magnetism, graphology, astrology, and alchemy, though Papus himself occasionally expressed skepticism about some of the work done under his auspices. Recent discoveries of x-rays, for example, provided the impetus for various laboratories to test the psychic potential of inanimate objects, such as ancient monoliths and potatoes, of all things, whose 'secret inscriptions' could now be read more easily.[32]

Official recognition and legitimation of Papus's work came in 1912 with the Ministry of War's request that he revise Emile Gary and Georges Polti's *La Théorie des tempéraments* (1889), which drew heavily on physiognomy and phrenology. Papus redefined the field as 'human morphology' in keeping with his notions of analogous relations between anatomy and personality, which he continued to develop long after his dissertation.[33] The triumph of Papus's application of science to the occult finally came with a series of lectures that he gave at the Théâtre Fémina and the Hôtel des Sociétés Savantes in early 1913. In keeping with his rising renown, Papus's audience included far more than the immediate enthusiasts of the occult, many more of them women who were also interested in a new public role.

Nowhere was this wider public for mysticism more evident than in Russia. By 1899 there were at least three Martinist lodges in St Petersburg, and their members arranged for the Russian Foreign Ministry to invite Papus to visit the country in January 1900. Following an impressive spiritist séance with the Romanoff court, he was invited again by the lodges to give a series of conferences thirteen months later. For three weeks Papus attempted to explain the 'Archémètre,' a type of spiritualist's Rubik's cube created by the late Stanislas de Guaïta, for keeping track of all manifestations of the immaterial. Papus's presentations did not go unnoticed by the Russian imperial family, who at the behest of the empress Alexandra granted him an audience just before he returned to Paris. This experience added still further luster to Papus's activities, which were now widely seen as having been sanctioned by the wife of a major European sovereign.[34]

Papus's apparent misogyny

The many misogynist elements of Papus's work are suggested in part by his problematic relations with his assorted female followers.[35] All of them were initially captivated by the considerable personal charm that he exercised in his occultist associations. One such was Anna Wronski, the daughter of Hoenë Wronski the alchemist, who served briefly as Papus's personal secretary and paramour before he abandoned her in order to marry Mathilde in 1895. Seven years later, however, Papus left – but did not divorce – his wife, eventually sharing more than mystical interests with another woman, Jeanne Robert, with whom he had a child, Philippe, in 1906. Meanwhile, Mathilde remained in contact with Papus, often *in extremis*, over this new relationship. Expressive of Papus's contempt for women, none of these quasi-marital ties was resolved by the time he died in Paris of the tuberculosis he contracted on the Western Front in 1916. He was just 51. As a consequence of Papus's evident disdain for sustained relationships, including two rival 'widows,' his spiritualist legacy remained equivocal for many decades, at least until his son Philippe assumed responsibility for the Martinist Order in 1960.[36]

From their inception the Martinists had initiated women, a very unusual ritualistic practice in secret organizations at the time. Only the mixed Masonic order, Le Droit Humain, under the leadership of Maria Deraismes, did the same, and it began doing so only in 1892, a full year after the Ordre Martiniste (the Theosophists included women even earlier, but their gatherings were not secret).[37] Anna Wronski and Marie-Anne de Bovet, the novelist and advocate of women's rights, were among the first women in Papus's new order.[38] But the initiations varied. The Martinists followed the traditional 'social model' for women initiates, admitting them in a gender-specific ritual and relegating them to qualified membership. None of them held responsible positions in the association; these posts were all reserved for men in keeping with Papus's early, unremarkably patronizing pronouncements about the complementary equality of women in his associations.

For the first ten years of the Martinist Order's existence, for instance, Papus generally regarded women as the guardians, the emotional center, of the occult tradition. 'It is by all that the Heart suggests to them that women led us to belief in the first principle,' he announced patronizingly during a meeting of the Groupe Indépendant d'Etudes Esotériques in February 1890. 'It is to them that the 20th century belongs.'[39] Dominating his comments, however, was the need for women to control their special occult powers, as if women required help with this in a way that men did not. In 1893, for example, Papus wrote on women's essentialist, mystical roles. Women, he believed, should 'take control of the tranquil' and 'dominate the active' in their effort to become 'hidden master' of 'unconquerable nature.'[40] Men were always the master of themselves and thus invited no such advice. This perspective remained with him for the rest of his life.

The most fully developed statement Papus made about the place of women in the occult is in his one and only novel, *Au pays des esprits, ou roman vécu des mystères de l'occultisme*, self-published anonymously in 1903. The preface explains the purpose of the work: to introduce the female reader to the lived experiences of the occult. It identifies some truly objectionable women who seem incapable of comprehension 'in a manner appropriate to [their] mode of sensibility,' namely, 'the bearded woman and the woman boxer.'[41] Papus expresses his manifest displeasure with 'some brains reasoning in a masculine way by bodies dressed in skirts,' who are insensitive to 'the feminine mind' as Papus explained it.[42] His overt hostility to public women and their efforts to redefine gender roles becomes even more apparent in the novel itself.

The story Papus tells is predictably filled with visions, clairvoyance, mesmerism, out-of-body experiences, magic, and the like, all of which the autobiographical *récit* presents as perfectly ordinary, everyday occurrences. Louis de B—, the scion of a distinguished but impoverished Hungarian nobility living in India, recounts his own initiation into 'the Fraternity,' clearly a Masonic association, which enables him to acknowledge the special powers he possesses, however coldly scientific this group's mystical erudition. But the otherwise honorable fraternity's only initiated woman, Mme Hélène Laval, is an evil figure, 'a veritable Medea' intent upon securing Louis's devoted wife, Blanche, for her brother. Blanche makes the mistake of allowing a hair-clipping of hers to fall into Laval's hands, putting her at the mercy of this 'witch.' In the end Louis cannot save Blanche and their new-born baby. They die, but Laval's spell is broken by the combined efforts of Louis and his Indian allies, the fakirs. Once Laval has been stripped of her powers, the protagonist can return home to Germany to tell his story to a Western audience.

Although Papus works hard to reassure his female readership of their importance to heterodoxy, he ultimately fails. The novel warns off all women from the experience he wants them to understand. In the right hands – men's hands – the occult, that is, the continuity of the material and immaterial worlds, is manageable. Otherwise serious problems arise in both this realm and the next. Miscommunication with the afterlife, Papus felt, brings great misery to the living and the dead. But this message is profoundly misogynist; women and the mystical, even in the formalized context of secret societies like the Martinists, do not mix. The occult is really only for men who have the strength of character to put it to best use. As Louis states in the end:

> I learned that communication between the inhabitants of our planet and the spiritual spheres constitutes the most elevated, the purest and most ordinary of religious faculties in our soul. The follies, the fantasies, the errors, and the imposters [women] who have dishonored the movement falsely called spiritualism, give to mortals only a very imperfect idea of the sublime truth…[43]

Evidently, given their incapacity to think mathematically, women are not up to this challenge. They must be stopped before they even try.

Papus's defensiveness about women in the occult arose, in part, from competing heterodox ideas and organizations at the turn of the century. As the bourgeois self found itself under siege from contending specialists in the new discipline of psychology – what Matt Reed refers to as the transition from 'alienation' to 'degeneration' in psychiatry – the spiritualists in France discovered new sources of inspiration and were much less susceptible to doctrinal and organizational regimentation.[44] With this fragmentation in occultist circles arose new opportunities for women to exercise leadership in secret societies as well as in professional life. The gender revolution of the twentieth century was not far off.

Conclusion

It is in this particular historical context, then, that we find the intersection of honor, gender, and misogyny in French mystical circles, at least among the neo-Martinists. Papus's quest to lend the prestige of medical science to vulgar mysticism led him to pursue a career in medicine largely in the service of his occultist publications and organizations. In this effort women played an equivocal role, as faithful and fee-paying audiences, but only as subordinate members of the special hierarchy the neo-Martinists created in the secrecy of their rituals.[45] Papus's own pronouncements about the natural but unregulated proclivity of women for the occult asserted widespread notions of mysticism that relegated women to well-defined, secondary roles in his associations. Similar prejudices appeared in his public expressions of disdain for leaders of the women's movement at the turn of the century.

It is thus no accident that Papus worked hard to undermine the organizational efforts of the Theosophists, led first by Hélène Blavatsky then by Annie Besant.[46] He ensured that this influential group, which was more open to women adepts, would take only shallow root in France, even though the mixed Masonic order of Le Droit Humain honored equally both its male and female leaders. A more rational, thoroughly egalitarian associational tradition – that of the Freemasons – supported the 'New Woman' it actively encouraged the ideas and activities of France's first feminists, women such as Nelly Roussel, Marie Bonnieval, and Madeleine Pelletier.[47] Evidently the occult, as Papus and his followers knew it, was much too traditional to embrace even complementary gender equality, much less the more legal-egalitarian variety we know today.[48]

From the perspective of one female follower, however, these concerns were subordinated to the power of Papus's synarchic doctrines. Céline Renooz shared Papus's interest in renewing Western manners of knowing, and happily wrote him about their mutual efforts. Renooz's ambitions were as outsized as those of her neo-Martinist fellow traveler. 'I hope to replace the

Ecole d'Anthropologie,' she told him grandiosely in 1891, out of interest in many of the same epistemological questions as Papus.[49] She had published a few years earlier a sweeping challenge to the scientific method in her auto-biographical account of a revelation she had that led her to dismiss Charles Darwin's theory of evolution by natural selection. 'The enormous power of thought,' she wrote, 'which overwhelmed me and made me see so clearly into nature's mysteries, was a moral force whose command it seemed to me I had to obey in order to save the old world.'[50] Papus himself could not have said it better; Renooz's occultist sympathies found a home in his neo-Martinist vision, despite his misogynist inclinations.

What recent historiography helps us understand is just how fragile were masculine codes of bourgeois honor in the nineteenth century. The physical set-tos between the likes of Papus and Jules Bois closely resembled the jour-nalistic and political duels whose primary implication was to publicize the 'honorable' calling of otherwise marginal professions in the Third Republic. Only the lunatic fringe of the occultist movement, such as Joséphin Péladan, a close associate of Papus's, would actually refuse to participate in a duel that could bring respectability to an obscure and passing feature of Parisian cul-tural life.[51] The mystical types Papus championed his entire adult life fit Bob Nye's model much better. For like other middle-class professionals seeking a secure footing in the shifting social landscape in fin-de-siècle France, the occultists needed to stand out as men. As Nye states:

> The scientific and popular articulation of a universal and 'natural' concep-tion of masculinity helped weaken the social and cultural distinctions that had divided men historically into different social, political, and cultural categories, each with its own codes and criteria of manly comportment. These older categories were not yet dead by 1914 or so, but they were being relentlessly supplanted by a form of male identity that was common to all men and that was rooted in male sex and in the masculine behavior appropriate to it.[52]

Papus and his followers in their version of the occult also shared in a misog-ynist transition, fiercely resisting the women's movement and the 'New Women' who animated it. These women were nothing less than an affront to bourgeois male *amour-propre* and heterodox power. The consequences of this historical clash can still be seen in France today. Until very recently, Philippe Encausse, Papus's son and heir-apparent to the leadership of the Ordre Martiniste maintained the same gendered initiatory rituals. Its membership includes fewer than a hundred initiates.[53] Meanwhile, the mixed Masonry of Le Droit Humain, another secret society, has increased its membership to several hundred thousand worldwide. The historical context of masculine codes of honor has changed and the roles of women have changed along with them. Martinism and its like have been left behind.

The historical consequences of these developments, I believe, also lie deep in contemporary French civil society. The evolution of a liberal society, one supportive of free and active associational life, always seemed elusive in modern France. As Alexis de Tocqueville pointed out, the centralizing authority of the eighteenth-century monarchy survived the Revolution and Napoleonic Empire nearly intact largely because the republican and Bonapartist state precluded the natural evolution of bourgeois society and its interest in association.[54] Although Pierre Rosanvallon has questioned the efficacy of these political and juridical limitations on civic life in France, it is clear from the conflicted activities of Papus and his fellow neo-Martinists that the internal dynamics of this evolution was itself troubled.[55] The exclusionary tendencies of such groups, forbidding equal access to women in particular, but also to other marginalized groups such as peasants and Catholics, meant that there could be no true civic life until the demise of the Third Republic's 'stalemate society' after 1968.[56] The modernization of the shifting boundaries of French gender roles would also have to wait, until the impact of Simone de Beauvoir's *Le Second Sexe* (1949) and the turmoil of 1968 finally gave birth to second-wave feminism.[57] Meanwhile, professional men still had their honor to uphold.

These implications are well illustrated in Eugen Weber's extended essay on the fin de siècle.[58] In a pervasive mood of pessimism, despite remarkable material and scientific progress – 'so much was going right ... [yet] so much was being said to make one think that all was going wrong'[59] – French professionals found it difficult if not impossible to accommodate the demands of rapid social change. The assertive appearance of organized feminism went hand in hand, it seems, with the revival of occultist activities, precisely the historical contradiction that Papus the physician celebrated in his efforts to draw women to his meetings and to sell them his publications and services, whatever he thought of his female clientele in reality. When Papus found himself at odds with fellow occultists, as he did briefly with Jules Bois in 1893, his leadership of this contrary development – of appealing to independent women, on the one hand, and of sustaining their ritualistically gendered hierarchies, on the other – became a matter of honor, which he defended notwithstanding the rise of mixed associational life in modern France. Through it all he resorted to his medical practice to provide the necessary credibility to his para-professional work. As Weber put it, 'If the science of man knew no limits, neither did his credulity,'[60] as the anti-Masonic confabulations of Léo Taxil demonstrated in the same period.[61] At this historical moment, the 'science' of minds, bodies, and spirits richly reflected the many cross-currents of a deeply conflicted modernity.

Notes

1. See J.-K. Huysmans, *Là-Bas* (1891; Paris: Gallimard, 1985), p. 332. (Unless otherwise indicated below, all translations from the French are the author's.) Note, Papus [Gérard Encausse], '*Là-Bas* par J.-K. Huysmans,' *L'Initiation* (May 1891): 97–114, in part a response to Huysmans's insult of Papus as 'se contenter de ne rien savoir': Huysmans, *Là-Bas*, p. 331. Huysmans's dismissive judgment of Papus was clearly derived from his principal source on the occult, the defrocked priest Joseph Boullan, one of Papus's many spiritualist adversaries. Compare Christopher McIntosh, *Eliphas Lévi and the French Occult Revival* (London: Rider, 1972), pp. 177–94, on Huysmans and the occult.

2. See a careful review of Joseph Boullan's allegations in Papus [Gérard Encausse], *Peut-on envoûter? Etude historique, anecdotique et critique sur les plus récents travaux concernant l'envoûtement* (Paris: Chamuel, 1893), pp. 3–19, whose criticisms of Boullan had apparently elicited Jules Bois's ire.

3. Jules Bois, 'L'Envoûtement et la mort du docteur Boullan,' *Gil Blas* (9 January 1893): 2. Bois is best known for his popular survey of satanic practices and magic, generously prefaced by J.-K. Huysmans, who endorsed Bois's thesis of the occult as a genuine force for evil: 'C'est cette étude que Jules Bois a tentée, dans ce volume qui est certainement le plus consciencieux, le plus complet, le mieux renseigné que l'on ait encore écrit sur l'au-delà du mal,' in Bois, *La Satanisme et la magie* (1894; Paris: Jean de Bonnot, 1996), p. xiii.

4. See the embroidered account of the duel by Jules Bois quoted at length in Philippe Encausse, *Papus le 'Balzac de l'occultisme.' Vingt-cinq années d'occultisme occidental* (Paris: Pierre Belfond, 1979), pp. 18–19. Many features of Bois's version of events are not corroborated by other sources. Compare the accounts in http://en.wikipedia.org/wiki/Papus and http://www.hermetic.com/sabazius/papus.htm with the much better informed http://fr.wikipedia.org/wiki/Papus, all three accessed 16 January 2007.

5. Philippe Encausse, *Papus (Dr. Gérard Encausse). Sa Vie. Son Oeuvre. Documents inédits sur Philippe de Lyon. Maître spirituel de Papus. Opinions et jugements. Portraits et illustrations* (Paris: Editions Pythagore, 1932), p. 18, repeated in idem., *Papus le 'Balzac de l' occultisme'*, p. 18. Compare Marie-Sophie André and Christophe Beaufils, *Papus biographie. La Belle Epoque de l'occultisme* (Paris: Berg International, 1995), pp. 105–6, a well-researched and thorough study of the occultist. Unless otherwise cited, background related to Papus in this chapter is taken from André and Beaufils's work.

6. I focus on Robert A. Nye's *Masculinity and Male Codes of Honor in Modern France* (New York: Oxford University Press, 1993), but also his *Crime, Madness, and Politics in Modern France: the Medical Concept of National Decline* (Princeton, NJ: Princeton University Press, 1984), where professional discourses play a more important role.

7. The historical literature on this phenomenon is rich. See, for example, James F. McMillan, *Housewife or Harlot: the Place of Women in French Society, 1870–1940* (New York: St Martin's Press, 1981); Karen Offen, 'Depopulation, Nationalism, and Feminism in Fin-de-Siècle France,' *American Historical Review*, 89(2) (1984): 648–76; and Mary Louise Roberts, *Disruptive Acts: the New Woman in Fin-de-Siècle France* (Chicago: University of Chicago Press, 2002).

8. A recent example is Elinor Accampo, *Blessed Motherhood, Bitter Fruit: Nelly Roussel and the Politics of Female Pain in Third Republic France* (Baltimore, MD: Johns Hopkins University Press, 2006).

9. Felicia Gordon, *The Integral Feminist: Madeleine Pelletier, 1874–1939* (Cambridge: Polity Press, 1990), pp. 16, 17, 88–9.

10. Judith F. Stone, 'The Republican Brotherhood: Gender and Ideology,' in *Gender and the Politics of Social Reform in France, 1870–1914*, ed. Elinor A. Accampo, Rachel G. Fuchs, and Mary Lynn Stewart (Baltimore, MD: Johns Hopkins University Press, 1995), p. 46.

11. Encausse, *Papus*, p. 42. This, years later, became the title to Encausse, *Papus le 'Balzac de l'occultisme'*.

12. This same point is well made by John Warne Monroe, *Laboratories of Faith: Mesmerism, Spiritism, and Occultism in Modern France* (Ithaca, NY: Cornell University Press, 2008), pp. 233–50.

13. Compare the perspective in Robert A. Nye, 'Medicine and Science as Masculine Fields of Honor,' *Osiris*, 12 (1997): 60–79.

14. Papus, *Hypothèses* (Paris: Coccoz, 1884), quoted in André and Beaufils, *Papus biographie*, p. 23.

15. See the extensive scholarly literature on the occult in modern France, for example, McIntosh, *Eliphas Lévi and the French Occult Revival*; Marie-France James, *Esotérisme, occultisme, franc-maçonnerie et christianisme aux XIXe et XXe siècles. Explorations bio-bibliographiques* (Paris: Nouvelles Editions Latines, 1981); René Le Forestier, *L'Occultisme en France aux XIXe et XXe siècles. L'Eglise gnostique*, ed. Antoine Faivre (Milan: Archè, 1990); and David Allen Harvey, *Beyond Enlightenment: Occultism and Politics in Modern France* (DeKalb, IL: Northern Illinois University Press, 2005).

16. See Eliphas Lévi [Alphonse-Louis Constant], *Dogme et rituel de la haute magie* (Paris: G. Baillière, 1856), 2 vols. The translation of the *Nuctameron* appears in the second volume. Compare McIntosh, *Eliphas Lévi and the French Occult Revival*, pp. 101–4.

17. Papus, 'Comment je deviens mystique,' *L'Initiation* (December 1895): 199. Emphasis in the original.

18. See a nearly comprehensive listing of Papus's work in Encausse, *Papus le 'Balzac de l'occultisme'*, pp. 185–212. Notably absent is Papus's novel, discussed below.

19. See 'William Emmette Coleman, "Sources of Madame Blavatsky's Writings,"' in Gertrude Marvin Williams, *Priestess of the Occult: Madame Blavatsky* (New York: Alfred A. Knopf, 1946), Appendix M, pp. 337–8.

20. Papus, *Qu'est-ce que l'occultisme?* (1900; Paris: Librairie et Editions Leymarie, 1989), p. 17.

21. On Papus's penchant for associational life, see Robert Amadou, 'Papus,' *Encyclopédie de la franc-maçonnerie*, ed. Eric Saunier (Paris: Librairie Générale Française, 2000), pp. 639–40.

22. Discussion of the strong personalities at odds over occultism is extensively discussed in the second half of Robert Amadou, 'Martinisme,' *Encyclopédie de la franc-maçonnerie*, pp. 550–5.

23. See André and Beaufils, *Papus biographie*, pp. 221–4.

24. See Johann Malfatti di Monteregio, *Studien über Anarchie und Hierarchie des Wissens, mit besonder Beziehung auf die Medicin* (Leipzig: F.A. Brockhaus, 1845), which first appeared in French translation as *Etudes sur la mathèse, ou Anarchie et hiérarchie de la science, avec une application spéciale à la médecine*, trans. Christien Ostrowski (Paris: A. Frank, 1849). The analogy that Papus appropriated was already widely known, however. For example, Geneviève Bréton, the prolific diarist, was much taken by Plato's tripartite scheme. See Bréton, *'In the Solitude of My Soul': the Diary of Geneviève Bréton, 1867–1871*, ed. James Smith Allen, trans. James Palmes (Carbondale, IL: Southern Illinois University Press, 1994), p. 47.

25. On Mathias Duval, see Edouard Retterer, 'Mathias Duval (1844–1907). Sa vie et son oeuvre,' *Journal de l'anatomie et de la* physiologie, 43(3) (1907): 241–331.
26. See the frontispiece to *L'Initiation* (January 1895). Emphasis in the original.
27. Harvey, *Beyond Enlightenment*, p. 6.
28. Ibid., p. 35.
29. Cf. Eugen Weber, 'Some Comments on the Nature of the Nationalist Revival in France Before 1914,' *International Review of Social History*, 3(2) (1958): 220–38, and idem., *The Hollow Years: France in the 1930s* (New York: W.W. Norton, 1994), pp. 111–46.
30. Papus, *Du traitement de l'obésité locale* (Paris: Chamuel, 1898), quoted in André and Beaufils, *Papus biographie*, p. 167. In 1911 Papus would actually advertise a paid course of instruction in physiology 'à l'usage des magnétiseurs, masseurs et gens du monde,' in *L'Initiation* (January 1911): endpage. He clearly knew his market.
31. See Monroe, *Laboratories of Faith*, pp. 199–233.
32. See Papus, 'Les Rayons invisibles,' *L'Initiation* (February 1896): 23–8.
33. Emile Gary and Georges Polti, *La Théorie des tempéraments et leur pratique* (Paris: G. Carré, 1889).
34. On Papus's trips to Russia, see André and Beaufils, *Papus biographie*, pp. 175–81, 207–9.
35. I draw on the broad definition of misogyny provided by David D. Gilbert, *Misogyny: the Male Malady* (Philadelphia: University of Pennsylvania Press, 2001), p. 9: 'Misogyny, then, is a sexual prejudice that is symbolically exchanged (shared) among men, attaining praxis. It is something that is manifest in the ways people relate to each other. It is, of course, specifically acted out in society by males, often in ritualistic ways.'
36. Philippe Encausse, 'A propos des groupements martinistes' (1960), in Encausse, *Papus le 'Balzac de l'occultisme'*, pp. 56–7.
37. For more on the place of women in Masonic and para-Masonic associations in modern France, see James Smith Allen, 'Sisters of Another Sort: Freemason Women in Modern France, 1725–1940,' *Journal of Modern History*, 75(4) (2003): 783–835.
38. According to André and Beaufils, *Papus biographie*, p. 126.
39. Quoted by Jules Bois in his report published in *L'Etoile* (February 1890), according to André and Beaufils, *Papus biographie*, p. 68.
40. Papus, 'Petit essai de politique féminine,' *Le Figaro* (August 1893), quoted in André and Beaufils, *Papus biographie*, p. 110.
41. Papus, *Au pays des esprits, ou roman vécu des mystères de l'occultisme* (Paris: Edition de l'Initiation, 1903), p. ii. Note the discussion of this novel in the context of the 'New Woman' phenomenon and the images of Masonic women in France, in James Smith Allen, '*Rebelles* without a Cause? Images of Masonic Women in France,' *Labour History Review*, 71(2) (2006): 43–56.
42. Papus, *Au pays des esprits*, p. ii.
43. Ibid., pp. 415–16.
44. Jan Goldstein, *The Post-Revolutionary Self: Politics and Psyche in France, 1750–1850* (Cambridge, MA: Harvard University Press, 2006), pp. 316–29; and Monroe, *Laboratories of Faith*, pp. 243–57.
45. These efforts to sideline women are made explicit in the secret rituals initiating women into the Martinist order. See the Bibliothèque Municipale de Lyon, Fonds Papus, dossier 5490. It is evident that the Martinist ceremonies are adapted with significant differences from the gender neutral Theosophists, whom Papus managed to marginalize in Paris.

46. See McIntosh, *Eliphas Lévi and the French Occult Revival*, pp. 157–8.

47. On the relationship between Freemasonry and the women's movement, see James Smith Allen, 'Freemason Feminists: Masonic Reform and the Women's Movement in France, 1840–1940,' in *Women's Agency and Rituals in Mixed and Female Masonic Orders*, ed. Jan Snoek and Alexandra Heidle (Amsterdam: Brill, 2008), pp. 219–34 and pictures 3–11.

48. Karen Offen, *European Feminisms: a Political History, 1700–1950* (Stanford, CA: Stanford University Press, 2000), pp. 20–3.

49. See Céline Renooz to Gérard Encausse, 28 December 1891, in Bibliothèque Historique de la Ville de Paris, Fonds Bouglé, Papiers Céline Renooz, box 2, dossier 1892, no. 20.

50. Céline Renooz, 'A Revelation,' trans. James Smith Allen, in *Nineteenth-Century Women Seeking Expression: Translations from the French*, ed. Rosemary Lloyd (Liverpool: University of Liverpool, 2000), p. 95. For more on the curious intellectual trajectory of one of Papus's female followers, see James Smith Allen, 'Writing the Body and Women's Madness: the Historiographical Implications of *l'Ecriture Féminine* in Céline Renooz's "Une Révélation" (1888),' in *Women Seeking Expression: France 1789–1914*, ed. Rosemary Lloyd and Brian Nelson (Melbourne: Monash Romance Studies, 2000), pp. 194–205.

51. Nye, *Masculinity and Male Codes of Honor*, pp. 213–14. Note Péladan's reasons for not dueling with a journalist: Péladan, the author of more than twenty books, did not consider his opponent a professional equal. Compare McIntosh, *Eliphas Lévi and the French Occult Revival*, pp. 165–8, 171–6.

52. Nye, *Masculinity and Male Codes of Honor*, p. 215.

53. Amadou, 'Martinisme,' pp. 554–5.

54. See the sensitive treatment of this theme in Richard Herr, *Tocqueville and the Old Regime* (Princeton, NJ: Princeton University Press, 1962).

55. See Pierre Rosanvallon, *The Demands of Liberty: Civil Society in France since the Revolution*, trans. Arthur Goldhammer (2004; Cambridge, MA: Harvard University Press, 2007), esp. pp. 247–65.

56. See Stanley Hoffmann's work on the stalemate society in his 'Paradoxes of the French Political Community,' in *In Search of France: the Economy, Society, and Political System in the Twentieth Century*, ed. Stanley Hoffmann et al. (New York: Harper and Row, 1965), pp. 1–117; and idem., 'The State: For What Society?' in *Decline or Renewal? France since the 1930s* (New York: Viking Press, 1974), pp. 443–86.

57. See Claire Duchen, *Feminism in France from May '68 to Mitterrand* (London: Routledge and Kegan Paul, 1986), pp. 1–13.

58. Eugen Weber, *France, Fin de Siècle* (Cambridge, MA: The Belknap Press of Harvard University Press, 1986).

59. Ibid., pp. 2–3.

60. Ibid., p. 35

61. See *Léo Taxil et la franc-maçonnerie. Lettres inédites publiées par les amis de Monseigneur Jouin* (Chatou: British-American Press, 1934) and Eugen Weber, *Satan franc-maçon. La mystification de Léo Taxil* (Paris: Julliard, 1964) for documentation of the unscrupulous activities of an entrepreneurial publicist who was once an ardent Masonic anti-cleric and then an equally ardent anti-Masonic writer. The occasional resemblance of his mystifications to those of Papus is no accident.

Part III
Morality, Honor, and Masculinity

Introduction to Part III

The claim that cities are hotbeds of vice has been a common refrain in the Western world, but this refrain has grown louder and more insistent since the advent of urban modernity in the eighteenth century. Jean-Jacques Rousseau's warnings about the increased likelihood of sexual precocity, immorality, and 'deviance' in urban contexts were repeated in various forms throughout the nineteenth century, and were echoed by fin-de-siècle physicians and moralists who agreed that prostitution, masturbation, sexual 'inversion,' and premarital sex were all more common in the city than in the country. Beyond these anxieties about sexual deviance, though, were more generalized concerns that the urban lifestyles and opportunities associated with modern bourgeois culture had a gender-blurring effect that threatened to minimize differences between the sexes. Men who worked at desks and rarely exercised, who used their brains rather than their muscles, and who allowed their manners to be softened for the purposes of increased sociability may have made good citizens, but they did not always measure up to traditional masculine ideals of action, bravery, and aggression that continued to circulate throughout the fin de siècle. Such men were also especially vulnerable to the enervating temptations of the big city. By the same token, women who pressed for and benefited from increasing educational and employment opportunities were seen as potentially 'unsexing' themselves by shirking their traditional roles as wives and mothers. Modernity thus had a potentially unsettling effect upon gender identities: capable of consolidating male privilege and conventional gender identities, it also provided the ingredients for their eventual subversion.

For republican elites seeking to reform the physical and moral 'health' of the body politic while neutralizing the influence of the Church, dealing with the myriad problems of city life was of paramount importance. Doing so might prevent the sexual predation of males overstimulated by urban modernity, thus supporting children and families while preserving the health of the nation. Although decrying as 'sin' what more secular observers might have diagnosed as pathology or decadence, the Protestant purity crusaders described in Steven Hause's chapter, which opens this section of the book, launched a critique of urban life fueled by organicist ideas of the body politic in decline. If the widely-diagnosed 'degeneration' of France conflated medical and moral theories about individual and collective health, religiously-oriented reformers proposed abstention for purposes that were every bit as concerned with health, morality, and the family.

Bourgeois men who failed to control their sexual impulses were thus perceived in complex ways. Given the sexual double standard of the period, a degree of libertinism seemed to validate the prowess of the sexual predator while stigmatizing as 'immoral' women who succumbed to his dangerous seductions. This portrait nevertheless had a flip-side. In addition to being seen as a potential carrier of syphilis infecting the unwary – and thus as some-one directly contributing to national decline – the sexual adventurer could be revealed as dishonorable if he failed to take responsibility for whatever pregnancies resulted from his actions. Whereas the duel remained for men the definitive site for resolving disputes about honor, women who felt they had been wronged by men could seek an alternative form of recompense through the legal system. In her chapter Rachel Fuchs shows how unwed mothers, though formally prevented from filing paternity suits against mar-ried men, could nevertheless sue men for damages wrought to their own reputations by refusing to acknowledge paternity. By calling attention to the consequences of male dishonor, these women effectively formulated versions of female honor. Andrea Mansker approaches the question of honor from a different perspective in her chapter, examining the ways in which feminists took advantage of ideals of male honor to shame men publicly if they shirked their responsibilities. If some men could not exercise self-restraint or at least take responsibility for their actions, growing numbers of women were willing to turn their much vaunted ideals of honor against male seducers.

While such measures had considerable efficacy among the solidly bour-geois, men on the margins of middle-class respectability engaged with the opportunities and limitations of modernity in more complex ways. If in the eyes of Protestant reformers and many feminists France teetered on the verge of moral collapse, it was the sheer popularity of the urban pleasures they described that fed their concerns. For many people mass urban entertainment represented a liberating release of sensations and experiences foreclosed by conventional bourgeois mores, which is why the stimulating distractions of the metropolis could also be framed in more positive terms, both for men and women. The aesthetic movements of Symbolism and self-styled 'decadents' offered just such a validation: reveling in the supposed cultural decay that worried many bourgeois elites, bohemian aesthetes perceived in intense expe-rience access to more authentic ways of being. As Michael Wilson explains in his chapter, among men associated with the bohemian artistic and literary circles of Montmartre the sensuality of popular urban entertainment in part promoted a critique of straight-laced bourgeois masculinity as well as a rejec-tion of bourgeois notions of female respectability. Yet lurking behind their claims to 'liberate' female sexuality was a more stylish version of the seducer who dreamed of sex without consequences and thus mirrored, in more flam-boyant terms, the sexual double standard practiced by the bourgeois males they despised.

6
Social Control in Late Nineteenth-Century France: Protestant Campaigns for Strict Public Morality[1]

Steven C. Hause

One of the best-established images of fin-de-siècle France depicts a decadent, or degenerate, culture. Eugen Weber devoted the first chapter of *France, Fin de Siècle* to decadence, giving us such vivid sketches as the contemporary claim that 'The degeneration of the race pours out of our every pore ... We are the mushrooms of ancient dunghills.'[2] Robert Nye wove the theme of degeneration through his path-breaking discussion of male sexuality, introducing us to the psychiatrists who invented the concept of degeneration and in whose work it reached its apotheosis, then teaching us how degeneration illuminates our understanding of population, reproduction, homosexuality, and masculine identity.[3] Roger Shattuck famously showcased the decadents in the cultural avant-garde in a world of 'pompous display, frivolity, hypocrisy, cultivated taste, and relaxed morals.'[4] Two generations of contemporary French medical scholars lamented the many manifestations of degeneration – from tuberculosis and syphilis to hysteria and neurasthenia.[5] David Barnes has skillfully connected medical history and social history to show 'the specter of the cabaret ... in turn-of-the-century fears of French decline and degeneration.'[6] The greatest attention to the social issues of decadent France has come from a generation of feminist scholars who have produced a large body of literature exposing the price women paid for, and the feminist responses to, an age of regulated prostitution, forbidden paternity suits, and unwanted pregnancy.[7] The work of Anne Cova, for example, has effectively shown the connection between degeneration (*dégénérescence*) and the role maternity played in overcoming it (*'La Mère: régénératrice de la race'*).[8]

Yet there is a noteworthy omission in our view of fin-de-siècle decadence, an especially surprising omission in the work of English-speaking scholars. Where are the evangelical Protestants fighting sin? To be sure, Protestants constituted less than 2 percent of the population after the loss of Alsace, but that is still more than half a million people, mostly devout Calvinist adherents to a stern morality.[9] It is impossible to ignore the history of Protestant France in many aspects of the history of the Third Republic, in the shaping of which, as political history has long acknowledged, Protestants played an exceptionally important role.[10] Protestants were so prominent in the creation of the Republic that the first cabinet named after republicans controlled all branches of the government was the William Waddington government of 1879; Waddington, the eldest son of a prominent Norman Protestant family (which also sent his brother Richard to the Senate), named a cabinet which included five practicing Protestants among its eleven members, plus a sixth member (Jules Ferry) who had married into the Protestant elite. Protestants held the portfolios for foreign affairs (Waddington), justice (Philippe Le Royer), finance (Léon Say), the navy and colonies (Admiral Jauréquiberry), and public works (Louis de Freycinet). And when the Waddington government fell, it was replaced by another cabinet headed by a Protestant (Freycinet, who would preside over no fewer than four governments in the late nineteenth century).

The influence of this Protestant community has been widely noted in many aspects of the history of the French Republic. The famous educational laws associated with Ferry, which created France's universal, compulsory, free, and laïc schools, were shaped to a significant degree by the Protestant educators whom Ferry appointed (including Ferdinand Buisson, Jules Steeg, Félix Pécaut, Julie Favre, and Pauline Kergomard). In economic history, the role of Protestants in nineteenth-century European industrialization was so large that it led to one of the most famous interpretations of modern history (the Weber Thesis). Even in France, Protestants added fuel to this much-debated interpretation with leading roles in textiles, heavy industry, railroads, and especially banking. The majority of the largest banks in France were Protestant (including such names as Andre, Hentsch, Hottinguer, Mallet, Marcuard, Mirabaud, Neuflize, Schlumberger, and Vernes) and at the peak of Protestant financial leadership, 70 percent of the regents of the Bank of France were Protestant.[11]

Much of the history of the early Third Republic contains this leitmotif. The history of the Dreyfus Affair and the French campaign for human rights is impossible to tell without taking into account the prominent role of Protestant Dreyfusards who shaped the campaign for revision (such as Auguste Scheurer-Kestner) and played a leading role in founding the League of the Rights of Man (whose early presidents were Protestants: Trarieux, Buisson, and Francis de Pressensé).[12] The history of women's movements in France included (as the present author has argued at length elsewhere) a prominent and disproportionately large Protestant leadership, such as the pastors' daughters who were the first heads of the National Council of French Women, Sarah Monod and Julie Siegfried.[13] And historians of France should be especially comfortable with this Protestant leitmotif. After all, a Protestant historian (Gabriel Monod) was the primary founder of the *Revue historique*, and Protestant scholars played a similar role in shaping historical studies at the École pratique des hautes études.[14]

So, where are the Protestants in the social debate over the decadence of France around 1900 (which is surely a quintessentially Protestant issue)? This chapter seeks to demonstrate the importance of the Protestant minority in this cultural debate. The generalization that French Protestantism was a religion of puritanical austerity is well-established, but this understanding has not led to the study of Protestant morality campaigns. Social control puritanism remained very strong in the orthodox mainstream of nineteenth-century French Protestantism. Two generations of pastors were trained in the spirit of Alexandre Vinet, the most influential French-language theologian of the nineteenth century, who taught a blunt standard: *Rien pour le plaisir, rien pour la vanité, tout pour le devoir.*[15] Social historians have noted the presence of this Protestantism in the largest moral reform campaigns of the late nineteenth century, the campaign against legalized prostitution and the campaign against alcoholism. But French Calvinists (and Methodists, Lutherans, and Baptists) fought many other battles against sin. As Pastor Elie Gounelle exclaimed, 'We need an entire army of soldiers to fight against alcoholism, gambling, horse-racing, lotteries, pornography, prostitution whether regulated or not, materialism....'[16] Pastor Louis Comte restated this list as war on all of the 'infamous debaucheries' of young men. (Feminists, such as Madame Abbadie d'Arrast, pointed out that demoralization was a larger issue.[17]) He included 'marriage without spiritual union' because that was 'merely approved prostitution.'[18] Others hastened to add suggestive dancing, birth control, tobacco, homosexuality, and blood sports to the condemned list, or to speak in favor of Sunday blue laws and to advise against life in cities (which they claimed were 'modern Babylons').[19]

Studies of the battles against alcohol and prostitution do not usually mention the vocabulary of the Protestant 'awakening' (*le Réveil*, the fundamentalist revival in France, *c.* 1814–49, which led to the creation of independent, evangelical churches and a French Methodism which shaped late nineteenth-century French Protestantism), which included references to sin, repentance, and redemption.[20] Instead, scholars who study these movements have focused on class and gender. From this perspective, temperance is about paternalistic industrialists seeking greater control over the workers they employed, and abolitionism is about paternalistic men who regulated commerce in women's bodies. These perspectives certainly express important truths, but they are insufficient truths. The songbook of the temperance league did indeed include songs like Mlle Sautter's *'Soyons des ouvriers fidèles'* (Be Loyal Workers / And Let Us Work Joyously), but it contained far more songs like *'Buveur arrête!'* (Drinker, stop! / Come, Your Place is Ready in the Ranks of the Elect). To present a fuller sense of the morality campaigns of the late nineteenth century, social history must reincorporate the latter song's Huguenot sense of sin.[21]

Campaign Against Prostitution

The campaign against prostitution is a good place to start recovering the Protestant sense of sin because it involves that most taboo of subjects, sexuality. Calvinist reformers were so uncomfortable with the thought of sexuality that they rarely used the word. Instead, they denounced '*plaisirs malsains*' or '*passions malsaines*' and, of course, '*la débauche.*'[22] Wrestling with unwholesome pleasures required a large arena. In the words of the foremost morality reformer, Pastor Tommy Fallot, 'Our ambition is to purify the entire country.'[23] This led to lessons on guarding virginity (for girls) or purity (for boys), fury at ubiquitous pornography, shock at licentious dances and entertainments, disapproval of elaborate coiffures and make-up, denunciations of the dangers of masturbation, and outrage at legal barriers to paternity suits, as well as the fight against legalized prostitution. All were part of a clear and consistent Protestant war on debauchery. Without some understanding of this morality, it can be difficult to understand why pioneering feminists who fought to abolish regulated prostitution might also oppose sex education (one Protestant called it 'medical pornography') or how they could even sponsor feminist lectures against birth control.[24]

The campaign to abolish legalized prostitution underscores other connections between Protestantism and feminism. Many of the women drawn to feminism began their public careers as moral reformers, not as feminists. Indeed, it was precisely their involvement in campaigns such as abolitionism that led them to feminism. Isabelle Bogelot, Sarah Monod, Julie Siegfried, Marguerite de Witt-Schlumberger, Mme Henri Mallet, and Ghénia Avril de Sainte-Croix all followed a route from abolitionism in the 1880s, to a broader mixture of philanthropy and social activism in the 1890s, and then to the feminist movement.[25] The campaign against regulated prostitution was, of course, so large that it crossed all religious lines – drawing significant support among Catholic and Jewish leaders as well as Protestants – but a surprisingly large number came from the sub-culture of Protestantism.[26] And it was a prominent Protestant, Marguerite de Witt-Schlumberger (the grand-daughter of Guizot), who led the abolitionist committee of the Conseil national des femmes françaises (CNFF) and represented the Fédération abolitionniste internationale in that alliance of women's organizations. She had come to the campaign against prostitution through the combined effect of Josephine Butler's creation of the Fédération abolitionniste in 1874 and Pastor Fallot's great morality campaign of 1883. Prostitution, de Witt-Schlumberger insisted, was a plague of such proportions that public opinion was not even disturbed by the hundreds, perhaps thousands, of minors who were inscribed with the Police des moeurs. De Witt-Schlumberger used her own resources to publish and distribute pamphlets on prostitution, such as her angry 'A Glance in the Lairs of Hell: the State as Regulator of Debauchery,' notable both for its anger and passion and its inclusion of masculine prostitution.[27]

The career of Sarah Monod is another excellent illustration of this activity of Protestant women. Monod was the daughter of Pastor Adolphe Monod, renowned as the conscience and the thundering voice of orthodox Protestantism and called 'the Protestant Bossuet.'[28] Sarah remained devoted to her father throughout her life, never marrying but giving her considerable intelligence and energy first to Sunday School teaching, then to charities and the diaconate, and finally to the women's movement. Monod's diary, preserved in a Protestant library rather than a feminist collection, leaves no doubt that her religion preceded and shaped her feminism.[29] The debates in the organizing committee for the foundation of the Conseil national des femmes françaises in 1901 show that at least one Catholic-born feminist (Maria Pognon) worried that Monod was too devoted to her religion (Pognon called her 'le porte-drapeau du protestantisme'), to lead a coalition of all women's organizations.[30] Jane Misme, one of the foremost feminist journalists before World War I (and born Catholic), similarly called Monod 'la papesse du protestantisme' ('the female pope of Protestantism') and described her in terms of her austere black clothing. But Misme subsequently concluded that Monod (the president of the 125,000 member National Council of French Women) 'alone possesses the means to assemble and to govern the entire spectrum of feminism' – a definition which included the feminist mainstream as well as some organizations of Catholic women on the right and socialist women on the left. [31]

An examination of other social control campaigns (such as anti-alcoholism) leads to conclusions about Protestant republicanism similar to those suggested by looking at the Protestant anti-prostitution campaign. The most helpful figure to focus upon in such a study is Pastor Tommy Fallot (1844–1904), whose ambitions for the nation and morality campaign of 1883 have already been mentioned above.[32] Fallot was born into a prominent Alsatian family noted for producing industrialists and Lutheran pastors; his maternal grandfather, the noted industrial reformer Daniel Legrand, was a bit of both. Fallot began engineering studies but became swept up in the passions of the mid-century Protestant Awakening. After studying in Paris for three years while living with Pastor Edmond de Pressensé, Fallot enrolled at the Faculty of Protestant Theology in Strasbourg. He graduated in 1872 with a *thèse* entitled 'The Poor and the Gospels.'[33] Fallot began his career as a Lutheran pastor in the *Reichsland* of Alsace, but he emigrated to France in 1875 rather than conduct official prayers for Kaiser Wilhelm I. De Pressensé secured a post for Fallot as pastor of an *église libre* in a poor district of Paris, and Fallot responded by preaching the Christian socialism foreshadowed by his thesis. Although he was certainly not a revolutionary socialist, Fallot shocked Protestant high society by preaching that 'Communism, complete communism, was the law of the first Christian associations.'[34] As he elaborated this socialism, it chiefly meant 'the application of the principles of justice and love proclaimed by Jesus Christ.'[35] He developed his ideas, however, through correspondence with August Bebel and Wilhelm Liebknecht (who admired his defiance of the Kaiser) and Benoît Malon

Relèvement
Anti-Porn.

(a friend whom de Pressensé and his wife had helped to escape at the end of the Commune).[36]

Tommy Fallot became the leader of Protestant moral reform campaigns in 1883 when he founded his League for the Recovery of Public Morality (*Ligue française pour le relèvement de la moralité publique*). The Morality League joined battle across the entire social control front, but Fallot devoted especial effort to an anti-pornography campaign.[37] France already possessed a large corpus of anti-pornography legislation. Napoleon's Penal Code of 1810 had covered 'songs, pamphlets, figurines, and images contrary to *bonne moeurs*.' In May 1819, the Bourbon restoration had established the crime of 'insults against public and religious morality' and under that concept had outlawed 'the display, the distribution, the sale, or the offering for sale of writings, printed matter, prints, engravings, paintings or emblems which insult public or religious morality.' The leaders of the Paris Commune shared some of this mentality: they had very little time for social reforms, yet managed to adopt two anti-pornography statutes in the spring of 1871 – reforms which would have pleased both the Bourbons and the Bonapartes. The 'government of moral order' polished that name with another statute (saying almost exactly the same things) in 1875. The historic Press Law of 1881, typically remembered as a landmark of liberalism, included an article suppressing 'flagrant insults against good morals committed by the press' (Article 28), but its only novelty was the inclusion of pornographic posters and placards.[38] The law of 1881 had initially been cheered by the Protestant press, which anticipated a 'pitiless' police campaign against the kiosks displaying 'filthy' (*immonde*) pictures and publications, but they soon concluded that wily pornographers were 'skillful at profiting from the least fissures in the law.'[39] The Chamber of Deputies soon heard their complaints of loopholes in Article 28 and hastened, by a vote of 426 to 47, to adopt another anti-pornography law, the Law to Suppress Insults against Good Morals of 1882. This act forbade 'the sale, the offer for sale, the public display, the posting, or the free distribution on the streets' of printed obscenity.[40]

Despite all of these laws, Fallot viewed France as inundated with pornography. He found it 'appearing on the sidewalks, in shop windows, in newspaper kiosks, on the walls [of Paris],' and he reported that 'its peddlers shove their merchandise at decent women and slip it into the hands of children as they leave school.'[41] The Morality League found so much indecent literature because its definition of pornography was so wide, encompassing the stories of Gyp, several of the novels of Emile Zola (especially the vivid *Nana*, which had appeared in 1880), and much of the naturalist school of fiction. Fallot attacked journalists for protecting pornographers behind freedom of the press, he denounced deputies (many of whom had voted for three anti-pornography laws) for ignoring pornography, he warned the nation that the railroads were carting Parisian filth into the countryside, and he urged people to report to him every indecent publication they found. Pornography, he insisted, was not merely wicked to read, but it caused wicked behavior. At the very least, it made men worse husbands, worse fathers, and worse soldiers.[42] Pastor Fallot chose to launch a political attack on pornography. He reasoned that an awakened public opinion would elect anti-pornography deputies; failing that, the campaign should stimulate greater action from current deputies. Fallot planned a petition campaign, coordinated with provincial lectures. The Morality League was already deeply involved in the fights against alcohol and prostitution. Fallot himself had accepted the presidency of the Paris section of the abolitionist league inspired by Josephine Butler, the Union of the Friends of Young Women (*Union internationale des amies de la jeune fille*).[43] Nonetheless, he and the league launched their assault on '*la presse immorale*' in early 1887. Professor Jalabert, a Protestant legal scholar on the Law Faculty of Paris, persuaded Fallot that the press laws of 1881 and 1882 contained adequate provisions against pornography, so Fallot stated a simple objective for the petition campaign: to convince the government to enforce the law. The league insisted that the Municipal Law of April 1884 gave local officials the power to act to assure public order, safety, and health, and these powers provided an opportunity to enforce the law against pornography.[44]

The Morality League's 1887–88 campaign against immoral literature was essentially a pastors' crusade. The chief speakers were Pastor Fallot, Pastor and Senator de Pressensé (who accepted the presidency of the Morality League while Fallot directed it as secretary-general), Pastor Louis Comte of St Etienne (the editor of the Morality League's publication, *Le Relèvement social*), Professor Jalabert, and Pastor Eugène Bersier (an editor of de Pressensé's *Revue chrétienne* and his cousin by marriage). De Pressensé had the largest reputation in this group and served as the featured speaker in most towns.[45] 'We are more and more submerged by the swelling torrent of unwholesome literature,' he told provincial France, singling out Zola's school of literature, 'which pretends to be "naturalist" but sees only the lowest, the most vile sides of nature, and erects them into a system depicting vice.'[46]

When the petition had acquired 33,000 signatures, Pastor de Pressensé deposited it with the French Senate, which filed it with the Commission on Petitions, which assigned as its *rapporteur* Senator de Pressensé. Judging by its 10–1 parliamentary support, this resolution probably did not need the full Calvinist fury that de Pressensé gave it in two speeches. The Senate sped instructions to enforce the laws to the Ministry of Justice and the Ministry of the Interior, with a copy to the Ministry of Religion. The respective ministers warmly endorsed the war on the unwholesome and forwarded instructions to *parquets*, *préfets*, and police.

The Morality League's campaign produced few lasting results. Whenever local preachers brought accusations against specific books or periodical vendors, they got action, especially in towns with Protestant voting strength, as happened in Nîmes, Montauban, and Bordeaux.[47] Tommy Fallot was so

Anti-Porn

determined to keep the attention of moral reformers focused on pornography that he founded another organization, the Anti-Pornography League (*Ligue nationale contre la pornographie*), so the Morality League could fight other *plaisirs malsaines*. By 1891, Fallot had burnt out. He took a quiet country pastorate in the Drôme and turned most of his work over to Louis Comte. Comte helped win additional anti-pornography legislation in 1895 (a law including foreign language pornography), 1898 (a law including obscene objects), and 1905 (a statute to outlaw the private sale of pornography). Comte carried this fight well into the twentieth century. He became a leader of the *Fédération des sociétés contre le pornographie* which published a manual for local leaders to press the fight against pornography, which battled to treat birth-control literature as pornography (winning several convictions), and which urged attention to the literature of pederasty and its connection to the prostitution of youths.[48] Comte was also one of the federation's organizers of an International Anti-Pornography Congress at Paris in 1908.[49] The Federation, like most morality leagues, was not an exclusively Protestant organization, but its Calvinist nature was clear from the composition of its board of directors: it included seven Protestant pastors and no Catholic priests. (Among the prominent Catholic groups in the anti-pornography campaign was Marie Maugeret's *Fédération Jeanne d'Arc*.[50]) Comte, Gounelle, Sarah Monod, Julie Siegfried, and the French YMCA (*Alliance des Unions chrétiennes des jeunes gens*) fought 'the pornographic peril' with so much passion that they made such puritanism one of the issues in fin-de-siècle anti-Protestantism.[51]

This brief glimpse of a Protestant campaign for moral reform should suggest the depth of Protestant social conservatism. Note that there was little difference between the anti-pornography legislation that they championed during the Third Republic and the anti-pornography laws of the Bourbon Restoration. Indeed, Protestant reformers were more conservative than the Bourbons. They demanded stricter controls over private behavior and morality, and they called for stricter police enforcement of such laws. The same Protestant churches which denounced Bourbon intolerance of differing personal beliefs, were themselves vehemently intolerant of differing private behavior.

The similarity between the social conservatism of Protestant republicans and the conservatism of the Bourbon Restoration is equally clear if one studies other campaigns of social control, especially the one pressing for Sunday blue laws. Monarchist Sunday closing laws of 1814 and 1837 had won the support of the monarchist National Assembly in 1874, but one of the first actions of the young Third Republic in 1879 had been to abrogate these laws. Almost immediately, prominent Protestants founded the *Société française pour l'observation du dimanche,* under the honorary presidency of General Chabaud-la-Tour (a Protestant) and two Protestant honorary vice presidents. The work of the society was directed by Louis Sautter (a Protestant) and three pastors. They sought to block postal service and railway operation on Sundays, in addition to the traditional targets of closing factories, offices, and shops. The financial backing for the society came from the highest level of *haute société protestante*, including the economic elite of Alfred André, the Hentsch brothers, Baron Hottinguer, seven members of the Mallet family, Madame Schneider of Le Creusot, Théodore Vernes, and Madame Schlumberger.[52]

This discussion of the social conservatism within French Protestantism calls for a readjustment of the political characterization of this minority. It must also be stressed that profound social conservatism coexisted with ardent republicanism. Most of the leaders of Protestant morality campaigns (like the great majority of Protestants in French politics) were active on the political left. Of the four figures cited most often in this chapter – Sarah Monod, Tommy Fallot, Edmond de Pressensé, and Louis Comte – one was a founder of the feminist movement, one a leader of non-Marxist socialism, one a founding father of the Third Republic, and the last a prominent provincial Dreyfusard and a founder of the League of the Rights of Man. Let the least known of these, Pastor Louis Comte, stand for the group. He was involved in two widely-discussed judicial proceedings at the end of the century. The first was in 1899 when he became a hero of the Dreyfusard left for preaching a vigorously pro-Dreyfus sermon (not his first) despite an explicit threat from the prefect to suspend him. He went ahead and called the general staff 'poltroons.' Dreyfusard supporters immediately raised double his salary, although Pastor Comte refused the excess. Comte's next day in court came in 1902, and that time he became a hero to social conservatives: cabaret owners sued him for calling them 'the exploiters of shady operations.'[53] He, like much of the Protestant community, typifies the social conservatism within republicanism.

Among the paradoxes of this blend of radicalism with conservatism, is the Protestant view of the role of the state. Protestant republicanism opposed state intervention into many aspects of private life. This was most obvious in Protestant economics, where Protestants were the leading champions of laissez-faire economics in France. (A Protestant, Jean-Baptiste Say, was arguably the foremost champion of Adam Smith and classical liberal economics in early nineteenth-century France; his grandson, Léon Say, continued this role as Minister of Finance in eight different cabinets of the early Third Republic.) This tradition of laissez-faire liberalism did not extend, however, to moral issues – there was no Protestant argument for a free market in sex, alcohol, or tobacco; instead, the state was expected to intervene, as Protestant legislators demanded in the campaign against pornography.

The French Protestant minority of the late nineteenth century – with their mixture of left-wing politics, social conservatism, and strong support for human rights and feminism – offer a helpful, supplemental perspective to studies of gender, and especially of men and masculinity such as Robert Nye's influential *Masculinity and Male Codes of Honor*. Protestant social and moral control placed its heaviest emphasis on men. *Ouvriers* drank too much, but *ouvrières* were a lesser concern. Men produced and consumed the pornography. Most of the gamblers, the smokers, and the crowd at animal blood sports were men. (There were certainly exceptions and complications to this generalization: women, for example, often obtained a *debit de tabacs* – as the wife of Pastor de Pressensé did – to sell tobacco through the state monopoly.[54]) Men perpetuated prostitution. The Protestant perspective on the women who engaged in prostitution was typically to found 'rescue' organizations, prison-visitation groups, and societies to help reintegrate former prostitutes into society. (Beyond the well-known leagues of the women's movement, which had a significant Protestant leadership, one should note such Protestant groups as the Comtesse de la Lozère's *Oeuvre du refuge de Paris*, a charity to rescue 'poor fallen women' by helping them towards domestic service or factory work.)

Where were the Protestants? Engaged in shaping virtually every morality campaign of late nineteenth-century France.

Notes

1. An earlier version of this chapter was presented as a paper at the Rudé Conference in Wellington, New Zealand. The author wishes to acknowledge the helpful commentary and discussion he received there.
2. André Derain, in an undated personal letter to Vlaminck, as quoted by Eugen Weber in *France, Fin de Siècle* (Cambridge, MA: Harvard University Press, 1986), p. 13.
3. Robert A. Nye, *Masculinity and Male Codes of Honor in Modern France* (New York: Oxford University Press, 1993), pp. 74–5. See especially chapters four and five for degeneration.
4. Roger Shattuck, *The Banquet Years: the Arts in France, 1885–1918* (Garden City, NY: Anchor Books, 1961), p. 3.
5. See, for example, the psychiatrists discussed by Nye, such as Bénédict-Augustin Morel and Valentin Magnan. For the late nineteenth-century physicians who studied syphilis in the belle époque, starting with Alfred Fournier, a good starting point is Claude Quétel's *History of Syphilis* (Baltimore: Johns Hopkins University Press, 1990), especially chapter six, 'The Great Turning Point (around 1900).'
6. David S. Barnes, *The Making of a Social Disease: Tuberculosis in Nineteenth-Century France* (Berkeley: University of California Press, 1995), pp. 167–8.
7. The numerous works of Rachel Fuchs, such as *Poor and Pregnant in Paris: Strategies for Survival in the Nineteenth Century* (New Brunswick: Rutgers University Press, 1992) and *Abandoned Children: Foundlings and Child Welfare in Nineteenth-Century France* (Albany: State University Press of New York, 1984), have pioneered this perspective on the belle époque. Another excellent illustration of the place of women in this debate is Elinor Accampo's evocatively sub-titled *Blessed Motherhood, Bitter Fruit: Nelly Roussel and the Politics of Female Pain in the Third Republic* (Baltimore: Johns Hopkins University Press, 2006). Accampo and Fuchs have joined with Mary Lynn Stewart to produce a collective volume which introduces many of the social

debates of the era, *Gender and the Politics of Social Reform in France, 1870–1914* (Baltimore: Johns Hopkins University Press, 1995).

8. Anne Cova, *Maternité et droits des femmes en France: XIXe–XXe siècles* (Paris: Anthropos, 1997), pp. 35–43. See also the pioneering essay by Karen Offen, 'Depopulation, Nationalism, and Feminism in Fin-de-Siècle France,' *American Historical Review*, 89 (1984): 648–76.

9. The last French census to identify respondents by religion, the census of 1872, reported a total of 600,000 Protestants (1.66 percent of the population), chiefly in the Église Réformée (540,000) and the Lutheran Church (60,000). These numbers are repeated in the *Annuaire Statistique* during the 1870s. The Église Réformée reported 550,000 members to the Sous-directeur des cultes non-catholiques in 1883. See for the Archives nationales, F19 10 031-1 for this report, or the statistical annex based on it in André Encrevé's remarkable thèse d'état, *Protestants français aux milieu du XIXe siècle* (Geneva: Labor et Fides, 1986), pp. 1081–97. Pastor Gambier, who edited the *Agenda Protestant*, a reference handbook for the Church, was still using almost the same numbers in the late 1890s. *Agenda Protestant: Recueil de renseignements relatifs aux églises et aux oeuvres du protestantisme de langue française* (Paris: Fischbacher, 1898), p. 154, reports 560,000 in the Reformed Church, 80,000 Lutherans, and 10,000 in independent churches.

10. The classic statement of this thesis is André Siegfried's *Tableau politique de la France de l'ouest sous la Troisième République* (Paris: Armand Colin, 1964). It has been restated with such frequency that it requires few reminders. For the period considered here (1860–1910), Protestants were prominent among the critics of the Second Empire (as were Edmond de Pressensé, Eugène Pelletan, Jean-Jacques Clamageran, Auguste Scheurer-Kestner, and Ferdinand Buisson) and leading champions of republicanism and opponents of monarchical restoration (Pressensé, Charles Freycinet, Léon Say, and William Waddington). For other overviews of the political role of French Protestants, see Stuart R. Schram, *Protestantism and Politics in France* (Alençon: Corbière et Jugain, 1954); Patrick Cabanel, *Les Protestants et la République, de 1870 à nos jours* (Paris: Editions complexe, 2000); and Philip Nord, *The Republican Moment: Struggles for Democracy in Nineteenth-Century France* (Cambridge, MA: Harvard University Press, 1995), esp. chapter five, 'Liberal Protestantism.'

11. André Encrevé and Michel Richard (eds), *Les Protestants dans les débuts de la Troisième République, 1871–1875* (Paris: Société de l'histoire du protestantisme français, 1979), p. 358.

12. For the Ligue des droits de l'homme, see William D. Irvine, *Between Justice and Politics: the Ligue des droits de l'homme* (Stanford: Stanford University Press, 2007) and Wendy E. Perry, 'Remembering Dreyfus: the Ligue des droits de l'homme and the Making of the Modern French Human Rights Movement' (PhD dissertation: University of North Carolina, 1998), UMI Number 9914888. Part Two (volume two) of Perry's dissertation is an especially valuable dictionary of the membership of the league.

13. Steven C. Hause, with Anne R. Kenney, *Women's Suffrage and Social Politics in the French Third Republic* (Princeton: Princeton University Press, 1984), esp. pp. 255–9; see also the same argument in Laurence Klejman and Florence Rochefort, *L'Egalité en marche: le féminisme sous la Troisième République* (Paris: Presses de la foundation nationale des sciences politiques, 1989).

14. See Pim Den Boer, *History as a Profession: the Study of History in France, 1818–1914* (Princeton: Princeton University Press, 1998), esp. pp. 330ff on 'The Historians'

Journal: the *Revue historique'*; and Benjamin Harrison, 'Gabriel Monod and the Professionalization of History in France, 1844–1912' (PhD dissertation: University of Wisconsin, 1972), UMI Number 72-31, 679.

15. *'Nothing for pleasure, nothing for vanity, everything for duty.'* Vinet was Swiss. Edmond de Pressensé studied under him, but Vinet died in 1847 and the other pastors mentioned in this paper were too young to study with him directly. For an assessment of his role, see the Dossier Alexandre Vinet: le théologien et son influence théologique pour la France, in the manuscripts collection of the Société de l'histoire du protestantisme français (54, rue Saint-Pères, Paris), MS 1137/Carton 8 (Hereafter, BSHPF).

16. Auguste de Morsier, *Appel aux chrétiens, suivi des déclarations de E. Gounelle et W. Monod* (Geneva: Kündig, 1909), p. 29.

17. See, for example, *La Femme*, September 1913 (a memorial issue on Abbadie d'Arrast's death). Her argument on games of chance, while understanding that most gamblers were men, sees gambling as part of a larger social issue of demoralization (pp. 137–8).

18. Louis Comte, *Faut-il que jeunesse se passe?* (Bordeaux: Relèvement social, n.d.), p. 8.

19. Pierre Poujol and Stuart Schram, 'Le Protestantisme rural: traditions, structures, et tendances politiques,' *Christianisme social*, 65 (1957): 549–72 ; quotation, p. 551.

20. See Alice Wemyss, *Histoire du Réveil, 1790–1849* (Paris and Lausanne: Les Bergers, 1977). Wemyss uses the starting date of 1790 (instead of 1814 given above) to provide a background chapter entitled 'Préparation, 1790–1812', then she too begins the discussion of the *Réveil* with the end of the Napoleonic wars.

21. Both songs are from the temperance society known as the Blue Cross which proclaimed a non-sectarian identity, but whose founders and leaders were Protestant. Léon Say and Dr Gustave Monod were the first presidents. Anonymous, *Chants de la Croix-bleue* (8th edition: Lausanne, 1892), pp. 211 and 135.

22. 'Unwholesome pleasures,' 'unwholesome passions,' 'debauchery.'

23. Fallot to Pastor Louis Comte, 14 February 1893, in the Papiers Pasteur Elie Gounelle, BSHPF, MS 1670, Dossier 5 (Louis Comte).

24. For the discomfort of French Protestants with subjects of human sexuality, see Isabel Lisberg-Haag, 'Les Protestants et la question sexuelle au tournant des XIXe et XXe siècles,' in Isabelle von Bueltzingsloewen and Denis Pelletier (eds), *La Charité en pratique: Chrétiens français et allemands sur le terrain social* (Strasbourg: Presses universitaires de Strasbourg, 1999); for a good illustration of it, see the preaching of Pastor Vinet (de Pressensé's master) against masturbation, in Jean Stengers and Anne Van Neck, *Histoire d'une grande peur, la masturbation* (Brussels: Université de Bruxelles, 1984), pp. 74ff. The leadership of the Conseil national des femmes françaises was predominantly Protestant during its early history, and the CNFF strongly opposed the neo-Malthusian feminism of women such as Nelly Roussel and Madeleine Pelletier. One of the first women physicians in France, Dr Blanche Edwards-Pilliet, was a member of this Protestant leadership and the person who delivered the CNFF lectures against birth control. See the discussion of this in Jennifer Waelti-Walters and Steven C. Hause (eds), *Feminisms of the Belle Époque: a Historical and Literary Anthology* (Lincoln: University of Nebraska Press, 1994), p. 242.

25. Although these women were all deeply involved in Protestant philanthropic and social activism, they were not all practicing Protestants. Avril de Sainte-Croix has been identified as a Protestant in several works, including by Michelle Perrot, 'Preface,' in Laurence Klejman and Florence Rochefort, *L'Egalité en marche: Le Féminisme sous la Troisième République* (Paris: des Femmes, 1989), p. 17: 'les philanthropes

protestantes, affranchise du conservatisme catholique: Avril de Sainte-Croix, Sarah Monod, Isabelle Bogelot, Emilie de Morsier...;' and by the present author: Steven C. Hause with Anne R. Kenney, *Women's Suffrage and Social Politics in the French Third Republic* (Princeton: Princeton University Press, 1984), p. 59: 'Avril de Sainte-Croix ... also came to feminism through Protestant philanthropy.' The thorough research on Avril de Sainte-Croix by Karen Offen suggests that she may have had Huguenot ancestors, and that she held several anti-Catholic attitudes, but she was probably not a practicing Protestant. See Offen's 'France's Foremost Feminist, or Who in the World is Madame Avril de Sainte-Croix?' *Archives du féminisme,* 9 (2005): 46–54; and her 'Intrepid Crusade: Ghénia Avril de Sainte-Croix takes on the Prostitution Issue,' *Proceedings of the Western Society for French History,* 33 (2005): 352–74. Materials in the Fonds CNFF at the Centre des Archives du Féminisme (Angers) show that when the foundation of the Conseil national des femmes françaises provoked some concerned discussion about the predominance of Protestants in the organization, Avril de Sainte-Croix stated that her own role in the leadership should be seen as proof that the council would be impartial. 'Procès-Verbal de la réunion du Comité d'initiative,' 10 April 1901, Fonds CNFF 2AF3, Folder 'Réunions, 1900–1901.'

26. A good illustration of the close cooperation of women across religious lines would be the Catholic Lefevre sisters, better known by the married names of Caroline de Barrau de Muratel (1828–88) and Marie d'Abbadie d'Arrast (1835–1913), who worked in numerous groups which were predominantly Protestant, such as the Conference de Versailles. Both sisters chose to work closely with Pastor Fallot's *Ligue française pour le relèvement de la moralité publique.* Fallot, in turn, called Barrau de Muratel 'a laïc saint.' Geneviève Poujol, *Un Féminisme sous tutelle. Les protestantes françaises, 1810–1910* (Paris: Editions de Paris, 2003), p. 194. Abbadie d'Arrast's obituary in *La Femme* stressed that she was especially concerned to collaborate in social campaigns 'sans distinction de culte.'

27. For a basic sketch of de Witt-Schlumber, see Poujol, *Un Féminisme sous tutelle,* p. 265. For her role in the campaign against prostitution, see her *Un Coup d'oeil dans les antres de l'enfer: L'état réglementaire du la débauche* (Paris: Chez l'auteur, n.d.); and her *Une Femme aux femmes. Pourquoi les femmes doivent étudier la question des moeurs* (Geneva: Fédération abolitionniste, 1908); p. 12 for minors as inscribed prostitutes.

28. Reported in Avril de Sainte-Croix's obituary of Sarah Monod for *L'Abolitionniste,* 1 January 1913.

29. Sarah Monod's diary ('Journal de Sarah'), in the Papiers Sarah Monod (MS 1546), BSHPF. *See Note 15*

30. 'Procès-Verbal de la réunion du Comité d'initiative,' 10 April 1901, Fonds CNFF 2AF3, Folder 'Réunions, 1900–1901.' It was Pognon's concerns which provoked Avril de Sainte-Croix's comments cited above in note 19. The resultant compromise was that Monod became president, Pognon and Julie Siegfried (a Protestant) became vice-presidents, and Avril de Sainte-Croix became secretary-general.

31. Jane Misme, 'Les Emancipatrices', *Le Figaro,* 7 July 1899.

32. For brief biographical sketches of Fallot, see: Jean Baubérot's entry in Jean-Marie Mayeur and Yves-Marie Hilaire (eds), *Dictionnaire du monde religieux dans la France contemporaine*: Volume 5; André Encrevé (ed.), *Les Protestants* (Paris: Beauchesne, 1993); and the entry in Roman d'Amat et al. (eds), *Dictionnaire de biographie française,* 13, p. 542. For a fuller study see Marc Boegner, *La Vie et la pensée de Tommy Fallot,* 2 vols (Paris, 1914–26).

33. Tommy Fallot, *Les Pauvres et l'évangile*, thesis, University of Strasbourg, 1872.
34. Quoted by Elie Gounelle in 'T. Fallot: un prophète au XIXe siècle,' *La Revue du Christianisme social*, 17 (1904): 470.
35. Fallot's speech 'Protestantisme et socialisme' which he published as an essay in *La Revue chrétienne* in December 1888. This phrase formed Article 2 of the statutes of the Association protestante pour l'étude pratique des questions sociales, adopted at Nîmes in 1888. The statutes were reprinted in *Le Protestant* (15 December 1888).
36. Baubérot, 'Tommy Fallot' in Encrevé (ed.), *Les Protestants*, p. 198.
37. The best available history of the anti-pornography campaigns of the Third Republic is Annie Stora-Lamarre, *L'Enfer de la IIIe République: censeurs et pornographes, 1881–1914* (Paris: Imago, 1990). It has a strong international perspective (finding the center of a pornography industry in Brussels and the center of an anti-pornography movement in Geneva) and a detailed treatment of 'l'enfer' at the Bibliothèque nationale (the section of the library for forbidden books), but it has little detail on the Protestant anti-pornography campaign. See pp. 88–91 and 116–19. The best accounts of the Protestant campaign are contained in Tommy Fallot's pamphlets. See especially his *Ligue française pour le relèvement de la moralité publique: notre nouvelle campagne* (Paris: Fischbacher, 1891).
38. The text of French anti-pornography legislation can be found in the *Journal officiel* under the dates of: 17 May 1819; 15 and 22 April 1871; 29 December 1875; and 29 July 1881.
39. For the reaction of the Protestant press, see: 'La Loi sur la presse,' *Le Christianisme au XIXe siècle*, 26 August 1881. For a survey of anti-pornography laws and the reaction to them, see Anonymous, *Congrès international contre le pornographie. Paris, 21 et 22 mai 1908. Rapports, discussion, voeux, et decisions* (Paris: Mouillot, 1908).
40. *Journal officiel de la République française* (2 August 1882).
41. Fallot, *Ligue française pour le relèvement de la moralité publique*, p. 11.
42. Ibid., *passim*.
43. Following Josephine Butler's speaking tour of France, Italy, and Switzerland in 1874–75, efforts were begun to create an international association to support the abolitionist cause. The *Union internationale des amies de la jeune fille* was founded in Geneva in 1877 by twenty-two representatives from seven countries. Sarah Monod led the French delegation. The Paris chapter of the union was led by women chiefly drawn from Protestant philanthropy and social work: Mme Fisch (the wife of a pastor), Julie Siegfried (the daughter of a pastor), and Mme Admiral Puaux. For Josephine Butler's role, see her *Personal Reminiscences of a Great Crusade* (London, 1896). For the Protestant leadership of the union, see Anne-Marie Käppeli, *Sublime croisade: ethique et politique du féminisme protestant, 1875–1928* (Geneva: Zoé, 1990). For the role of French Protestant women, see the Protestant press, especially: 'L'Union internationale des amies de la jeune fille,' *Le Protestant*, 9 November 1895. For the leadership role of Tommy Fallot, 'L'Union internationale des amies de la jeune fille,' *Le Protestant*, 16 April 1887. See also the summary in an unidentified obituary of Monod by J. Davaine, available in the Monod Papers (MS 1546), BSHPF.
44. Fallot produced several pamphlets during this campaign. In addition to *Ligue française pour le relèvement de la moralité publique*, cited above, see especially his *Communication sur l'organisation de la lutte contre la pornographie* (Nice: Relèvement social, 1891); *Vers un nouveau régime des moeurs: un programme d'action municipale* (Bordeaux: Relèvement social, n.d.). See also the coverage of this campaign in the Protestant press, for example, *Le Protestant*, 31 December 1887 and 11 February 1888. Stora-Lamarre does not cover this campaign in *L'Enfer de la IIIe République*,

chiefly examining the morality league in later years (under Pastor Louis Comte) and looking at its Swiss connections; see pp. 88–91.

45. For more on Edmond de Pressensé, see: Steven C. Hause, 'A Pastoral Family in French Politics: Edmond, Elise, and Francis de Pressensé,' *Proceedings of the Annual Meeting of the Western Society for French History*, 17 (1990): 383–91; Jules Calas, *Edmond de Pressensé: un libéral chrétien* (Rouillac: Etendard évangélique, 1892); Henri Cordey, *Edmond de Pressensé et son temps, 1824–1891* (Lausanne: Bridel, 1916). For his role in the morality league, see Cordey, pp. 486–9.

46. De Pressensé's speech at Lyons, 18 December 1887, repeated at several provincial stops (at Rouen and unspecified other towns), and in Paris, 10 February 1888, as quoted in *Le Protestant*, 31 December 1877, 11 February 1888, and 3 March 1888.

47. Some evidence of this survives in departmental archives. In the archives of the Gard (at Nîmes), for example, series J contains many of the Protestant consistorial records. These files include the records of Pastor Auguste Grotz's efforts to press the mayor and the *procureur général* to act. Archives départmentales – Gard, Dossier 'Rapports avec l'autorité civile' in the Fonds Consistoire de Nîmes, 4 J 193.

48. Fédération des Sociétés contre la pornographie, *Manual pratique pour la lutte contre la pornographie* (Paris: the Fédération, 1909). The manual reports that they had just won two convictions for 'publications anticonceptionnelles,' resulting in one and two-month prison sentences, plus 200 and 500 franc fines. Ibid., pp. 6–7. For homosexual pornography, p. 42.

49. The new legislation can be found in the *Journal officiel* for 22 January 1895 and 16 March 1898. Louis Comte was not so prolific a writer as Fallot, but his thinking can be seen in *Faut-il que jeunesse se passe?* (Saint-Antoine, Dordogne: Relèvement social, nd.) and in his regular contributions to *La Revue du Christianisme social*. Biographical sketches are available in Encrevé, *Les Protestants*, pp. 135–6 and in the *Dictionnaire de biographie française*, 9, pp. 426–7. The fullest study is by one of his collaborators, Elie Gounelle, *La Vie et l'oeuvre de Louis Comte* (Alençon, 1927). The Papiers Elie Gounelle at the BSHPF (MS 1670) contain many materials on Comte, especially in Carton 8. For the congress, see: Anonymous, *Congrès international contre le pornographie. Paris, 21 et 22 mai 1908. Rapports, discussion, voeux, et decisions* (Paris: Mouillot, 1908), which includes a summary of anti-pornography legislation. *see note 15*

50. BSHPF, Rapports/T606, Fédération des Sociétés contre la pornographie, *Liste des Sociétés contre la pornographie, Janvier 1910* (Paris: Desfosses, 1910).

51. See 'Encore une lettre de Zola,' published in *La Croix*, 22 January 1898, although originally written in defense of *Nana* in 1881. Zola denounces 'the Protestant spirit' in vehement terms. 'Under the often hypocritical pretext of morality, they have a hunger to discipline ... [but] we are in France, not in Germany!' For the anti-Protestant context of these remarks, see Steven C. Hause, 'Anti-Protestant Rhetoric in the Early Third Republic,' *French Historical Studies*, 16 (1989): 183–201.

52. See the files of the society at BSHPF, Rapports/T538, Société française pour l'observation du dimanche. Officers and financial contributors are drawn from the Comité de Paris *Rapport, 1884–1885*.

53. For his suspension, see the files on Comte in the records of the Ministère des cultes at the Archives nationales. The most helpful files are in the series of complaints against pastors, F19 10,443. For a sketch of him, Idelette Chapelle, 'A Propos du pasteur Louis Comte, 1857–1926,' *BSHPF*, 133 (1987): 471–9. (For his suspension over Dreyfus, pp. 477–8.)

54. Archives du préfecture de police, Dossier Ba 1228 (Dossier de Pressensé-Dehault), police report of 8 July 1891.

7
Paternity, Progeny, and Property: Family Honor in the Late Nineteenth Century

Rachel G. Fuchs

'Honor is a masculine concept,' Robert Nye has eloquently argued. 'It has traditionally regulated relations among men, summed up the prevailing ideals of manliness, and marked the boundaries of masculine comportment ... Women had no real place in this system of honor. They were only permitted to safeguard their sexual honor, which in truth belonged to their husbands, fathers, and brothers, who were ultimately responsible for its integrity and defense.'[1] Building on these important concepts, this chapter explores notions of honor, masculinity, progeny, and property embodied in a man's legal actions to disavow children born to his wife in the nineteenth and early twentieth centuries. It also demonstrates that although paternity suits were illegal, unwed mothers still had some legal and honorable recourse against men who had dishonored them. They used tort law and sued men for damages resulting from fraudulent seduction and a resulting baby and asserted their rights as adult human beings. Men had been using tort law for decades when another man materially wronged them. By using tort law in courts, just as men had done, and by blaming men for damaging them, women attempted to restore their lost integrity, self-respect, and status in their community, thereby broadening the field of female honor. Both categories of legal action involved men's denial of paternity and the honor (or dishonor) in sexual relations between individual men and women.

In an effort to protect men's property and honor from progeny which a man wished to deny, the men who framed the Civil Code of 1804 designed article 340, which prohibited paternity searches through the turn of the nineteenth century. In an era without blood-type analysis or genetic (DNA) testing as proof of paternity, issues of evidence dominated discussions. Only in 1912, after decades of debate, did legislators finally allow a woman to bring a paternity suit within a framework of specified circumstantial evidence – such as producing a man's letters to her in which he wrote of 'his' child in a manner that judges could interpret as an avowal of paternity, or by summoning witnesses stating that the couple had cohabited during the possible time of conception. Paternity suits, however, affected only unmarried men. From

150

1804 to 1972, a married man was exempt from paternity suits for children born of his adultery.

Since the bourgeoisie associated property with honor, the need to preserve the integrity of marriage and to prevent outsiders from intruding on the family bloodline and property were inherent in the Civil Code.[2] The Code's redactors at the beginning of the nineteenth century and legislators throughout the century feared that a poor single mother, whom they often portrayed as deceitful and scheming, would bring false charges against an honorable man, and thus diminish his honor, his property, and that of his family. The fear of the adulteration of a family's estate became one of the biggest obstacles to permitting paternity searches. By denying the possibility of paternity suits, the Code enabled men's sexual freedom and absolved a man of all legal, fiscal, moral, and social responsibility if he were not married to the mother of his child. Unwed mothers and their children thus suffered materially and legally when a father refused to acknowledge them. The children had no right to his name, support, or affection, nor could they receive any inheritance from him.

Despite the Civil Code's prohibition of paternity suits and the towering emotional and financial hardships they faced along the way, women entered the public sphere of the courtroom with their private dramas and dreams, looking for public redress of private wrongs in intimate matters. They sought damages and reparations for the harm men had done to them through seduction and abandonment, and which left them with a child to support. Undoubtedly, the publicity of going to court and putting their sexual life before a critical audience inhibited many. For others, desperate or emboldened by successes they or their lawyers had heard about, and quite savvy about legal procedure, to admit a dishonor in a public courtroom could paradoxically enable them to shift the dishonor on to the men, reclaim their own honor, and obtain financial indemnification for their loss. Sometimes, though, their efforts were futile. When a woman lost her honor through an extranuptial pregnancy and resulting baby, her family also lost honor in the community. A woman, and her family, however, could try to regain that lost honor by telling the courts, and the community, that the man, not she, had behaved dishonorably through forcing her into sexual intercourse, sometimes by means of a false marriage promise or by the abuse of his position and authority. In these court cases, women and their lawyers avoided any semblance of paternity suits. Shifting the narratives from paternity to property damage and broken contracts allowed women redress within the legal system. These court cases helped define the unwritten codes of honor and behavior.

As women attempted to mitigate the scandal of a non-marital pregnancy and obtain some reparations, in their suits for damages they fashioned their narratives to demonstrate that they had been young, innocent, virtuous, and from a respectable family, before the men deprived them of their honor by means of force or deception. Until mid-century, a young woman's father sometimes sued for damages in the name of his daughter, based on the assumption that a young, unmarried woman was the property of her father who bore the responsibility to protect her from damage. From this perspective, it was the father's property, and thus his honor, that a man had damaged by seduction and a broken marriage promise. After mid-century, however, fathers were absent from the damage suits; hereafter women sued in their own names. This significant shift could be attributed to an increasing emphasis on women's rights, primarily as workers and mothers. As more women left their families for employment outside the home, they became more independent and more vulnerable. Seduction, pregnancy, and childbirth damaged their ability to earn a living and their right to work. The concept of 'right to work' became an important aspect of the discourse. Furthermore, during the 1840s and later, the increased activity of feminists and other social reformers, predominantly the Utopian Socialists, may have empowered women to act in their own names. The women who sued for damages were exercising their right to work as well as their rights to court hearings and to make contractual agreements as citizens. Since unwed mothers and their lawyers were not targeting a man's putative paternity, condemning his adultery, or asking him to provide his name and support to a child, they could, and did, pursue adulterous married men as well as single men for damages. They only sought redress for the wrongs the men had done them personally. Although a few asked the man to behave honorably and provide some monetary support to the child, this occurred primarily during the last third of the century.[3] Men's honor then came to include not only fulfilling contractual agreements and making reparations for a civil wrong done to the women, but also providing for the child.

The key, however, was that there had to have been a baby as a visible sign of damage. Otherwise, the damage would only have been the destruction of a woman's reputation and of her virginity, and hence the consequent reduction of her material value on the marriage market. It was difficult to sue successfully for damages for intangible consequences, such as pain and suffering. Moreover, if there were no pregnancy and child, it was unlikely that an innocent young girl from an honorable family who had been seduced and abandoned or who had a premarital love affair after a marriage promise would go to court and publicize that relationship. If she remained silent, her transgression and humiliation could remain secret – unless the man bragged. However, if a pregnancy ensued, there would be no way to keep the illicit affair a secret from her community. Even if she left home, as thousands did, suspicion, if not full knowledge of the pregnancy would remain. In these circumstances, it might have been in her interest to lodge a complaint and put herself under the aegis of the magistrates, believing, correctly or not, that she might receive public support and that the law could punish a man who had betrayed her. It was a better alternative than suicide or infanticide as a means to reclaim personal and family honor. It would also help salve her wounds if judges could place the blame on the man who had violated her body, her heart, and her sense of reason by false promises, abuse of authority, or a broken engagement. He had behaved dishonorably by taking advantage of the young poor girl; she, in turn, would behave honorably by going to court to make him assume some financial responsibility. Given the frequency of prosecutions for infanticide and the astoundingly high rates of child abandonment during the century, the women who went to court could also show the world that they were indeed honorable mothers; they were raising the children themselves.[4] Regardless of what the Civil Code prescribed or proscribed, women had their own codes of behavior sanctioned by the community. A woman's ideal of honor included marriage and family; women blamed dishonest men for keeping them from that ideal, and used the arena of the courtroom to avenge themselves. Nevertheless, for poor working women, the cost of childbirth and raising an infant were uppermost in their pleas for reparations. Financial desperation drove them to court.

Men sought honor and dreaded shame, but their sense of shame was different from that experienced by women. A man's fear of shame may have been sufficient reason to abandon his pregnant lover and flee from marriage if there had been the slightest bit of gossip about her immorality or 'loose conduct.' The trepidation over a misalliance may have arisen from an alarm over diluting his property with the blood of others; he had to be certain the child was his. Honor also entailed marrying someone of a similar level in society. A good marriage for both men and women included an increase of property or status. If he broke an engagement at his mother or father's request, it was not dishonorable; rather he demonstrated that he was honorable in sanctifying his parents' wishes and not giving in to what he, his parents, or his lawyer described as the wiles of covetous women. For a man, abandoning a woman was not inherently dishonorable; there were no community sanctions of honor to make him stay with a woman beneath his station, even if they had a baby. Accusing her of a lack of virtue would provide a sufficient and honorable excuse for breaking a marriage promise.   *Contract*

In taking a man to court over a broken contract that both the man and woman had entered into, women based their actions on forms of honor inherent in contract law that usually pertained only to male citizens. Increasingly during the last third of the century, by suing for damages from a broken marriage promise, women began exercising – and bringing public attention to – their unwritten rights as citizens. During the nineteenth century, an engagement or marriage promise had the force of a legal contract if the family and community knew of it. If a person broke it without due cause, they or their family could be sued.[5]

Issues of honor, the contractual nature of the marriage promise, and the consequences for breaking it were all open to judicial interpretation. The Civil Code did much to disempower women, but members of the judiciary could work within and around the Code to empower women. Those magistrates who considered a marital engagement as a contract between a man and a woman implicitly acknowledged women's right to enter into legal agreements. Some magistrates considered a marriage promise, especially if it were a formal engagement, as a reciprocal contract between the two families, not just the man and woman. Breaking that promise would entitle the other family to reparations. Others, unsurprisingly, disagreed. They alleged that a marriage promise amounted to a private commitment bound by conscience, with no pecuniary consequence if ruptured.

Magistrates may have interpreted a marriage promise as an act of honor, but they also gave it the force of a contract in civil law. Jurisprudence on the obligations of marriage promises reveals that they remained part of a moral web of individual and familial rights and duties. It became incumbent on magistrates to interpret those moral obligations and give them the force of law. Magistrates decided that if a person broke that promise without due cause, thereby harming another, he or she would have an obligation to pay monetary reparations for that harm. They based their decision on article 1382 of the Civil Code, which specified that anyone who has wronged another person would be obliged to make reparations for that wrong and must bear responsibility by paying an indemnity, or *dommages-intérêts.* Due cause for breaking an engagement occurred if the man could prove that the woman had had sexual relations with another man. The reverse was not true; a woman could not break the agreement if the man had sexual relations with another. Men may have wanted to avoid the courts, but the wronged women, with help from sympathetic lawyers and judges, forced the men there.

Not only did magistrates decide on the nature of marital promises as contractual agreements, but they also had to decide what constituted 'fraudulent seduction.' The sine qua non in their decisions was the demonstrable virtue of the young woman and her virginity prior to the seduction. A woman's word alone was insufficient to win her suit. Written proof of a marriage promise and witnesses who could speak to her innocence and her behavior as a dutiful daughter were crucial. As several reformers intoned, it was the father's duty to protect his daughter's virtue, but if he could not, then society and its laws had that duty. Alexandre Dumas (fils), for example, demanded that the 'law protect the virginity of girls, which I call their capital.'[6] Virginity constituted social as well as material capital, assuring a good marriage and commanding a better price on the marriage market. Nothing could replace this capital if a seducer stole it or a woman lost it. Nevertheless, not all agreed that seduction amounted to theft of property. Moralists considered an unmarried woman's virginity less as capital and more as a virtue. If it was a virtue, it could not be stolen and property laws should not apply. This was not to say that moralists thought dishonorable men should get off scot-free. Rather, depriving a woman of her virtue, they reasoned, should be treated by the law as extortion, swindle, and abuse of confidence, or as inciting a minor to debauchery.[7]

Definitions of seduction and the nature of a marriage promise depended on the age of the woman and the circumstances. In their awards, magistrates took into account testimony about the age of the mother at the time of seduction, as well as her reputation and that of her family. The 'fault' of the man had to have been manifest. Seduction of minors differed from that of women who had reached their majority at the age of twenty-five. Magistrates maintained that 'a woman of twenty-five or thirty years could defend her virtue herself, had sufficient experience to understand the consequences of a fault, and sufficient discernment to thwart or frustrate the insidious promises of a Lothario.'[8] If these women had consented to seduction, they could not have been virtuous, but rather knowingly guilty of committing a fault.[9] Those between the ages of fifteen and twenty-five had more discernment than young girls, but they still needed protection from fraudulent seduction.[10]

Although the hope of marriage to a man of property and wealth could have facilitated the process of seduction among poor women, differences of social class were rarely apparent in the cases of fraudulent marriage promises that women brought to court. Most of the women going to court were not pursuing men of higher income or status, or married men with families. On the contrary, these were cases where, for instance, a laundress sued a cab driver, a domestic servant legally pursued a valet, a female mechanic brought a plumber to court, or a woman employee sought damages from a co-worker.[11]

Cases with class differences did occur occasionally, such as a domestic servant suing her master, a young delivery girl and her family suing an older, richer landowner, or a seamstress seeking damages from a medical student. These became the focus of the popular press. For example, in April 1902, Adèle Hartmann met Maurice Cohen on the streets of Paris. He was a medical student and she was a seamstress about ten years older than he. Intimate relations followed. Though they never had a dwelling in common, in May 1903 they had a child. In one letter, Maurice confessed that he had acted 'in a regrettable caprice' and wanted to end the relationship. In response, Adèle sent him a 'menacing letter' leading him to seek police intervention to avoid a 'scandalous situation.' The judge refused her both child support and damages because Cohen never acknowledged being the father, regretted his involvement with her, and never provided anything for the child's needs. Furthermore, she was older than he, and the judge may have considered her less his victim and more his seducer.[12]

An 1864 landmark case often cited and discussed throughout fin-de-siècle France established a precedent involving a young girl seduced by an older man. In the village of Vire in western Normandy, fifteen-year-old Mademoiselle G..., a baker's daughter, was delivering bread to Monsieur L..., a thirty-three-year-old married man of considerable property.[13] She claimed that he seduced her after her initial resistance. Their relations continued, and when she was eighteen she left for Paris. By the time she was twenty-six she had six children. Then, in 1861, Mlle G... brought a case for damages against L... before the Civil Tribunal in Vire to ask for 70,000 francs from him. She produced his letters as proof of his paternity and evidence that he had paid the wet nurse for the children. The local tribunal awarded in her favor, ordering L... to pay her damages as well as child support for all her children. He appealed, but lost. Unsatisfied, he took his case to the Cour de Cassation, the highest court in France, where he lost again.

Themes of honor run throughout this case. It might have been a loss of honor for Mlle G...'s father to admit openly that he allowed his daughter deliver bread to this man. Judges and the community could have accused him of inadequately supervising his teenage daughter.[14] Judges repeatedly referred to 'honor' when speaking of her. She could have been an 'honorable mother' and good worker, they said, if only his seduction had not prevented her. Furthermore, the judges declared that he had behaved 'dishonorably' in seducing an innocent young girl whose honor had been beyond reproach.

Magistrates had the power to declare financial settlements as well as restore a woman's honor that a man had stolen. To use the language of melodramas, a judge could play the role of the hero to save the woman's honor from the villainous scoundrel, even ex post facto. But, judges only did so if a woman had been young, innocent, and pure and had then tried to lead a virtuous life as a mother after succumbing to the man's strength, entreaties, or false promises. In this case, judges ruled that since L... had behaved dishonorably, he had to repair the damage he had caused. The courts also blamed him for her condition, and provided a sufficient financial award so she could resume her life as an 'honorable working woman.' Magistrates' decisions demonstrated to the world that she had been innocent, and her loss of virtue was not her fault but his.[15] She was trying to do the honorable thing and raise her children. She could have behaved dishonorably and abandoned all of them at the foundling hospice in Paris, as so many in her position had.[16] Finally, in awarding in her favor, the judges restored her family's good name in the village. This path-breaking decision set the stage for increasing numbers of women to sue for the damages of seduction and to win.

Emblematic cases from 1875 and 1901 provide examples of women winning their suits. In 1875, a judge ruled that a putative father had to pay damages and a *pension alimentaire* because he had written to the mother promising support: 'Whether or not my father approves of you as my wife, I will not be less the father of your child, and as a result I will contribute as much as possible to make you happy. Believe me, you can always count on my aid and protection.' Although the judge viewed these spontaneous promises as having the power of a legal contract, several lawyers faulted the judge's ruling in this case, complaining that the man had neither promised marriage nor seduced her fraudulently – implying that he had therefore behaved honorably. Nonetheless the judge's ruling in favor of the mother stood.[17] In

1892, a Paris Civil Tribunal allowed a mother to have both reparations and child support, in part because she was a fifteen-year-old domestic servant whose forty-one-year-old master had abused his authority by seducing her. The Appeals Court in Paris supported the award of damages but denied her child support.[18] In 1901, the Cour de Cassation reaffirmed that a man had to make reparations for seduction and a broken marriage promise. Throughout this period, numerous issues of the *Gazette des Tribunaux* contained dozens of reports with headlines such as 'Seduction – Pregnancy – Paternity of the Seducer – Damages.'

The key in having the courts award the single mother reparations was having her prove, usually by a written letter from the putative father, that he seduced her after promising marriage – and that until then she had been honorable. The mother and her lawyer had to make clear that she was asking for damages for herself because of the seduction, and that she was not filing a paternity suit. Court decisions raised and only partially resolved complex issues, deciding that consensual non-marital sexual relations did not entitle a woman to damages; rather they had to have been preceded by force, fraud, abuse of authority, or a written promise of marriage, that is, dishonorable action by men.[19] Awarding damages to single mothers for the wrongs men did to them indicates a changing climate of attitudes toward seduction, honor, paternity, the family, and the rights of both men and women toward the end of the century. Yet, as we will see, men continued to have the right to deny paternity.

Disavowal of paternity

In a typical double standard, a married man had the right to commit adultery, unless he brought his mistress into his marital home, but he did not have to bear responsibility for the resulting child. A married woman, on the contrary, had no legal right to commit adultery, and her husband could even kill her and her lover if he caught them together in his home. Needless to say, a woman held no such right over her husband.[20] A married woman's sexual fidelity was the key element in maintaining family integrity, the husband's line of inheritance, and the public moral order. Therefore, the Penal Code considered a woman's adultery a criminal offense. If the husband could prove his wife's adultery, the Code punished her by a fine and a prison term ranging from three months to two years. Judges, however, were lax in enforcing penalties. And rather than bringing criminal charges against his adulterous wife and her lover, the husband often sought separation, divorce (after it became legally possible in 1884), and to disavow paternity of his wife's child. Moreover, if the wife went to prison for adultery and the husband had not disowned her children prior to her sentencing, he would have sole responsibility for them. Denying paternity preserved a man's honor more, and hurt him and his children less, than sending their mother to jail for adultery.

Legally, paternity belonged only to the man who was officially married to the mother of his child, but a married man could disavow paternity when he could prove his wife's adultery, and thus her dishonorable behavior. According to article 312 of the Civil Code, 'the husband is the father of the child born within marriage,' responsible for contributing materially and morally to rearing and educating the child, acting as a father, and providing the child with a civil status and inheritance. Yet the same article went on to say that the husband could disavow the child if he could prove that he could not possibly have physically cohabited with his wife during the legal time of conception.[21] A law of 6 December 1850 reinforced the Civil Code, making it easier for a married man to deny paternity of a child born to his wife. The bases of proof were: significant geographical separation; his physical inability to conceive children; and her departure, with the knowledge of friends and family, from the marital household. These conditions had to have existed during the legal time of conception (estimated at 180–300 days before the birth of the child). A wife who concealed the pregnancy and birth from her husband would provide further evidence that the child was not his.

A man directed his reproductive and marriage strategies toward ensuring an inheritance for his heirs and maintaining his family honor and bloodline. Therefore, his biological connection to his children was of prime importance. Before blood groupings or the use of genetic testing, those family connections depended on the sexual behavior of the women. A wife's public infidelity resulting in a child doubly dishonored him, and when he went to court to absolve himself of paternity for that child, he could save both his honor and his property. If his legal action to disavow paternity of a child born to his wife was successful, that child could no longer carry his name or inherit a portion of his estate. Marriage linked biological paternity and social fatherhood. By denying biological paternity of a child born of his wife's adultery, a man also denied his social and emotional responsibilities of fatherhood.

A man may have found it preferable, or more honorable, to protect his family's property than to admit the shame that might accompany publicly acknowledging his wife's adultery. A husband was supposed to protect his wife's sexual honor and fidelity as a component of his own honor, much as a father was to guard his daughter's sexual virtue. When a wife's adultery had become public knowledge, she had already shamed her husband and deprived him of some element of his honor. He, therefore, had little to lose and much to gain by denying paternity; at least he could salvage elements of his pride and property. Taking action to preserve his family property and name from those outside his bloodline enabled him to assert control and regain some honor and respect in his family and community. A husband's denial of a child born to his wife, when he did not think the child was of his blood, was meant to keep order in his family.[22] The denial of paternity could create disorder in the short term to maintain order in the longer term.

Children of an adulterous woman posed problems to society when they entered the family of a man who was not biologically their father and polluted his bloodline. Although anthropologist Mary Douglas did not specifically discuss children of adultery, these children were (to use her apt phrase) 'matter out of place' and a source of pollution for the legally and religiously sanctioned conjugal families, their honor, and the transmission of their property.[23] Because female adultery was a far greater taboo than male adultery, women were the greater polluters of families. Their children, as symbols of disruptive matter outside the established familial order, represented a danger to the established family ties and the honor of the men. When a husband disavowed those children, he not only deprived them of his name and a portion of his legacy, he also engaged in a ritual cleansing of his honor and family connections.[24]

In court cases, women did not seek to disrupt the power of the male bloodline, but they did assert power to restore their own honor as they shamed their betrayers and won financial benefit. However, blood relations trumped female agency. Since honor was linked to property, and blood relations were an aspect of the mechanism of power, according to Michel Foucault, then denial of paternity kept inheritance along bloodlines intact and reinforced male power. Foucault's analysis of the discourse of blood and power, and his statement that 'the blood relation long remained an important element in the mechanisms of power, its manifestations, and its rituals' applies to discussions of paternity and progeny.[25] In fin-de-siècle France, the courts customarily assigned or denied paternity in terms of blood, but without biological proof. Moreover, the distinction between blood kinship and emotional kinship was not clear-cut. In the absence of blood and genetic tests, court-determined paternity was complex, involving language about past behavior and public perceptions. Sex became a public issue encompassing the mother, father, the community, and the courts. In cases of paternity denial, as in those brought by women against men for damages, power resided in the civil courts with the reliance on the verbal and written testimony of the men and women involved – but it relied especially on the word of family and neighbors. As a point of honor, married men insisted on being the *géniteurs*, tied to the child by blood or semen. Unmarried men protected their right to choose, or deny, their progeny.

Two major questions surround married men's disavowal of paternity. First, was it more honorable to deny paternity and thus deprive the child of a legitimate civil status and family ties than it was to live with the idea that marriage indicates paternity, as custom and the Code dictated? Second, was it more honorable to accuse one's wife of adultery in a public courtroom than to provide one's name and property to progeny who may not have been of the same blood? Court cases involving female adultery suggest that a wife and her lover stole her husband's honor, and her husband reclaimed it by disavowing paternity. Furthermore, by disavowing paternity a man protected his honorable reputation and that of his family, as well as his property.[26]

To deny paternity, a husband most frequently summoned family and community witnesses to testify on his behalf that they knew his wife left his home to be with her lover.[27] Men rarely invoked other possible evidence of her adultery, such as their own impotence or infertility. A husband sometimes claimed ignorance of his wife's pregnancy and childbirth as evidence that he was not the father of her child.[28] The key was her *public* infidelity; if friends, family and community knew about it, his honor would dictate that he divorce his wife and deny paternity of the child she conceived. His successful legal action disavowing paternity required an alteration of the child's birth certificate, removing his name as the father and as the child's surname, if it had been there in the first place.[29] This was not complicated. In more than half the available records, the mother did not provide a father's name – the birth certificate simply said, '*père non dénommé*,' and she gave the child her own name or that of her lover. A successful disavowal suit also meant the man would have nothing to do with the child. This was not often a problem since his wife usually had already left his home before she gave birth.

At first glance, it would appear that if a man went to court to deny paternity of his wife's child, that public action would dishonor him and show the world he was a cuckold. In most cases, however, his family and community already knew, so he lost little by going to court. Moreover, action against his wife could reinstate his honor and pride. Avoiding ridicule resulting from a wife's adultery was, as Nye has discussed, paramount to protecting honor.[30] Denial of paternity was probably better than going to prison for stabbing one's rival, an action to which Henri Gaveau resorted. Gaveau, a forty-year-old roofer, had married a 'charming woman' who left him and went to live with one of his friends. In an effort to avenge his honor, Gaveau invited his rival to his house. Although quite cordial throughout the meeting, as Gaveau was seeing the man to the door he stabbed him seven times in the back; his rival collapsed but was not gravely wounded. Gaveau went to prison where he awaited trial on assault charges.[31]

The key in determining if a husband won his case for disavowal of paternity, which he usually did, was that his wife had 'abandoned the marital home.' Realizing its legal and persuasive power, men commonly used this phrase in a formulaic fashion. Disavowal, however, was not a simple procedure; it required that a man bring a civil suit against his wife and prove her adultery. The testimony of witnesses – family, friends, and neighbors – usually supplied the proof that the wife had committed adultery. In a typical case, Oscar Caron went to court in June 1898 to disavow Raymond Caron, his wife's son born the previous month, because of 'the physical impossibility of cohabitation' during the legal period of conception. Members of their community testified that his wife had 'abandoned him,' had left their 'marital home' in Cambrai during the legal time of conception and had gone to Paris where she had an 'irregular conduct.' Furthermore, she hid her pregnancy from him, and he only found out about the child from the list of recent births published in the local newspaper; she had returned to Cambrai to give birth. He may have been suspicious in order to have looked at that list in the first place. He brought the charges as soon as he learned of the baby's birth. The judge, however, took two years to evaluate all of the documents and witnesses' testimony and decide in this case. This delay was not unusual in paternity cases because of the need to gather evidence from both sides, and the general sluggishness of legal proceedings.[32]

In 1902, a year after lodging his court action, Victor Rouelle, an employee at the gas works in the working-class Paris suburb of Aubervilliers, won his suit against his wife, Eugènie, and her lover, Jules Lemaire, as her accomplice. Rouelle successfully disavowed a girl born in 1897 and a boy born in 1900. The daughter had Victor Ruelle's name on her birth certificate as her father, but by 1900 Eugènie Rouelle and Lemaire were cohabiting, and the boy's birth certificate bore Lemaire's name as the father, even though Eugènie was still legally married to Victor Rouelle, and according to the Civil Code, Rouelle was the legal father. Rouelle based his demand on the 'moral impossibility' of having lived with his wife during the legal period of conception for either child because she was not living in his home, but with a lover. He also filed a criminal suit accusing his wife of adultery with Jules Lemaire. His wife and Lemaire were convicted of the *délit* (misdemeanor) of adultery and were fined. Moreover, Rouelle also brought forward witnesses who attested that his wife displayed 'irregular conduct,' thus putting the dishonor on her and attempting to reclaim his own honor. Eugènie Rouelle admitted that before her adultery with Lemaire she had sexual relations with another man and that her daughter was born of that relationship.[33]

When a husband and his witnesses mentioned a wife's immorality, his wife usually did not contest that ignominious charge. One man brought nine witnesses attesting that his wife abandoned her marital home and lived in a *hôtel meublé*, which indicated furnished rooms that were often the alleged abode of prostitutes and women of loose morality. These witnesses reported that a man (but only one) joined her in the evening and did not leave until morning, adding that they never saw her at the home of her husband, who lived alone.[34] In another example, in 1901, Louis Bail brought his case for disavowal of paternity against his wife, Charlotte. Unlike other cases of paternity denial, Bail and his wife were not in the process of a marital separation or divorce. On the baby's birth certificate, Charlotte Bail gave her maiden name, and in the space for the father's name, she left only a blank. To win his suit, Louis Bail had to prove the 'impossibility of conjugal cohabitation at the time of conception.' A witness on his behalf testified that Charlotte Bail had loose morals and adulterous relations during the time of conception. That witness further alleged that Charlotte believed that the child was not her husband's, which was why she refused to provide a father's name. Charlotte did not contest the paternity.[35]

Generally, however, disavowal of paternity did not necessitate that witnesses specifically state that a woman had 'loose morals' or an 'irregular conduct' – tropes that might indicate prostitution. To accuse her of having left her husband's bed for that of another man provided sufficient evidence of her adultery. Almost all the cases for disavowal of paternity were rather formulaic with witnesses supplying the oral testimony that the husband and wife did not live together at the legal time of conception, and that she had taken a lover. The testimony of witnesses was crucial; they provided the evidence of the very public nature of the women's adultery. Victor Stier denied his paternity of a girl, Augustine, whom his wife delivered in 1900 and whose birth certificate stated that she was the daughter of Augustine Béné; the father was not named. Victor Stier declared, and many witnesses agreed, that his wife left their conjugal home in 1899 and since then she had intimate relations with Henri Girard, which continued during the legal period of conception of young Augustine. If that were not sufficient grounds for paternity denial, at the legal period of conception Stier was away from home performing his military service.[36] When Georges Gaudy won his civil action to disavow a baby boy born to his wife in 1902, he had only one witness, Mlle Tixier, who worked as a domestic servant in the same household as his wife. She attested that during the legal time of conception Mme Gaudy never visited her husband, nor did he come to see her. She was convinced that when Mme Gaudy became pregnant, it did not result from relations with her husband, and Mme Gaudy had told her as much. The tribunal found this testimony sufficient to establish Gaudy's adultery. Furthermore, the birth certificate revealed the absence of a father's name.[37]

One characteristic case based on witnesses and letters dates from 1907 when August Roux, an employee in the administration of Postes et Télégraphe, sought to deny the paternity of a child born to his wife while she was still legally married to him. One witness said, 'At the time when Roux told me about his wife's childbirth, I knew only that she had left him eight or nine months before.' Two other witnesses put the departure of Mme Roux from her husband 'well before the birth of the child.' They added that Roux was surprised by the child's birth and did not even know that his wife was pregnant. Her estrangement from her husband was borne out by her own testimony that after she left her husband she did not have any relations with him. In a letter to her husband at the time of divorce proceedings, but prior to the court case he brought denying paternity, she wrote: 'What do you want to do with my child? ... It shows that you really have no honor and are nothing but a coward to have as your instrument of vengeance a little being who is not yours. My child is cherished, lacks for nothing, and does not need the protection of a stranger. I do not think it surprises you to learn that my daughter is not yours!' Unsurprisingly, the judge allowed him to disown the girl. The mother's admission that the child was not her husband's was typical. Cases in which the husband denied paternity of his wife's child were generally uncontested, but still required court proceedings.[38] A man's honor was a complicated matter. He could divorce his wife and disavow the child, but in doing so, he also had to behave honorably and not harm the child. In paternity disavowal cases, judges attributed bad conduct and dishonor to the mother and her lover, but not her husband.

Some couples had not lived together for years. In 1907, Pierre Dauget, a roadman in Paris brought a suit against his wife, Marie Dauguet, and Jean Bourre, a sculptor, as her accomplice. Pierre Dauguet and Marie Chaumont had married in 1880 and she gave birth to a son in 1881. However, shortly after their son's birth, Marie left her son and husband, disappearing from his life. Pierre then went to Paris in search of work. Twenty-six years later, in 1907, Marie asked Pierre Dauguet for his consent to the marriage of her oldest daughter, who was legally his child. This is how he learned Marie's whereabouts, as well as of the existence of this daughter born in the nearby department of the Eure. He thereafter learned of six other children born to Marie, all of whom had his name listed as their father because he was still legally married to Marie, although he had not lived with, nor seen her for over twenty-five years. He won his case to disavow all seven children.[39]

When a man brought a case for paternity disavowal to court, it usually indicated that the marriage had irreparably broken down and the couple was legally separated and divorcing, living apart from one another. Since divorce usually occurred three years after the legal separation, many a woman's child who was not her husband's was born during that time. These were often the children disavowed. In August 1900, Louis Bisselin, a retired administrator, successfully disavowed the paternity of Ernest Louis whom his wife, Ernestine Louise delivered in December 1899. During that year they had separated, but were not yet divorced. According to the terms of article 312, in case of divorce or separation, the husband could disavow a child born 300 or more days after the separation or divorce, as long as the couple did not have the same residence.[40] When Mme Ragon filed for divorce in 1911, she received a ruling of non-conciliation and lived apart from her husband but did not get divorced. When she gave birth to a daughter in 1914, her husband disavowed the child.[41] Camille Lucien Prudhomme initiated divorce proceedings when his wife left his home and went to live with her lover in Nice. She had a child during the course of the divorce proceedings, but named Camille as the father. Camille filed not only for divorce, but also for paternity disavowal.[42] Even when a woman gave birth after the divorce, if during the possible time of conception she was still legally married, her husband was still considered the child's father and could disavow the baby – if he could prove that she lived with another during that time.[43] This action may have been less a question of his honor, than of absolving himself of moral and financial responsibility for a child who was not his.

Few mothers contested the disavowal. In such situations, both husband and wife summoned witnesses who testified about whether the couple had spent time together during the legal time of conception. If a man continued to have sexual relations with his wife, if he visited her or she went to visit him, even though she had a lover, he could not succeed in his efforts to disavow those children.[44] In one instance, a man failed to find witnesses to his wife's adultery and to his cessation of sexual relations with his wife during the possible time of conception. Witnesses agreed that the couple lived separately at one time, but they did not know if it was a continuous separation or if they had re-established their life in common. The husband's brother testified that he had heard that his brother did not live with his wife and that she had sexual relations with another man, and had children by him. However, he could not positively affirm that his brother never had relations with his wife since he saw his brother only three or four times a year. All agreed that she left her husband for another man, but no witness could testify that husband and wife were never together during the legal time of conception. He lost his suit to disavow the child.[45]

Disavowal of paternity was irreversible. A night watchman divorced his wife in 1896 and disavowed the child she had given birth to in 1895. However, a short time after the divorce, he and his wife resumed life together and he said that he had always considered the child as his own, that he had helped raise him, and had supported him both materially and affectively as a father. His wife died in 1921 and in 1928 he sought to adopt this child, now a thirty-three-year-old man. The court rejected his attempt to adopt because he had once disavowed paternity.[46]

In fin-de-siècle France, with the deep-rooted political and social concerns about degeneration, depopulation, and the nation's future, having and protecting children became an honorable thing for men to do – from the point of view of the politicians and the judiciary. Motherhood had always been honorable for women. However, in situations of paternity denial, the man's honor and blood ties with his family and his biological children took legal precedence over the well-being of extranuptial children, despite the child-centered rhetoric of the Third Republic. A man still found it more honorable to deny paternity of his wife's child, and thus deprive the child of a legitimate status and family ties, than it was to live in a marriage with legal but not biological paternity, especially if his family and community knew of his wife's adultery.

* * *

Since paternity derives from sex, when issues of paternity go to court sexual power is formulated and contested in a public space. Discourse in the Civil Tribunals, on the most apparent level, focused on children's survival and on protecting the property of the father and his family; but it was also about sexual power. Women and men used their power in court, in a complex interplay between law and gender as they navigated and made use of the courts, of the law, and of the current concepts of gendered honor within and outside marriage.

Marriage served both emotional and material functions. In addition to procreation, raising a family, and transmission of property, marriage also served as a bond of mutual affection and pleasure.[47] When men and women took their affection and pleasure elsewhere, that aspect of conjugal family life faded. Law and customs tolerated male adultery without imposing consequences, but for women, any form of adultery was fraught with dishonor because it would weaken the power and property of her husband, and indicate her sexuality as being beyond his control and outside the social and moral order. Cases of disavowal of paternity, and those when a woman sought damages, indicate the public nature of intimate lives. However, only a few men denied paternity or were objects of women's suits for damages. The untold majority, whose life stories never appear in the records, may have been responsible fathers, whether or not they were legally married to the mothers or biologically related to her children.

In a culture in which a man's reproductive and marriage strategy depended upon transmission of patrimony, certainty that the children his wife bore were biologically his own held prime importance for his preservation of his property and honor. A married woman was presumed to be faithful, and women's sexual behavior was key to the maintenance of masculine honor. If she were publicly unfaithful, she took his honor from him. To regain that honor, he had to renounce the children and his wife for her immoral behavior. Likewise, for a young unmarried woman, virginity was equated with virtue and a symbol of her honor. If a man stole her virtue by means of fraud or a broken marriage promise, leaving her with a child, he also stole her honor. At the turn of the twentieth century, women increasingly, and publicly, accused men of behaving dishonorably, and in so doing could restore their honor by successfully putting the blame on the men. Perhaps inspired by the feminist movement, perhaps as a result of increased participation in urban life, and perhaps even as a result of state policies that increasingly empowered them as mothers, women were publicly acting in a more sexually liberated manner. Men, who had sought to avoid the courts, were forced there by the women, and by circumstances, to disavow children who were not biologically theirs.

Honor and dishonor were transferable in the public arena of the courts, especially when it pertained to paternity, property, and progeny. To transfer honor, both women and men had to have held it in their own rights, which they did in fin-de-siècle France.

Notes

1. Robert A. Nye, *Masculinity and Male Codes of Honor in Modern France* (New York: Oxford University Press, 1993), p. vii.

André-Jean Arnaud, *Essai d'analyse structurale du Code civil français: La Règle du jeu dans la paix bourgeoise* (Paris: Librairie générale de droit et de jurisprudence, 1973); Suzanne Desan, *The Family on Trial in Revolutionary France* (Berkeley: University of California Press, 2004).

3. For a more detailed discussion and evidence from court cases see Rachel G. Fuchs, *Contested Paternity: Constructing Families in Modern France* (Baltimore: Johns Hopkins University Press, 2008), pp. 68–96. For further elaboration on the reasons for the mid-century shift, see specifically pp. 75–80.

4. Historians can only know the frequency of prosecutions for infanticide, not the actual rates. See Fuchs, *Contested*, p. 143; idem., *Abandoned Children: Foundlings and Child Welfare in Nineteenth-Century France* (Albany: State University of New York Press, 1984), pp. 142–5; Albert Millet, *La Séduction* (Paris: Cotillon, 1876), p. 138.

5. I found no evidence in the records of the Civil Tribunal of Paris of men suing women for breach of a marriage promise.

6. Alexandre Dumas (fils), *Les Femmes qui tuent et les femmes qui votent* (Paris: Calmann Lévy, 1880), p. 27.

7. Paul Coulet and Albert Vanois, *Etude sur la recherche de la paternité* (Paris: Marescq, 1880), pp. 114–28; Millet, *La Séduction*, pp. 117, 179–81.

8. Millet, *La Séduction*, p. 61.

9. Coulet and Vaunois, *Etude sur la recherche de la paternité*, p. 142.

10. Janine Mossuz-Lavau, *Les lois de l'amour: Les politiques de la sexualité en France de 1950 à nos jours* (Paris: Payot, 1991), pp. 189–90.

11. Fuchs, *Contested*, pp. 83–96, 110–12.

12. The judgments of the Tribunal Civil (D1U5), Assistance Judiciaire (AJ) at the Archives de Paris (AP), contain court cases of suits for *désaveu de paternité, dommages-intérêts,* and *pension alimentaire.* I examined a random sample of forty-five bound volumes (one in twenty) from over 800 volumes of civil suits of all varieties brought to the courts with the aid of *Assistance judiciaire* of the Tribunal Civil judgments for Paris for the years 1890 through 1939 to get a composite picture of the less well-to-do segments of society, those who qualified for what we might call legal aid. For this case see AP, Tribunal Civil, D1U5 (AJ 100), January 1906, case 2955 of 1905, Judgment of 18 January 1906. See also D1U5 (AJ 150), November 1909, case 3609 of 1909, Judgment of 16 November 1909. In at least half the available cases, women won their suits.

13. Sources for this case come from the *Gazette des Tribunaux* (*GT*) (10 September 1864): 885–6; and Millet, *La Séduction*, pp. 69–72.

14. As Robert A. Nye, cogently argued, 'A man's ability to control his daughter's sexuality counted heavily in his perception of his own honor.' See Nye, *Masculinity*, p. 30.

15. For a discussion of men as cads and scoundrels in cases of bigamy and abortion see Angus McLaren, *The Trials of Masculinity: Policing Sexual Boundaries 1870–1930* (Chicago: University of Chicago Press, 1997), pp. 31, 38, 86–8. For a discussion of gendered narratives and melodramas in the courtroom see Fuchs, *Contested*, pp. 62–3, 68–9, 93–4, 240–1.

16. Rachel G. Fuchs, *Poor and Pregnant in Paris: Strategies for Survival in the Nineteenth Century* (New Brunswick: Rutgers University Press, 1992), pp. 219–26.

17. Jugement de Tribunal civil de la Seine, 24 February 1876 in Coulet and Vanois, *Etude sur la recherche de la paternité*, pp. 71–5.

18. *GT*, 24 March 1892 and 12 October 1992. Seduction by abuse of authority is the legal terminology for *le droit de cuissage,* and could range from sexual harassment

to unwanted sexual advances, and rape. Marie-Victoire Louis, *Le Droit de cuissage: France, 1860–1930* (Les Editions de l'Atelier/Editions Ouvrières, 1994), pp. 179, 200–9. In several court cases the judge awarded in favor of the young woman accusing the man of *l'abus de situation sociale et d'autorité*.

19. Léon Giraud, *La Vérité sur la recherche de paternité* (Paris: F. Pichon, 1888), p. 31; Francis Félix Dubois, 'Les Fiançailles et promesses de mariage en droit français,' thesis, Université de Rennes, Faculté de droit (Angers: A. Burdin, 1897), pp. 142–68.

20. For a husband's adultery see article 230 of the Civil Code (repealed in 1884) and paragraph two of article 324 of the Penal Code for a husband's right to kill his wife and her lover if he found them *en flagrant délit* in their marital home. For a discussion of property and bourgeois male honor, see Nye, *Masculinity*, chap. 4.

21. One of the major redactors of the Code, Bigot de Préameneu, was obsessed with protecting the male line of inheritance and provided a variety of ways in which a husband could deny the paternity of his wife's child. P.-A. Fenet, *Recueil complet des travaux préparatoires du Code civil* (Paris: 1827), Livre Premier, *Des personnes*, Titre septième, *De la paternité et de la filiation*, présentation au Corps législatif et exposé des motifs par M. Bigot-Préameneau, 2 germinal an XI (24 mars 1803), vol. X, pp. 135–41, in François Ewald (ed.), *Naissance du Code Civil* (Paris: Flammarion, 1989), pp. 223–8.

22. Emile Carbon, *Le Désaveu de paternité*, Thèse pour le doctorat des sciences juridiques (Montpellier: Firman et Montane, 1925), pp. 20–2.

23. Mary Douglas, *Purity and Danger: an Analysis of the Concepts of Pollution and Taboo* (London: Routledge, [1966] 2002), pp. 35, 166–74.

24. Discourse on hygiene, pollution and degeneration was not uncommon, but no other scholar has explicitly linked Douglas's concept of pollution and matter out of place to female adultery and family dynamics. For women as the embodiment of disorder and degeneration see the works of Gustave Le Bon and Gabriel Tarde cited by Daniel Pick, *Faces of Degeneration: a European Disorder, c. 1848–c. 1918* (New York: Cambridge University Press, 1989), pp. 40–2, 92.

25. Michel Foucault, *The History of Sexuality: an Introduction*, vol. 1 (New York: Vintage, 1990), pp. 64, 83, 87, 147–8; quotation from p. 147.

26. Nye, *Masculinity*, pp. vii, 9.

27. If a wife were still living with her husband, even though she committed adultery, and the neighborhood knew, her husband did not stand a chance of winning his case of paternity disavowal.

28. See AP, Tribunal Civil, D1U5, *Assistance judiciaire*. All cases for *désaveu de paternité* were recorded in a formulaic fashion, providing circumstantial evidence indicating that the wife had left the marital home. Judgments of the Civil Tribunal usually occurred a year after the man first brought his case to court. I supplemented these sources with those brought by a man without aid of *Assistance judiciaire*, usually those who had some degree of financial resources.

29. The right to carry the patronymic is important because the patronymic is a form of property.

30. Nye, *Masculinity*, p. 171.

31. *Le Matin*, 9 March 1925: 2B. His fate is unknown. For another case of disavowal that appeared in the press see *Le Matin*, 22 February 1923: 1D.

32. AP, D1U5, Tribunal Civil (AJ10) August 1900, case 3980 of 1898.

33. AP, D1U5, Tribunal Civil, (AJ30) March 1902, case 5154 of 1901.

34. AP, D1U5, Tribunal Civil, (AJ80) 27 December 1904.

35. AP, D1U5, Tribunal Civil, (AJ30) March 1902, case 688 of 1901.
36. AP, D1U5, Tribunal Civil (AJ30) March 1902, case 1249 of 1901.
37. AP, D1U5, Tribunal Civil (AJ 60) December 1903, case 4878 of 1902. For similar stories of witnesses attesting that the wife left her husband to live with her lover see: AP, Tribunal Civil, D1U5 (AJ 80) December 1904, cases 5737 of 1903 and 3885 of 1904.
38. Arch. Paris, D1U5, Tribunal Civil (AJ 120) 1–30 April 1907, cases 3541 and 3542 of 1905, Judgment of 23 April 1907.
39. AP, D1U5, Tribunal Civil (AJ120) April 1909, case 392 of 1907.
40. AP, D1U5, Tribunal Civil (AJ10) August 1900.
41. AP, DU5, Tribunal Civil, 1ère chamber (not AJ), case 1804 January–June 1915.
42. AP, DU5, Tribunal Civil, 1ère chamber (not AJ), case 9317 January–June 1915. For a similar case see AP, D1U5, Tribunal Civil (AJ 208), March1913, case 5844 of 1912.
43. AP, DU5, Tribunal Civil, 1ère chamber (not AJ), case 531 January–June 1915.
44. AP, D1U5, Tribunal Civil (AJ 610), 27 December 1904.
45. AP, D1U5, Tribunal Civil (AJ80), December 1904, case 610 of 1904.
46. AP, Requêtes d'adoption dans le Chambre du Conseil du Tribunal Civil de la Seine, Côte, 1277 W, Judgment of 30 November 1928, case CE57841.
47. For a conceptualization of the material and emotional attributes of families see Hans Medick and David Warren Sabean (eds), *Interest and Emotion: Essays on the Study of Family and Kinship* (Cambridge: Cambridge University Press, 1994).

8

Shaming Men: Feminist Honor and the Sexual Double Standard in Belle Époque France

Andrea Mansker

The Second International Congress of Women's Charities and Institutions held at the Universal Exposition of 1900 featured a debate on the 'repeal of all exceptional measures applied to women in the sphere of morals.' Planned under the patronage of the French government, this event was one of two major congresses spearheaded by republican feminists at the turn of the century world's fair in Paris. Considered the more 'moderate' of the two by scholars, the Congress of Women's Charities focused its philanthropic attention on combating national degeneration and shied away from addressing overtly political issues such as the vote.[1] Despite their reluctance to discuss women's suffrage, congress members nonetheless spotlighted sexual politics. Following a report condemning state-regulated prostitution by the secretary-general of the French branch of the International Abolitionist Federation (FAI) Auguste de Morsier, Maria Pognon took the floor and attempted to infuse a more radical feminist hue into the debate. Pognon, pacifist free-thinker and president of the Ligue française pour le droit des femmes (LFDF), argued that women's right to control their own bodies had to be highlighted as central to the 'moral question' and insisted that the double sexual standard touched much more broadly on the lives of middle-class women than Morsier had indicated. Framing her attack in terms she felt would generate the most outrage among the majority of bourgeois feminists present,[2] Pognon asserted that:

> There is a right that does not belong to the man, but that he has accorded to himself very gratuitously, just as he procures all rights in our society. The man does not have the right to contract diseases and to transmit them to his home [*foyer*]. The man does not have the right to marry a pure and well-raised young woman [*jeune fille*] when he knows that he is completely unworthy of this young woman.

Basing her indictment of men on widely publicized medical reports about the 'venereal peril,' Pognon argued that these realities called for action among

169

women in particular: 'I would like for a woman to make her voice heard on this subject; I find that we do not rise up violently enough against such a denial of justice towards our sex.'[3]

Attempting to link the plight of 'honorable women' [*honnêtes femmes*] to those members of the female sex who lacked 'the means to live honorably,' Pognon rather hypocritically highlighted a situation that applied principally to middle-class households. Dramatically relating a doctor's account of a male patient who contracted a venereal disease just prior to his wedding, Pognon claimed that the doctor, being a 'very honorable man,' told his patient, 'You are a coward, and I do not understand why you do not buy a revolver instead.' Though the fiancé authorized the doctor to inform the bride's father that he was ill and that he needed to call off the engagement, the father chose not to cancel the wedding due to financial considerations. Pognon's anecdote had its desired effect; the meeting notes indicate 'lively protestations' and 'exclamations' among the audience. Pognon followed up her points immediately by endorsing a legal proposal made by prominent abolitionist Dr Louis Fiaux. She demanded that 'any man who infects a woman – whether his own, or I will gladly say another, but especially his own – be sent to prison.' Her speech was followed by a unanimous congressional vote approving a single morality for both sexes.[4]

For Pognon, as for many republican feminists at the turn of the century, the 'moral question' focused not only on prostitution and legal equality, but belonged to a particular sexual economy regulated by the French honor system. In her speech, Pognon publicly denounced men for failing in their fundamental protective duty to women and sought to expose the harmful effects of male sexual irresponsibility on the family. Furthermore, her focus on honor and familial patrimony left little doubt as to which class concerned her, ironically reinforcing the double standard to an extent. Branding men's actions as 'cowardly' and arguing that such behavior constituted a 'denial of justice towards our sex,' Pognon suggested that middle-class women had a particular obligation to speak publicly about these matters. The nineteenth-century honor code dictated that the family's reputation had to be safeguarded at all costs and surrounded the household's private and sexual affairs with a veil of silence.[5] Yet, as Pognon's statements reveal, pre-war feminists now seized on the language of honor to expose men's private sexual violations to public view.

Scholarship on 'social feminists' during the Third Republic emphasizes their liberal rhetoric on legalized prostitution and the double moral standard. The turn of the century abolitionist fight for individual rights and its defense of common law coincided with the republican coalition governments' counteroffensive against the Church and against nationalist, anti-Dreyfusard agitators. Historians have also elucidated the Protestant roots of this strain of feminist moral philanthropy, which allowed women to position themselves and their own role at the center of the 'social question.'[6] 'Social feminism' is a term scholars apply to a prominent bourgeois, largely Protestant faction of the women's movement during the Third Republic. This particular brand of feminism can be described as a subset of what Karen Offen refers to as 'relational feminism,' but the qualification is primarily meant to explain how this cohort positioned itself in relation to the growing struggle for women's suffrage and more radical demands for sexual liberty.[7]

Positing a broader framework within which to examine campaigners' understanding of citizenship and abolitionism, this chapter explores reformist feminists' new political voice on sexuality from the perspective of the French honor code. Studies based on prescriptions of honor in the nineteenth century beg the important question of how individuals of both sexes applied the code to their daily lives, and a survey of men and women's concrete experiences points to revealing gaps between rhetoric and practice. My study suggests that in their speeches and published appeals, feminists engaged in a public shaming ritual of men, empowered as they were by their particular role in the honor system as custodians of the family's sexual virtue and unblemished lineage. By taking independent action to defend the household's honor against men's corrupt sexual practices, women positioned themselves as moral regulators of male sexual behavior and transformed the code to legitimate their own roles as actors in civil and civic society. As such, feminists considered 'moderate' by historians adopted an exclusionary masculine code of behavior to formulate an early critique of the personal dimensions of republican citizenship.

'There is only one honor, or there is no honor:'[8] a democratized code?

The Larousse *Grand Dictionnaire* article on *honneur* described the difficulties of defining the word's meaning in nineteenth-century France given the concept's national and class-based adaptations over the past centuries. The author pointed out that the French had borrowed the term from the ancient Romans, who privileged 'honor' as a regulatory and status-based notion. However, he noted that the French had developed a completely different interpretation. Among the Romans, 'The honorable man was he who had served in public offices. The "honor" of a family consisted less in the virtue of each of its members than in the high functions they had exercised.'[9] The article implied that the modern French code, by contrast, did not principally emphasize public and political functions, but rather, the private virtues of the family and each individual member's worth. Indicating that the system of honor in France stemmed from the country's feudal origins and its system of noble patrimony, the author argued that democratization had altered the code's character, but not its overall form. At base, the word meant 'high regard for one's self, corroborated by the respect of others.' Furthermore, despite variations in the class-based interpretations of honor, 'all of these forms of honor rest on common principles, which are composed of a single virtue. In this sense, men of all classes understand as soon as this word "honor" is exchanged between them.'[10]

Though French honor partly referred to male 'virtue, courage or talents' in the professional and public realms, it privileged a distinctly private dimension centered on the household and marital economy. Encyclopedic entries suggest that nineteenth-century commentators focused on honor as rooted in the sexual and social relations of the conjugal model. As the 1885 Littré *Dictionnaire* specified about familial honor: 'In speaking of a husband, honor [refers to] the good reputation reflected on him by his wife's fidelity.'[11] Larousse also included a quote by Rousseau about the importance of lineage and virtue: 'The honor of a chaste woman is under the protection of men of estates.'[12] Despite this recognition of gendered relations based on property as the foundation of the system, editors referred readers to the separate entry *chasteté* for specific definitions of female honor. Under *chasteté* one finds that *honneur, sagesse* (proper behavior) and *vertu* (virtue) had different meanings when applied to the female sex. 'Virtue' had a broad reach for men: 'The virtuous man is good in all respects; he is the man of duty and sacrifice. In [the term] "virtue," there exists an idea of strength capable of conquering the passions and avoiding bad examples. To develop virtue in the soul of citizens would be the main objective of legislation, politics and philosophy... '[13] When applied to women, however, these same three terms were synonyms for 'chastity,' 'continence,' and 'purity.' For women, '*honneur* assumes the will to remain laudable in the eyes of society; *sagesse* entails the idea of a great reserve, of the prudence a woman uses to avoid dangerous opportunities; *vertu* makes one imagine the strength of spirit, the courage a woman would use to resist attacks by seducers.'[14] Though signifying a certain sense of self-control, as did the male definition, woman's honor had a principally sexual meaning which solidified her exclusion from the active virtues of citizenship and rooted her identity more firmly in the family than the man's. What made a man a citizen in France – 'conquering the passions and avoiding bad examples' – did not translate into an aptitude for civic responsibility in women. Furthermore, as many of the quotes suggest, the woman's sexual honor was not technically her own, but accrued to the head of the household. Woman's inferior physical strength was a prominent factor leading to her exclusion from the public code, which required individuals to back up their words with violence if necessary. This translated into a lack of willpower for all women, thereby negating the 'selfhood' on which citizenship rested. This explains why, when a man entered into a marriage contract, he made an unspoken agreement to protect his wife's sexual honor and by extension, that of the family.[15]

This sexual division present in the French bourgeois definition of 'honor' was widely commented on by republican women's activists at the turn of the century. The feminist Harlor, novelist and literary critic for Marguerite

Durand's daily women's rights publication *La Fronde*, wrote specifically of this issue in a 1901 article entitled 'Feminine Honor:'

> Moreover, is there anything more humiliating for the woman than the completely sexual meaning of the title 'honorable woman' [*honnête femme*]? What hatred this implies of the woman's intelligence and character, since it essentially declares her to be unworthy of a different praise, incapable of serving the human community by an activity whose importance would necessarily make of a certain virtue what it has done for the man.

While male honor appeared to contain key features that equipped men for a broad civil identity in French society, female honor narrowed women's social and professional options and, in reality, could be considered an emblem of their exclusion from public life. Furthermore, Harlor noted, the duty of dominating the passions did not carry over into the sexual realm for men in the same way as it did for women:

> The entire life of the woman, in the bourgeoisie especially, is governed by a commandment which does not exist at all – or only exists in appearance – for the man. This is a commandment of the physiological order, demanding of the young woman a virtue from which the young man is exempted and which would even make him ridiculous with time.[16]

Explicitly linking the problem of the double moral standard to the honor code, Harlor pointed to a disjuncture within the system that many feminist commentators would underscore in their public discussion of sexual politics. The honor code actively encouraged men to demonstrate their sexual prowess and, Harlor suggested, may have generated social censure when men adhered to the familial model of monogamy.

In his book on male honor, Robert Nye argues that the fin-de-siècle honor system held men to a strict code of sexual behavior as it did for women, and that this code centered on the conjugal heterosexual model. This model assumed national importance in late nineteenth-century France due partly to the country's falling birth rate and widespread fears of national decline.[17] Yet feminist comments on double morality reveal that while men were reproached for 'aberrant' forms of male sexuality and effeminate comportment, they did not feel an imperative to limit their sexual behavior to the family. For Harlor, the male honor community may have paid lip service to sexual fidelity, but in reality, a man's violation of this prescriptive dictate did 'not at all blemish honor' as it did for the woman. Asking whether this 'law' of sexual honor was 'legitimate' and where it came from, Harlor exposed the hypocrisy of the gendered honor system.[18] This contradiction between the Larousse definition of male honor as rooted in the family and the social code that sanctioned and even expected sexual conquests of men was a sign of the nineteenth-century honor culture's schizophrenic character. As Harlor elaborated, the double standard was a sacred tenet of bourgeois, rather than aristocratic, morality. Were a woman from the upper class, she argued, 'where moral principles are greeted more often by smiles than by severities,' the code would not require such strict sexual conduct from her.[19] Thus, above all, the democratization of the honor system was responsible for this new dualistic regiment of behavior between the sexes. French middle-class men, while attempting to align honor to their own regime of property and moral comportment, had nonetheless retained elements of the aristocratic system of honor. This former code not only tacitly acknowledged male sexual promiscuity, but used such conduct as an active measure of manliness and courage. In fact, the retention of this meritorious aspect of the honor culture may be indicative of bourgeois men's need to restore lost masculinity in the crisis-ridden atmosphere of fin-de-siècle France.[20] In critiquing the double moral standard, then, belle époque feminists pointed to both the gendered contradictions of the democratized honor system and a broader gap between the code's philosophy and practice after the French Revolution.

Abolitionism and the language of shame

Sexual honor became a central issue for republican women activists in these years in conjunction with developments in international feminism and widespread sexual anxieties that arose in fin-de-siècle France. As Morsier's presence at the 1900 feminist congress indicates, feminists were active in the French branch of the FAI. The French chapter had been formed in 1897 after a visit to the continent by English activist and founder of the British and Continental Federation for the Abolition of Prostitution, Josephine Butler. French feminist abolitionists drew heavily from the language and concepts of the English social purity movements that Butler spearheaded in the 1870s and 1880s. These movements, which spawned an international crusade, form a vital context in which to understand the feminist focus on the sexual question. The Contagious Diseases Acts introduced by the British government in the 1860s provoked a massive sixteen-year repeal campaign led by Butler. Protesting these acts permitting the compulsory examination, detention, and treatment of suspected prostitutes, Butler and the eventual mass political network of vigilance committees to which her initiatives gave rise condemned what they referred to as state-sanctioned 'male vice' or 'lust.'[21] As Judith Walkowitz has pointed out, Butler portrayed 'fallen women' as 'victims of male pollution, as women who had been invaded by men's bodies, men's laws, and by that steel penis, the speculum.'[22] Butler's fight against the CD Acts, in conjunction with the success of W.T. Stead's infamous 'Maiden Tribute' exposé, which provoked public outcry concerning the procurement and violation of 'unwilling virgins,' resulted in a new resolve among English feminists to speak publicly about sex.[23]

This confluence of events created a feminist insistence on the centi the 'double moral standard' to women's inferior status, an emphasis tl... ...u a profound influence on the English suffrage campaign of the early twentieth century. From the 1880s to World War I, English feminists argued that a single moral standard had to be enforced for both men and women, and that the basis of women's unequal status in society was their experience of 'sexual objectification, sexual violence, and lack of bodily autonomy' that was perpetrated by men.[24] Butler's numerous travels to Paris between 1874 and 1880 gave rise to several French liberal associations, which demanded the elimination of the vice squad – the special police force which arbitrarily arrested and detained suspected prostitutes. The Association pour l'abolition de la prostitution réglementée, a French section of the British and Continental Federation, brought together radicals, feminists, and Protestant abolitionist groups in a common fight against the system of legalized prostitution in Paris. Feminists were prominent in this campaign from the beginning. Maria Deraismes, for example, joined this group and presided over the morality section of the Société pour l'amélioration du sort des femmes, which sent a petition to the Chamber of Deputies in 1879 demanding eradication of the registration of underage girls. Deraismes's actions helped lay the groundwork for later broad-based feminist support of abolitionism.[25]

Despite the fact that by the 1880s calls for an end to the 'French system' were widely supported in the women's movement, feminist discourse on prostitution and sexuality only began to reach a broader audience near the turn of the century. According to the Swiss-born feminist abolitionist Emilie de Morsier who helped propagate Butler's campaign in France, as late as 1884 reformers were unable to say 'that there has been in this country a genuine movement of public opinion in favor of the abolition of state-regulated vice.' For Morsier, part of the problem was French women's trepidation and passivity. While numbers of women had joined the different abolitionist associations in France, Morsier argued that, 'it must be admitted that it is not the feminine element which had predominated' in these groups. Unfortunately, this aspect of the 'Woman Question' had not 'awakened their interest.' Morsier chided women for their apathy: 'It has been said that "women make the morals" but it would be more correct to say they *accept* them.' Suggesting that women 'tacitly accept men's opinions and yield to their wishes,' Morsier asserted that French women exercised a 'culpable complaisance' in the continued sanctioning of state-run prostitution.[26]

French women's weak support for Butler's initiatives was partly a result of the early faltering of the French abolitionist movement. The radical attack on the vice squad in France was not simply a feminist effort, but was part of a broader struggle for individual liberties threatened by conservative governments in the late 1870s. According to Alain Corbin, though many politicians supported the libertarian aspect of the program, they could not work with the evangelical and moralizing elements. In 1878 and 1881, the opportunist majority in the Chamber rejected the campaign being carried out by the Parisian extreme left, and many radicals refused to commit themselves too strongly to the abolitionist cause. By the turn of the century, the coalition had made few political gains.[27]

However, a broader movement against the vice squad revived in France between 1898 and 1901, fueled by the creation of the French branch of the FAI. The FAI's campaign coincided with the formation of the Leftist Bloc and the 'Government of Republican Defense' in 1899. Once again, politicians of the Third Republic proved sympathetic to the abolitionist rhetoric on individual liberty and equality before the law, this time to counter nationalist, right-wing threats to the public order. These developments, along with the rise of the mass press and the flowering of feminist publications, gave new impetus to the feminist effort to insert republican women's voices into political discourse on sexuality. The international feminist congresses of 1900 represented a new stage of visibility and awareness for the feminist abolitionists and an insistence on sexual morality as the key to women's rights, as we saw in Pognon's speech.

The sexual double standard was not only a prominent theme among the Protestant feminists who organized the Congress of Women's Charities and Institutions, but was also highlighted at the subsequent International Congress on Women's Condition and Rights. This latter congress featured a speech delivered by the feminist crusader Ghénia Avril de Sainte-Croix on the subject of regulationism. Avril de Sainte-Croix became secretary-general of the FAI in 1901 following Auguste de Morsier's tenure, and was a leading agitator against the international white slave trade. She also co-founded the largest feminist umbrella organization in France, the Conseil National des Femmes Françaises (CNFF) in 1901.[28]

While Avril de Sainte-Croix drew on the universalist language of the Rights of Man to demand liberty for prostitutes, she also framed the topic broadly around the idea that women needed to break the silence surrounding male sexual behavior within the family. Double morality, she argued, 'has been the most certain source of women's misery, immorality and oppression.' It was 'bizarre' and 'incomprehensible to everyone' that more than a century after the Revolution, feminists had to inscribe a paragraph in their program 'demanding the unity of morality for both sexes and the abolition of regulated prostitution.' Referring to the taboo that had existed for many years in France against women speaking publicly of sexual matters, Avril de Sainte-Croix declared that it was impossible for them to continue to maintain silence on an issue that so profoundly affected their interests. Stating that, 'I know that many believe these are questions that women must leave outside of their deliberations,' she called on women specifically to act: 'We must, on the contrary, raise our voices that much higher, so that men will hear – men who have usurped the title of moralists, who say to us that it is especially to protect honorable women, to safeguard the family, that they want to maintain the institution [of regulationism].'[29]

Avril de Sainte-Croix's emphasis on exposing men's behavior applied not only to the prostitute's rights in a democratic republic, but referred more broadly to the code attached to the French family. Men claimed to 'safeguard the family' by accepting legalized prostitution. According to this rationale, the state provided a class of women to satisfy men's sexual appetites and thus 'protect' 'honorable women' from unrestrained male lust. Echoing tenets of French regulationism's early theorist, Parent-Duchâtelet, the neoregulationists associated with Senator René Bérenger most prominently elaborated this argument after the turn of the century. The state's logic was partly that 'proper' married women could not satisfy their husband's sexual drives and that public health thereby required a controlled outlet for these needs. Additionally, neoregulationists suggested that the complete abolition of *maisons de tolérance* would flood the streets with disrespectable *filles publiques*, thereby exposing honorable women and their daughters to the dangerous specter of venal sex.[30] Dismissing such claims as detrimental to women, Avril de Sainte-Croix suggested that women must reject this form of male 'protection.' Quoting Swiss feminist Emma Pieczynska, she insisted, 'If it is a question about us, then it is a matter of justice that we make our voices heard. Silence would imply our consent. We cannot accept a protection that is exercised by such means.'[31] Avril de Sainte-Croix thus broadly denounced men's breach of the code, indicating that they had failed in their private responsibilities towards women and the family. Arguing that men 'have usurped the title of moralists,' she drew on women's traditional roles in the honor system as self-disciplined guardians of the family's virtue to insist on their special authority as moral regulators of the household and community. According to Avril de Sainte-Croix, this was a duty that men had illegitimately appropriated. The 'sexual question' thus not only required women to defend the customary notion of the 'honest woman' but also simultaneously to take an active stance that broke from women's submissive roles in the honor culture.

Avril de Sainte-Croix recognized that the mass press was crucial in exposing men's behavior and gaining public acceptance for this new feminist rhetoric on sexual honor. She indicated that Durand's *La Fronde* had allowed the abolitionists to publish a series of articles in 1897–98 about prostitution when, 'despite our assiduous collaboration with many major newspapers, we were never able to get [our articles] published elsewhere.'[32] Women's discussion of sexuality thereby proliferated with the birth of new feminist publications as well as in mainstream liberal newspapers, which began to welcome feminist discussion of the topic after the turn of the century. Avril de Sainte-Croix's 1900 congressional speech also made a profound impact on the French women's movement, as feminist commentators' correspondence and memoirs attest.[33] Moderates and militants alike began to speak out more forthrightly and insistently on the issue of sexuality in the press and at public meetings.[34]

Pognon's call to arms among women in the face of men's sexual infection of their wives additionally indicates that these congresses were held against the background of a growing public fear about the 'venereal peril.' Such concerns filtered into the republican feminists' rhetoric on sexual honor. Disturbing medical studies revealed the ubiquitous nature of syphilis in France in the last decades of the century and warned of the facility with which it was contracted. In addition to generating international conferences on sexual disease in 1899 and 1902, syphilitic anxiety spawned a highly influential neoregulationist league in 1901, the French Society of Sanitary and Moral Prophylaxis (SFPSM).[35]

Many feminists sympathetic to the programs of the moral and neoregulationist leagues echoed Pognon's concerns about how such a scourge would affect the French family and bourgeois women in particular. Elucidating the significance of the venereal peril to the women's movement in a 1911 article in *La Suffragiste*, the militant feminist Remember argued in frank terms that:

> ¾ of the male race *comes to marriage* with this filthy and *incurable* malady that has been given the scientific name 'syphilis.' It is transmitted with the greatest facility. Men thus struck by it contaminate their wives, and this is the cause of repeated abortions. To communicate such a disease *is a crime that is currently very frequent*. To give birth to syphilitic children *is another crime*, for they are born with numerous defects![36]

Describing syphilis in the language of male criminality as did Pognon, Remember stressed men's insult to women and to the French household more generally. She highlighted the venereal peril to counter natalist diatribes against 'New Women,' who were often accused of egotistically pursuing their own educational and professional aims rather than sacrificing themselves to the family and nation.[37] Remember's rhetoric reflected studies of prominent clinicians in the capital, particularly those of Alfred Fournier, head of the syphilis and skin disease clinic at the Saint-Louis hospital and founder of the SFPSM. Fournier warned in 1887 that virginal bourgeois wives infected by their husbands accounted for at least 20 percent of the cases of female syphilis he treated in his Parisian office. Furthermore, he suggested that innocent children who suffered from the diseases of their mothers or from contact with badly cleaned medical instruments made up 5 percent of all syphilitics. Fournier's writings had a profound impact on public opinion, particularly due to his gruesome descriptions of chaste young women whose bodies were covered in lesions, who silently suffered because their shame prevented them from seeing doctors.[38] The neoregulationist discourse propagated by Fournier's SFPSM emphasized the 'outrage' of honest woman by syphilis, though Fournier had tended to focus on men as innocent victims of prostitutes.[39] Along with the oppositional abolitionist initiatives, neoregulationist discourse provided an opening for 'honorable women' to enter the debate. The SFPSM sought to disgrace infected men to a certain extent and offered prescriptions for what type of sexual responsibility an 'honest man' owed to society.

Feminists argued that women's vulnerability to such forms of male injustice was compounded by the fact that the state left them defenseless against their husband's sexual behavior. The Parisian activist and writer, Cleyre Yvelin, cited Swiss anthropologist J.J. Bachofen in an article she penned for the feminist publication *L'Entente* in 1906: 'Woman, abandoned without protection to the sexual excesses of man, fatigued to the point of death by his pursuit of pleasure, experiences the need for purer mores!'[40] As she further elaborated in a 1911 letter to her colleague Arria Ly, women came to marriage as virgins while their fiancés, 'more or less tainted, condescend to ask [these women] to marry them in order to initiate them into the sexual debaucheries that [men] have gotten used to, and to profane them with their ignoble caresses ... The law is clear: obligation of conjugal duties! ... What a shame!'[41] Yvelin noted with disgust that despite women's awareness of men's depravity and the risks they ran of contracting disease from them, they were nonetheless required by French law to sleep with their husbands. She referred to sections of the Civil and Penal Codes on marital obligations that were coming under heavy feminist scrutiny by the late nineteenth century. Though the Civil Code contained no explicit article requiring consistent sexual relations between husband and wife, the application of both separation and divorce legislation later in the century clarified its implicit understanding of this imperative. Jurisprudence specified that the 'persistent refusal' of either spouse to fulfill his or her conjugal duty was considered an *'injure grave'* and thereby constituted grounds for marital rupture.[42] In highlighting the double moral standard, feminists also frequently recalled article 324 of the Penal Code, which specified that a husband had a right to kill both his wife's lover and his spouse if he caught them *en flagrant délit* in the home, though a wife who took the same action was considered a criminal. Under the Penal Code, an adulterous wife was liable to imprisonment, whereas an adulterous husband was subject only to a fine, which could be enforced only if his adulterous act took place in the conjugal home. Article 230 of the Civil Code had also specified that the husband could only be convicted for adultery if he brought his mistress into the family dwelling, though this article was repealed in 1884.[43] Such legal endorsement of the double standard meant that not only were men considered not to blame, but the state collaborated in this disregard for the family's well-being. This situation, Yvelin pointed out, made a mockery of the institution of marriage and a young woman's virginity, both of which were considered foundations of female honor. According to her, such sanctioning of men's behavior also 'provoked [woman's] resistance' and 'armed her' for the struggle, 'first for her defense and then for her vengeance.'[44] As

La Fronde journalist Camille Bélilon similarly wrote, the contemporary 'code of morality' was 'injurious to women.'[45] Feminists drew a connection between women's sexual oppression and their inferior legal status in French society. The association between female honor and sexuality severely circumscribed women's lives, meaning that not only did laws have to be changed, but the entire French moral structure needed to be altered.

As French feminist commentary on male sexuality and the venereal peril suggests, the discourse of women as victims of male affronts proved to be a powerful weapon for feminists to wield in their claim of women's fitness for full citizenship. The honor code emphasized the inviolability of the family based on women's sexual purity and self-discipline. Men broke the code by infecting women and by abandoning their duty of protection. This breach allowed women to recoup the role of moral police from men. Feminists could thereby position themselves as the main defenders of the 'traditional' family code as a tactic to gain public sympathy. Whereas activists who framed sexual demands more starkly in the language of individualism were often perceived as waging a 'sex war' and as threatening the basis of the French family, reformist feminists who positioned themselves as defenders of a time-honored notion of sexual honor were able to garner greater support for important legal and social reforms after 1900.[46]

A feminist honor code

The double morality conflict reappeared in the spotlight in 1908 during senatorial debates over the Jullien Law regarding divorce and its multiple moral and sexual ramifications. The Jullien Law was an amendment to the 1884 Naquet Law granting limited divorce by fault. The 1908 legislation allowed the separated spouse to convert his or her separation into a divorce after three years upon the request of either partner. As Jean Pedersen has shown, the idea that a wife guilty of adultery might be able to divorce a 'spotless spouse' gave rise to fears among many senators. These fears centered especially on the suspicion that women would be given greater license to commit adultery and that they might begin to treat marriage as little more than a free union. Senator Bérenger played on this anxiety to argue for judges' discretion in such cases. Proponents of the bill, by contrast, focused on the 'unhappily married man' required to remain chaste while separated, a situation which some characterized as 'particularly ridiculous for men.'[47]

Such continuing support in parliament and in broader public opinion for men's sexual prerogatives led the mainstream feminist newspaper of the CNFF, *La Française*, to launch an opinion survey among its readers in 1909 on the question of the double moral standard. The survey results, which were published at regular intervals from 7 November 1909 to 20 March 1910, featured commentary by many leading lights of the feminist, medical, and literary world. Such responses make clear that for contemporaries, 'double morality' touched on a number of connected sexual topics during the prewar years. Addressing the venereal peril, adultery, venal sex, and medical views on male continence, commentators struggled to expose the crux of the problem related to the perceived breakdown of the French family as well as the broader degeneration of the population. Though some readers focused on men's 'natural' need for promiscuity, many argued that the moral problem was not biological, but social – a code of behavior that delineated different rules for men and women based on sexual preconceptions.

Writer Colette Yver, author of the critically acclaimed 1907 novel *Princesses de Science*, framed the parameters of the debate with her controversial response. Referring to the 'tacit code' that allowed men to escape punishment for their sexual adventures, Yver suggested that this code was largely created by public opinion. Nonetheless, she argued that it was not completely arbitrary and outdated, but had a concrete function in French society, justifying women's disadvantaged position. For Yver, traditional 'customs' did not require an 'inflexibly severe' stance towards the husband's infidelity, since his sexual behavior was 'less prejudicial to the family than that of the woman.' Yver explained that a 'woman's fault [could] introduce foreign subjects into the home. Responsibility [for these children] would fall uniquely onto the head of the family, to the detriment of legitimate children.' For Yver, this need to protect the legitimacy of the family line and to maintain its property intact provided a 'simple and clear reason whose overall good sense will satisfy everyone.' Even though she admitted that the father's indiscretion could 'divert the property of life, activity and wealth outside of the family, resources which should be reserved for the little organism of which he is the head,' Yver nonetheless asserted that women needed to tolerate a certain amount of sexual inequality to maintain the household. This task was made easier by the fact that women's sense of propriety was 'less offended' by the husband's violation of the marital contract than by the 'stain of this sacred temple that is the family, this drama of the familial nest where one day, eggs of a sparrow hawk are hatched.' Yver thereby championed the wife who forgave her husband in service of not disrupting the family. According to the antifeminist French author, the code particularly charged the woman with a duty to safeguard the family organization – she was a *'gardienne du foyer.'*[48]

Other respondents echoed Yver's reasoning that property was the root of the double moral standard in French society. Another female novelist, a married woman who wrote under the pen name of Stanislaus Meunier, argued that while society considered the adulterous wife guilty and even criminal when she gave birth to a child from an illicit union, the adulterous husband did not commit a criminal action. Meunier explained that this was 'because he cannot fraudulently introduce his bastards into the conjugal home.' For her, this social and legal prejudice meant that feminists would have a hard time equalizing the moral code between men and women: '[Men's] lapses are infinitely less serious than those of women. Men know this and feminism will never convince them to be as severe on themselves as they are on their companions.'[49]

As such opinions suggest, the nineteenth-century French honor code was firmly rooted in noble and commoner inheritance practices stemming from the Middle Ages. Nye argues that the bourgeoisie's idea of patrimony in particular 'included a distinctive set of inheritance practices and a related ideology of sex and sexual behavior.'[50] The French family centered its identity on stringent fertility and marital strategies designed to keep its property intact, and this was made more important for the middle classes than it had been for the nobility due to legal obstacles commoners faced during the Old Regime. Inheritance laws required an equal division of family property between children and stipulated that land would revert to collateral lines in the absence of direct heirs. The French Revolution had institutionalized this system of middle-class inheritance and the conjugal model that it supported. All family members thereby had to work towards the common goal of social reproduction, making sexual, marital, and economic sacrifices where necessary to ensure the success of the unit's patrimony. Women's sexual virtue played a crucial role in facilitating this task. Nye suggests that 'biological reproduction now served the family's grand agenda for attaining honor.'[51] This ultimately meant that the family's inviolability centered on women's sexual purity, which protected legitimacy based on property. As *La Française* readers pointed out, this idea of sexual female honor still held sway in the years prior to the Great War, despite signs of a more sympathetic public opinion towards illegitimate children.[52]

Yet many feminists who participated in the debate sought to expand this narrow definition of honor beyond a woman's sexual virtue, suggesting that 'fidelity' broadly conceived formed the basis of numerous tenets of French civil life. Jeanne Oddo-Deflou, founder of the Groupe française d'études féministes (GFEF), established that 'by *morale*, we are here uniquely referring to the rule of sexual relations between the man and woman,' and argued that no question was 'more important to the future of feminism.' Yet Oddo-Deflou protested against the 'narrow and exclusive meaning' of the concept in French society: 'Chastity is certainly an attractive virtue, but it is neither the only one nor the primary one. And, to cite only one [of these virtues] whose social import is very superior, we will limit ourselves to mentioning *sincerité*, with the diverse nuances which modify its name based on its different applications.' According to Oddo-Deflou, 'sincerity' or 'integrity' formed a foundation of civil and social relations in post-revolutionary France, ensuring the proper functioning of the state: 'We can imagine a society living in the most generous and freest sexual promiscuity; we can hardly conceive of one where the veracity of speech and the fidelity to contracted engagements do not form the ordinary base of relations.' Loyalty to one's word pledged in a binding contract was an extension of fidelity, suggesting that the notion underlying female honor actually formed the basis of a much more far-reaching principle in France. Women were not only responsible for maintaining the family's sexual honor in a narrow sense, but were the special guardians of civil society and social relations more generally. Such definitions went far beyond property concerns, and by suggesting that this concept buttressed other types of relationships, Oddo-Deflou accused men of breaking their contract made to the family unit. Exposing the injustice of society's castigation of the unfaithful wife, Oddo-Deflou asked 'If the misconduct of the woman leads to particular consequences, shouldn't that of the husband make him fall from the preponderant rank of director that he has assumed in the family? Should it not withdraw from him every right to control the education and supervision of his children?' Men's violation of the family compact disqualified them for their leadership roles within the home, and by extension, Oddo-Deflou implied, for the active virtues of citizenship. Appealing to the prescriptive definition of male honor outlined in the Larousse encyclopedia discussed earlier, Oddo-Deflou sought to carve out an expanded niche for women in the honor system. Women, she suggested, had to act on behalf of the household, usurping men's traditional roles in order to restore familial honor.[53]

This emphasis on men's violation of their 'word' resonated throughout the debate as feminists consistently linked male adultery to an infraction of the customary 'law' of family loyalty. As several participants pointed out, male adultery was largely ignored by French legislation, so feminist denunciations of men appealed to an unwritten code that existed outside normal legal channels. Augusta Moll-Weiss, director of the Ecole des Mères, disputed the idea that women's adultery was more serious because of the danger posed by illegitimacy. She argued that, 'For the moralist, the breach of one's given word carries the same name among men and women, whatever disasters flow from it.' For the pragmatist, however, it was necessary to know whose violation of the 'conjugal code' – the husband's or the wife's – carried 'a greater prejudice to society or to the family, wherever their action especially exerts itself.' For Moll-Weiss, the consequences of the wife's adultery were much more detrimental to the family. However, this was not due to property concerns. Rather, she suggested that the wife's fault was more important because 'it is especially on the woman that the entire morality of the family depends.' The family is modeled in her image, and she has a 'much greater influence on the evolution of the race than the man.'[54] Moll-Weiss thereby appealed to women as moral regulators of the family and the nation, suggesting that they had to hold themselves to a stricter code of sexual comportment than men due to their greater responsibilities. In this way, respondents converted the conventional notion of women's passive honor into a more active understanding of behavior consistent with the demands of citizenship.

For many feminists in the debate, the duty entrusted to women to protect against illegitimacy had lost meaning thanks to men's disregard of the family's public reputation. Chief editor of *La Française* Jane Misme commented extensively on Yver's response and sought to expose the fallacy of her thinking regarding the French household. Misme agreed that at stake in leveling the moral standard were not women's individual rights to sexual liberty. In fact, all debate participants made a point of reiterating that the women's movement was firmly opposed to the principle of 'free union.' For Misme, adultery not only hurt the spouses individually, but constituted a wrong done to the family itself. The problem was that the husband did not appear to have the same interest as the wife in shielding family stains and transgressions from public view. The dilemma, in other words, centered on protecting the family's honor; its public reputation needed to be preserved in an environment where slander and libel were more damaging to it than the actual adulterous offense.[55] For Misme, in nearly every case where the family suffered from the wife's wrongdoings, it was the 'pride of the husband who, in order to punish her, publicized them.' Since making something private into public knowledge was fundamental to the honor code, Misme reasoned that there was a social code beyond the familial one that pressured men to reveal their wives' infidelity. Specifically addressing Yver's praise of women who hid the sins of their husbands in order to save the household, Misme argued that 'true feminism has never taught otherwise;' it holds that the family's reputation must be safeguarded. Yet, did the husband not also make a commitment to the family to keep its secrets, even when faced with a wife's adultery?[56]

Paul Bureau, a prominent Catholic member of Senator Bérenger's League against Licentiousness in the Streets and author of *La crise morale des temps nouveaux*, specifically blamed the honor code for sanctioning men's sexual misdeeds:

> The Penal Code and public opinion recognize exceedingly extensive rights for the offended husband [*mari outragé*]; if one analyzes these alleged rights, one will see that they are nothing other than the most certain violation of a duty. Our pagan notion of honor is so vulgar and egotistical that, very often, the first duty of a man of honor is to close his ears to the deceitful advice that it suggests to him.[57]

Bureau thereby suggested that husbands must learn to forgive their wives' transgressions in order both to demonstrate their reciprocal duties and to save the family. In mentioning the rights of the 'offended husband,' Bureau referred to the inequitable treatment of male and female adultery by the French Penal Code as outlined earlier. He pointed out that these legal measures also formed the basis of the male code of honor in French society, which granted men certain privileges in return for their responsibilities towards the family. Yet, for Bureau as for other readers, the French 'pagan notion of honor' sanctioned actions that actually destroyed the unit it sought to protect. He thereby appealed to a code beyond the law that required men to conform to a unified moral standard. Mlle Lucie Bérillon, professor at the Lycée Molière and a recognized lecturer, similarly wrote that while society expected faithfulness from women, for men this same virtue created 'a kind of ridicule in the eyes of society [*le monde*].' Changing the social code would thus require men to be courageous and to brave the derision of their peers. According to Bérillon, women must especially initiate this adjustment of masculine honor. Customs would be modified 'under women's influence.'[58]

Some readers additionally highlighted the broader consequences of adulterous men's infractions. For a female schoolteacher who signed her letter L. Fourets, the disloyal husband was guilty of destroying two families through his behavior: 'If the husband's adultery does not introduce bastards into the conjugal home, it introduces them into the home of others.' For Fourets, a guilty husband would not only create a burden on a separate household, he would generate additional shame for his wife in the form of the mistresses' affronts to her. Fourets recounted the story of a married man who seduced a young woman, and as a result, the young woman became pregnant. The husband mistreated his wife in favor of his mistress, causing the former to commit suicide. For Fourets, both the mistress and husband were 'criminals' but 'the man is still more so than the young woman.'[59] As Misme similarly noted:

> Is it only the woman's misconduct which places so many abandoned children under the state's dependency and which throws so many others into vice and crime? The man's responsibility augments here since, nearly always, the mother who abandons a child is poor while very often it is a rich father who has made her pregnant.[60]

For respondents, male immorality had implications that reached beyond the family. Addressing the social consequences of such behavior for the nation, many appealed above men's authority to the state to rectify the situation. Part of the feminist project was thus to expose and question men's behavior, to use shame as a device to silence those who would support the principle of dual morality. Commentators argued that destroying such an implicit and pervasive code required women's direct and independent action. As many emphasized, women had a special duty to exercise social censure on men who cheated. For Oddo-Deflou, bringing male sexuality in line with the conjugal code would help rectify the slide into decadence the French state was experiencing: 'Without a doubt, a reform of [masculine] morals would have the happiest repercussions and the best utility for our national existence.' This meant encouraging young men to 'come pure to the wedding day.' Abstinence before marriage was widely promoted for young men by the SFPSM and by numerous abolitionists in this period. But Oddo-Deflou argued that this task would be difficult, not because of the supposedly negative effects of continence on male health, but due to the accolades accorded to promiscuous men in broader social circles. Reform of male sexual practices would only succeed 'when the sinner, instead of taking pleasure in his sin, will have

Avril de Ste Croix

honor and glory withdrawn from him (as is paid to him today), and will be conscious of it and feel regret. He will guard himself against falling back [into sin].' Oddo-Deflou suggested that women in particular were 'obliged to hasten this moment.' She thereby attributed a central role to women in the public system of honor: Women 'must crown the leaders [*coryphées*] of masculine gallantry with thorns and not roses. Matrons must exile them from their salons, richly-dowered young women must unmercifully refuse them their hand; let them be flagellated with hatred or ridicule, excluded forever from every suitable alliance ... and their cohort will quickly vanish.'[61] Oddo-Deflou's response was thus an appeal to women to act in the face of men's blatant disregard for the family's interests. Reader Ida R. Sée similarly argued that 'when mothers will cease to smile at the "conquests" of their sons, and to declare that "youth will pass," the female servant, worker, and the "young undowered woman" will perhaps cease to know the anguishes of maternities that an odious lie declares "shameful."'[62] Women, then, were principally responsible for enforcing the family honor code, using their special positioning in it to ostracize men from society and to restore national health.

Participants additionally drew a link between the duties of sexual honor and citizenship. Bureau suggested that sexual self-control was a civic 'duty' and 'one can only have [rights] insofar as one shows oneself suited to respect his duties.'[63] No one made this connection more clearly than Avril de Sainte-Croix, who also participated in the *La Française* survey. She condemned women who dared to defend 'the unlimited right of the man in matters of love.' Insisting that women were aware of these realities, Avril de Sainte-Croix argued that, 'their attitude is all the more inexcusable as there are those who, by their indulgence, which is accommodating to the strong only, help to maintain laws and rules in our codes, in our administrations. From the woman's point of view, [these laws] represent the negation of all justice.' She thereby placed the sexual question at the base of all other feminist demands and at the root of women's exclusion from French law and politics. She noted that the feminist fight to obtain legal reforms for women in the family would mean nothing so long as general opinion continued to praise men for their sexual escapades while condemning women: 'For example, do we believe that the abrogation of Article 340 of the Civil Code on paternity suits will have reestablished justice so long as the general mentality has not changed...?' Avril de Sainte-Croix noted that despite her legal recourse, the *fille-mère* 'will remain dishonored [*déshonorée*] in her daily life while her seducer, after paying his due, will be able to leave with his head held high and collect the smiles that today greet our low-class Don Juan.' Thus, women had to apply themselves to changing general opinion, to inculcating sexual responsibility in their male children, and to showing intransigence on this issue. When the equality of morality was realized, 'Women will be able to see the extension of their civil rights; they will be able to obtain the amelioration of their economic situation; they will even come to enjoy their political rights...'[64]

For Avril de Sainte-Croix, civil and civic rights flowed from the elimination of the double standard.

Conclusion

By a particular sleight of hand, turn of the century republican feminists highlighted sexual morality in order to formulate a more active notion of female civic identity. In fact, their heightened rhetoric on an equal moral standard helped make sexual discipline a key qualification of republican citizenship on the eve of the war. This stance was based on women's particular role in the nineteenth-century honor system. By arguing that they were protecting the family's reputation in the face of men's dishonest sexual behavior, feminists could position themselves as defenders of a reassuring vision of gender roles in a republican social order that, in the eyes of many commentators, had fallen into decadence. Activists' more independent sense of honor in these sexual debates can also be linked to a broader public sympathy demonstrated toward 'slandered' women in turn-of-the-century France. This phenomenon manifested itself in lenient attitudes by juries and judges towards 'wronged women' who committed crimes of passion and towards those who sued their seducers for damages to their sexual reputations.[65] The 'honest woman' was imagined in this period as attempting to restore a conventional sense of honor in the face of a corrupt political and social environment. Yet, by breaking the silence and declaring themselves the overseers of male sexuality, feminists subverted the patriarchal implications of the code and insisted that the personal was political. Though they couched their demands partly in customary language, these women nonetheless advocated a complete reform of French sexual culture and saw the single moral standard as the foundation of political change. Such contested notions of honor ultimately mark the attempted adaptation of a code based primarily on blood and patrimony to the demands of republican citizenship for both men and women.

Notes

1. Laurence Klejman and Florence Rochefort, *L'Egalité en marche* (Paris: des femmes, 1989), pp. 137–9; Steven C. Hause and Anne Kenney, *Women's Suffrage and Social Politics in the French Third Republic* (Princeton: Princeton University Press, 1984), pp. 30–1.
2. For the middle-class character of the feminists who organized and participated in this congress, see Hause and Kenney, *Women's Suffrage*, pp. 30–44, 58–60; For the bourgeois tenor of the congress in general, see congress program in *Deuxième Congrès international des oeuvres et institutions féminines tenu au Palais des Congrès de l'Exposition Universelle de 1900*, compte rendu des travaux par Madame Pégard, vol. 1 (Paris: Charles Blot, 1902), pp. 14–15.
3. Maria Pognon at the plenary session of 19 June 1900, *Deuxième Congrès international des oeuvres et institutions féminines*, vol. 1, p. 73.

4. Ibid., pp. 73–4; For Fiaux's proposal to criminalize *contamination intersexuelle*, see his report summarized by Morsier at the 1900 congress: Dr. Louis Fiaux, 'L'abrogation de toutes les mesures d'exception à l'égard de la Femme, en matière de moeurs,' *Deuxième Congrès international des oeuvres et institutions féminines*, vol. 2, pp. 574–86; Fiaux gives a history of debates that took place on this issue at the 1899 Conférence internationale de prophylaxie and the 1901 Congrès de la Fédération internationale pour l'abolition de la Police des moeurs in his *Le Délit pénal de contamination intersexuelle* (Paris: Félix Alcan, 1907), pp. 1–38.

5. William Reddy argues that 'Both men and women were expected to conceal serious infractions of morality – this is the other dimension of preserving honor – whether the infractions were their own or committed by their spouses or close relations.' Honor was 'a collective, familial state.' Reddy, *The Invisible Code: Honor and Sentiment in Postrevolutionary France, 1814–1848* (Berkeley: University of California Press, 1997), p. 72; See also Rachel Fuchs, 'Paternity, Progeny and Property: Family Honor in the Late Nineteenth Century,' Chapter 7 in this volume.

6. Anne-Marie Käppeli, *Sublime croisade: Ethique et politique du féminisme protestant, 1875–1928* (Carouge-Geneva: Editions Zoé, 1990); Geneviève Poujol, *Un Féminisme sous tutelle: Les protestantes françaises, 1810–1960* (Paris: Les Editions de Paris, 2003); Alain Corbin, *Women for Hire: Prostitution and Sexuality in France after 1850*, trans. Alan Sheridan (Cambridge, MA: Harvard University Press); Karen Offen, 'Intrepid Crusader: Ghénia Avril de Sainte-Croix Takes on the Prostitution Issue,' *Proceedings of the Western Society for French History*, 33 (2005): 352–74; Hause, 'Social Control in Late Nineteenth-Century France: Protestant Campaigns for Strict Public Morality,' Chapter 6 in this volume.

7. Karen Offen, 'Defining Feminism: a Comparative Historical Approach,' *Signs: Journal of Women in Culture and Society*, 14(1) (Autumn 1988): 119-57; Hause and Kenney, *Women's Suffrage*, pp. 25–6.

8. Harlor, 'Honneur féminin,' *La Fronde*, 13 March 1901.

9. Pierre Larousse, *Grande Dictionnaire Universel du XIXe Siècle* (Paris: Administration du Grand Dictionnaire Universel, 1873), p. 377.

10. Ibid.

11. Émile Littré, *Dictionnaire de la Langue Française*, vol. 2 (Paris: Hachette, 1885), p. 2041.

12. Larousse, *Grande Dictionnaire*, p. 377.

13. Ibid., p. 376.

14. Larousse, *Grande Dictionnaire Universel du XIXe Siècle* (Paris: Administration du Grand Dictionnaire Universel, 1867), p. 1063.

15. Robert A. Nye, *Masculinity and Male Codes of Honor in Modern France* (Berkeley: University of California Press, 1993), p. 46; Julian Pitt-Rivers, 'Honor,' *International Encyclopedia of the Social Sciences* (New York: Macmillan, 1968), pp. 505–6; Mansker, '"Mademoiselle Arria Ly Wants Blood!" The Debate over Female Honor in Belle Époque France,' *French Historical Studies*, 29(4) (Fall 2006): 621–47.

16. Harlor, 'Honneur féminin,' *La Fronde*, 13 March 1901.

17. Nye, *Masculinity and Male Codes*, pp. 98–126.

18. Harlor, 'Honneur féminin.'

19. Ibid.

20. For the continuing influence of aristocratic culture and mores over the belle époque bourgeoisie and the idea that men's sexual competition for desirable women was a part of the honor code in this period, see Edward Berenson, *The Trial of Madame Caillaux* (Berkeley: University of California Press, 1992), pp.181–207;

Christopher E. Forth, *The Dreyfus Affair and the Crisis of French Manhood* (1 more: Johns Hopkins University Press, 2004), pp. 39–44. In fact, anthropologist Julian Pitt-Rivers makes a compelling case that male honor in the Latin countries of Europe has long included these elements of sexual rivalry and conquest over women as enhancing men's prestige, whereas within the family the imperative of sexual purity has been restricted to women as a result of its moral division of labor. Honor, Pitt-Rivers argues, continues to submit to 'the reality of power' throughout a man's life, and this includes sexual as well as economic, military and political power. See Pitt-Rivers, 'Honor,' pp. 504–6.

21. Susan Kingsley Kent, *Sex and Suffrage in Britain, 1860–1914* (Princeton: Princeton University Press, 1987), pp. 60–79; Lucy Bland, *Banishing the Beast: Sexuality and the Early Feminists* (New York: New Press, 1995), pp. 95–123.

22. Judith Walkowitz, *City of Dreadful Delight: Narratives of Sexual Danger in Late-Victorian London* (Chicago: University of Chicago Press, 1992), p. 92.

23. Ibid., p. 90; Bland, *Banishing the Beast*, pp. xii–xviii.

24. Bland, *Banishing the Beast*, p. xiii; Walkowitz, *City of Dreadful Delight*, pp. 132–3.

25. For a brief history of feminist abolitionist efforts in France, see 'Rapport de Mme Savioz de Sainte-Croix,' *Congrès international de la condition et des droits des femmes tenu à Paris en 1900* (Paris: Impr. Des arts et des manufactures, 1901), pp. 106–8.

26. Emilie de Morsier quoted in Theodore Stanton, *The Woman Question in Europe: a Series of Original Essays* (New York: G. P. Putnam's Sons, 1884), p. 266.

27. Corbin, *Women for Hire*, pp. 220–30.

28. Offen, 'Intrepid Crusader,' pp. 352–61.

29. Ghénia Avril de Sainte-Croix, 'Rapport,' pp. 97–8.

30. For this early twentieth-century debate between neoregulationists and abolitionists in which Bérenger took a leading role, see especially meetings of 13 and 20 January 1905 in *Commission Extraparlementaire du Régime des Moeurs. Procès-Verbaux des Séances* (Melun: Imprimerie Administrative, 1909), pp. 266–307. Avril de Sainte-Croix was an active member of this extra-parliamentary commission. For Parent-Duchâtelet, see Corbin, 'Présentation,' in *La Prostitution à Paris au XIXe siècle*, texte présenté et annoté par Alain Corbin (Paris: Seuil, 1981), pp. 7–49; Jill Harsin, *Policing Prostitution in Nineteenth-Century Paris* (Princeton: Princeton University Press, 1985), pp. 96–130.

31. Avril de Sainte-Croix, 'Rapport,' p. 98.

32. Ibid., p. 107; For Avril de Sainte-Croix's exposé of living conditions of prostitutes at the Saint-Lazare prison, see 'Les Femmes à Saint-Lazare,' *La Fronde*, 15–17 December 1897; See also series 'La Serve,' *La Fronde*, 21–23 January 1898.

33. See, for example, Arria Ly's testimonial of the impact Avril de Sainte-Croix's speech had on her activism in Ly, 'L'Horrible révélation!' n.d., Fonds Arria Ly (FAL), Box 8, Fonds Marie-Louise Bouglé (FMLB), Bibliothèque historique de la ville de Paris (BHVP).

34. For press clippings on a sample of the brochures, meetings and speeches given by feminists on the sexual question after the turn of the century, see Dossier Avril de Sainte-Croix, 1897–1907 (6 microfilm reels) and 351 Pro (Dossier Prostitution), 1900–1919 at the Bibliothèque Marguerite Durand (BMD). A growing emphasis on fighting double morality can also be traced in the congresses and committees of the major feminist organizations. The International Council of Women (ICW) had a committee on 'White Slave Traffic and Equal Moral Standard,' which Avril de Sainte-Croix chaired from 1904. The Union française pour le suffrage des

femmes (UFSF) tended to highlight a single moral standard in their propaganda and meetings, especially under the influence of Marguerite de Witt-Schlumberger, who served as UFSF president from 1913. The CNFF did not create an actual section on 'l'unité de la morale' until 1916, but it showed a dedicated interest in the issue from the organization's foundation in 1901. See Offen, 'Intrepid Crusader,' p. 352; Dossier Marguerite de Witt-Schlumberger, BMD and the Assemblées générales of the UFSF from 1910 in 1 AF 2, Fonds Cécile Brunschwicg, Centre des Archives du Féminisme (CAF); Christine Bard, *Les Filles de Marianne: Histoire des féminismes* (Paris: Fayard, 1995), pp. 66–7.

35. Judith Surkis, *Sexing the Citizen: Morality and Masculinity in France, 1870–1920* (Ithaca: Cornell University Press, 2006), pp. 185–205.

36. Remember's emphases. Remember, 'Faut-il instruire les jeunes filles des réalités du mariage?' *La Suffragiste*, October 1911.

37. For this rhetoric on depopulation, see Offen, 'Depopulation, Nationalism, and Feminism in Fin-de-Siècle France,' *American Historical Review*, 89(3) (June 1984): 648–76.

38. Corbin, *Women for Hire*, p. 249.

39. Surkis, *Sexing the Citizen*, pp. 198–9.

40. J.J. Bachofen cited by Cleyre Yvelin, 'Mademoiselle et Madame,' *L'Entente*, February 1906, FAL, Box 10, FMLB, BHVP.

41. Yvelin to Arria Ly, 7 August 1911, FAL, Box 3, FMLB, BHVP.

42. See examples nos 43-46 under Art. 2 in Dalloz, *Jurisprudence générale, Troisième Table Alphabétique de Dix Années du recueil périodique, 1887–1897* (Paris: Bureau de la Jurisprudence générale, 1897), p. 418.

43. H.D. Lewis, 'The Legal Status of Women in Nineteenth-Century France,' *Journal of European Studies*, 10(39) (1980): 178–88.

44. Bachofen cited by Yvelin in 'Mademoiselle et Madame.'

45. Camille Bélilon to Ly, n.d., Série 83 féminisme, Dossier CP 4249, FMLB, BHVP.

46. In belle époque France, only a small number of feminists pressed for women's right to birth control and abortion, since such reforms were seen as extremely radical in a country plagued by a slowing birth rate. Those activists who did so, such as Madeleine Pelletier and Nelly Roussel, tended to frame their arguments primarily in the language of individualist, natural rights philosophy. The public and the mainstream women's movement branded Pelletier's feminism as hostile to men and as inappropriate to the 'feminine' character of the French women's movement. Reactions to Roussel were similar, even though she deliberately framed her arguments in the context of birth control improving marriage and motherhood, as well as being a woman's right; she also publicly shamed men about the double standard they practiced. On Pelletier, see Felicia Gordon, *The Integral Feminist: Madeleine Pelletier, 1874–1939. Feminism, Socialism and Medicine* (Cambridge, UK: Polity Press, 1990), pp. 134–40; and Charles Sowerwine and Claude Maignien, *Madeleine Pelletier, une feminist dans l'arène politique* (Paris: Les Éditions Ouvrières, 1992), pp. 213–33; on Roussel, see Elinor Accampo, *Blessed Motherhood, Bitter Fruit: Nelly Roussel and the Politics of Female Pain in Third Republic France* (Baltimore: Johns Hopkins University Press, 2006), esp. chapters 3 and 4. For successful attempts by women to regain their sexual honor in the public forum of the courtroom, see Rachel G. Fuchs, 'Seduction, Paternity, and the Law in Fin de Siècle France,' *Journal of Modern History*, 72(4) (2000): 944–89.

47. Jean Elisabeth Pedersen, *Legislating the French Family: Feminism, Theater, and Republican Politics, 1870–1920* (New Brunswick: Rutgers University Press, 2003), pp. 87–97.
48. Colette Yver, 'Notre Enquête,' *La Française*, 24 October 1909.
49. Stanislaus Meunier, 'Notre Enquête,' *La Française*, 14 November 1909.
50. Nye, *Masculinity and Male Codes*, p. 13.
51. Ibid., pp. 31–46, quotation p. 38.
52. On illegitimacy, see Pedersen, *Legislating the French Family*, pp. 121–9.
53. Emphases in the original. Jeanne Oddo-Deflou, 'Notre Enquête,' *La Française*, 21 November 1909.
54. Augusta Moll-Weiss, 'Notre Enquête,' *La Française*, 5 December 1909.
55. Berenson, *The Trial of Madame Caillaux*, pp. 174–86, 198–9.
56. Jane Misme, 'Notre Enquête: Conclusions,' *La Française*, 27 February 1910.
57. Paul Bureau, 'Notre Enquête,' *La Française*, 19 December 1909.
58. Lucie Bérillon, 'Notre Enquête,' *La Française*, 30 January 1910.
59. L. Fourets, 'Notre Enquête: Opinions des lecteurs,' *La Française*, 12 December 1909.
60. Misme, 'Notre Enquête: Conclusions,' *La Française*, 6 March 1910.
61. Oddo-Deflou, 'Notre Enquête.'
62. Ida R. Sée, 'Notre Enquête: Opinions des lecteurs,' *La Française*, 12 December 1909.
63. Bureau, 'Notre Enquête.'
64. Avril de Sainte-Croix, 'Notre Enquête,' *La Française*, 23 January 1910.
65. For crimes of passion, see Ruth Harris, *Murders and Madness: Medicine, Law, and Society in the Fin de Siècle* (Oxford: Clarendon Press, 1989), pp. 208–42; Ann-Louise Schapiro, *Breaking the Codes: Female Criminality in Fin-de-Siècle Paris* (Stanford: Stanford University Press, 1996), pp. 136–78; on seduction suits, see Fuchs, 'Seduction, Paternity, and the Law,' pp. 944–89.

9

'Capped with Hope, Clad in Youth, Shod in Courage': Masculinity and Marginality in Fin-de-Siècle Paris

Michael L. Wilson

Among the many destabilizing consequences of modernity is, as Robert Nye has argued in *Masculinity and Male Codes of Honor in Modern France*, that in the modern period 'masculinity is always in the course of construction but always fixed, a *telos* that men experience as a necessary but permanently unattainable goal.'[1] The paradoxes of modern French manhood and the multiple stresses to which masculinity is subject seemed particularly acute to contemporary observers at the fin de siècle.[2] A century of political and social upheavals appeared to have unmoored all hierarchies, including gender hierarchies, from their seemingly inevitable and natural ground. Modern forms of capitalism threatened to render all relationships impersonal, abstract, and fungible. Productive labor, especially for the middle class, was increasingly sedentary and bureaucratic. As Steven Hause discusses in Chapter 6 in this volume, anxieties about depopulation, national degeneration, and decadence were widespread and gave rise to social protest movements urging moral renewal. The status of women was vigorously and publicly debated, with clear consequences for the status of men. Andrea Mansker demonstrates in Chapter 8 how fin-de-siècle feminists appropriated and transformed notions of honor in order to create new models of female citizenship, while Rachel Fuchs in Chapter 7 shows how women across social classes used the courts to attempt to restore their honor and that of their children. Within this context, the meaning of manhood was clearly open to question and critique.

Nye's path-breaking work is self-consciously focused on upper-class masculinity, on the elaboration of codes of masculine behavior for and by traditional elites and the bourgeoisie that would come to imitate, supplant, and transform them. Nye outlines what we may take to be the normative form of French masculinity between the Revolution and the 1920s, constructed around productive capacity, reproductive fitness, political and familial authority, and the public display of honor through dueling. Such a model of masculine identity is striking, not only for the ways in which it excludes women from participation in most domains of public life, but for the ways in which it systematically excludes many (if not most) men as well. Nye's account of the *doxa* of male identity challenges us to consider how masculinity was experienced and articulated by those men who fell outside the norms of bourgeois masculinity. As a preliminary contribution to such a project, I wish here to examine a small group of men who at the fin de siècle deliberately rejected normative masculinity and were thus forced to construct individual and collective identities for themselves on the margins of French life, the odd assemblage of would-be writers, artists, composers, and idlers known as 'bohemians.'

'Bohemia' is generally understood to be a subculture common to Western societies but with a distinctly French origin.[3] Bohemia is a self-chosen community, loosely associated with social marginality, youth, poverty, devotion to art, and rebellious behaviors and attitudes. In the 1830s, when bohemia was first identified and celebrated as a precinct of artistic life, observers felt it was not just a French phenomenon but a uniquely Parisian one. By the latter half of the nineteenth century, the history of Parisian bohemia formed a rich and varied tradition, one as much literary as social.

From 1881 through the First World War, the most prominent locus of French bohemian life was the Parisian neighborhood of Montmartre. The bohemians of Montmartre, while drawing upon the received traditions of bohemian life, were unusual in appropriating the tools of the modern consumer economy; the *montmartrois* established their own cafés and cabarets, many of which also published their own satirical newspapers.[4] These publications promoted the work of the artists who frequented the establishments as well as the cafés themselves, trying to attract a public for both. The newspapers were a forum in which bohemian Montmartre constructed its image and identity for itself and for a wider, perhaps unknown, audience.

The texts produced by and about bohemian Montmartre reveal a great deal about how a group of self-styled marginals negotiated masculinity at the fin de siècle. Like previous generations of bohemians, these men saw the 'fraternal misery' of being artists as central to their identity. If mainstream society declared, like Lucien Arréat in his 1892 volume, *Psychologie du peintre*, that their sensitivity, sympathy, and selfishness make artists 'the most feminine of men,' the bohemians of Montmartre cast these characteristics as inherently masculine. For *la bohème montmartroise* the term 'artist' had, as a member later admitted, 'a more elastic meaning than elsewhere.'[5] To be an artist in this context meant more than, and was not dependent upon, the production of art, literature, or music. Rather, an artist was one who possessed certain philosophical and social attitudes and expressed them through particular forms of behavior.

The members of bohemian Montmartre constructed their notions of masculinity as distinct from the available models of male identity and experience. While the majority of the inhabitants of bohemian Montmartre were of petit bourgeois origin, they rejected or failed to maintain the social concomitant

★ individs respond to norms
active/self-conscious self-fashioning

of that economic identity. They lived among and at the standard of living of the working class, yet were neither forced into manual labor nor integrated into working-class culture. The bohemians felt a deep sense of identification with the socially marginalized but that relation was largely imaginary and based in the romantic valorization of bohemian sensibilities. The *montmartrois* articulated their alternative notions of masculinity through several related tactics. First, the bohemians deliberately and explicitly rejected the hallmarks of bourgeois masculinity: productive labor, marriage and family life, and participation in civic life. Second, the bohemians stressed that they were genuinely connected to the 'real' French heritage; unlike their 'modern' counterparts, they understood the Gallic virtues of festivity, irreverence, bodily expression and exuberance. Finally, bohemian discourse emphasized the hypertrophic heterosexuality of artists, the enormous energy for desire and being desired, their pursuit and conquest of women. The bohemians' challenge to hegemonic masculinity operated by redeploying signifiers of traditional masculinity and ironically inverting norms of bourgeois manliness; bohemian masculinity insisted on, rather than questioned, male privilege. The *montmartrois* were adamant in their writings that bohemian men were superior to most men and all women, thereby reproducing if not exceeding bourgeois norms of appropriate gender identity.

The most concise sketch of the bohemian model of masculinity as creative transgression is found in a text by Émile Goudeau, a founder or participant in every major bohemian undertaking between 1881 and 1908. Goudeau wrote this piece in 1888 to coincide with the publication of his memoirs, *Ten Years of Bohemia*. Goudeau begins his account of the 'great road of Bohemia' within the thematic terms of bohemian life as set down by Henry Murger in the late 1840s: 'It was an army! Men capped with hope, clad in youth, shod in courage. They entered into life, bearing the banner of their twenty years, a banner which flapped in the wind beneath the blistering sun.'[6]

Goudeau's invocation of an army of artists is telling in several ways. Military service was an exclusively male experience, one common to most men of Goudeau's generation. The French army was held, until the advent of the Dreyfus Affair, to extend the revolutionary traditions of fraternity and equality and the soldier was an exemplary figure in popular culture (Goudeau's is an army without officers). As a national institution, the military was widely thought to be above social and political conflicts.[7] Martial imagery also evokes older notions of male honor, a term that rarely arises in bohemian discourse. The military metaphor allows Goudeau to characterize the irregular, mostly mental activities of bohemia in terms of discipline, austerity, and physical challenge. He warns those who choose this route that the road is narrow and rough, fraught with perils. The worst of these is the temptation to rejoin bourgeois society:

the way of the simple-minded, the way of the good folks who, if they've never experienced extraordinary laughter, have never felt as too heavy the burden of an existence that is well-considered, balanced, bureaucratic, a life chosen for them by their wise and ponderous fathers ... the way of the simple-minded where await provincial fiancées and chubby-cheeked wet-nurses.[8]

Casting the pillars of bourgeois morality – marriage, reproduction, and paternal authority – as 'simple-minded,' Goudeau depicts bohemia as superior in its cultivation of exceptional men freed from such strictures. He accentuates the fellowship of like-minded comrades, a fellowship unavailable to most men. Here, among 'the crowd of your companions,' the bohemian would be 'suddenly seized by an intoxication of ideas or of wine, of poetry or of absinthe, of love or of hashish.'[9] Camaraderie, laughter, and intoxication are thus seen as privileged means of escaping what bohemians saw as the joyless constraints of bourgeois life and labor. This creative intelligence, more than actual cultural production, marks one as an artist: 'in our brains the marvelous flower of Imagination can unfold!' Among Goudeau's army of poets, 'some are equipped with pencil or paintbrush, others with nothing at all.'[10] Yet even possessing the right sensibility does not suffice. Of those who begin on the 'great road of bohemia,' not everyone will endure:

Of the laughing companions, some fall ... The road is filled with debris: lost hopes, mud-soiled illusions, ephemeral loves ... To emerge victorious from this merciless ascent demands muscles and stamina. At the top, one flexes one's biceps; they are good, the calves strong, the shoulders large, the chest filled wide with the pure air of the mountaintop.[11]

By the end of this text, then, bohemian masculinity is explicitly figured in terms of the traditional masculine virtues of somatic virility, sacrifice, and self-command. Goudeau's narrative transforms bohemian life – a self-identification as creative, the invisible labor of ideation, practices of leisure and café sociability – into a trial of physical daring, martial self-discipline, and spiritual renunciation. Importantly, this bohemia has no set aesthetic program, no specific ideological content, and no particular goal save what Goudeau calls the 'goal of life – which is simply to live before one dies.'[12]

Few of the texts produced by the bohemians of Montmartre are as condensed and explicit in their staging of a transfigured masculinity as Goudeau's. We are able, though, to trace the construction of bohemian masculinity through and across the larger corpus of texts produced within this subculture. We might start with the bohemians' relation to a crucial inheritance of the French Revolution: the close identification of citizenship, political activity, and masculinity. The bohemians from the start insisted that their community was *montmartroise*, part of a realm far apart physically, culturally, imaginatively from the official world of Paris. When the Chat Noir cabaret, the founding institution of bohemian Montmartre, began publishing its newspaper, *Le Chat noir*, it was subtitled 'An organ of the interests of Montmartre' and its masthead portrayed Montmartre's two remaining windmills. The bohemians' enthusiasm for Montmartre involved their deliberate rejection of the modern world which had produced the 'bourgeois' Third Republic and its failures. An early entertainment at the cabaret was the coronation of its owner, Rodolphe Salis, as King of Montmartre, a mock-archaic ceremony culminating in the singing of the 'Chanson à Grévy,' an old favorite from the Latin Quarter in which the President of the Republic is depicted as doddering, lacking in virility, and decidedly bourgeois.[13] A more pointed rejection of the bourgeois republic came during the municipal elections of May 1884. In an effort to 'render the electoral period less banal, less pale, less monotonous,' posters appeared throughout Montmartre announcing the campaign of Rodolphe Salis, 'candidate of literary, artistic, and social protests.'[14] Salis's appeal to the voters of the eighteenth arrondissement begins with a deliberate paraphrase of Abbé Sieyès's provocative 1789 pamphlet, *What is the Third Estate?*:

> What is Montmartre? – Nothing.
> What should it be? – Everything!
> The day has finally come when Montmartre can and should reclaim its right of autonomy from the rest of Paris ... Montmartre is rich enough in finance, art and intelligence to live its own life. The Butte, this breast at which fantasy, science and all the truly French arts are fed, already has its own voice, *Le Chat noir*. Starting today, it must have its own representative, a representative worthy of the name.[15]

Like many *montmartrois* texts, Salis's appeal relies on a simple inversion such that the marginal becomes central and the central marginal. We should note that, despite this inversion, the source of festive creativity is figured as female but its expression is still cast in terms of masculine activity.

The parodic operations of this poster (and a second one posted on the eve of the election) had been developed in the previous several years in the pages of *Le Chat noir*. Politics is a prominent focus of the paper's humor; for example, the entire issue of 28 October 1882 was devoted to reporting Grévy's *coup d'état* of 2 November 1882, five days in the future. The articles in this issue are remarkable for their lampooning of prominent political personalities, their imitations of how official journalism would cover such an event, and their imagining of a variety of responses to the coup by the *montmartrois* themselves.[16] In later years, the attacks on politics were more modest in scale and depended far more on reacting to current events. The legislative elections of 1885, for instance, represented an important opportunity for 'radical' republicans to gain more power in the Chamber of Deputies. In response, Salis once again issued an appeal to the citizens of Montmartre:

> VOTERS,
> Down with modern politics,
> Long live Art, the Politics of the future,
> Down with what divides us,
> Long live what unites us!
>
> PEOPLE,
> Chosen by the literary men and artists of Montmartre to represent you in the Chamber.
> Enough of bellies! – Brains instead!
> Enough of phrase-makers, – singers instead!
> No more lawyers, – Orpheuses instead!
> Leave the pharmacists to their glass jars,
> The veterinarians to their stables,
> The doctors to their cholerics,
> The spiders to their ceilings,
> The night watchmen to their carriages,
> The lawyers to their bars,
> The canaries to their cages,
> The refiners to their beetroots,
> The clowns to their stages.[17]

Fake election campaigns became a repeated bohemian amusement, culminating in the 1893 crusade launched in *Le Chat noir* for Captain Cap, an imaginary 'anti-bureaucratic and anti-European candidate.'[18] This bit of satire – Captain Cap's slogan was 'No more bureaucracy! No more European routine! No more white savages!'– so offended the new owner of the paper, Émile Boucher, that George Auriol lost his position as editor.[19]

Auriol's dismissal is surprising, in large part because bohemian discourse insists so strenuously that political opinions simply do not matter. Political positions or ideology seldom figure as such in bohemian discourse. The bohemian papers constantly ridicule the institutions of and participants in parliamentary politics, but very few lines of critique emerge. The president is a buffoon;[20] petty disputes between representatives create governmental disorder;[21] the governmental bureaucracy is too large and inefficient;[22] foreign relations are so ridiculous that the French appear almost as foolish as other nations.[23] All these critiques also appeared within the nightly entertainment in bohemian cabarets, with *chansonniers* such as Henri Fursy, Léon Xanrof, Vincent Hyspa, and Jacques Ferny specializing in songs mocking local and national politics.[24] These themes, especially the disdain for parliamentary republicanism, are precisely those taken up in contemporary political satire.[25] What distinguishes bohemian attacks on electoral politics is their underlying assumption that the present system of government is *incapable* of representing bohemian interests. Thus, politics is dismissed as meaningless, its particular content irrelevant.[26] As in Salis's electoral announcement of 1885, bohemian discourse insists that politics is simply another aspect of the bourgeois culture that must be rejected in favor of Art.[27]

Even art, though, is not in itself a secure terrain for the establishment of masculine identity. Many articles in bohemian papers are concerned with the complicity of the most acclaimed writers and painters of the era with the bourgeoisie, and with the entrenched power and creative sterility of cultural elites:

> Ah well! you bureaucrats of the Conservatory, decorated members of the Comédie-Français, municipal councilmen of literature and art, frighten if you will! ... Not all poets, oh dear dependents on the state, are able to be office managers; they do not insist on receiving the high regard of the imbecilic bourgeois society that oppresses the art of the Third Republic.[28]

Most of the pieces take a more oblique, humorous approach to these same concerns. One article, for example, invents changes in style and subject matter for a number of *Salon*-bound painters, often reversing or muddling their best-known mannerisms. Manet, for instance, is listed as presenting 'Bonaparte in the camp at Bologna at the moment he embraces the first sapper he has decorated,' and the *juste milieu* painter Carolus-Duran is said to be submitting 'A self-portrait by Velasquez.'[29] The literary reportage takes aim at the parallel set of affectations attributed to literary figures. A good deal of this scorn is directed at Emile Zola, but even Victor Hugo, generally treated as a hero by the bohemians, comes in for criticism. In one article Hugo is taken to task for presiding over an expensive banquet in his honor. The author of the piece emphasizes his devotion to Hugo, but explains that this means 'I cannot indulge in spending 40 francs to watch you eat.'[30] The articles on art and literature formulate an implicit contrast of bohemian attitudes towards cultural production with those celebrated in the mainstream press. The texts insist both that the world of art is significant and worthy of attention and that it must not reproduce the relations of power and exclusion operating throughout bourgeois society.

This insistent need to establish bohemian identity and community in opposition to bourgeois norms can also be seen in a second major tactic the *montmartrois* deployed in articulating their transgressive masculinity: displays of hypertrophic heterosexuality. The desiring, pursuit, and conquest of women is one of the most consistent themes in bohemian discourse. As memoirist Maurice Donnay would later put it, 'We didn't think about war, nor about Bolshevism, we only thought about love.'[31] Representing bohemian love required attention not so much to male behavior as to the appropriate female object of desire and the sorts of relationships possible between an artist and the ideal woman.

Bohemians, to begin with, rejected bourgeois notions of appropriate female behavior. Each stage of a proper lady's life – innocent girlhood to matrimony and motherhood – is ridiculed. Particular (and exhaustive) disdain is reserved for the requirement of female chastity before marriage and for those young women who adhere to it. While occasional texts do valorize women who are chaste and remote,[32] bohemian writers more often deride virgins for their ignorance of 'the sole good that life grants these damned ones' and for their neglect of 'the supreme duty of Woman.'[33] So fervent is the disapprobation towards virgins that one poem addresses the Virgin Mary, divining the deprivations she must have experienced and 'the regrets which filled your heart and your feelings.' The poet concludes: 'I pity you / for having not, at least, known the love of a man.'[34] Bohemian writers ridiculed virgins' lack of sexual experience less because these women have been denied sexual pleasure than because they lack knowledge of the 'sole good' of being the object of male desire. That is, the chastity and sexual self-regulation so centrally at stake in the discursive and social practices documented by Fuchs, Mansker, and Hause was, from the point of view of the *montmartrois*, a fundamental misunderstanding of the proper role of women.

If female 'purity' is rejected, so too is the ideal of the *femme au foyer*, the modest and pious woman devoted to maternity and domesticity, a cornerstone of bourgeois morality. While prominently represented in dominant discourses, the *femme au foyer* makes only rare appearances in bohemian discourse, and then largely as a figure of ridicule.[35] She is rebuked not only for holding bourgeois ideals but, paradoxically, for not living up to them. Maurice Donnay argued that, if men have little respect for women, it is because they have learned hypocrisy from their mothers. From these women, they have learned:

> the good morals of ... this fine bourgeoisie in which the most solemn mothers readily declare: 'A young man must sow his wild oats.' But sow them where, you good mothers who can't doubt the importance of choosing the woman who will form the young man's first idea of women?[36]

This gap between the proclaimed morality of the *bourgeoise* and her 'actual' existence is a favorite occasion for bohemian humor. To be 'an honorable woman,' the *chansonnier* Xanrof declares, 'is pretty tedious.'[37] This is why, his song suggests, so few women remain honorable. That bourgeois wives, whatever their pretensions, are unfaithful is simply assumed. Thus, the double standard in sexual relations is seen by the bohemians as not only embodied in bourgeois women but regulated and enforced by them. The *montmartrois* drew attention to the double standard in sexual morality just as feminist activists did, but they did so in order to claim that men were the real victims of this hypocrisy, not women. The bohemians, in rebelling against the customs constraining sexual expression in bourgeois society, retain and forcefully reassert its normative gender hierarchy.

Set against this image of constrictive and often grotesque bourgeois womanhood, bohemian discourse constructs an ideal woman, the desire for whom is a favorite topic in bohemian newspapers. This ideal woman is never imagined to be an equal; indeed, the bohemians foreground sexual difference in describing her. Ideal femininity is here, as is usually the case in nineteenth-century culture, inscribed bodily and figured in conformity to classical standards of beauty, especially delicate facial features, a voluptuous torso, and 'shapely' legs. The bohemians' ideal woman is youthful: the beauty of a young woman is like a flower and fades quickly.[38] Those who conform to these standards are truly women, 'God's masterpiece':

> God took stars, snow and roses in His holy hands
> And, dreaming a masterpiece with this amalgam,
> Made of the rose a face, of the snow two breasts,
> Of the stars two eyes, and made of it all a Woman.[39]

Like this poem, which does not grant 'God's masterpiece' intelligence, many love poems published in bohemian newspapers are little more than lists of the beloved's physical features:

> She would be very sweet, she would be very good,
> With the eyes of a child, large, blue or black,
> Which my intoxicated eyes would make their only mirror.
> Roses would blossom upon her pretty mouth.
>
> In her hair, wild and golden, or shadow-dark and gleaming,
> In strophes of kisses, under the pallor of night,
> As the mad birds sing of my Hopes …[40]

The young woman is here rendered explicitly child-like, her only purpose to reflect the poet's gaze narcissistically back to himself. Other texts are even less subtle, taking up the archaic literary form of the blazon to fetishize body parts like the mouth, throat, breasts, or lower legs.[41] The descriptions in these texts are predicated on a physiognomy of desire: a woman's face and body are held to be of paramount importance because they *constitute* her character and identity.

Still, beauty, however important, is not enough – as bohemian descriptions of virgins attest. These young women must also be sexually accessible:

> Everyone of course thinks of girls like flowers, yet they aren't treated like flowers if they grant ... their favors to everyone. Is this logical, this squeamishness? We love flowers, their balm enchants us ... Why shouldn't it be the same with girls, who are worth more than flowers, though they fade just the same.[42]

The woman favored by bohemian discourse is imagined as combining physical attractiveness with 'freedom': the liberty to engage in pre- and extramarital sexual relations, to cohabit outside marriage, and to work outside the home. This liberty is identified exclusively with young working-class women. As a consequence, the bohemian papers contain innumerable texts, like 'La Bouquetière,' which seek to evoke the particular charms of a working-class woman.[43] The young flower-seller, for example, is described as:

> A little of the ideal, lost
> On a badly-lit street.
>
> A little of the ideal that captures
> The most indifferent heart.
>
> A little of the ideal which caresses,
> Charity for each soul that passes by.[44]

As is conventional in these texts, the poem reveals little about the woman who is its subject, merely contrasting her physical charms with her modest surroundings. This combination of physicality, sexual availability, and financial independence exercised a powerful attraction for bohemian men. The sort of imagined heterosexual relationships they represented are all the more striking for their asymmetry of power and regard. While bohemian discourse does challenge a particular class-bound concept of 'femininity,' allowing women a limited role in the public sphere and valuing their participation in sexual experience, it offers an equally restrictive concept in its stead. It can be summarized in the caption for one caricature: 'Women, they don't belong in art. I only let them into my bed.'[45] That the precise place imagined for women in bohemia is in bed is made clear from the first issue of *Le Chat noir*; the envoi of the poem entitled 'Ballad of Joyous Bohemia' addresses women directly:

> Woman, don't be too hard on us:
> The artist, in your satiny arms
> Doesn't cut such a bad figure,
> Whether painter, poet or actor.[46]

Women are seen here as benefiting from their proximity to talent, even if they must be coaxed to provide comfort and support.

On the other hand, the knowledge that men are tied to women emotionally and sexually, and are thus vulnerable to them, only exacerbates the bohemians' anxiety that their ideal woman will use and then betray them.[47] The fear and loathing of what female flesh may extract from the male spirit pervades bohemian discourse, expressed as a facile and cynical misogyny:

> At bottom, it's all a question of whether the harm they will have caused us sufficiently balances the hours of happiness they'll have given us, and whether the cruelty of their ingratitude must erase from our thankful souls the joys spread there by their caresses, even the fleeting and deceitful ones.[48]

What the 'harm' and 'cruelty' of women might be is suggested elsewhere in bohemian discourse: infidelity, smothering domesticity, sapping of creative energies, and rejection of bohemians' elevated sensibilities. Noticeably absent is any discussion of possible paternity and its repercussions; female honor and male responsibility as examined by Rachel Fuchs are simply ignored. Given such an understanding of the possible relations between men and women, it is hardly surprising that one article counsels artists to avoid all but the most transitory encounters: 'The truly happy ones – sly devils – are the incurable bachelors. They've foreseen the danger and defended themselves to the utmost.'[49] The author admits, though, that few men are so lucky; most enter into some sort of alliance with a woman: 'Without being on their guard they fall into the trap ... They are defeated; and forever more they are the broken down companions of some sludge in dirty skirts, with whom they live and love among the combs and dishwater and toothbrushes!'[50] Bohemian discourse stresses, however, that while it is common for men to enter into relationships with women, 'these ideal unions are not within the morals, within the good morals of the bourgeoisie.'[51] The principal way to avoid the bourgeois model, and a particularly effective way for a man to retain some of his power in relation to a woman, is to remain unmarried:

> Mother Nature has her laws,
> And, when she speaks,
> Listen closely to her voice.
> So, to extinguish the flame
> That sets my heart on fire,
> Wisely, I took a woman...
> But I am not married.[52]

About the experience of such relationships bohemian discourse is oddly silent. Although many of the founding figures of bohemian

Bohemian Domesticity

Montmartre – including Rodolphe Salis, his brother Gabriel, the illustrator Adolphe Willette, and the *chansonnier* Aristide Bruant – did cohabit for long periods and even marry, only a very few bohemian texts describe the wives or the home lives of artists.

In all of the texts that take up the topic of bohemian domesticity, relations between the sexes are depicted as fraught with deception and compromise; any domestic arrangement risks reproducing what bohemians considered the less desirable aspects of bourgeois marriage. The most ambivalent of these texts suggests that the unhappy lives of women involved with bohemians are sacrificed to the demands of art:

> The mistresses of poets are skinny ... The mistresses of poets are plain, but their plainness is full of a charm that could make you cry ... The mistresses of poets are dead. In their life on this earth, so short, they were called Lillith, Antigone, Sperata! – and it is these women, who died of love, that today we seek to kiss on the lips.[53]

While the text portrays these women as faded copies of a feminine ideal, it at least accords them some (perverse) dignity and value. More often in these texts, the women desired by bohemians, once in a relationship, soon reveal themselves to possess the very worst characteristics ascribed to their gender: they are manipulative, deceptive, vain, cruel, and promiscuous.[54] Moreover, as companions, these women are no longer suited or able to provide creative inspiration.[55] In a cartoon by Forain, a woman says to her distracted lover: 'Read me the sonnet again, you know, where you compare me to a living spring...'[56] The woman who inspired that poem has, from the perspective of the artist, disappeared. Thus, no relationship is safe from the routine, boredom, and infidelities of domesticity. Just as the charms of every woman must fade, every alliance must end:

> Then, the kisses lose their charm,
> Having lasted several seasons.
> The mutual betrayals
> Lead to an end one day, but without tears ...
>
> It's death to hold on too long
> With flowers, with women.[57]

If passion or even love cannot endure – and the bohemians assume they cannot – the fault lies with women. Bohemian discourse suggests that the very qualities which draw men to particular women make men blind to the possibility that all women are alike and in their similarity present a particular danger. While relationships with women are necessary, it suggests, they are *women artists*

unreliable. The trustworthy, enduring, meaningful relations remain those between men of spirit, relations founded on higher principles of intellect and creativity, untainted by the weakness and duplicity of the (female) body.

Thus we see the crucial importance within bohemian discourse of protecting bohemian identity not just from competing forms of masculinity but from those women who assume the masculine prerogative of creation. These women are identified by the hyphenated, hermaphroditic appellations of *femme-artiste*, *femme-peintre*, or *femme-auteur*. Bohemian discourse suggests that the spirit of an artist can dwell only uneasily within the female: 'It is truly incredible that such an artistic temperament is contained in so young and charming a wrapper.'[58] In this unnatural accommodation, one identity must dominate at the expense of the other. Should artistic ambition prevail, the woman will, at the least, be un-sexed. A woman with literary aspirations, one poem suggests, becomes a blue-stocking, a singular being 'who is not a woman and lacks the virility of a man.'[59] A more unsettling possibility is that women artists will come to resemble men in more than their vocation: 'There is nothing feminine about the woman painter. She wears a masculine stand-up collar and jacket. The wrinkles in her dress are stiff and disgraceful. All her movements are brusque and devoid of elegance.'[60] Such masculinization need not signal a lack of artistic merit – quite the opposite. For example, in a much-circulated anecdote, the poet Marie Krysinska, the only woman in bohemian Montmartre to be treated as an artistic peer, is revealed to wear men's shoes under her skirts.[61] Sarah Bernhardt was admitted to the meeting of the Hydropaths, the literary club that formed the nucleus of bohemian Montmartre, only if she took the title of *Monsieur* Bernhardt. The original occasion for this *travesti* was to elude police regulations against cross-dressing, but the charade continued after its legal necessity, becoming both an inside joke and an honorific. The sixth issue of the Hydropath's journal devoted its cover to Monsieur Bernhardt, and inside proclaimed, 'What a good young man, and what a remarkable young man!'[62] *Le Chat noir* took up the joke, even announcing Bernhardt as the Messiah. This masculine identification is meant as tribute not just to Bernhardt's dramatic skill but to her work in sculpture and painting. At the same time, *Le Chat noir* ran excerpts from *Dinah Samuel*, a *roman-à-clef* which casts the actress as a virago; and, as Bernhardt withdrew from bohemian circles, she was increasingly feminized, appearing as the paper's wire service (that is, as a gossip) and finally as 'queen of the bourgeoisie.'[63]

Bernhardt's fall from grace represents what, for the bohemians, is the debilitating potential within every *femme-artiste*: femininity is always in danger of smothering creativity.[64] Second-rate women's work becomes personified in bohemian discourse by the Société (later, the Union) des Femmes Peintres et Sculpteurs, whose annual exhibitions at the Palais de l'Industrie were routinely reviewed in Montmartre's journals.[65] The *montmartrois* treated these artists with irony and skepticism. The tone of the reviews is light, the attitude condescending. Each exhibition is hailed as an improvement over the previous one, yet after eight years the same reviewer's highest praise is 'that this twelfth exhibition is as interesting as is possible.'[66] This perceived lack of quality is attributed directly to the gender of the artists. The exhibition is described as 'this little festival of mothers' and, in an over-wrought conceit, as a 'caesarian operation' after which 'the one hundred fifty-five mamas of the displayed new-borns' can find comfort that 'the three hundred fifty-six infants will survive.'[67] Here female artists are completely identified with the biological processes of reproduction, processes that bohemian discourse elsewhere shuns. Artistic motherhood, though, is achieved through unnatural means, requiring assistance and leaving the fate of the 'new-borns' in question. Further, even the subjects of the works themselves are too feminine for *Le Chat noir*: 'we continue to deplore the absolute absence of genre paintings. Still lives, landscapes, flowers (oh! too many flowers!)' Another critic expresses the same sentiment in a single sentence review: 'It's just like a bouquet of flowers!'[68] The bohemian gender ideology which equates artistic merit with masculinity cannot address the *femmes-artistes* as simultaneously female and creative: insofar as they are women they cannot be true 'artists,' and insofar as they are artists they cannot be true 'women.'[69]

Bohemian discourse thus engages gender in terms that appear similar to those dominant in bourgeois society. Both assume a gender hierarchy in which society and culture are created and sustained by men, in which men are fundamentally superior to women, and in which female sexuality is bound to male desire. Moreover, the bohemian understanding of gender transgression itself seems a variant of, or contribution to, wider public discourses. The representation of the *femme-artiste* forms part of the debates, provoked in large part by the French feminist movement, about the place of (bourgeois) women in the public sphere and particularly about the dangers of the masculinization of women who compete economically with men.[70] Both the bohemians and bourgeois society were strongly resistant to the discussions of female citizenship that Mansker describes.

While these similarities are striking, they are also misleading. Bohemian discourse deploys these prevailing gender norms to a different end; they form part of an assault *against* marriage and the bourgeois family, *against* propriety and respectability. They are integral to the counter-discourse of bohemia, the effort to mount a critique of bourgeois society from within its own discursive space. By rejecting the institutions and practices that articulate and undergird bourgeois masculinity, the bohemians of Montmartre constructed their sense of male privilege around an imagined monopoly on intellect, imagination, and sensibility. In place of productive labor, they celebrated fantasies, fictions, and festivity; in place of citizenship and public responsibility, they valorized camaraderie and private fraternal ties; in place of monogamy and reproduction, they honored the open expression of heterosexual desire, unconstrained sexual activity, and freedom from family responsibilities. This fragile and unstable formulation of bohemian identity – transgressive genius as the ground of masculinity and vice-versa – had to be defended, on the one hand, against bourgeois society and its prescriptive manhood; but it also had to be defended, on the other hand, against 'femininity' as such. Bohemian Montmartre's embodiment of masculinity is, thus, inseparable from its counter-discursive strategy to valorize marginality as authenticity, to imagine a small, shifting group of men at the periphery even of Parisian literary and artistic life as warriors 'capped with hope, clad in youth, shod in courage.'

Notes

1. Robert Nye, *Masculinity and Male Codes of Honor in Modern France* (New York: Oxford University Press, 1993), p. 13.
2. Landmark works on masculinity in France during this period are Annelise Maugue, *L'identité masculine en crise au tournant du siècle, 1870–1914* (Paris: Rivages, 1987); Venita Datta, *Birth of a National Icon: the Literary Avant-Garde and the Emergence of the Modern Intellectual* (Albany: State University of New York Press, 1999); Christopher E. Forth, *The Dreyfus Affair and the Crisis of French Manhood* (Baltimore: Johns Hopkins University Press, 2004); and Judith Surkis, *Sexing the Citizen: Morality and Masculinity in France, 1870–1920* (Ithaca: Cornell University Press, 2006).
3. The scholarly literature on bohemia is voluminous. Signal works on French bohemianism include Roger Shattuck, *The Banquet Years: the Arts in France, 1885–1918* (New York: Harcourt, Brace, 1958); César Graña, *Bohemia versus Bourgeois* (New York: Basic Books, 1964); George Levitine, *The Dawn of Bohemianism* (University Park, PA: Penn State University Press, 1978); Luce Abélès, *La Vie de bohème* (Paris: Éditions de la Réunion des musées nationaux, 1986); Jerrold Seigel, *Bohemian Paris: Culture, Politics, and the Boundaries of Bourgeois Life, 1830–1930* (New York: Viking, 1987); Elizabeth Wilson, *Bohemians: the Glamorous Outcasts* (New York: I.B. Tauris, 2000); and Mary Gluck, *Popular Bohemia: Modernism and Urban Culture in Nineteenth Century Paris* (Cambridge, MA: Harvard University Press, 2005).
4. For a brief introduction to bohemian Montmartre during the fin de siècle, see my 'Portrait of the Artist as a Louis XIII Chair,' in Gabriel Weisberg (ed.), *Montmartre and the Making of Mass Culture* (New Brunswick, NJ: Rutgers University Press, 2001), pp. 180–204. See also Jerrold Seigel, *Bohemian Paris*, pp. 215–41.
5. Maurice Donnay, *Autour du Chat Noir* (Paris: Grasset, 1926), p. 15.
6. 'C'était une armée! Des gars coiffés d'espérance, vêtus de jeunesse, chaussé de courage. Ils entraient dans la vie, portant l'oriflamme de leurs vingt ans, une oriflame qui claquait au vent, sous le soleil fou.' Émile Goudeau, 'Au Bout de Dix Ans,' *Le Pierrot*, 6 July 1888.
7. Forth, *Dreyfus Affair*, pp. 43–7, *passim*. See also David M. Hopkin, *Soldier and Peasant in French Popular Culture, 1766–1870* (New York: Boydell Press, 2003).
8. '... l'allée des simples, l'allée des bonnes gens, qui, s'ils n'ont jamais de rires extraordinaires, ne sentent point trop lourde l'existence bien façonnée, équilibrée, bureaucratique, choisie pour eux par leurs pères sages et pondérés ... l'allée des simples où t'attendaient les fiancées provinciales et les nourrissons joufflus.' Ibid.

9. '...la foule de tes compagnons, subitement secoués par une ivresse d'idée ou de vin, de poésie ou d'absinthe, d'amour ou de haschich.' Ibid.
10. 'les rires extravagants et les fêtes nocturnes' ... 'en notre cervelle puisse s'épanouir la merveilleuse fleur de Fantaisie!' ... 'les uns [sont] munis du crayon ou du pinceau, les autres de rien du tout.' Ibid.
11. 'Des compagnons rieurs, quelques-uns tombent ... La route est pleine de débris: espérances fanées, illusions souillées de fange, amours éphémères ... Pour sortir vainqueur de cette ascension sans merci, il fallait des muscles et du poumon. Alors, on ausculte ses biceps: ils sont bons, les jarrets solides, le épaules larges, la poitrine se gonfle d'air pur sur la crête de la montagne.' Ibid.
12. '...but de la vie – qui est simplement de vivre avant de mourir.' Ibid.
13. '[I]l y eut l'élevation de Salis au grade de roi de Montmartre. Il dut revêtir un costume en or, des étoffes inoïes, se munir d'un sceptre. Après avoir reçu les hommages des peuples, il s'en alla prendre possession du Moulin de la Galette. Il s'y rendit, cachant ses vêtements royaux sous un ulster, accompagné par des peintres et des poètes armés de hallebarde, qui, tout le long de la butte, à l'ahurissement des populations, criaient: Vive le roi! ... Il est vrai qu'on chantait de temps à autre *Grévy le Jurassique*, et le *Vive Grévy!* si ironique fût-il, compensait le séditieux: Vive le roi!' Goudeau, *Dix ans*, pp. 266–7. For another instance of mock monarchism, see Xernard Fau, 'L'Entrée du Comte de Paris à Montmartre,' *Le Chat noir*, 28 March 1885.
14. '... rendre la période électorale moins banale, moins pâle et moins monotone ... candidat des revendications littéraires, artistiques, et sociales.' 'Élections municipales du 4 mai 1884,' *Le Chat noir*, 10 May 1884.
15. 'Qu'est-ce que Montmartre? – Rien. Que doit-il -re? – Tout! Le jour est enfin venu où Montmartre peut et doit revendiquer ses droites d'autonomie contre le restant de Paris ... Montmartre est assez riche de finance, d'art et d'esprit pour vivre de sa vie propre ... *La Butte*, cette mamelle où s'allaitent la fantaisie, la science, et tous les arts vraiment français, avait déjà son organe le *Chat noir*, à partir d'aujourd'hui, elle doit avoir son représentant, un représentant digne de ce nom.' Ibid.
16. See also A'Kempis [Goudeau], 'Le grand complot du 13 à l'Hôtel de Ville,' *Le Chat noir*, 15 July 1882.
17. 'ÉLECTEURS, A bas la Politique moderne, / Vive l'Art, la Politique future, / A bas ce qui nous divise, / Vive ce qui nous réunit! // PEUPLE, Choisis des lettrés et des artistes de Montmartre pour te représenter à la Chambre. Assez de ventres! – des cerveaux! Assez de phraseurs, – des chanteurs! Plus d'avocats, – des orphées! Laisse les pharmaciens à leurs bocaux, Les sous-vétérinaires à leurs écuries, Les médecins à leurs cholériques, Les araignées à leurs plafonds, Les vidangeurs à leurs voitures, Les avocats à leurs barres, Les serins à leurs cages, Les raffineurs à leurs betteraves, Les pitre à leurs tréteaux.'] Rodolphe Salis, 'Électeurs,' *Le Chat noir*, 30 October 1885.
18. George Auriol, 'Le Bénedicité,' *Le Chat noir*, 21 January 1893; Alphonse Allais, 'The Meat-Land,' *Le Chat Noir*, 1 April 1893; Auriol, 'Les Elections,' *Le Chat noir*, 12 August 1893; 'Captain Cap,' *Le Chat noir*, 19 August 1893; and Georges Marx, 'La Bureaucratie au Captain Cap,' *Le Chat noir*, 2 September 1893.
19. 'Plus de bureaucratie! Plus de routine européene! Plus de sauvages blancs!' Quoted in Armond Fields, *George Auriol* (Layton, UT: Peregrine Smith Books, 1985), pp. 59–60.
20. See, for example, 'L'Album de Monsieur Grévy,' *Le Chat noir*, 19 December 1885; Pimodan, 'La Loge de Monsieur Carnot,' *Le Chat noir*, 25 October 1890; 'Le Compas

de M. Carnot,' *Le Chat noir*, 27 February 1892; Raoul Ponchon, 'Sarcey, président,' *Le Courrier français*, 8 July 1894; and Paul Dollfus, 'Le Boulevard, Félix Faure,' *Le Chat noir*, 26 January 1895.

21. See, for example, D. Cavé, 'Séance à la Chambre,' *L'Auberge des Adrets* No. 7 [1886]; Tiret-Bognet, 'La Déclaration Ministérielle,' *Le Chat noir*, 23 January 1886; Adolphe Willette, 'L'Épiphanie,' *Le Pierrot*, 4 January 1889; Jules Jouy, 'Une Séance à la Chambre,' *Le Chat noir*, 21 May 1892; Armand Masson, 'Élégie sur l'Instabilité Ministérielle,' *Le Chat noir*, 4 February 1893; Jean D'Arc, 'Élections législatives,' *Le Courrier français*, 6 August 1893; and 'La Devinette ministérielle,' *Le Chat noir*, 2 February 1895.

22. See, especially, the campaign devised for Captain Cap (notes 14 and 15 above); and Un Bureaucrate, 'La Lettre d'un bureaucrate,' *Le Chat noir*, 26 August 1893.

23. See, for example, Le Diplomate, 'Politique Étrangère,' *Le Chat noir*, 18 March 1882; Baron V., 'Lettres sur la politique étrangère,' *Le Chat noir*, 13 June 1891; Émile Goudeau, 'La Chine et Montmartre,' *Les Quat'z'Arts*, 9 January 1898; and Dr V., 'La Question cubaine,' *Les Quat'z'Arts*, 24 April 1898.

24. See, for example, Léon Xanrof, *Chansons à Rire* (Paris: Flammarion, 1891); Jacques Ferny, *Chansons Immobiles* (Paris: E. Fromont, 1896); Henri Fursy, *Chansons Rosses* (Paris: P. Ollendorf, 1898); and Vincent Hyspa, *Chansons d'humor* (Paris: Enoch, 1903).

25. See Jacques Lethève, *La caricature et la presse sous la IIIe République* (Paris: A. Colin, 1961), pp. 94–124; and Philippe Roberts-Jones, *La caricature du 2e Empire à la Belle Époque* (Paris: Club français du livre, 1963), pp. 5–9.

26. See, for example, A'Kempis [Émile Goudeau], 'Bulletin politique,' *Le Chat noir*, 1 July 1882; Louis Legrand, 'Les Décorations du 14 juillet,' *Le Courrier français*, 14 July 1889; Raphaël Shoomard, 'L'Affaire des Philippines,' *Le Chat noir*, 29 June 1891; Adolphe Willette, 'Ah! Ah! funiculi funicula!' *Le Courrier français*, 3 July 1892; and Hugues Delorme, 'La Politique,' *Les Quat'z'Arts*, 20 November 1897.

27. This general disdain for politics is punctuated by moments in which the realm of bohemian concerns and that of politics appear to draw near to one another and even to intersect, most notably the Boulanger Affair, the anarchist 'crisis' of 1893–94, and the Dreyfus Affair.

28. 'Eh bien! messieurs les bureaucrats du Conservatoire, messieurs les décorés de la Comédie-Français, messieurs les conseillers municipaux de la littérature et de l'art! effarez-vous si vous voulez ... Tous les poètes, ô chers budgetivores, ne peuvent pas être chefs de bureau, ils ne tiennent pas tous à la haute consideration de l'imbécile société bourgeoise qui opprime l'art de la troisième République!' Emile Goudeau, 'Bulletin littéraire,' *Le Chat noir*, 29 December 1883.

29. 'Bonaparte au camp de Boulogne au moment où il embrasse le premier sapeur qu'il a décoré ... Le portrait de Velasquez peint par lui-même.' Rodolphe Salis, 'Le Salon avant Wolff,' *Le Chat noir*, 4 March 1882. See also, Constant Chanouard, 'Le Salon avant Wolff,' *Le Chat noir*, 11 March 1882; Emile Goudeau, 'Peintures and Peinture,' *Le Chat noir*, 6 May 1882; Rodolphe Salis, 'Chat Noir-Salon,' *Le Chat noir*, 27 May 1882; A'Kempis [Goudeau], 'Bulletin Artistique,' *Le Chat noir*, 30 December 1882.

30. '... ne me permettent pas de dépenser 40 francs pour vous voir manger.' Olympio, 'A Victor Hugo,' *Le Chat noir*, 3 March 1883. See also Rodolphe Salis, 'Que souffle, Messieurs!' *Le Chat noir*, 18 February 1882; A'Kempis [Goudeau], 'Voyage des découvertes,' *Le Chat noir*, 18 March 1882; 'Ce que Je Veux,' *Le Chat noir*,

18 March 1882; Emile Goudeau, 'Lettre de M. Jacquet à M. Dumas fils,' *Le Chat noir*, 19 June 1882; Goudeau, 'Bulletin littéraire,' *Le Chat noir* (30 September 1882).
31. 'Nous ne pensions pas à la guerre, ni au bolchevisme, nous ne pensions qu'á l'amour.' Maurice Donnay, *Autour de Chat Noir* (Paris: B. Grasset, 1926), p. 43.
32. See Jules de Marthold, 'Virgo,' *Le Chat noir*, 12 July 1884; and Rodolphe Darzens, 'Sonnet Virginal,' *Le Chat noir*, 10 June 1885.
33. '... le seul bien que la vie accorde à ses damnés ... le devoir suprême de la Femme.' Edmond Haraucourt, 'Vierges Mortes,' *Le Chat noir*, 21 March 1885; Hugues Delorme, 'Vierges,' *Le Chat noir*, 26 March 1892. See also Dubut de Laforest, 'Les Vierges Contemporaines,' *Le Chat noir*, 5 August 1882; Noel Gontran, 'Pour rester Vierge,' *Le Courrier français*, 29 April 1888; Raphael Chaignaud, 'Vierge stérile,' *Le Chat noir*, 18 May 1889; Georges Briquet, 'Considérations sur la jeune fille,' *Les Quat'z'Arts*, 4 January 1908.
34. '... les regrets dont ton coeur et tes sens étaient pleins ... je te plains / De n'avoir pas, au moins, connu l'amour de l'homme.' Victor d'Auriac, 'Sonnet à la Vierge,' *Le Chat noir*, 21 October 1882.
35. See, for example, Marcel Capy, 'Entre deux feux,' *Le Chat noir*, 7 March 1891; Guillaume, 'Eclairage Levant,' *Le Chat noir*, 4 June 1892; Hermann Paul, 'La Dame de province,' *Le Courrier français*, 30 September 1894; Hermann Paul, 'Quel délicieux concert!' *Le Courrier français*, 31 March 1895.
36. '... les bonnes moeurs de ... cette bonne bourgeoisie où les mères les plus gourmées disent couramment: "Il faut qu'un jeune homme jette sa gourme." Mais où la jeter, bonne mères qui ne vous doutez pas de l'importance du choix de la première femme pour la première idée que le jeune homme se fait de la femme?' Maurice Donnay, *Des Souvenirs* (Paris: A. Fayard et Cie., 1933), pp. 285–6.
37. Léon Xanrof, 'Femme Honnête,' *Le Courrier français*, 12 July 1891.
38. See Pierre de Rensard, 'Sur un bouquet,' *La Lanterne Japonaise*, 27 October 1888; and Charles Cros, 'Lendemain,' *Le Divan Japonais*, 28 June 1891.
39. 'Dieu prit étoiles, neige et rose en ses doigts saints, / Et, rêvant un chef-d'oeuvre avec cet amalgame, / Fit de la rose un front, de la niege deux seins, / Des étoiles deux yeux, et du tout une Femme.' Jean Rameau, 'Le Chef d'Oeuvre de Dieu,' *Le Chat noir*, 10 January 1885. See also Alfred Mortier, 'Idéal,' *Le Chat noir*, 26 July 1890.
40. 'Elle serait très douce, elle serait très bonne, / Avec des yeux d'enfant, de grands yeux bleus ou noirs, / Dont mes yeux enivrés feraient leurs seuls miroirs; / Les roses fleuriraient sur sa bouche mignonne. / Dans ses cheveux d'or fauve, ou d'ombre qui rayonne, / En strophes de baisers, sous la pâleur des soirs, / Comme des oiseaux fous chanteraient mes Espoirs...' Bénoni Glador, 'Elle,' *Le Chat noir*, 1 February 1890. See the equally obsessive detailing of features in Ogier d'Ivry, 'Rose Blond,' *Le Chat noir*, 9 October 1886.
41. Victor d'Auriac, 'La Chanson des seins,' *Le Chat noir*, 23 December 1882; Maurice Vaucaire, 'Bras et Jambes,' *Le Chat noir*, 4 November 1882; Rodolphe Darzens, 'Vos Seins,' *Le Chat noir*, 4 July 1885; Maurice Donnay, 'A ta gorge,' *Le Chat noir*, 26 January 1889; Armand Masson, 'Litanies des seins,' *Le Chat noir*, 28 November 1891; Albert Tinchant, 'Aux Lèvres,' *Le Divan Japonais*, 5 March 1892; Eugène Cross, 'Les Bas,' *Le Courrier français*, 7 January 1894; Pierre Trimouillat, 'Ballade en l'honneur d'un beau cou,' *Les Quat'z'Arts*, 12 December 1897.

42. 'Tout le monde donc considère les filles comme des fleurs, mais cependant il ne les traite pas comme des fleurs, si elles concèdent ... leurs faveurs à tout le monde. Est elle logique, cette délicatesse? Nous aimons les fleurs, leur baume nous enchante ... Pourquoi ne doit-il pas être de même des fille, qui valent mieux que les fleurs, quoiqu'elles se fanent de même?' Didi, 'Extrait Liebig,' *Le Divan Japonais*, 25 July 1891.

43. See, for example, Fernand Crésy, 'La Dompteuse,' *Le Chat noir*, 13 May 1882; Edmond Harancourt, 'La Parisienne,' *Le Chat noir*, 7 October 1882; Alexandre Chevalier, 'Vive la Parisienne,' *L'Auberge des Adrets*, no. 4 [1886]; Jehan Serrazin, 'Pour une jeune institutrice,' *Le Divan Japonais*, 4 September 1891; Sarrazin, 'La Chanson de la blanchisseuse,' *Le Divan Japonais*, 30 January 1892; Claude Lauzanne, 'Marchande de Plaisir,' *Le Chat noir*, 30 April 1892; Raoul Gineste, 'La Brodeuse,' *Le Chat noir*, 15 October 1892; Aristide Bruant, 'A Grenelle,' *Le Mirliton*, 2 November 1892; Edouard Beaufils, 'Aux Modistes de Paris,' *Le Courrier français*, 31 March 1895; and Thomas Chesnais, 'Nos Trottins,' *Le Grand Guignol*, 15 January 1898.

44. 'Un peu d'idéal, égaré, / Sur un trottoir mal éclairé. / Un peu de l'Idéal qui prend / Le coeur le plus indifférent. / Un peu d'Idéal caressant, / Aumôme à l'âme passant.' Charles Clerc, 'La Bouquetière,' *Les Quat'z'Arts*, 13 March 1898.

45. 'La femme, je ne l'admets pas en art. Je ne l'admets que dans mon lit.' Louis Legrand, 'La femme ...' *Le Courrier français*, 17 December 1893.

46. 'Femme, ne nous soyez point dure: / L'artiste, en vos bras de satin, / Ne fait pas mauvaise figure, / Peintre, poète ou cabotin.' Eugène Torquet, 'Ballad de joyeuse bohème,' *Le Chat noir*, 14 January 1882.

47. A few texts even suggest that men are drawn to the women who will most abuse them. A very pointed example of this is Léon Gandillot, 'Les Trois filles,' *Le Chat noir*, 9 June 1988.

48. 'Au fond ... toute la question est de savoir si le mal qu'elles nous auront fait équilibre suffisamment les heures de bonheur qu'elles nous auront données, et si la cruauté de leurs ingratitudes doit effacer de nos âmes reconnaissantes les joies qu'y ont semées leur caresses, mêmes passagères et trompeuses.' Georges Courteline, 'Sanguines et Fusains,' *Le Mirliton*, 1 August 1886.

49. 'Les vrais heureux, – les malins, – ce sont les incurables célibataires. Ceux-là ont prévu le danger et se défendent à outrance.' Jules Bois, 'Petites décadences: Femmes d'artistes,' *Le Courrier français*, 17 August 1890.

50. 'Sans y prendre garde ils sont tombés dans le piège ... Ils sont vaincus; les voilà pour jamais les compagnons affalés de quelque gadoue aux jupes sale, avec qui ils aiment et mangent parmi les peignes et l'eau de vaiselle et les brosses à dents!' Ibid.

51. '... ces unions idéals sont pas dans les moeurs, dans les bonnes moeurs de la bourgeoisie.' Maurice Donnay, *Des Souvenirs*, p. 285.

52. 'La mère Nature a ses lois, / Et, quand elle parle, quand même, / Il faut bien écouter sa voix. / Aussi, pour éteindre la flamme / Dont mon coeur est incendié, / Sagement, j'ai pris une femme .../ Mais je ne suis pas marié.' Jules Jouys, 'Pas Marié,' *Le Chat noir*, 7 June 1884. See also Alphonse Allais, 'Délicatesse,' *Le Chat noir*, 14 January 1888; and Quinel, 'Ballade de Sous-sol,' *Le Courrier français*, 27 March 1892.

53. 'Les maîtresses de poètes sont maigres ... Les maîtresses de poètes sont laides, mais leur laideur est pleine d'un charme à faire pleurer ... Les maîtresses des poètes sont mortes. Durant leur vie terrestre, si courte, elles s'appelèrent Lilith, Antigone, Sperata! – et c'est d'elles, les mortes d'amour, que nous cherchons le baiser sur les

lèvres d'aujourd'hui.' Gabriel de Toulouse-Lautrec, 'Les Maîtresses des poètes,' *Le Chat noir*, 14 November 1891.

54. See, for example, Jean Floux, 'Marcelle,' *Le Chat noir*, 2 July 1887; Henry Papin, 'Frou-Frou: Épisode de la vie de Bohème,' *Le Pierrot*, 5 October 1888; François Morel, 'Femmes d'amis,' *Le Chat noir*, 20 October 1888; Jule Bois, 'Petites Décadences'; Maurice Donnay, 'La Bonne Maîtresse,' *Le Chat noir*, 13 December 1890.

55. See, for example, Roedel, 'Femmes d'artistes,' *Le Courrier français*, 31 July 1892 and 23 October 1892.

56. 'R'dis moi donc l'sonnet, tu sais, où tu m'compares à une source vive ...' J.-L. Forain, cover drawing, *Le Courrier français*, 18 March 1894.

57. 'Puis les baisers perdent leurs charmes, / Ayant duré quelques saisons. / Les réciproques trahisons / Font qu'on se quitte un jour, sans larmes ... On meurt d'avoir dormi longtemps / Avec les fleurs, avec les femmes.' Charles Cros, 'Lendemain,' *Le Divan Japonais*, 11 June 1891.

58. 'Il est vraiment incroyable qu'un pareil tempérament d'artiste ait pu s'être logé dans aussi jeune et aussi charmante enveloppe!' E. Ch., 'Femmes Peintres et Sculpteurs!' *Le Chat noir*, 28 February 1885.

59. '... qui n'est point femme et n'a ... la virilité de l'homme.' Jean Goudezki, 'Bas-Bleu,' *Les Quat'z'Arts*, 28 November 1897. See also 'Bonnes Vieilles Blagues,' *Le Mirliton*, 1 September 1886.

60. 'La femme peintre n'a rien de féminin. Elle porte le col droite et le veston masculins. Les plis de sa robe sont roides et disgracieux. Tous ses mouvements sont brusques et dépourvus d'élégance.' Toto Carabo, 'Types montmartrois: La Femme peintre,' *La Lanterne Japonaise*, 10 November 1888. See also the drawing by Georges Auriol, 'La femme peintre,' *Le Divan Japonais*, 18 July 1891.

61. Anne de Bercy and Armand Ziwès, *A Montmartre ... le soir: Cabarets et chansonniers d'hier* (Paris: B. Grasset, 1951), p. 23. The respect accorded Krysinska is, of course, relative. She appeared in *Le Chat noir* only 17 times in the journal's fourteen years of weekly publication; four other women were published, each no more than twice.

62. 'Quel bon garçon, et quel singulier garçon!' Georges Lorin, 'Monsieur Sarah Bernhardt,' *Les Hydropathes*, 5 April 1879.

63. *Le Chat noir*, 15 April 1882; *Le Chat noir*, 27 May 1882.

64. This belief in the opposition between 'femininity' and 'creativity' and the attendant ascription of inferiority to art produced by women is by no means limited to bohemian Montmartre, but is a pervasive feature of modern Western culture. See Linda Nochlin's 'Why Have There Been No Great Women Artists?' in *Art and Sexual Politics*, ed. Elizabeth C. Baker and Thomas B. Hess (New York: Collier, 1973), pp. 1–39, and Griselda Pollock, *Vision and Difference* (New York: Routledge, 1988). Anne Higonnet suggested that all nineteenth-century critical discussions of artists and art works were conducted in gendered terms in 'Writing the Gender of the Image: Art Criticism in Late Nineteenth-Century France,' *Genders*, 6 (Fall 1989): 60–73.

65. On the Union des Femmes Peintres et Sculpteurs, see Tamar Garb, *Sisters of the Brush: Women's Artistic Culture in Late Nineteenth-Century Paris* (New Haven: Yale University Press, 1994); and C. Yeldham, *Women Artists in Nineteenth-Century France and England* (New York: Garland, 1984), I: pp. 98–105.

66. '... que cette douzième exposition-là est intéressante au possible.' E. Ch., 'XIIe Exposition de l'Union des Femmes Peintres et Sculpteurs,' *Le Chat noir*, 11 March 1893.

67. '... cette petite fête de mères de famille ... les cent cinquante-cinq mamans des nouveaux-nés exposés ... les 356 enfants sont nés viables.' E. Ch., 'Union des Femmes Peintres et Sculpteurs,' *Le Chat noir*, 25 February 1888; E. Ch., 'Les Femmes Peintres et Sculpteurs.' *Le Chat noir*, 20 February 1886.

68. '... nous continuons à déplorer l'absence absolue des tableaux de genre. Les natures mortes, les paysages, les fleurs (oh! trop de fleurs!)' E. Ch., 'Union des Femmes Peintres et Sculpteurs,' *Le Chat noir*, 25 February 1885; 'Que c'est comme un bouquet des fleurs!' Pierrot [Adolphe Willette], 'Union des Femmes Peintres et Sculpteurs,' *Le Courrier français*, 28 February 1886.

69. I discuss the *montmartrois* attempt to resolve this 'contradiction' through the trope of gender inversion at greater length in '*Sans les femmes, qu'est-ce-qui nous resterait?*: Gender and Transgression in Bohemian Montmartre,' in Julia Epstein and Kristina Straub (eds), *Body Guards: the Cultural Politics of Gender Ambiguity* (New York: Routledge, 1991), pp. 195–222.

70. See Angus McLaren, *Sexuality and Social Order: the Debate over the Fertility of Women and Workers in France, 1770–1920* (New York: Holmes and Meier, 1983), Chapter 10; and Karen Offen, 'Depopulation, Nationalism and Feminism in Fin-de-Siècle France,' *American Historical Review*, 89 (3) (June 1984): 648–76.

Part IV
Gender and the Dreyfus Affair

Introduction to Part IV

The modern anxieties discussed in previous chapters – from debates about the gender of the public sphere and the specter of mental and physical degeneration to disagreements about the proper comportment of men – were condensed in the national crisis that was the Dreyfus Affair, though this fact has only come into focus for historians in recent years. From the arrest and trial of Captain Alfred Dreyfus for treason in 1894 through his eventual pardon in 1906, the rifts created by the Dreyfus Affair divided French political life for decades and still reverberate even in the present. Historians have long explained, and not without reason, how the Dreyfus Affair dramatized fundamental disagreements about the course of a nation poised between the modernizing impulses of the fragile Third Republic and the still potent forces of pre-revolutionary traditions, symbolized most vividly in the army and the Church. This dualistic vision of pro-modern defenders of Dreyfus struggling against resolutely anti-modern defenders of military glory and religious institutions has been problematized in recent decades by historians on both sides of the Atlantic. Acknowledging the profound divisions wrought by the Dreyfus issue, recent scholarship shows how Dreyfusard and anti-Dreyfusard factions shared many common concerns and cannot be neatly divided into pro- and anti-modern camps, especially if one adopts a more complex view of modernity. Both sides of the Dreyfus divide were anxious about the effects of urban modernity on the bodies and minds of the country; both expressed misgivings about what consequences modernity had for the masculinity of men and the femininity of women; and both, it seems, were deeply troubled about the association of Jews and this modernity. That they used their engagement in the Dreyfus case partly as means of negotiating these worries reveals just how complex the Affair really was. As the chapters in Part IV reveal, the affirmation of conventional gender distinctions through debates about 'heroism' could also be challenged by women, who sought ways of overcoming such constraints.

Venita Datta's chapter probes this complexity by examining the vexed question of whether or not Alfred Dreyfus qualified as a 'hero' at the fin de siècle. The concept of heroism is laden with premodern connotations, often martial in nature and almost always emphasizing courage, action, or some kind of innovation. Moreover, a cult of heroism pervaded the fin de siècle, and provided the polemics of the Affair with some of their most potent imagery. What, then, prevented the unjustly imprisoned and suffering captain from being seen as a hero, both during the fin de siècle and even in recent years, when requests to transfer Dreyfus's remains to the Panthéon were rejected by President Jacques Chirac? The answer to that question draws the reader into the complexity of a culture beholden to spectacles of heroism on the stage yet seemingly unable to tell the difference between fantasy and reality.

In many respects Ruth Harris's chapter on the ~~salonnières~~ Gyp and the Marquise Arconati-Visconti brings the themes of this volume full circle. Here we have the case of two aristocratic women who, though aligned with opposing sides of the Dreyfus Affair, engaged in this public crisis through different avenues, from private salons and writing for the press to hiring street thugs to disrupt meetings of the opposing camp. Aware of how unstable distinctions between private and public spheres really were in everyday life, both women took advantage of whatever means they could to assert themselves in the largely male-dominated politics of the Affair, thus seeking creative means of coping with the 'gender turmoil' that the Third Republic imposed and upon which it depended. The ways in which these women 'acted out' their deeply held beliefs – particularly their abilities to connect emotionally with men and wield power over them with regard to their respective political positions, both rational and irrational – demonstrate the degree to which the Affair itself was not just about Dreyfus, but was a culminating expression of all the interlocking tensions produced by the subjective experiences of gender, national identity, and democracy in the early Third Republic.

10

From Devil's Island to the Pantheon? Alfred Dreyfus, the Anti-Hero

Venita Datta

Since the beginnings of the Dreyfus Affair, its protagonist Alfred Dreyfus has been viewed both by other actors of the Affair and by historians either as a minor detail or even as a potential anti-Dreyfusard. Indeed, one well-known book by Marcel Thomas is even entitled *L'Affaire sans Dreyfus* (1961). Only in recent years have scholars begun to examine Alfred Dreyfus himself. The aim of Vincent Duclert's monumental biography is to restore Alfred Dreyfus to his true place in the Affair.[1] Following the lead of Dreyfus's grandson Jean-Louis Lévy, Duclert argues that without Dreyfus's heroic determination to survive and fight the charges against him, there would have been no Affair, but merely a footnote in history.[2]

Although Dreyfus himself could arguably fit the Dreyfusard ideal of the hero – a selfless, modest man who exhibited moral courage in the face of widespread opposition, and some did indeed depict him in this manner – he was frequently viewed with antipathy even by his allies. While both Dreyfusards and anti-Dreyfusards exalted heroes, their visions differed significantly. The former valued moral courage and singled out civilian heroes, whereas the latter favored physical prowess and military heroes who obeyed orders.[3] Although the suspicion of soldiers among some antimilitarist Dreyfusards might make Dreyfus seem potentially less acceptable as a hero, such an explanation cannot suffice since Colonel Picquart, the soldier who risked his career and defied his superiors in order to reveal the army cover-up of the Dreyfus case, became (along with writer Emile Zola) the standard bearer of Dreyfusard heroism.[4] The fact that Dreyfus was Jewish contributed, in part, to hostility toward seeing him as a hero. Anti-Semitism was so widespread that not even Dreyfus's allies were immune to the contemporary image of the Jew as a coward.[5] As I aim to illustrate in this chapter, other factors also played a role in the emergence of this negative portrait of Dreyfus.

Although Dreyfus was rehabilitated by the Cour de Cassation in 1906, collective memory of the man remains that of an anti-hero. In some sense, this image represents the 'revenge' of the anti-Dreyfusards. Indeed, the recent commemorations in France of the centenary of Dreyfus's rehabilitation have sparked some controversy in the wake of Duclert's call to move Dreyfus's remains to the Pantheon and President Jacques Chirac's subsequent refusal of his request. A closer examination of representations of Alfred Dreyfus reveals not only that many Dreyfusards believed he acted with determination and force to prove his innocence at his retrial in Rennes in 1899, but that they also perceived him as a hero, although some at the time did regret that he didn't seem to play the hero effectively enough for an unsympathetic press and public. Dreyfus received many letters of support from his admirers, all of whom cited his heroism, both in the wake of the second guilty verdict at Rennes, and even after he accepted the pardon offered by President Emile Loubet. Although accepting this pardon did not have an immediate impact on perceptions of Dreyfus among his allies, it did lead soon after to the breakdown of the Dreyfusard coalition, and in retrospect, hardened his former supporters' views of him as antipathetic. Such attitudes were in evidence at the time of Dreyfus's rehabilitation by the Cour de Cassation in 1906. Posterity has retained this latter image of Dreyfus, forged not only by anti-Dreyfusards in the years after the Affair, but also by his own supporters, rather than the snapshot of Dreyfus at the time of his trial at Rennes, when he remained a valiant hero.

The aim of this chapter is twofold: first and foremost, through an examination of sources from the time of the Affair, I would like to shed light on fin-de-siècle discussions of heroism. Second, by analyzing the works of scholars who have written about Alfred Dreyfus himself, notably Vincent Duclert and Philippe Oriol, as well as through a perusal of the press coverage of the recent failed attempt to 'pantheonize' Dreyfus, I seek to explore the relationship between history and memory.[6] As historians have noted, the Dreyfus Affair, like the French Revolution, belongs to the present as well as to the past, to history as well as to memory.[7] While the Affair has marked national memory and has become what historian Pierre Nora dubbed a 'lieu de mémoire' ('realm of memory'), that is, a person, place, or event that has been absorbed into the national consciousness, Dreyfus himself remains a 'non-lieu de mémoire,' and indeed, until recently, a 'non-lieu d'histoire' as well. Thus, Dreyfus as a man (rather than a symbol) has been erased both from French history and memory.[8] Fin-de-siècle notions of heroism, imbued with a culture of spectacle and theatricality, have to a great extent forged contemporary views of Dreyfus as a non-hero and are thus directly related to Chirac's refusal to transfer Dreyfus's remains to the Pantheon, although fear about stirring up anti-Semitic tensions might also have played an important role in his decision. An examination of the representations of Alfred Dreyfus, then and now, thus sheds light on the impact of late nineteenth-century constructions of heroism and national identity on the present.

In order properly to understand why Dreyfus did not become a hero in public consciousness, we need first to examine the backdrop of fin-de-siècle discussions about heroism as well as the conventions of heroism itself. Following defeat in the Franco-Prussian War, the cult of the hero gained great popularity in France, manifesting itself in all aspects of national life, from the curriculum of the primary schools, to the colonial and sporting movements, to literature and the arts. But heroes did not have to be national figures. The democratic creed of the Third Republic encouraged the idea that ordinary men and women could become heroes. Indeed, the Académie française distributed *prix de vertu* for 'daily acts of courage.'[9]

The search for heroes at this time was a result of the widespread sense of inferiority vis-à-vis Germany, as well as a collective guilt about the egoism of modern consumer society.[10] Thus, the celebration of heroes was part of a concerted effort toward national regeneration: heroes restored the honor and glory of a France that had lost the war. For republicans, the use of heroes not only cemented national solidarity, it also legitimized the Republic by rooting it in traditions of the past. Military heroes were, of course, popular during this time, but so were civilian heroes like Louis Pasteur and Victor Hugo.[11]

Although the era's obsessive quest for heroes led during the Dreyfus Affair to the emergence of two rival visions of the hero – pitting the Dreyfusard, who incarnated moral and intellectual courage, against the anti-Dreyfusard, who celebrated physical courage and the cult of the army – even these rival visions shared much common ground.[12] Heroism was founded, above all, on courage, both physical and moral, and on the supposedly male qualities of self-control and scorn of danger. Although heroism was not limited to males (witness the popularity of Joan of Arc), heroic virtues were seen as specifically masculine. Heroes were depicted as having a great strength of will and a strong sense of self. They also had a highly developed belief in honor and duty. They were willing to sacrifice themselves, not for egotistical reasons, but rather for the greater good, most often, the good of the nation.[13] While there were far fewer historical female heroes than male ones at the fin de siècle, Joan, along with Napoleon, represented the two most popular heroes of the period. Moreover, there is ample evidence illustrating that women sought such role models. Thus, writers such as Anna de Noailles, Gérard d'Houville, Marie Lenéru, and Daniel Lesueur, all used Nietzsche to promote their ideal of 'superwomen,' while other writers, like Gyp, used the image of Napoleon to create a feminine version of the military hero in her novel *Napoléonette* (1913).[14]

Female heroism, like that displayed by Joan of Arc, could be widely celebrated, but could also be explained away as a product of Joan's faith in God and country. Similarly, the heroism of the society women who perished in the 1897 Bazar de la Charité fire (a charity bazaar which caught fire and in which 125 people, mostly women, died) was lauded but at the same time minimized by representing it as the product of filial or motherly duty, even though the women in question could have escaped but instead opted to try to rescue their companions (some lost their lives in the process). Despite the fact that these women had chosen to place themselves at risk, they were viewed by contemporaries as having acted for egotistical reasons, in order to save loved ones. Women's heroism thus was distinguished from its male counterpart: it was seen as more visceral, the product of the heart rather than of the conscious *male* choice of the mind. Contemporaries (as during other eras) seemingly ignored the fact that Joan of Arc with her gender blurring was a subversive figure, a fact that did not escape Sarah Bernhardt, who played her twice in two different productions over the span of twenty years, transforming herself in the process into a national hero, one who could unite 'beyond politics.' The heroic qualities of the historical figure were increasingly linked in the minds of contemporaries with the traits of the actress who portrayed her.[15] Furthermore, some of the traits associated with heroism, in particular the notions of sacrifice and abnegation, were traditionally seen as female characteristics, as more than one feminist commenting on Nietzsche's view of the *surhomme* ('superman' or 'overman') realized.[16] Thus, the cult of heroes, which was supposed to shore up gender divisions, actually revealed cracks in the ideal of strictly delineated gender categories.

One way in which these cracks were revealed is through the emphasis of human qualities over military prowess in the portrayal of the three most celebrated military heroes of the time, Joan, Napoleon, and Cyrano de Bergerac. Napoleon, for instance, was depicted in his dressing gown, fretting about the potential betrayal of his wife, while Joan was a young girl who cried. The eponymous Cyrano, who played to full houses at the height of the Affair, was as much a lover, albeit a failed one, and a poet, as a fighter. Moreover, his sacrifice for the woman he loved was selfless, 'Christ-like' and even 'feminine.'[17]

How then do we reconcile the popularity of sensitive, democratic heroes who blurred gender lines with the 'crisis of masculinity' during the fin de siècle?[18] The concerns about honor and manhood *were* acute; witness the battle that pitted Dreyfusards and anti-Dreyfusards, both of whom laid claim to real honor and manhood. Nevertheless, the pervasive popularity of heroes who blurred gender categories complicates our understanding of the crisis of masculinity, suggesting, as Lenard Berlanstein has noted, that a real 'breakthrough in understandings of gender' was made during these years. Without denying the power of antifeminist rhetoric of the time, Berlanstein illustrates in his work on theater actresses of the nineteenth century that women increasingly assumed more prominence in public life as role models than was thought previously.[19] The popularity of sensitive heroes along with the emergence of actresses as national symbols also signals profound changes in the way that women and traditional 'female' traits were viewed in French society. Although most males did not advocate abandoning the traditional role of women as wives and mothers, women at the fin de siècle were increasingly incorporated into an understanding of the nation both as theatergoers and as role models and symbols of national identity. Furthermore, in an era in which French honor was sorely tested, any figure, male or female, who brought glory to the nation, was celebrated.[20]

Perhaps the crisis of masculinity was due less to the rise of women in the public sphere than to the loss of the war, as Berlanstein suggests.[21] Such an explanation would account for the simultaneous appeal of sensitive and military heroes, and moreover, of heroes who faced their destiny with dignity. The fates of Napoleon, Joan, and Cyrano all mirrored France's situation at the fin de siècle – hence, in part, their success with contemporary audiences. While sensitive heroes did not necessarily supplant all other types of heroes, their emergence may have worked against Alfred Dreyfus, who, in the eyes of some supporters, conformed to an earlier, more classical model of male heroism.

Images of heroes were shaped in large part by a literary culture in which theatrical conventions flourished. Writers did a great deal to popularize the cult of the hero: witness the avant-garde's celebration of Nietzsche's superman, who served as an example for men and women of the time, and Maurice Barrès's quest for 'professors of energy.' The theater, in particular, was responsible for the large-scale marketing of heroes, as illustrated by the phenomenal success of plays representing Napoleon and Joan of Arc, who were listed in surveys as the two most popular heroes of the era.[22] Real-life heroes, especially in the theater, were transformed into objects of popular consumption, reduced to their human qualities and thus rendered more accessible to the increasingly democratic audiences who attended the plays. Moreover, these real-life heroes, including the obscure seventeenth-century poet Cyrano de Bergerac, were portrayed by the most celebrated actors of their day. Not only were these fictional representations 'theatrical' in every sense of the term, they were also imbued with the charisma and celebrity of the actors who played them: Félix Duquesne, in the case of Napoleon, Sarah Bernhardt with l'Aiglon and Joan, and finally, Constant Coquelin, in the role of Cyrano. In such an atmosphere of theatricalized heroism, it is not surprising that the modest Alfred Dreyfus could not compete.

Vanessa Schwartz and others have studied the transformation of real-life events into spectacles, both in the press and in other venues where the line separating fiction from reality was increasingly blurred. Other scholars, among them James Lehning, have argued that the melodramatic genre in France shaped the political culture of the nation.[23] Contemporaries were highly aware of the theatrical nature of actual events, particularly at Alfred Dreyfus's degradation ceremony and in the courtroom during his two trials, as the press coverage of these events amply illustrates.[24]

Christopher Forth has demonstrated how questions of race and gender were intertwined in representations of Alfred Dreyfus such that it was possible to employ a gender technique that 'could also function as a euphemized racial commentary so that besmirching the manliness of Dreyfus could be read as an implicit indictment of his Jewishness.'[25] The fact that Dreyfus was *degredation ceremony*

also the symbol of a new kind of officer, promoted not necessarily for his courage in battle, but rather for his technocratic qualities, only reinforced this image.[26] Yet latent, widespread anti-Semitism was only one factor of his contemporaries' refusal to see Dreyfus as a hero. Just as important were expectations of his behavior. The 'performances' (in both senses of the term) of Alfred Dreyfus at the degradation ceremony and at the trials simply did not fit contemporary expectations of a hero. Ironically, it was because he was not theatrical enough that Dreyfus was seen as having performed badly, like a bad actor who didn't know his lines or who couldn't deliver them convincingly.[27]

Above all, representations of Alfred Dreyfus at his degradation forever shaped images of him. In his monumental *Histoire de l'Affaire Dreyfus*, Joseph Reinach referred to the ceremony both as a 'public festival' and as a 'book burning.'[28] For their part, journalists often described the degradation ceremony as an 'execution.'[29] What they probably meant was that it was tantamount to a castration – hence, in part, the desire of some military men for a real execution that might have preserved the manhood of a fellow officer, however reprehensible they found his actions. Without belaboring the point, the stripping of Alfred Dreyfus's military insignias and the breaking of his sword was a metonym for the stripping of his manhood and a loss of his honor. As Reinach noted, the tattered rags of Dreyfus's military vestments on the ground served as a stark reminder of the honor that had also been stripped away.[30] Indeed, the journalist for *Le Petit journal* argued that Dreyfus was 'no longer even a man.'[31] The fact that Dreyfus protested that an innocent man was being condemned seemed to have had little lasting impact on collective memory.[32] This image of Dreyfus's degradation was a powerful one, and difficult for contemporaries to overcome as well as for those of our own time. Witness the controversy over placing Tim's statue of Alfred Dreyfus in the courtyard of the Ecole Militaire, with President François Mitterrand commenting that one did not commemorate a humiliation.[33]

Moreover, during the degradation ceremony, along with the two trials, even those who were sympathetic to Dreyfus found his behavior incomprehensible. It did not conform to public perceptions of what heroic or even innocent behavior should be. He did not cry like a stock villain of melodrama, thereby showing his remorse.[34] Unlike heroes of fiction, particularly those of melodrama, he did not display sufficient emotion. As a military man, Dreyfus was trained to restrain his emotions; but his own reserved personality reinforced this military behavior. Reinach noted that those most likely to understand such behavior were the very soldiers who condemned him, while his defenders were both wary of military comportment and more inclined to view theatrical displays of emotion with approval. In some sense, then, Dreyfus was too controlled, such that his behavior was likened to that of an automaton, even by Reinach who explained his behavior with such lucidity.[35]

really smart

Devil's Island to the Pantheon? Alfred Dreyfus, the Anti-Hero 223

Rennes

Reinach, as much as the journalists and writers whose reactions he described at Rennes, was the product of a profoundly literary culture. His descriptions of the trial and of Dreyfus abound with references to literature, especially to drama.[36] In fact, Reinach and others describe Dreyfus's appearance in the courtroom at Rennes as a long-awaited theatrical entrance, which did not fail to elicit pity even among the most hardened of his adversaries: 'What we especially anticipated was Dreyfus himself. It was the man coming back from this hell that we were going to see.' The Dreyfus who walked into the courtroom was 'a bag of bones' 'whose body had melted.' His frail body could barely be supported by his legs, which buckled under him.[37]

Yet, from the very beginning, Dreyfus's strategy was not to inspire pity but rather to appeal to reason, as he himself noted.[38] Reinach observed that Dreyfus answered all the questions with a 'clear assured voice, not at all this "metallic," bitter, atonal voice' that he was reproached for later, a view confirmed by other spectators.[39] Reinach further noted that even though the memory of his degradation ceremony in 1894 was painful to Dreyfus, 'his sensitivity was still turned inward, preventing him from crying for himself, [he was] hypnotized to the very end by his heroic idea of a military superman ...'[40] The reference to Nietzsche's superman, a popular image of male energy at this time, is significant, since a Nietzschean hero was one who mastered his emotions. Indeed, for Nietzsche, the superiority of such an individual lay in overcoming such base emotions as self-pity. Yet it is clear from his use of the word 'hypnotized' that Reinach was frustrated by the extent of Dreyfus's self-containment and commitment to military discipline.

Describing Dreyfus's behavior during the Rennes trial in a speech commemorating the trial ten years later, Victor Basch noted with some regret that the accused had based his defense on reason and the law rather than deploring his own sufferings. It was Dreyfus's modesty, Basch suggested, that prevented him from sharing the 'wounds of his soul.'[41] Thus, even among Dreyfusards who celebrated reason and individualist values, there was a fear of an excess of cerebral qualities. Moreover, there was such a thin line between showing too much emotion and not enough that these standards of manhood were quite fluid.[42] A further examination of Basch's speech on his memories of the Rennes trial is illuminating:

> We are so steeped in literature and especially in dramatic literature that it is difficult for us to imagine things differently than from a dramatic angle. All of us, more or less, had imagined Dreyfus as a dramatic or melodramatic hero. For some, he was going to speak, like a character out of d'Ennery [a melodramatic author], at length about his sufferings.

Later in the same passage, Basch talks further about contemporary expectations that would have Dreyfus behave like a hero in the theater: 'Others had made him into a dramatic hero, a Hernani [the eponymous hero of Victor

Hugo's play] or a Mounet-Sully [the celebrated actor]. They would have had him 'tempestuous, gesticulating, declaiming.' In fact, what the public and the Dreyfusards themselves wanted was an actor playing the role of Dreyfus. Indeed, André Antoine, a leading actor of the day who was in attendance at the Rennes trial, claimed he could have done a better job than Dreyfus in moving his audience.[43]

These contemporary impressions hardened over the years such that even supporters like Basch emphasized not Dreyfus's strength, but instead characterized his appearance on the witness stand and his defense of himself as having been weak. When a colleague interrupted Basch's speech, telling him that Dreyfus had indeed proclaimed his innocence, Basch dismissed the comment, stating that he had not done so 'with violence.'[44] The answer to this dismissal is, in part, explained by Basch's own earlier comment about a lack of theatricality of Dreyfus's 'performance,' a comment further developed by Reinach:

> Thus, Dreyfus brought with him to his cross-examination the same simple and stoic pride that he brought to all the acts in his life, but this again was not understood except by a few ... those who knew that real innocence rejects tirades and theatrics ... he shed a veil over his sufferings, reclaiming only his honor, and appealing uniquely to conscience, to the force of truth and reason.[45]

If Dreyfus was viewed as a hero at all it was as one of the stoic types, thus, more in line with the classical heroes of the seventeenth-century theater, especially those of Pierre Corneille, rather than the melodramatic heroes popular at the fin de siècle. Even Cyrano, who harkened back to the seventeenth century, was a baroque hero rather than a classical one.

As Reinach further noted, the conventions of the theater prevented contemporaries from valuing the lack of Dreyfus's 'performance' and for confusing content with style: 'It was ... inevitable that in a country where the esthetics of the theater dominates, that in this affair, where everything, for the last two years, had the appearance of drama, the inability of Dreyfus to express his emotions and his lack of charisma worked to his detriment once again.' Anti-Semites were happy that the behavior of their victim was so understated; had his 'performance' been any 'good' they would have accused him of acting, yet they would have equally reproached him for a 'bad' performance. But his inability to play a role gave them an easy out, representing him as less than human. As for the public and most of Dreyfus's supporters, Reinach concludes that they, who had been 'no less infected by romantic notions,' also wanted a performance: 'they would have wanted this ghost who came back from the dead, this resurrected Lazarus – to give them goose bumps or the delight of a melodramatic show, that before responding to his judges, he curse his torturers, at least that he let himself go ...' Even if they realized on an intellectual level that Dreyfus needed to keep his composure in order to survive, they were nevertheless disappointed:

> They too were to this extent incapable, as real Frenchmen, of judging men and things in a light other than that of the theatrical spotlight and of understanding an innocent man other than as shaking, beating his chest, displaying his wounds and accusing destiny. They would have wished him to shed tears; they reproached him for those he held back or that he dried too quickly. An actor was needed and he was a soldier.[46]

Yet the contemporary accounts of Reinach and others, who claim that Dreyfus defended himself both admirably and forcefully, contradict lore about Dreyfus as presenting a weak figure on the stand and as having defended himself poorly.[47] According to Duclert, it was not Dreyfus's job to uncover the machinations of a cover-up against him. Instead, it was to persist in proving his innocence through hard facts and a faith in the democratic processes of justice. Indeed, it is because Dreyfus presented a reasoned defense based on facts and truth against a vast conspiracy of the state that Vincent Duclert sees Alfred Dreyfus as a hero.[48] According to Duclert, not only did Alfred Dreyfus's defenders not understand the man but they also did not recognize the real importance of the Dreyfus Affair, which was the defense of individual rights by an individual fighting on the basis of facts and truth rather than emotions.

Yet it is for this very reason that contemporaries of the fin de siècle and perhaps those of our own time as well did not see him as a hero. They expected a performance that was never forthcoming. Not only did Dreyfus not perform well enough, but he did not perform at all. More precisely, he performed a different role than the one that contemporaries expected of him – the role of the logical lawyer rather than that of the righteously indignant defendant. The followers of Dreyfus thus tried to explain away his behavior. *Le Matin* noted that Dreyfus seemed almost 'classical.'[49] (Was this irony lost on anti-Dreyfusard monarchist Charles Maurras?) In fact, Reinach compared Dreyfus's main lawyer Edgar Demange, known for his understated defense, to a Cornelian hero.[50] Other revisionists attempted to deconstruct heroism, stating that it need not conform to the conventions of the theater and popular fiction. Not only did this approach help to vindicate Dreyfus, but it also helped to explain his refusal to perform and highlighted the virtues of not performing.[51]

Beyond the theatrical aspects of heroism as represented in the Affair, there are other factors related to fin-de-siècle constructions of heroism that prevented contemporaries from seeing Dreyfus as a hero. Male heroes, unlike female ones, were perceived as active agents. They could be victims but they had to have chosen their sacrifice. Indeed, Georges Clemenceau noted that the real victim and also hero of the Affair was Colonel Georges Picquart because he had chosen to tell the truth about the government cover-up, knowing full well the consequences of his actions.[52] A similar view was held by playwright Edmond Rostand, who admired Picquart immensely because he believed him to have deliberately chosen his fate, comparing him to his fictionalized hero Cyrano de Bergerac.[53] According to contemporaries, Dreyfus did not choose his fate but had it imposed on him. Moreover, Dreyfus was not seen as fighting for a principle but rather for himself. It is much the same argument that Chirac made when refusing the request to pantheonize Alfred Dreyfus, stating that he was a victim not a hero. Dreyfus was also not seen as a hero because he was a symbol rather than an individual; in other words, he was at best a puppet controlled by others, at worst a cipher to be made use of as others dictated. Indeed, Barrès referred to Dreyfus as a 'tragic Guignol,' on whose strings his masters pulled every time he spoke at his trial in Rennes. This image of a puppet to describe a man during this time was a reference to powerlessness and thus effeminacy; it was a way of denying him manhood.[54] Viewed as a symbol rather than an individual, Dreyfus could be neatly erased from the narrative of the Dreyfus Affair.[55] Ironically, as Duclert himself notes, it was because Alfred Dreyfus refused to be seen as hero that he was able to give universal meaning to the Affair which bears his name.[56]

At a time when heroes were destabilized and transformed, as were Napoleon and Joan, into more human and accessible figures, contemporaries still wanted them to have 'star' quality, that is, to be better, improved versions of themselves. Even Sarah Bernhardt, who played Joan to sell-out crowds during this time, complained that audiences did not want to see a coarse Joan of Arc but rather a sanitized image of the young peasant girl, one which would correspond to the period's ideals of female heroism.[57] Not only was Dreyfus too ordinary, he was also a figure of division at a time when French men and women, weary of such infighting, increasingly sought refuge in the fictions of the theater and the glories of the past enacted therein to find a unity 'beyond' politics. Although the Right ultimately co-opted these heroes more successfully than the Left, the theatrical representations of Joan and Cyrano (and Napoleon much less so) did succeed in temporarily uniting fin-de-siècle audiences around national figures, regardless of political affiliation.[58] While heroes in the theater did at times transcend contemporary divisions, the real-life Dreyfus did nothing but reveal these divisions and, moreover, he exposed the contradictions and anxieties underlying contemporary definitions of heroism.

Finally, Dreyfus's acceptance of a pardon, while it did not immediately transform the contemporary image of him as non-heroic, did have important long-lasting consequences. It led, eventually, to the breakdown of the Dreyfusard coalition. Reinach, for his part, was convinced that Dreyfus would never survive more jail time, while Clemenceau and Jean Jaurès argued against accepting the pardon. As Clemenceau and others realized, Dreyfus as a symbol would have less power if he were at home among his loved ones than if he were continuing to serve a jail sentence.[59] Reinach observes that it would have been more theatrical to refuse the pardon offered by President Loubet, but eminently less practical, noting wryly that a dead Dreyfus would have effectively put an end to any attempts to overturn the guilty verdicts. Yet even Reinach conceded Clemenceau's point that accepting the pardon put an end to the 'heroic' part of the Dreyfus Affair.[60] Despite the sympathetic portrayal of Dreyfus by Jules Huret, who recounted Dreyfus's train journey home for the readers of *Le Figaro*, in the eyes of many of Dreyfus's supporters, accepting the pardon was not heroic.[61] Not only did it not depict Dreyfus in a heroic light, it also minimized the heroism of his defenders, whose efforts now appeared to have been politicized. On the other hand, Emile Zola, writing to Lucie Dreyfus after the pardon, noted that Dreyfus was 'a greater hero than others, because his sufferings have been greater.'[62] As for his enemies, it gave them a way to continue to maintain Dreyfus's guilt, since they could claim that an innocent man would and should not have accepted a pardon.

Dreyfus was doubly wronged by the army in that he never regained the lost years on Devil's Island as years in rank. Unlike Picquart, who ended his career as a general and who, moreover, served as Minister of War under Clemenceau, Dreyfus retired from active duty in 1907; despite his rehabilitation by the Cour de Cassation in 1906, only after his service in the First World War did he achieve the rank of lieutenant-colonel. Furthermore, the ceremony in which he was granted the Legion of Honor was pro forma for a man of his rank, and moreover, a private rather than a public act.[63] Duclert concludes his biography of Alfred Dreyfus by examining the way in which Dreyfus was erased from national memory after 1906 and the emergence of an image of Dreyfus as antipathetic and anti-heroic. He notes, rightly, that Dreyfusards themselves were as much if not more responsible for this construction than the anti-Dreyfusards, although it essentially endorsed the position of the latter.[64] Although Dreyfusards may have won a political battle against their opponents, they lost a battle in the field of rhetoric about manhood,[65] and – I would also argue – about the very nature of heroism itself. In some sense then, they failed to realize the irony that in their defense of the rights of individuals, they had forgotten the very individual they were defending, instead 'dehumanizing' him in order to transform him into a symbol. For Duclert, it is precisely Alfred Dreyfus's ordinariness which makes him a hero.[66]

Vincent Duclert has compared the erasing of Dreyfus from public memory to other acts of forgetting, like the difficult events of the Second World War, particularly the role of the Vichy government in the treatment of the Jews of France. But while Chirac recognized (at a ceremony on 18 January 2007 at the Pantheon) the ordinary citizens who saved the lives of French Jews during the war ('les justes'), he was not willing to view Dreyfus as an ordinary hero, or even as a hero at all.[67] For his part, Vincent Duclert sees the heroism of Alfred Dreyfus to some extent through the lens of later historical events, especially those of World War II, by viewing Dreyfus's battle against the machinery of a state as a precursor of the resistance of individuals against totalitarian states of the twentieth century. So it is interesting to note that one of Dreyfus's 'rivals' for pantheonization was Marc Bloch, historian, Jew, and member of the Resistance.[68] But while the pantheonization of Marc Bloch, which was not without its own obstacles, would illustrate the triumph of good over evil, of light against darkness (note the same rhetorical devices in Zola's 'J'Accuse,' de Gaulle's 'Appel du 18 juin' and Chirac's recent speech), the pantheonization of Dreyfus would offer no such assurances.

Dreyfus as a victim is a symbol of the Republic triumphant, a sign of the victory of the forces of 'progress' against the 'retrograde forces of the past.' Writers, artists, and politicians fought to protect his rights and freedoms. This is an image neatly wrapped in the mythology of the Affair. On the other hand, Dreyfus as a hero is a symbol of the failure of the Republic to live up to its democratic ideals. If Dreyfus is to be celebrated as an individual battling the machinery of the state, this means that the Republic itself is no longer viewed in heroic terms but rather as a villain perpetrating an injustice. Indeed, for Duclert, the Affair illustrates the gap between the rhetoric of the Third Republic and the reality of undemocratic practices under it.[69] It is one of the reasons he cites for studying the Affair – to examine precisely how through the course of the Affair the Republic truly became a democracy. But French political elites are perhaps not yet ready to examine more critically the injustices of the Third Republic, preferring to retain an unproblematic view of its triumph over its enemies at the time of the Affair. This reticence may be due, in part, to weariness with obsessive national soul-searching about the Vichy regime and its role in the Holocaust.

While Chirac, who has done much to get the French to face the difficulties of their past, recognized Dreyfus's courage and his faith in the Republic in his presidential address commemorating the centenary of Dreyfus's rehabilitation on 12 July 2006, he seemed unable to take the final step to accept Dreyfus as a bona fide hero.[70] In part, his hesitation may have had something to do with the lack of unity even among Jewish organizations about moving Alfred Dreyfus's remains to the Pantheon, including disagreement among various members of the Dreyfus family. Undoubtedly, the recent violence of youths of Arab origins in the *banlieues* in the late fall of 2005 also played a role in Chirac's decision. Anti-Semitism in France today is less the product of the extreme right-wing National Front (although the National Front continues to fan such flames) and instead comes increasingly from the disaffected youths of the *banlieues*, reflecting tensions in the Middle East. It is quite possible that Chirac may have feared touching off another controversy that could set anti-Semitic sentiments aflame.

While these external factors certainly played a role in the president's refusal, the image of Dreyfus as a victim and fin-de-siècle notions of heroism which equate heroism with manhood (itself associated with agency) remain instrumental in his decision. Thus, the case for Alfred Dreyfus as a hero needs to continue to be made. Just as the work of such historians as Robert Paxton has contributed to a re-examination of public memory of World War II, perhaps the new work of Vincent Duclert and others will have an impact on the public memory of the Dreyfus Affair, one which restores Alfred Dreyfus to his rightful place in it.

Notes

1. Vincent Duclert, *Alfred Dreyfus: L'honneur d'un patriote* (Paris: Fayard, 2006). See also Duclert, *Dreyfus, voyage au cœur du Panthéon* (Paris: Gallaade Editions, 2007).
2. Jean-Louis Lévy, 'Alfred Dreyfus, anti-héros, et témoin capital,' in Alfred Dreyfus, *Cinq années de ma vie* (Paris: Maspéro, 1982), pp. 239–60.
3. On rival notions of heroism, see Venita Datta, 'The Sword or the Pen? Competing Visions of the Hero at the Fin de Siècle' in *Birth of a National Icon: the Literary Avant-Garde and the Origins of the Intellectual in France* (Albany: SUNY Press, 1999), pp. 135–82.
4. Dreyfusards admired less the military ideal in Picquart than the man of culture. Not all Dreyfusards, however, were antimilitarist and some genuinely admired the army while deploring its tactics in condemning Dreyfus.
5. On fin-de-siècle images of Jews as cowards, see Sander L. Gilman, *Jewish Self-Hatred: Anti-Semitism and the Hidden Language of Jews* (Baltimore, MD: Johns Hopkins University Press, 1986); Pierre Birnbaum, *Anti-Semitism in France: a Political History from Léon Blum to the Present,* trans. Miriam Kochan (Cambridge, MA: Basil Blackwell, 1992) and Birnbaum, *The Jews of the Republic: a Political History of State Jews in France from Gambetta to Vichy,* trans. Jane Marie Todd (Stanford: Stanford University Press, 1996).
6. See Philippe Oriol's introduction, 'L'Affaire de Dreyfus,' to the re-edition of Alfred Dreyfus's *Carnets (1899–1907)* (Paris: Calmann-Lévy, 1998), pp. 7–21.
7. Vincent Duclert 'Dreyfus, de l'oubli à l'histoire,' *Cahiers de l'Affaire Dreyfus,* 1 (2004): 71. On history and memory, see Pierre Nora's introduction 'Entre mémoire et Histoire' to *Les Lieux de Mémoire,* vol. 1 (Paris: Gallimard Quarto, 1997), pp. 23– 43; Jacques Revel, 'Histoire vs. Mémoire en France aujourd'hui,' *French Politics, Culture and Society,* 18(1) (Spring 2000): 1–12, and Susan Suleiman, 'Narrative Desire: the "Aubrac Affair" and the National Memory of the Resistance' in *Crises of Memory and the Second World War* (Cambridge, MA: Harvard University Press, 2006), pp. 36–61. The journal *Esprit* in February 2006 published a special issue on 'guerres de mémoire à la française' in which the debates about colonialism and the 'lois mémorielles' are discussed.
8. Pierre Nora, *Les Lieux de Mémoire.* The books have been translated into English as *Realms of Memory: Rethinking the French Past,* 3 vols, trans. Arthur Goldhammer (New York: Columbia University Press, 1996–98).
9. Paul Gerbod, 'L'éthique héroïque en France (1870–1914),' *La Revue historique,* 268 (1982): 424.
10. See Robert A. Nye, *Masculinity and Male Codes of Honor in Modern France* (New York: Oxford University Press, 1993), p. 225.
11. Christian Amalvi, *Les héros de l'histoire de France* (Paris: Editions Phot'oeil, 1979); and Jean-François Chanet, 'La Fabrique des héros: Pédagogie républicaine et culte des grands hommes de Sedan à Vichy,' *Vingtième Siècle,* 65 (January–March 2000): 13–34. On imperial heroes, see Edward Berenson, 'Unifying the French Nation: Savornan de Brazza and the Third Republic,' in Barbara Kelly (ed.), *Music, Culture*

and *National Identity in France 1870–1939* (Rochester: University of Rochester Press, 2008), pp. 17–39. Professor Berenson elaborates further on imperial heroes in *The Congo Story: Exploration and Empire in England and France* (forthcoming).

12. Datta, *Birth of a National Icon*, pp. 117–82.
13. Gerbod, 'L'éthique héroïque en France,' pp. 424–5.
14. Gyp, *Napoléonette* (Paris: Calmann-Lévy, 1913). This chapter is part of a book project entitled *Legends and Heroes of Fin-de-Siècle France: Gender, Politics, and National Identity*. I have also explored these issues in 'Superwomen or Slaves? Women Writers, Male Critics and the Reception of Nietzsche in Belle-Epoque France,' *Historical Reflections/Réflexions historiques* (Fall 2007): 421–48 and ' "L'Appel au Soldat": Visions of the Napoleonic Legend in Popular Culture of the Belle Epoque,' *French Historical Studies* (Winter 2005): 1–30.
15. See Venita Datta, 'Sur les boulevards: les représentations de Jeanne d'Arc dans le théâtre populaire,' *CLIO: Histoire, Femmes et Société*, 24 (2006): 127–49. Historians Mary-Louise Roberts and Lenard Berlanstein have argued that Bernhardt chose to play Joan in order to adopt a more respectable stance and to transform herself into a symbol of the nation: Berlanstein, *Daughters of Eve: a Cultural History of French Theater Women from the Old Regime to the Fin de Siècle* (Cambridge, MA: Harvard University Press, 2001), p. 235; Roberts, *Disruptive Acts: the New Woman in Fin-de-Siècle France* (Chicago: University of Chicago Press, 2002), pp. 217–18.
16. Françoise Benassis, 'Une Erreur de Nietzsche,' *La Fronde*, 6 April 1903: 1. On Nietzsche, see Christopher E. Forth, *Zarathustra in Paris: the Nietzsche Vogue in France, 1891–1918* (De Kalb, IL: Northern Illinois University Press, 2001). On women writers and Nietzsche, see Datta, 'Superwomen or Slaves?'
17. I am grateful to Professor Lenard Berlanstein for this observation.
18. On masculinity and male honor codes, see Nye, *Masculinity and Male Codes of Honor* and Berenson, *The Trial of Madame Caillaux* (Berkeley: University of California Press, 1992), pp. 186–98. On the crisis of masculinity, see Annelise Maugue, *L'Identité masculine en crise au tournant du siècle, 1871–1914* (Paris: Editions Rivages, 1987).
19. Berlanstein, *Daughters of Eve*, p. 239.
20. Ibid, p. 204.
21. Ibid., p. 239.
22. Among the plays representing Napoleon were Sardou's *Mme Sans-Gêne*, for example, as well as Edmond Rostand's *L'Aiglon*, in which Napoleon's doomed son, the Duke of Reichstadt, was portrayed by Sarah Bernhardt. Bernhardt also played Joan in Jules Barbier's *Jeanne d'Arc* in 1890 and Emile Moreau's 1909 play based on trial transcripts.
23. Vanessa R. Schwartz, *Spectacular Realities: Early Mass Culture in Fin-de-Siècle Paris* (Berkeley: University of California Press), 1998; James Lehning, *The Melodramatic Thread: Spectacle and Political Culture in Modern France* (Bloomington: Indiana University Press, 2007). See also Jean-Yves Mollier, 'La littérature et presse du trottoir à la Belle Epoque' in *La lecture et ses publics à l'époque contemporaine: Essais d'histoire culturelle* (Paris: PUF, 2001), who speaks of the esthéticization of politics at this time and observes that the Right during the Dreyfus Affair (I would add the Left too) was obliged to treat current events as a melodrama, representing traitors as villains in boulevard plays: p. 153. Suzanne Kaufman too uses this trope to describe the women who went to Lourdes to be cured in *Consuming Visions: Mass Culture and the Lourdes Shrine* (Ithaca: Cornell University Press, 2005), pp. 96–7. One of the earliest works to use this approach is that of Judith Walkowitz, borrowing from the

work of literary scholar Peter Brooks. (See his *The Melodramatic Imagination* (New Haven: Yale University Press, 1976).) See Walkowitz, *City of Dreadful Delight: Narratives of Sexual Danger in Late-Victorian London* (Chicago: University of Chicago Press, 1992).

24. See Christopher E. Forth's chapter 'Masculine Performances: Alfred Dreyfus and the Paradox of the Jewish Soldier' in *The Dreyfus Affair and the Crisis of French Manhood* (Baltimore: Johns Hopkins University Press, 2004), pp. 21–59.

25. Ibid., p. 22.

26. On the army, see Jérôme Hélie, 'L'Arche sainte fracturée,' in *La France de l'affaire Dreyfus*, ed. Pierre Birnbaum (Paris: Gallimard, 1994), pp. 226–50.

27. Forth, *Dreyfus Affair*, p. 49. See pp. 27–34 for a discussion of the theatricality of trials at this time.

28. Joseph Reinach, *Histoire de l'Affaire Dreyfus*, 2 vols (Paris: Editions Robert Laffont, 2006), Vol. 1, pp. 276–7.

29. Léo Marchès, 'La dégradation du capitaine Dreyfus,' *Le Siècle*, 6 January 1895. See also Forth, *Dreyfus Affair*, p. 25, and Duclert, *Alfred Dreyfus: L'honneur d'un patriote*, pp. 208–14.

30. Reinach writes of the sword: 'The warrant officer pulls it and with one fell swoop, breaks it on his knee, letting it fall to the ground, in the mud, its two sections broken "dead in the place of honor."' The expression 'morts à la place de l'honneur' is a quote from Léon Daudet: Reinach, *Histoire de l'Affaire Dreyfus*, Vol. 1, p. 282.

31. The reference to Dreyfus as no longer a man comes from Thomas Grimm, 'L'Expiation,' *Le Petit journal*, 6 January 1895.

32. 'I am innocent! Long live France!' quoted by Reinach, *Histoire de l'Affaire Dreyfus*, Vol. 1, p. 283.

33. Didier Sicard, 'La Statue errante du Capitaine Dreyfus,' *Les Temps modernes*, February–April 2003: 3–6. Mitterrand quoted in an article by Jean Daniel in *Le Nouvel observateur*, 5–11 January 2006: 11. The statue is now located in an out of the way spot on the corner of the boulevard Raspail and the rue Notre-Dame-des-Champs A large facsimile of the statue can be found in the courtyard of the Musée d'art et d'histoire du judaïsme. See 'Un beau discours et pas de statue pour le capitaine Dreyfus,' in *Libération* of 12 July 2006. Jack Lang also wrote to Chirac calling for the pantheonization of Dreyfus. See Duclert's 'Antisémitisme, république et démocratie: Le modèle Dreyfus,' *Les Temps modernes*, (7) (July 2002): 171–4. Duclert states that Dreyfus represents the civic courage and patriotic fidelity of an ordinary citizen. It is for this reason that Dreyfus represents a democratic model, according to Duclert.

34. In his 1908 trial for high treason, naval ensign Charles-Benjamin Ullmo, who was guilty, cried profusely. I examine this trial in *Legends and Heroes*.

35. Reinach notes: 'But Dreyfus, at once too military and too weak ... became the machine that is a subordinate in front of a superior who has one more stripe than he,' *Histoire de l'Affaire Dreyfus*, Vol. 2, p. 505. See also Forth, *Dreyfus Affair*, pp. 43–50.

36. This idea of the culture of spectacle is very much in evidence. Reinach notes that the women on both sides were more passionate, thus commenting indirectly on the feminine nature of the culture of spectacle. Reinach, *Histoire de l'Affaire Dreyfus*, Vol. 2, p. 501. Indeed, Anne-Marie Thiesse describes the newspaper as a sexually divided space such that *faits-divers*, trials, and dramatic public representations of private events occupied the intermediate zone separating the masculine space of politics from the feminine space of the serialized novels, which was located, in

her words, on the 'rez de chaussée' (below the fold) of the newspaper: Anne-Marie Thiesse, *Le Roman du quotidien: Lecteurs et lectures populaires à la Belle Epoque* (Paris: Le Chemin Vert, 1984), p. 20.

37. Reinach, *Histoire de l'Affaire Dreyfus,* Vol. 2, pp. 501–2.
38. Dreyfus stated: 'that one should seek to elicit pity when one is at fault, this is conceivable. An innocent [man], however, should appeal only to reason,' quoted by Reinach, *Histoire de l'Affaire Dreyfus,* Vol. 2, p. 502.
39. Among them, Jules Claretie, cited by Reinach, *Histoire de l'Affaire Dreyfus,* Vol. 2, p. 507, who called Dreyfus's voice 'very masculine.'
40. Reinach, *Histoire de l'Affaire Dreyfus,* Vol. 2, p. 507.
41. Victor Basch, 'Discours de Victor Basch sur l'affaire Dreyfus prononcé au Congrès de la Ligue des Droits de l'Homme à Rennes, 29 mai 1909,' reproduced in Françoise Basch, *Victor Basch, De l'affaire Dreyfus au crime de la Milice* (Paris: Plon, 1994), pp. 356–7.
42. Dreyfusard Henry Bérenger, in common with anti-Dreyfusard Barrès, feared the rise of an intellectual proletariat no longer sufficiently manly to lead France. See Datta, *Birth of a National Icon,* pp. 123–4.
43. Victor Basch quoting Antoine in 'Alfred Dreyfus et l'Affaire,' *Cahiers des Droits de l'Homme,* 31 July 1935: 503, cited by Françoise Basch, *Victor Basch,* pp. 68–9. Dreyfus himself recognized the public's need for theatricality on his part in his memoirs: Alfred Dreyfus, *Carnets,* pp.182–3. See also Duclert's discussion of this point: *L'honneur d'un patriote,* pp. 741–2.
44. Victor Basch, in Françoise Basch, pp. 356–7.
45. Reinach, *Histoire de l'Affaire Dreyfus,* Vol. 2, p. 508.
46. Reinach, *Histoire de l'Affaire Dreyfus,* Vol. 2, pp. 508–9.
47. A reading of the trial transcripts seems to indicate that Dreyfus defended himself admirably and forcefully, as Vincent Duclert notes. Nevertheless, fin-de-siècle notions of manhood shaped representations of Alfred Dreyfus. Furthermore, present-day historians cannot capture the impression that Dreyfus's 'performance' may have had on those in attendance in the courtroom. While anti-Dreyfusard Maurice Barrès, who was in attendance at Rennes, admitted to feeling some pity for Dreyfus, he found Dreyfus to be 'monotonous,' like a 'phonograph,' concluding that Dreyfus's tone detracted from the nobility of the words he was uttering. Barrès was admittedly an opponent of Dreyfus, but his characterizations were shared by some Dreyfusards. See Barrès, *Scènes et Doctrines du nationalisme* (Paris: Editions du Trident, 1987), p. 103. See also p. 105, where he speaks of Dreyfus's 'dry' voice. At a time when Sarah Bernhardt used her 'golden voice' to convince audiences she really was the young Joan of Arc (rather than a middle-aged woman), the role of voice in a public 'performance' was important.
48. Duclert, *L'honneur d'un patriote,* p. 641.
49. Quoted in Forth, *Dreyfus Affair,* p. 49.
50. Reinach, *Histoire de l'Affaire Dreyfus,* Vol. 2, p. 634.
51. Forth, *Dreyfus Affair,* p. 49.
52. The undated quote from Clemenceau states: 'Dreyfus was the victim, Picquart the hero,' quoted in Duclert, *L'honneur d'un patriote,* p. 27.
53. See Léon Parsons, 'L'Opinion d'un poète,' *L'Aurore,* 7 March 1898: 1. Furthermore, even if Picquart himself was not theatrical, the idea of a man who risked all for honor had great theatrical appeal.
54. Barrès, *Scènes et doctrines,* 119. Witness the use of the word to disparage Oscar Wilde years earlier and to denigrate representations of a devirilized Napoleon,

clad in his dressing gown as played by actor Félix Duquesne in Victorien Sardou's *Mme Sans-Gêne*.

55. It is also clear that from the beginning Dreyfus was seen as a symbol rather than as an individual. For most people, he was 'a name, a symbol, of innocence or infamy, an unknown,' Reinach, *Histoire de l'Affaire Dreyfus*, Vol. 2, p. 499. In fact, Barrès calls him an 'enigma': *Scènes et Doctrines*, p. 106.

56. Duclert, 'Dreyfus, de l'oubli à l'histoire,' pp. 79–81.

57. Sarah Bernhardt, *Ma double vie* (Paris: Editons Phébus, 2000), pp. 99–100.

58. Richard Vinen notes that for many French men and women during World War II, the head of the Vichy regime, Marshal Pétain, was viewed as a national hero 'above politics.' Vinen quotes Catholic philosopher Jean Guitton, as stating that 'the national leader incarnates the tradition of the nation. In extreme necessity, he can be a woman or a young girl (Joan of Arc for us), Pétain is above all a national leader.' In this manner, contemporaries of the Second World War could separate loyalty to Pétain from disapproval of the actions of the Vichy regime: *The Unfree French: Life under the Occupation* (New Haven: Yale University Press, 2006), p. 57. In some respects, this desire for a national hero above politics was presaged by the search for unifying heroes under the Third Republic. Such a concept of a national leader also allows for the possibility of a female hero.

59. Reinach quotes Clemenceau as declaring before Rennes that a guilty verdict would be 'more beautiful:' *Histoire de l'Affaire Dreyfus*, Vol. 2, p. 652. To which Reinach replies that real individuals are not marionettes in the theater nor are they chess pawns to be pushed around. Note that Zola's article about the guilty verdict at Rennes was called 'Le Cinquième Acte.' Published originally in *L'Aurore*, 12 September 1899, it is reproduced in Emile Zola, *The Dreyfus Affair: 'J'Accuse' and Other Writings*, ed. Alain Pagès, trans. E. Levieux (New Haven: Yale University Press, 1996), pp. 136–43.

60. Reinach, *Histoire de l'Affaire Dreyfus*, Vol. 2, pp. 647, 651.

61. See Jules Huret, 'En liberté.' Orginally published in *Le Figaro*, 22 September 1899, this piece was republished in *Tout yeux, tout oreilles* (Paris: Bibliothèque Charpentier, 1901), pp. 335–62.

62. This letter to Madame Dreyfus, published in *L'Aurore* on 22 September 1899, is also reproduced in the Pagès volume, p. 146. Zola goes on to characterize Dreyfus as a martyr. It is interesting to note that Dreyfus himself, writing to Lucie on the eve of his degradation in 1894 had distinguished between physical courage and heroic martyrdom: 'Alas, I have the courageous soul of a soldier, I wonder though if I have the heroic soul of a martyr!' Alfred and Lucie Dreyfus, *Ecris-moi souvent, écris-moi longuement*, ed. Vincent Duclert (Paris: Mille et une nuits, 2005), pp. 122–3. Ruth Harris is currently working on a project on Lucie's heroism. See her article 'Letters to Lucie: Spirituality, Friendship and Politics during the Dreyfus Affair,' *French Historical Studies*, 28 (Fall 2005): 601–27.

63. When spectators cried out 'Long live Dreyfus!' he turned to them and stated, 'No, long live the Republic, long live truth!' Quoted in Duclert, *L'honneur d'un patriote*, p. 982.

64. Duclert, 'Dreyfus, de l'oubli à l'histoire,' p. 64, and *L'honneur d'un patriote*, p. 1032.

65. Forth, *Dreyfus Affair*: see especially the introduction and the conclusion, pp. 1–16, 235–42.

66. See also Duclert's article in *Le monde* of 17 June 2006, in which he proposed the pantheonization of Dreyfus for this reason.

67. See the text of Chirac's speech about 'les justes,' in *Le monde*, 19 January 2007. On Chirac's refusal of Duclert's request, 'Dreyfus célébré, sans Panthéon,' *Le monde*, 7 July 2007. The article quotes former Justice Minister Robert Badinter, who agrees with Chirac's decision: 'Dreyfus is certainly a victim of exceptional courage but a victim nevertheless. The hero of the Affair is Zola and he is in the Pantheon.'

68. 'Panthéon: le match Bloch-Dreyfus,' *Le Point* (22 June 2006), at http://www.lepoint. fr/actualites-chroniques/2007-01-17/polemique-pantheon-le-match-bloch-dreyfus/ 989/0/12019 (accessed 29 June 2009). Indeed, Pierre Birnbaum warned against pantheonizing Dreyfus as a Jew since he saw himself foremost as a Frenchman. The same could also be said of Marc Bloch.

69. See Duclert, 'Dreyfus, de l'oubli à l'histoire,' who states: 'It took the Affair to reveal this gap, that is, the divorce between democracy and the Republic,' p. 74.

70. See Chirac's speech from 12 July 2006: 'Allocution de M. Jacques Chirac à propos d'Alfred Dreyfus en 2006,' at http://fr.wikisource.org/wiki/Allocution_de_ M._Jacques_Chirac_%C3%A0_propos_d%27Alfred_Dreyfus_en_2006 (accessed 29 June 2009).

11
Two *Salonnières* during the Dreyfus Affair: the Marquise Arconati Visconti and Gyp

Ruth Harris

Conventional political history is notorious for the 'maleness' of its exposition, and standard accounts of the Dreyfus Affair all too readily conform to this stereotype. As an espionage tale, the Affair falls within the masculine arenas of diplomatic and military history, while as a story of political crisis, its main characters remain ministers, jurists, and polemicists.[1] The history of the struggle between 'intellectuals' and 'anti-intellectuals,' moreover, focuses attention on the leading lights of French academia and literature, almost all men, who tussled over the primary values of French politics and society.[2]

Women *are* mentioned in conventional accounts, but often to add feminine spice to an otherwise very male story. Who would not find a place for Mme Marie Bastian, the charwoman-turned-spy who collected the rubbish from Maximilien Schwarzkoppen's bin in the German Embassy and delivered the infamous *bordereau* that was the chief evidence against Dreyfus? It would be impossible not to describe Colonel Ferdinand Walsin Esterhazy's relationship with his mistresses Marguérite Pays and Mme de Boulancy, who became embroiled in the Affair through their connection to the real culprit.[3] There was also the 'Veiled Lady,' a shadowy figure who seems to have sprung from the pages of a second-rate adventure story, and who, Esterhazy claimed, had offered him photographs of confidential documents that the pro-Dreyfus Colonel Georges Picquart had acquired that proved Dreyfus's guilt.[4] The list of interesting and important women could go on and on, from the feisty female reporters of the feminist newspaper *La Fronde* through the tear-stricken Berthe Henry to the stoical Lucie Dreyfus who, more than anyone else, was responsible for her husband's ultimate return to France.[5] Indeed, new work on these figures – both recent and in the making – shows that the participation and representation of women in the Affair will soon join the avalanche of historical work produced since the beginning of the centennial commemorations.[6]

In this chapter, I have deliberately chosen two women of opposing political views – the Dreyfusard Marquise Arconati-Visconti and the anti-Dreyfusard

Gyp (Sybille Gabriel Marie Antoinette de Martel de Janville) – because they showed many similar psychological traits and emotional preoccupations. Both were remarkably important within their respective coalitions, and both displayed contradictions and conflicts, as well as the centrality of aggression and humor in sustaining and channeling the political emotion that the Affair had liberated.

Unlike the women cited above – who tended to reinforce prevailing visions of women as servants, mistresses, and wives – as important activists both the Marquise and Gyp challenged gender categories. By the time of the Affair, Gyp was already a best-selling novelist, and contributed to events as an anti-Semitic journalist. She paid right-wing thugs to fight Zola's supporters during his trial for libel, and contributed articles in *La Libre parole* to spread her anti-Semitic beliefs.[7] The Marquise did not have the same radical public persona, but she was equally influential among the Dreyfusards. She connected academic men to Dreyfusard politicians and patronized republican professors who used their expertise to demonstrate that Dreyfus could not have been the author of the *bordereau*.[8] Her money and influence established key posts and research institutions for these same men and other Dreyfusard colleagues (particularly at the Sorbonne and the Ecole de Chartes) who were central to mainstream republican ideology.[9]

Examining the discourse and behaviors of these two women provides a means through which to approach the strange nature of the *'cause célèbre'* as a form of exceptional politics. The Affair was characterized by unforeseen and often unlikely political alliances based on a perception of a common cause against a dangerous, monolithic enemy. Whereas rhetoric in politics always has a tendency to create Manichean divisions, the Affair intensified this inclination to an extraordinary degree. Actors discussed human and moral values in often existential terms, and both the Marquise and Gyp were exemplary in promoting almost outrageous forms of anti-clericalism and anti-Semitism. This chapter argues that understanding such a political world demands an investigation of the psychological dynamics underpinning the Affair, especially the myriad intimate connections between friends and associates in which these women played key roles.

For all their power and influence (and Gyp's extraordinary public persona), they occupied a different political and emotional space to activist men. Both the Marquise and Gyp were *salonnières*, and hence fulfilled a demanding role that was defined by their gender. Mature in years and resourceful by temperament, they, like the other *salonnières* of the era, were omnipresent in the social and political networks they helped to sustain.[10] They had to work hard, to be charming, witty, welcoming, severe, critical, informed as required, to spot future talent, to oversee kitchens as well as menus, wine-cellars and décor. The *salonnière's* work was demanding both in terms of emotional resources and social choreography.[11] But they did more than create a context. As the crisis over Alfred Dreyfus deepened and people chose different sides, friendships

broke apart and alliances became brittle. By jumping head-first into the maelstrom, women like the Marquise and Gyp helped to reshape the political
world and its agenda. Their activities show that the Affair cannot be analyzed
within the tidy confines of conventional history: the private and the political
overlapped with dinnertime conversation, intimate correspondence, literary
and historical production as well as political advocacy.

Their impact was profound but also double-edged. Denied citizenship and
access to the centers of political decision-making, they never engaged in the
Affair on terms of equality with men. Although as extraordinary as the men
they patronized (and who patronized them in return), both the Marquise
and Gyp lived this tension through bouts of exhibitionist anger, moments of
mad despair, vilification of opponents and idealization of the men on their
own side. Neither showed any great admiration for their husbands (by the
time of the Affair, the Marquise was a merry widow), but they worshiped the
political, literary, and artistic 'great men' whose careers they encouraged.[12]
Their fantasies of achievement thus often depended dangerously on the men
they groomed and sparked into action. But they could never join the masculine club, nor could they envisage working in solidarity with other women
because of a strong streak of misogyny. It is not an exaggeration to suggest that they lived in a kind of gender turmoil. The jagged emotion that
their position produced contributed to the political effervescence of the crisis but it also meant that they lived its ups and downs with an often painful
intensity.

Although both *salonnières*, the Marquise Arconati-Visconti and the
Comtesse de Martel shared little else besides some temperamental similarities. The Marquise was a serious patroness of the historical establishment
and responsible for endowing the chairs and libraries of famous historians
and research institutes.[13] She was both omnipresent and hidden from view,
both a facilitator and an agitator during the Affair. In the first role she provided a forum, mostly through her dinners on the rue Barbet for intellectuals
and politicians. Her capacity to straddle these two worlds made her central
to the coalition. She introduced disparate sympathizers to each other, and
recruited new ones, strengthening the sense of mission and identification
which set the Dreyfusards apart. She corresponded with the political elite
and condemned the Brisson Ministry ('the cowards, the villains, the histri-
onic politicians') for not championing the revisionist cause more strongly in
the wake of Colonel Hubert-Joseph Henry's dramatic suicide.[14] Despite the
growing cracks in the coalition, she would become one of Alfred Dreyfus's
most loyal friends after his pardon at Rennes in September 1899, even abandoning her friendship with the 'second hero' of the Affair, Colonel Picquart,
partly because of his anti-Semitism.[15]

Gyp, in contrast, was a society novelist, famous for the wit and lightheart-
edness of her fast-paced dialogue novels as well as her 'advanced' anti-Semitic
views. Before the Affair, she knew men and women from across the political

spectrum, but with the crisis she no longer tolerated anyone with Dreyfusard sympathies and excluded everyone from 'that camp.'[16] Friends with the novelist Anatole France for fifteen years, she broke with him, even dismissing servants she suspected of Dreyfusard loyalties.[17] She believed that Picquart's role 'had been the shadiest and the dirtiest in the Affair' and was outraged when Mme Ribot, the wife of the prominent republican politician Alexandre Ribot, had the temerity to exclaim, 'Well yes, if I had a daughter, I would be proud to offer her to this admirable man!'[18]

While the Marquise knew the Dreyfusard centrists and Radicals and even became close to the socialist leader Jean Jaurès, Gyp was connected to those who opted for right-wing populism and authoritarianism. She found other loyal friends through monarchism or anarchism, showing again her own political malleability as well as the novel – and, at first glance, surprising – political alliances of the era. Gyp was a common point among various splinter groups, whose contacts in the aristocratic world, journalism, literature, and politics meant that she was the 'consummate insider.'[19] Not only did she have conversations with General Roget, the man whose support the right-wing politician Paul Déroulède sought during his attempted coup d'état of February 1899,[20] but she was also acquainted with Félix Faure, the President of the Republic.[21] She was Déroulède's conduit for information, keeping in touch with Jules Guérin, the head of the Ligue antisémitique, and relayed Maurice Barrès's optimistic view of the Rennes trial back to associates in Paris.[22] Through her cousin, she even had links to the Orléanist monarchists, whom she despised.

Gyp loved the air of violence that the Right promoted during the Affair, and relished the aggression of political quarrels when they became personal. For example, she delighted in telegraphing Barrès to warn him that Octave Mirbeau – an anarchist Dreyfusard whom she detested – had a bought a 'light revolver' after reading Barrès's threats in a newspaper. She was clearly put out when Barrès was unimpressed by these 'puerile' reactions, and she happily contemplated Dreyfus's exoneration because it would allow her to continue her anti-Semitic campaign.[23] In rehashing the 1899 retrial at Rennes, she was delighted that Dreyfus's lawyer, Fernand Labori, had been shot, and was unashamed to remark that Alfred Demange, his other counsel, might also receive a bullet in the back.[24] She breathed in the heady air of conspiracy. When she was once again reviewing events surrounding the Affair to Déroulède, she thanked him warmly for the 'gorgeous stylet' that he had sent her as a gift and which she now wore – with point and wire – as a 'ravishing jewel' that also served as 'an excellent weapon.' All around her, she proclaimed to her friend, were 'bizarre people' who bothered her; 'all the time' she received anonymous letters that they would soon kill her.[25] Speaking of a rock thrown through her window, she concluded: 'I am afraid of firearms, and this fear means that I can't use them, while knives and sticks don't upset me in the least.'[26]

Gyp actively supported nationalist candidates during the elections of 1898, and rejoiced with Déroulède and Marcel Habert (his lieutenant and a mutual close friend) in the victory of right-wing candidates. Although Barrès lost his seat in Nancy by the slightest of majorities in May 1898, she nonetheless had the pleasure of knowing that the detested Joseph Reinach, the Jewish Republican who did much to organize the Dreyfusard campaign, had also been rejected by the electorate in Digne (Basses-Alpes). With their gains during the Affair, the nationalists believed that they were on the road to a mass movement, and the trouncing of Reinach was the sweetest part of their victory.

Gyp poses problems for feminist historians, for they are obliged to take seriously a powerful woman who is not a role model, let alone a heroine. She is almost an embarrassment, for her ideas and comportment fit only too well into the stereotype of the 'irrationalist' right, with all its aggressive hatreds and fantastic beliefs. If anything, an investigation of Gyp seems to reinforce the dichotomy between the destructive madness of the anti-Dreyfusard feelings and the high-minded rationality of their opponents.

But aspects of the Marquise also cause embarrassment. Historians have long neglected the Marquise's correspondence to Joseph Reinach during the Affair, preferring to concentrate on the period after 1899 when she and her salon fostered the extreme anticlericalism of the Bloc des Gauches.[27] It is easy to pay homage to the woman who subsidized the Sorbonne and gave history prizes to the Ecole des Chartes, but harder to accommodate the Dreyfusard *salonnière* who stilled her nervous crises by taking laudanum, consulted her father's spirit at his graveside when in need of advice, delivered coarse insults in Italian, and fantasized vividly about massacring and dismembering her enemies.

Nonetheless, the patroness of historical enquiry, political firebrand, and flamboyant friend were all of a piece. Her Dreyfusard advocacy and academic interests cannot be severed from the theatricality of her person and her reinvented sixteenth-century chateau in Gaesbeck in Belgium, where she hosted the Dreyfusards and named her garden's *allées* after the most illustrious devotees to the cause. Her creativity centered, literally, on creating a republican pedigree, one which she imaginatively connected to her restored castle.[28] Its renaissance owner Lamorraal van Egmond, she believed, represented republican beliefs in embryo: he was martyred during the Dutch Revolt of the 1540s and was hence the hero of national independence and Protestant free-thinking who struggled against Spanish absolutism and Catholicism.[29]

When she looked for her political roots, however, the Marquise generally sought ideals closer in time and place to her own. Her correspondence with Reinach displayed how she searched for the 'fathers' of the political tradition that defined her life, and she came to regard Reinach and his activism during the Affair as central to the rejuvenation of her political dreams. For the

Marquise, the Republic was, quite literally, a personal matter. She worshiped both her father and Gambetta as republican heroes, and believed they had both died on the same day and in the same hour.[30] Her father, Alphonse Peyrat, was an insurrectionary journalist during the Second Empire who became famous when Gambetta quoted his slogan: 'The clergy are the real enemy.'[31]

She was proud to be considered Gambetta's mistress, an allegation she always denied, although not enough to kill the story; indeed she seems to have been not unhappy when anti-Dreyfusards revived the tale during the Affair.[32] In his letters, Gambetta did call her 'Mia Chocciola' [my snail], 'Dear pet,' or 'the most fragrant of bouquets,' but any possibility of a love affair was blocked by the fact that she found Gambetta physically repulsive.[33] Her ambivalence arose partly because he was dangerously implicated in her paternal infatuation. Similarly, Reinach's appeal was that he was Gambetta's heir apparent, the man whose political apprenticeship had taken place at Gambetta's newspaper, *La Republique française*, and who compiled the Great Man's political discourses for posterity.[34] She offered her passionate and platonic adoration to Reinach instead, for he was now the living embodiment of the Peyrat-Gambetta tradition.

His importance to her grew with the central role that he played during the Affair. Joseph Reinach was the oldest of a triumvirate of brilliant Jewish brothers famed for their academic success and wealth (they were the sons of a Frankfurt banker).[35] Joseph was the most public of the trio, fiercely meritocratic, anti-clerical, and devoted to the Republic. He lived in style with liveried servants and private secretaries, enjoyed hunting, and had contacts among the great and the good across Europe. He was polyglot, and wrote to his brother Salmon for fun in English, while also being equally adept in German. But he was tainted by his father-in-law's complicity in the Panama Canal scandals of the early 1890s, financial peculations which encouraged the anti-Semitism that reached new heights during the Affair. Because of these negative associations, Reinach frequently operated in the background to coordinate the campaign, while also intervening publicly in the Dreyfusard newspaper *Le Siècle*.

The Marquise and Reinach thus shared a taste for grand residences, art and, above all, a certain kind of republican politics. Both of them were newly-rich, if not *nouveaux-riches*. The Marquise frequently recalled the single dress and inadequate shoes that were her only dowry when she married the wealthy Marquis Arconati-Visconti, a fey man with a syphilitic aura who died two years after their marriage. The Marquis's family detested their heir's republican and anticlerical bride, who refused to take her place at the Italian court. Despite her republicanism (and self-professed populism), she was enthralled by the new power that rank and wealth bestowed. She never married again. She remodeled the chateau at Gaesbeck, became a serious art collector and donated her collection, valued at a million dollars, to the Louvre in 1914.[36]

Above all, she patronized professional history and was widely regarded, and regarded herself, as 'Clio,' an important patron of professional history. In theory, the Marquise championed the 'people,' but she meant to shape their vision of the past through elite institutions, money, and objects.

Of all the Dreyfusard *salonnières*, the Marquise played the most with gender norms. She was famously misogynistic, remarking to the Belgian scholar Franz Dumont: 'Do not think, Monsieur, that many people are invited to my home; first I never receive women' (she later explained that her idol Gambetta had advised her to exclude women, and their rivalries, from her salon).[37] At times she embodied the most clichéd femininity and at others reveled in a theatrical boyishness. She dressed in the sumptuous robes, frills, corsages, and jewelry of a fin-de-siècle dame, hosting 'her' men at her *hôtel* on the rue de Barbet or at Gaesbeck. She loved enacting the past, and her favorite photograph showed her at around sixty as a renaissance page, in clothes made by Sarah Bernhardt's costumier.

Like the Marquise, Gyp also constructed an interlocking personal and political lineage. Whereas the Marquise was elevated to the aristocracy through marriage but insisted on her links with the people, the Comtesse de Martel was born of the famous Mirabeau family, and popularized the anti-Semitism of the salon and the street. As Willa Silverman has masterfully shown, Gyp's psychic life was completely rocked by her discomfiture with womanhood. The last in an aristocratic line, Gyp regretted that she was not born a man, an 'inadequacy' that her family never let her forget. She saw herself in increasingly masculine terms, her muscularity and sporting prowess suggesting a freakish tendency outside the feminine norm.

Gyp constructed her 'maleness' in conjunction with a political identity of sentimental Bonapartism. She even wrongly claimed that she was born on the same day as Napoleon, a fib which mirrored the Marquise's desire to associate her father's date of death with that of Gambetta's demise. While Gyp was nostalgic for certain aspects of her aristocratic inheritance – as the offspring of legitimists she despised the Orléanists – her political yearnings centered on men closely associated with Bonapartism. She admired General Ernest Boulanger, Déroulède, and Barrès, who all rejected the compromises of parliamentarianism and embraced populist authoritarianism. Above all, she assumed a male identity in her fiction and became 'Bob,' a boy who, although immaculately dressed, voices his cheeky assaults on authority.[38] As Silverman has shown, Bob was very much as Gyp saw herself, a charming anarchist, but like her, too, he showed the same sentimentalism for Bonaparte, an idealization of army and valor, and a nostalgia that separated him from the anarchists of the Left.

Obliged to maintain her family house in Neuilly and a second home in Brittany in order to uphold her society credentials, Gyp sat up nights turning out pages of prose. She topped the list at her Jewish publishers, Calmann-Levy, famous for their ability to reach a mass market and also publish serious works.

She wanted to leave these 'Rothschilds,' but she depended on their willingness to advance her money.[39] When they wanted to place stricter editorial controls on her anti-Semitic ravings, she hated these Jewish 'spoilers' all the more. She felt herself foiled by their 'monopoly' at every turn, as Jewish impresarios turned down her plays in theaters.

The Marquise and Gyp were both almost naive in their adoration. Sometimes the Marquise saw Joseph Reinach as a helpmate with whom she could discuss the purchase of antiques and the installation of a refurbished renaissance portal at her chateau. She allowed Reinach to pay her bills when she was traveling or to do other favors that cost money, knowing that such exchanges passed between equals. In this sense there was a kind of cozy, even matrimonial dimension to their friendship, in which she never once mentioned Reinach's wife or children. Ease in friendship did not mean that the Marquise wanted to acknowledge Reinach's home life.

But this amicable side of their relationship coexisted with her adoration, especially in the early years of the Affair. She worshipped Reinach, in the same way she worshipped Gambetta and her father. She wrote 'How I love you!!!! [underlined seven times] I speak like Shakespeare's heroine: "how beautiful is a man;"'[40] 'I kiss you with all the force of a heart which, for some time, only beats for you.'[41] She followed with rapt attention his journalistic interventions, which demonstrated Reinach's unerring, intelligent analysis of events, despite the incessant anti-Semitic diatribes launched against him. Her excitement, however, was often overcome by moments of despair, 'You will tell me that I see everything in black – this is true. In seeing what has passed in the last two years, I am like someone who has had a religion and lost it.'[42]

In thus describing her predicament, she showed how much she identified with the Republic and took the turn of events during the Affair personally: she believed that her father was turning in his grave with shame and disappointment. When events went against her and against the cause – as they did time and time again – she retreated into spasms of hysteria and illness, taking doses of chloral, ether, and digitalis to soothe her frayed nerves.[43] She wrote endlessly about the wickedness of their opponents and her desire to die rather than to live and witness the destruction of all her political hopes.

She retreated to bed, summoned her physician (a Dreyfusard, as she had dismissed another who thought differently) and studiously read Voltaire, the only 'tonic' that could restore her to calm.[44] She repeatedly begged Reinach to give her a 'shot of panglossism,' referring to the savant in Voltaire's *Candide* who repeatedly assured the young heroine that 'All was for the best in the best of all possible worlds.'[45] Dr Pangloss was something of a fool when faced with evil in the world. There seemed a part of her that disdained Reinach for his irrevocable optimism; and yet this quality – which she possessed so little of – was a balm to her disjointed spirit, continually upset by the reverses that the Dreyfusards suffered.

In a similar way, Gyp adored the dashing General Boulanger. Not only would he return France to the French and purge the country of political corruption, Jews, and foreigners, but he was also the symbol of the Napoleonic virtues that she had admired in her father and grandfather.[46] While the Marquise judged Reinach correctly – he was energetic and optimistic, despite the assaults against him – Gyp's objects of devotion were a perpetual disappointment. Boulanger was a broken reed, and after him she turned to Déroulède who was a similar failure. Although an orator with charm and the allure of a *chef*, Déroulède repeatedly misjudged people and bungled events. His coup d'état attempt in February 1899 was a fiasco, while his exile in Spain left him the 'absent man,' always in the thoughts of his followers but out of action.[47]

Both women were famed for their aggressive humor which sustained and enlivened the men on their side. They were outrageously funny precisely because they did and said things which unsettled gender conventions. They were unladylike in their defiance, transgressive in their cruel imaginings, and proud of flights of bad language wittily delivered. During the heat of the conflict, probably in 1898, the Marquise told Reinach how she regularly posted pro-Dreyfusard placards outside her home, and then lay in wait with jugs of water attached to a rope to douse anyone who dared deface them.[48] Although French to the bone, the Marquise used Italian as a foil – for romance, melodrama, humor, especially for bad language. She always addressed Reinach with Italian diminutives, calling him 'Beppo mio,' 'Carrissimo,' and 'mio Caro.' She described Du Paty de Clam as 'the mortadella of Bologna, half pig and half donkey.'[49] She was delightfully crude in Italian, indulging a kind of Rabelaisian humor that sought to use the epithets and expressions of the populace to mock the men on the other side.

She also specialized in conjuring up satisfying (and sometimes scary) fantasies of violence, repeatedly fantasizing about executing, disfiguring, and torturing her opponents. She repeatedly instructed Reinach to brand the anti-Dreyfusards with a 'red hot iron' and she dreamed of erecting gibbets to hang Mercier, Henry, Lauth, and Roger, officers involved in the military conspiracy.[50] As Clio she evoked examples from the past, another one of her father's idols, Robespierre, whom she called by his first name: 'we were cleaner in the time of Maximilien! I prefer the guillotine than that ocean of mud in which this country seems to want to sink.'[51] Occasionally she signed her letters as 'Maximilienne,' a fantasy of becoming the feminine embodiment of revolutionary virtue. She admired Fouquier-Thinville, the famous inquisitor of the Terror who, rather than hearing witnesses, sent hundreds to the guillotine without a thought. In her view, such ruthless men were better than 'all these bandits without balls [in Italian] of this good Republic who will pay nothing at all!!!'[52] She thus offered an image of castrated impotence, that she as a woman unable to work in the public arena knew only too well.

Gyp's violent urges focused on Jews. To a legitimist republican with Bonapartist longings, the Jew represented the bourgeois parvenu, who now 'monopolized' positions once reserved for the aristocratic elite.[53] Moreover, they lacked *panache*, a quality which Gyp, with her *lorgnon* held up to her eyes and her provocative *tenues*, possessed in spades. Like all the anti-Semites of her generation, Gyp both magnified Jewish power and despised Jews for their physical puniness and emasculation (circumcision was seen as confirmation of this view). But her hatred of Jews was also based on deep fears about her own powerlessness and fears of victimization, so potent in a woman who depended on the 'syndicat' for her income.

Gyp's wit was also acerbic, even scintillating. Related to Jean Sabran-Pontevès, a monarchist officer and gentlemen who ran unsuccessfully for election in May 1898, Gyp nonetheless detested the Orléanists for what she saw as their double dealing. She attacked the Duc d'Orléans for condemning Jews but taking their money (something, of course, which she did herself) and believed that they had helped undo her beloved Déroulède through their disloyalty to him in February 1899. She described an avaricious pretender and the sycophantic Jewish matrons who paid court to him in biting language which explains her success as an author:

> Isn't the Duke of Orleans a pretty character ... in marrying an ugly woman, older than he, who will not have children and is very rich? And, what's more, he still fastens together the money of the distracted old Jewesses who drool with envy over the stool that they would be able to have *at the Court*!!![54]

While both Gyp and the Marquise specialized in the humor of disdain, the Marquise also sought examples from the past to inspire and uplift. She shared with many nineteenth-century contemporaries a love of the Italian poet, Dante, and saw in his personal history another story of tormented innocence.[55] She saw the politics of the Third Republic in the machinations of fourteenth-century Florence, when Dante was forced into exile for his hostility to Church authority. She wrote eloquently to Reinach of the poet's sense of ill-treatment and put Dante in the same category as Voltaire, who had been forced into exile in Switzerland like many republicans who had fled the authoritarianism of Louis Napoleon. In one letter she described to Reinach a sojourn in Italy during which the Comtesse de Borromeo gathered together Italian Dreyfusards and toasted the 'martyr.'[56] Present at the gathering was the Marquis de Malaspina, whose forebear had given refuge to Dante in the past, and who declared his willingness to offer the same hospitality to Dreyfus now. The parallel between the two 'victims' was obvious to everyone present.

Perhaps the greatest difference between the two women was their entirely different relationship to Jews. The Marquise's passionate friendship with Reinach showed devotion to a man who was the ultimate target of anti-Semitic attack. She showed the same dedication to Alfred Dreyfus once he returned to France, never indulging in the anti-Semitism that distinguished

Dreyfusards like Georges Picquart exhibited as the coalition dissolved in disenchantment and recriminations after Rennes.

Moreover, she was lucky insofar as some of her aggressive fantasies could be partially resolved through the history-writing that she hoped to inspire. She wrote to Reinach in 1901 after the first volume of his work on the Affair finally brought relief: 'New Dante, you have marked them on the shoulder, all the Hanotaux, Dupuy and other wretches and miserable cowards! As to Mercier, your book is a gibbet where he will swing for eternity.'[57] For her, shaming through good history was sweet revenge, a metaphorical 'marking' that was probably even better than physical violence. When Dreyfus was finally rehabilitated, she also had the pleasure of knowing that Reinach's history sat proudly as a canonical text on the shelves of the university that she had done so much to patronize.

The Marquise's vicious anticlericalism, which intensified in the Affair's aftermath, corroded Dreyfusard humanitarianism. Even Joseph Reinach, who shared her view of the dangers of 'Jesuitism,' was repulsed by the manner in which Combes separated Church and state in 1905, and believed that the premier's policies would bring bitterness and electoral defeat.[58] But the Marquise's anticlericalism and Gyp's anti-Semitism can never be fully equated. Certainly, the Marquise saw the Church as the generator of conspiracy in much the same way that Gyp condemned the Jewish 'syndicate' as the fount of cosmopolitan subversion. Nonetheless, anticlericalism was an attack on an institution – and particularly the power of the Jesuit order – while anti-Semitism was an assault on a people, conceived all at once as deicidal murderers, exploitative capitalists, and racial polluters. Although both women were grand haters, Gyp won this dubious competition.

The importance of their antics, stories, and letters lies in the way that the Affair as a *cause célèbre* is incomprehensible without them. Men like Joseph Reinach and Paul Déroulède have long figured in histories of the Affair, but the motor of their advocacy and its tone drew strength from these intimate connections. The Affair's political intensity was formed in the crucible of passionate friendships, relationships sustained through face-to-face contact at the women's salons and carried on in conversations in letters. Joseph Reinach repeatedly confessed that his female councilors were essential to him in formulating his ideas and strategies. When the Marquise embroidered Dante's life story to make it relevant to the current crisis, she delved into history as a psychic goldmine, helping Joseph to re-fashion their dreams of republican revitalization. An important part of Déroulède's persona lay in his masculine appeal. Letters from devotees flooded in to support and extol him in terms similar to those which Gyp employed. Gyp offered not only her idealization, but also contributed to the atmosphere of adventurism, plotting, and putschist antics that defined Déroulède's political activism during the Affair.

The *salonnières* demonstrate the extent to which the very notion of political 'modernity' needs rethinking. Historians have focused on the emergence

→ Reminds us of what is old + alien about this era

of mass society, with its crowds, mass circulation press, and love of the spectacular and celebrity.[59] With its café society, emerging consumerism, international exhibitions, and imperial extravaganzas, the fin de siècle seems to epitomise the democratization of politics and culture. The baying crowds at Alfred's degradation, the vociferous exchanges in the newspapers, the anti-Semitic riots outside the Cour d'assises during Zola's trial, all testify to such tendencies. At the same time, however, the period remains a foreign country, permeated by aristocratic codes of honor, magico-religious beliefs and, above all, salon culture, which appear strangely out of step with contemporary society. No two *salonnières* better encompass the duality of these tendencies than the Marquise and Gyp. The former was an impoverished daughter of a republican firebrand elevated to the aristocracy through marriage, the latter a descendant of one of the greatest families of the French *noblesse* who wrote popular anti-Semitic novels and reveled in the excitement of street violence. That they incarnated these contradictions reveals a new way of analysing the Affair both as *cause célèbre* and gender politics.

Notes

1. See Douglas Johnson, *France and the Dreyfus Affair* (London: Blandford Press, 1966) and Jean-Denis Bredin, *The Affair: the Case of Alfred Dreyfus*, trans. Jeffrey Mehlman (London: Sidgwick and Jackson, 1987); for remarkable work which shows the new possibilities in military history see André Bach, *L'Armée de Dreyfus: Une histoire politique de l'armée française de Charles X à l'Affaire* (Paris: Tallandier, 2004).

2. See Pascal Ory and Jean-François Sirinelli, *Les intellectuels en France de l'Affaire Dreyfus à nos jours* (Paris: Armand Colin, 1986) for an earlier generational 'take' on the intellectuals, as well as Jean-François Sirinelli's *Intellectuels et passions françaises* (Paris: Fayard, 1990); see also the pioneering article by Jean and Monica Charlot, 'Un rassemblement d'intellectuels: La Ligue des Droits de l'Homme,' *Revue française de science politique*, 9 (1959): 995–1019; for more classic statements of the role of the intellectuals in the Dreyfus camp (as well as their opponents) see Christophe Charle, 'Champ littéraire et champ du pouvoir: Les écrivains et l'Affaire Dreyfus,' *Annales, ESC*, 32 (1977): 240–64 and his later *Naissance des 'intellectuels': 1880–1900* (Paris, Editions de Minuit, 1990). For more reconceptualization see Michel Winock, *Le Siècle des intellectuels* (Paris: Seuil, 1997), which examines the relationships between the two sides. Much important and focused work on these debates has been conducted by Vincent Duclert who sums up much of his research in his 'Anti-intellectualisme et intellectuals pendant l'affaire Dreyfus,' *Mil neuf cent. Revue d'histoire intellectuelle*, 15 (1977): 69–83. There are many other important strands in the historiography and increasing material on the relationship of institutions of the state to the political crisis, as well as cultural and social histories of anti-Semitism and popular political mobilization.

3. Marcel Thomas's classic *Esterhazy ou l'envers de l'Affaire Dreyfus* (Paris: Vernal/Philippe Lebaud, 1989) gives a brilliant sense of Esterhazy's world and the place of women in it.

4. Ibid., pp. 283–90.

— also, individuals crafting their identities...

5. See Mary Louise Roberts, *Disruptive Acts: the New Woman in Fin-de-Siècle France* (Chicago: University of Chicago Press, 2002) for more on female journalists, pp. 107–30; see also Michelle Perrot, 'Lucie et Alfred' (Avant-propos), in Vincent Duclert (ed.), *'Ecris-moi souvent, écris-moi longuement ...': Correspondance de l'île du Diable (1894–1899)* (Paris: Ed. Mille et une nuits, 2005), pp. 9–21, and Duclert's introduction. Duclert's magisterial biography, *Alfred Dreyfus: l'Honneur d'un patriote* (Paris: Fayard, 2006) gives Lucie her due throughout. For more on women's ecumenical and compassionate impulses see my 'Letters to Lucie: Spirituality, Friendship and Politics during the Dreyfus Affair,' *French Historical Studies*, 28 (4) (Fall, 2005), pp. 601–28. Elizabeth Everton, 'Women and the Anti-Dreyfusard Movement: Representation and Participation,' an unpublished proposal for a doctoral dissertation in history at the University of California at Los Angeles, cited with kind permission of the author.

6. Gender analysis has also contributed to new perspectives, with Christopher Forth's book on diverging visions of masculinity leading the way; see his *The Dreyfus Affair and the Crisis of French Manhood* (Baltimore: Johns Hopkins University Press, 2004) for the first examination of 'body politics.'

7. Willa Z. Silverman, *The Notorious Life of Gyp: Right Wing Anarchist in fin-de-siècle France* (New York, Oxford University Press, 1995), p. 142.

8. See the story of the 'philology' experts in Bertrand Joly, 'Ecole des Chartes et l'Affaire Dreyfus,' *Bibliothèque de l'Ecole de Chartes*, 147 (1989): 611–71. For more on the Marquise, see Franz Cumont, *La Marquise Arconati-Visconti (1840–1923): Quelques souvenirs* (Gaasbeek, 1977) and Carolo Bronne, *La Marquise Arconati: La dernière châtelaine de Gassbeek* (Brussels: Les Cahiers historiques, 1970).

9. For the important role of historians in the struggle see Madeleine Réberioux, 'Histoire, historiens et dreyfusisme,' *Revue historique*, 240 (1976): 407–32. The Marquise was particularly connected to Gabriel Monod, whose intervention in the Affair was crucial; see Rémy Rioux, '"Saint-Monod-la-critique" et "l'obsédante Affaire Dreyfus,"' *Comment sont-ils devenus dreyfusards ou anti-dreyfusards? Mil neuf-cent, Revue d'histoire intellectuelle*, 11 (1993): 33–8.

10. For an overview, see Anne-Martin Fugier, *Les salons de la IIIe République: Art, littérature et politique* (Paris : Perrin, 2003); see Steven Kale, *French Salons: High Society and Political Sociability from the Old Regime to the Revolution of 1848* (Baltimore: Johns Hopkins University Press, 2004) and Sylvie Aprile in 'La République au salon: vie et mort d'une forme de sociabilité politique, 1865–1885,' *Revue d'histoire moderne et contemporaine*, 38 (1991): 473–87. There are many anecdotal accounts that are helpful: André de Rouquières, *Cinquante ans de panache* (Paris: Pierre Flore, 1951) and Cornelia Otis Skinner, *Elegant Wits and Grand Horizontals: Paris-La Belle Epoque* (London: Michael Joseph, 1963) and Joanna Richardson, *The Courtesans: the Demi-Monde in 19th-Century France* (London: Phoenix, 2000).

11. For the arguments about 'performance' see Mary Louise Roberts, *Disruptive Acts* and her 'Acting Up: the Feminist Theatrics of Marguerite Durand,' *French Historical Studies*, 19(4) (Fall 1996): 1103–38, as well as the collection of essays edited by Jo Burr Margadant, *The New Biography: Performing Femininity in Nineteenth-Century France* (Berkeley: University of California Press, 2000).

12. Mme Arman de Cavaillet, the famous muse of Anatole France, literally relegated her husband to the kitchen while she 'fronted' intellectual matters in the study, dining room, and drawing room. She lived for France's literary career, edited his work, and sometimes even inserted her own prose into his literary criticism. See Jeanne Pouquet, *Le Salon de Mme Arman de Cavaillet* (Paris: Hachette, 1926).

13. She endowed a chair for the famous historian Gabriel Monod at the Collège de France, another for Gustave Lanson at the Sorbonne, and offered scholarships and prizes in history at the Ecole de Chartes, the centre of French paleography and curatorship. Moreover, she bought the library of Gaston Paris – a famous professor of comparative literature – for the Ecole pratique des Hautes Etudes, the research centre of the French humanities, and bequeathed her massive art collection to the Louvre, the Musée Carnavalet and the Musée des Arts Décoratifs.

14. Bibliothèque nationale, NAF (nouvelles Acquisitions françaises), 25 October 1898, ff. 207–9, undated.

15. Her relationship to Dreyfus was entirely different from her relationship to Reinach. See Bibliothèque Victor Cousin (Sorbonne) for his missives to her, Correspondance de la marquise Arconati-Visconti, manuscripts 271–275 (1901–1923); and her correspondence to him, Musée de l'histoire et de l'art du Judaïsme, 4 cahiers, September 1899–1910. This is the way she described her allegiance to Alfred in a letter to Reinach when she confronted Picquart on his unjustified bad feeling towards Dreyfus: 'He does not forgive me for having given him my opinion on his attitude towards the Captain … I don't care and am like Corinne "on the side of the victims,"' 303–4 BN NAF 24888, ff. 303–4, undated.

16. Archives nationales, AP (Archives personelles) 451 carton 9 Gyp to Paul Déroulède 39849, n.d.

17. Silverman, *The Notorious Life of Gyp*, pp. 138–9.

18. AP 451, carton 9 Gyp to Déroulède 41083, undated.

19. Silverman, *Notorious Life of Gyp*, p. 140.

20. AP 451, carton 9 Gyp to Déroulède 41164, undated.

21. AP 451, carton 9, Gyp to Déroulède 48483, undated.

22. Ibid.

23. AP 451, carton 9, Gyp to Déroulède 48483, undated.

24. Ibid. Admittedly, she did acknowledge that the bullet should be made of cork.

25. AP 451, carton 9, Gyp to Déroulède 7545, undated.

26. Ibid.

27. Gérard Baal, 'Un Salon dreyfusard, des lendemains de l'Affaire à la Grande Guerre: La Marquise Arconati-Visconti et ses amis,' *Revue d'histoire moderne et contemporaine*, 28 (1981): 433–63.

28. She constructed a massive forty-meter tower over the entry and installed decorative tableaux in the salle des Chevaliers. Executed by the French architect, Edmond Bonnaffé, these narrative pictures of the Chateau's history (replete with historical errors) look more like stage sets than frescoes from an old manor house. They also captured the Marquise in contemporary costume.

29. This view was enshrined in Goethe's play of 1788, which had incidental music written for it by Beethoven in 1809. Historical weight was added to this view by the American historian, John Lothrop Motley in his *The Rise of the Dutch Republic* (1876)

30. NAF 24888, ff. 299–300, undated.

31. Gabriel Monod, 'Les débuts d'Alphonse Peyrat dans la critique historique,' *Revue historique*, 96 (1908): 1–49. Monod wrote this article in recognition of the Marquise's patronage of historical scholarship in France.

32. BN NAF 24888, ff. 181-2.

33. Bronne, *La Marquise Arconati*, p. 82.

34. See Corrine Casset, *Joseph Reinach devant l'affaire Dreyfus: un exemple de l'assimilation politique des Juifs de France au début de la IIIe République*, thèse de l'Ecole nationale des chartes, 1982, and Jean El Gammal, *Joseph Reinach*

(*1856–1921*) *et la République*, thèse de 3e cycle d'histoire, université Paris X-Nanterre, 1982.

35. For more on the brothers see Jean-Yves Mollier, *Le scandale de Panama* (Paris: Fayard, 1991), pp. 209–38, and Pierre Birnbaum, *Les fous de la République: Histoire politique des Juifs d'État de Gambetta à Vichy* (Paris: Fayard, 1992), pp. 13–28.
36. *New York Times*, 20 March 1914: 4.
37. Cumont, *La Marquise Arconati-Visconti (1840–1923)*, p. 8.
38. Silverman, *Notorious Life of Gyp*, pp. 63–4.
39. Ibid, pp. 57–60.
40. BN NAF 24888 ff. 221-1, undated.
41. BN NAF 24888 ff. 210–11, 1 November 1898.
42. BN NAF 24888, ff. 201–2, undated.
43. BN NAF 24888, ff. 262–3, undated.
44. BN NAF 24888, ff. 201–2, undated.
45. BN NAF 24888, ff. 313–14, undated.
46. Silverman, *Notorious Life of Gyp*, pp. 89–91.
47. See the authoritative Bertrand Joly, *Déroulède: L'inventeur du nationalisme* (Paris: Perrin, 1998).
48. BN NAF 24888, ff. 181–2, n.d.
49. BN NAF 24888, ff. 238–9.
50. BN NAF 24888, ff. 200, undated. She dreamed about 'un Montfaucon,' an allusion to a Parisian medieval gibbet where the military conspirators would be shamed (Mercier, Henry, Lauth, and Roget).
51. BN NAF 24888, ff. 198–9, undated.
52. BN NAF 24888, ff. 315–17, undated.
53. Silverman, *Notorious Life of Gyp*, p. 79.
54. AP 451, carton 9 Gyp to Déroulède AN 39864, undated, emphasis in original.
55. She was not unusual in her cult for the Italian, which swept across Western Europe in the nineteenth century, reaching its height perhaps in England with the works of Gabriel Rossetti and Robert Browning. For the Marquise, as well as others further to the Right, Dante was the incarnation of the Renaissance whose writing in the vernacular prepared others to foster national cultures. In the French historical establishment, and hence among Dreyfusards, Dante was part of a politico-intellectual project that sought to investigate the origins of romance languages. In 1872, close associates of the Marquise, Gaston Paris and Paul Meyer, founded the academic journal, *Romania*, in which the study of Dante was important. The Marquise's personal obsession with Dante was fed by these sources. As much as she was a French Republican, she was also an Italian patriot, with her husband's father noted for his support of the *Risorgimento*.
56. BN NAF 24888 ff. 162–3.
57. BN NAF 24888 ff. 450–5, undated.
58. Baal, 'Un Salon Dreyfusard,' p. 440.
59. See Vanessa R. Schwartz, *Spectacular Realities: Early Mass Culture in Fin-de-siècle Paris* (Berkeley: University of California Press, 1998); 'Walter Benjamin for Historians', *American Historical Review*, 106(2001): 1721–43; Leo Braudy, *The Frenzy of Renown, Fame and its History* (New York: Oxford University Press, 1986); Gregory Shaya, 'The *Flâneur*, the *Badaud*, and the Making of a Mass Public in France, circa 1860–1910,' *American Historical Review*, 109 (2004): 41–77 ; Dominique Kalifa, *La culture de masse en France, vol. 1 (1860–1930)* (Paris: La Découverte 2001); Jean-Pierre Rioux and Jean-François Sirinelli (eds), *La culture de masse en France de la Belle Epoque à aujourd'hui* (Paris: Hachette, 2002).

Conclusion

Elinor Accampo and Christopher E. Forth

Engaging with the complexities and contradictions of modernity is an ongoing fact of life for societies across the world – Western or non-Western, developed or developing – yet for many in Europe the full force of these tensions was keenly felt in the fin de siècle. This volume has concentrated on the ways in which French men and women faced a wide variety of challenges and opportunities that influenced their individual identities as well as the identity of their nation as a whole. The delicately balanced Third Republic had to gird itself against sometimes violent challenges from both left and right wings of the political spectrum, while tensions with the Catholic Church reached a peak. As the chapters of this book show in various ways, however, the ideological and moral underpinnings of the Third Republic were complex and contradictory. The gendered roles upon which republicanism relied in the practice of daily life, the definitions of 'male' and 'female' individuals and their respective responsibilities for national well-being, were unstable and in the process of rapid evolution. In this concluding chapter we briefly consider how the French engagement with modernity during the fin de siècle evolved through the First World War and the collapse of the Third Republic.

Even though France's first three republics excluded women from exercising full political rights over the course of 150 years, bourgeois republicanism certainly did not confine them to the private sphere; moreover, it armed them and their male supporters with the rhetorical weapons to carve a place for women in civic life and to insist on their recognition in the justice system. Several chapters have shown how women – feminist or not – brilliantly employed the coded language of republicanism and male honor to gain power for themselves and point to the contradictions inherent in 'universalism' and the double standard in human rights. By appropriating honor codes for their own ends women exposed the hypocrisy of male behavior in the context of national ideals. Their success in shaming men publicly – in the courts, in the press, and in public lectures – exposed the incompatibility of male sexual prowess and exploitation with the modern bourgeois values of citizenship.

In broad terms, then, the so-called 'Woman Question' indeed found its complement in the 'Man Problem,' often in the form of 'sexual rebel' which, as Modris Eksteins points out, became a 'central figure in the imagery of revolt' during this period.[1] Those who, like bohemian artists, claimed to dismiss bourgeois republican values would find little contradiction between a principled rejection of domesticity and the sexual objectification of women. Indeed, the bohemian culture and its anti-bourgeois poetic and artistic celebrations exemplify the possibilities of self-fashioning beyond the reach of mainstream culture, the parliament, and courts. But they too developed their own codes of exclusivity in the artistic world. As we have seen, Papus's pursuit of the occult similarly rejected bourgeois republican values and reinstated a hierarchy of distinction based on 'science,' gender, and unconventional sexual behavior.

As traditional hierarchies disintegrated and secular culture undermined church authority, professional experts created a new knowledge-base for adjusting human behavior to the demands of modern society, especially in the face of fears about hereditary degeneration and the crisis of depopulation. Yet if the science of sexology scrutinized 'abnormal' sexual practices, it also gave voice to those on the margins by acknowledging them and soliciting their testimonies, especially in the wake of Oscar Wilde's trial when the mass press and medical literature made homosexuals increasingly visible.[2] André Gide, after a long struggle, admitted his homosexuality. Serge Diaghilev, whose ballet had become a Paris institution, made his homosexual proclivities quite public.[3] France's anarchist-dominated neo-Malthusian movement advocated female sexual liberation through birth control devices advertised in its journals and in informational brochures distributed and discussed in well-attended lecture circuits.[4]

Examples of male and female personal liberation abound in this period, invigorated and sustained by a wide variety of counter-cultural movements. But countervailing forces were at work as well. From the 1890s, an army of demographers, politicians, government officials, doctors, social hygienists, and moral reformers had become obsessed with France's low birth rates, producing a flood of books and articles about the depopulation crisis – and how it both reflected and contributed to French national degeneration. It also meant that France would not be able to compete militarily against its European neighbors. Founded in 1896, the National Alliance for French Population Growth immediately attracted 400 members, and it continued to grow in the years prior to World War I, acting as a pressure group on the French parliament to ban birth control and encourage higher fertility. Concerns about French reproduction and public health became more acute as the Moroccan crises of 1905 and 1907 escalated the international tensions that would lead to the Great War. A new national mood took hold by 1911 as the nationalist right became more bellicose and a revived Catholicism rejected modernism, scientism, and secularism.

The rejuvenation of the French Right was already under way even as the case of Alfred Dreyfus was resolved in his favor. The long-suffering captain received an official pardon in 1899 and was rehabilitated to the military in 1906, but the ideological cleavages widened by this national scandal hardly closed with the apparent conclusion of the Affair. In fact the Right continued to gain political mileage through its critique of the physical and moral weaknesses of both intellectuals and middle-class professionals committed to brain work rather than more physically strenuous pursuits. Even erstwhile opponents of militarism experienced a new-found belligerence in the years leading up to the First World War, and serious political divisions persisted during the war itself, despite the much vaunted *Union sacrée* that was supposed to signify an intellectual truce for the sake of the war effort.[5] The end to the Dreyfus Affair and the ultimate separation of Church and state in 1905 brought some stability to the Republic, but certainly did not end the French culture wars.

Within the context of contested culture, women generally gained considerable agency in the fin de siècle, as individuals and as groups. The feminist movement reached a peak by 1910; it could boast more than one hundred organizations and the support of influential politicians – all of which portended an optimistic future for women's status. Historians have devoted considerable attention to how the Great War transformed gender roles, and to the extent that it did, how permanent these transformations would prove to be. Feminists joined the majority of the French population in the *Union sacrée*, placing the interests of the nation above their demands for women's rights. If they did not silence themselves on the subject, press censorship did. They believed, moreover, that their contributions to the war effort – particularly in taking on men's jobs in industry and farm labor, or working for the Red Cross – would ultimately advance their cause for full citizenship. But most commentators viewed women's efforts during the war as an expression of their 'natural' disposition for self-sacrifice, and fully expected that they would return to the home when the war ended.[6]

Post-war labor shortages, however, kept many women in the industrial labor force, including in the previously male-dominated industries of metallurgy. But as the works of Laura Lee Downs and Laura Frader have shown, employers created a gendered system of labor stratification, confining women to poorly-paid, monotonous, repetitive, unskilled work associated with their 'natural' qualities as women – dexterity, perseverance, speed. Employers and unions continued to view women's wage work as supplemental to the family, and women's maternal functions as indispensible to its well-being, and they joined public officials and pronatalists in a profound concern over France's low birth rate and depopulation 'crisis.' Union leaders sought family wages for male 'breadwinners' so their wives could stay home to reproduce and raise children. But they also sought to assist women in reconciling work and maternal responsibilities because the male-depleted French economy depended heavily on their workforce participation. Family allowances (determined by family size) and other forms of support increased during the Depression, but so did the attacks against women's right to work in the face of rising unemployment among male breadwinners.[7]

Feminists consistently defended women's right to work outside the home; but they also adapted themselves and their rhetoric to the preoccupations of the epoch. In the years prior to World War I, their efforts, along with those of natalists, resulted in obligatory maternity leave for working women, the right to sue for paternity, and assistance to large families with insufficient resources. As historian Anne Cova has shown, during the interwar period feminists most frequently demanded that motherhood be viewed as a social function, and therefore that mothers receive some sort of compensation. The feminist movement, she noted, 'often glorified motherhood in order to use it as a trump card in the acquisition of other powers.' By defining motherhood as a social function, feminists sought access to social citizenship (the right to protection) as a means to political citizenship (the right to vote).[8] But feminist historians have also argued that the social rights women received failed to advance their social equality. Family allowances and social services – in lieu of improved skills and higher wages – undermined women's economic rights and made them more dependent within the family. Government and employer family-oriented policies that bolstered the earning power of the male breadwinner and weakened that of the working mother (and thus women in general) culminated in the Family Code of 1939.[9]

The pressure of maternalist and pronatalist rhetoric not only failed to raise birth rates, but did not succeed in domesticating women or regulating male behavior, at least not in any hegemonic way. New trends in urban pleasure provided ample opportunity for the sort of self-fashioning noted in the fin de siècle. The wave of popular hedonism and mass entertainment that met the end of the war has been viewed in various ways. Eksteins describes it as a collective effort to deny the disastrous implications of the slaughter by self-immersion in pleasures and a cult of youth.[10] However we perceive these developments, they too had consequences for perceptions of gender roles. While women who participated in the war effort might be lauded for their self-abnegation, the same was not true of the more problematic New Woman who, according to soldiers' stories, lived it up on the home front while their boyfriends, husbands, and fathers were away at the front. As we will see, in stark contrast to the 'good' women who resumed their domestic roles after the war, those who opted for individualistic pleasures were perceived as having shirked their duties to the nation by postponing or even forgoing having children.

This apparent deterioration of identity and morality was vividly illustrated in the culture surrounding jazz, which took Paris by storm in the 1920s. The modern music par excellence, jazz seemed to embrace the machine-like and primitive all within one movement. Its African and African-American provenance evoked ongoing racial fears, exacerbated no doubt by the influx of West African immigrants invited to assist in the reconstruction effort. The nature of this unusual music was a problem in its own right. For traditionalists, its syncopated rhythms and breathless pace seemed to place additional stress upon the nerves, thus reviving earlier concerns about the 'hyperstimulus' of urban life. Seemingly unleashing inner impulses and causing dancers to lose control, jazz threatened to collapse the personal boundaries of the individual. Dancers were thus seen as potentially overwhelmed by their own 'primitive' natures while swinging to the rhythms of the machine. Some, like the critic André Warnod, embraced this exhilarating experience: 'The jazz band is the panting of the machine, the trepidation of the automobile, the train that squeaks on the rails, the tramway that passes shaking the clock.'[11] Others, especially on the Right, saw in this culture a further slip into racial mixing, depopulation, and venereal disease, and thus as one more nail in the national coffin.[12]

Like many cultural perceptions of modernity, the gender-bending and inversions that took place in the jazz club and in other popular venues were seen as symbolized by and as particularly affecting women, bringing about a 'civilization that no longer has sexes' that, according to the proto-fascist writer Pierre Drieu la Rochelle, was unsettling for conventional gender ideals. The problems posed by this boundary-crossing female, often dubbed *la garçonne* after Victor Margueritte's 1922 novel, have been carefully analyzed by Mary Louise Roberts. Viewed largely as a product of the war, this modern woman was perceived as going so far as to smoke, drink, cut her hair, drive automobiles, don unconventional (even male) fashions, get jobs, and engage in premarital affairs, sometimes with other women – all of which suggested a disastrous subversion of 'natural' gender roles. Although usually not directly involved in feminist politics, such women acted out an implicit politics of refusal through their own unconventional behavior.[13] Many took active steps to remake their bodies through a variety of physical exercises or, acknowledging how important personal appearance had become in the modern world, even by undergoing surgery to improve their prospects for romance and employment.[14]

In the world of formal politics a more conservative stance carried the day. Although a 1919 law for women's suffrage passed the Chamber of Deputies by a large majority, it was radical republicans – invoking old fears about women's allegiance to religion and other conservative elements – whose ongoing debates about the issue rendered it too controversial even to be brought before the Senate. Although hopes for women's suffrage were more or less aborted by 1922, women certainly remained in the minds of legislators – especially in light of the huge losses France suffered in the war. In 1920 and 1923, the government passed laws to stiffen penalties for abortion and outlaw propaganda for and sale of all female forms of contraception (condoms remained legal for the prevention of venereal disease). The laws for the most part silenced proponents of neo-Malthusianism, and sent several of its most important leaders to prison for two to three years.[15] Such measures did not have the desired effect of increasing the French birth rate, for couples continued to practice traditional methods of birth control – withdrawal and clandestine abortion – and no doubt smuggled contraceptive devices into France.

Less attention has been paid to the 'new man' created by the Great War, but masculine ideals were also buffeted by new waves of crisis during the 1920s. Historians have emphasized that the battlefield experience upset long-held assumptions about what it meant to be a man. Traditional codes of masculinity that depended upon hand-to-hand combat, movement, and conquest dissolved in the trenches as soldiers became passive victims of artillery shells and experienced the un-heroic results of shell shock and lost limbs, all the more humiliating once they returned home.[16] Many returning veterans discovered that modern society's growing emphasis on appearance would have disastrous consequences for their identities and employment prospects, especially if they returned from the front with horribly disfigured faces.[17]

For all sorts of reasons, then, the bodies of soldiers understandably became subject to medical scrutiny during and after the war. Among pronatalists this was particularly true with regard to their sexual health. The rapid spread of venereal disease by 1915 and the huge military losses provoked deep concern in the Chamber of Deputies and among military doctors. In addition to the efforts to regulate men's use of prostitutes and treat venereal disease, military doctors waged a propaganda campaign to convince soldiers that it was their duty to remain faithful to their wives and girlfriends so that they would be able to produce healthy families. Doctors increasingly stressed the honor and duty of soldiers to procreate for the nation, reinforcing the association between national defense and reproduction.[18] A series of wartime postcards exhorted soldiers on leave to procreate, and strongly associated virility and weapons with fertility. (One such card portrayed happy babies in carriers dangling from a bayonet – the product of a soldier's patriotic 'good thrust,' as the caption indicated.)[19]

Such injunctions flew in the face of the new trends towards personal pleasure that were being encouraged in the 1920s. Returning veterans also fled the hardships of war by immersing themselves in the new pleasures of the city, as did a whole generation of males who had been too young to fight. This postwar hedonism was experienced as exhilarating by some and worrisome by others. According to some observers, beautiful young men with a penchant for mascara and drugs were common fixtures of the jazz scene, and the way they moved and gestured seemed to imitate the comportment of women.[20] Those who steered clear of such venues did not necessarily do so out of an allegiance to traditional values or a lack of concern with appearances. Physical culture, which had gained in popularity in the decade before the war, witnessed a flowering after 1918, for both women and men. According to the writer François Mauriac it was the young man's narcissism that ultimately saved him from dangerous modern excesses and encouraged him to develop his muscles instead: 'He cares for his body, exercises it lovingly, muscle by muscle, weans himself from pleasures, consents to the sacrifice of overly acute pleasures in favor of his sovereign force.'[21] Like so many examples of modernity in action, such activities rejected one aspect of modern life (potentially unhealthy habits) in order to promote another (a narcissistic attachment to personal appearance).

The proto-fascist movements that sprang up during the 1920s, partly as continuation of political ideas festering since the Dreyfus Affair, were also a reaction against these changes, prompting calls for the dissolution of the Republic along with the liberal democratic values that seemed to promote such corruption. As Cheryl Koos has argued, depopulation, more than ever before, became a locus for right-wing activism in the 1930s. By 1938 deaths had exceeded births for three consecutive years, and the French were replacing their population at a rate of only 87 percent. It was in this period that the National Alliance for French Population Growth achieved far greater resonance than it had earlier by linking their rhetoric about population decline to broader issues of male and female roles and sexual identity. Their arguments echoed those of Mussolini and Hitler in their attacks against individualism, and the 'Modern Woman' became one of their systematic targets. As the pronatalist campaign became invigorated in the 1930s, Koos deftly argues, its rhetoric, and use of gender therein, helped 'propel France philosophically towards the Vichy regime, which would have at its center the already familiar tenets of *Travail, Famille, Patrie*.'[22]

With the outbreak of World War II and the French defeat in June 1940, rightist extremists finally got their wish. From the ruins of the Third Republic the Vichy regime implemented reforms aimed at restoring men and women to the 'natural' roles and duties that had been supposedly disrupted by the corrupting influence of republican individualism and mass consumerism. This included a strong emphasis on natalism, family, and attempts to forge rugged males through various outdoor youth programs.[23]

The Third Republic was France's longest-lived democratic regime, but the demise of this self-conscious experiment in 1940 should not be hastily viewed as the triumph of anti-modern forces. As this volume has endeavored to show, modernity is a complex and multifaceted development capable of generating diverse and seemingly contradictory ideas and responses. Ironically, some of the most vituperatively anti-modern movements also betray their attachment to modernity. These chapters show that the ideology of republicanism in a modernizing context does not pave a smooth path to universal liberation, particularly when patriarchal and hierarchical traditions and codes of male honor are deeply entrenched. They demonstrate as well how inextricably linked the French Third Republic – and by implication, any political order – is to sexual and gender identity, and the regulation of sexual practices.

Notes

1. Modris Eksteins, *Rites of Spring: the Great War and the Modern Age* (New York: Doubleday, 1989), p. 34.
2. Michael Penniston and Nancy Erber, *Queer Lives: Men's Autobiographies from Nineteenth-Century France* (Lincoln, NE: University of Nebraska Press, 2007).
3. Eksteins, *Rites of Spring*, p. 34.
4. Elinor Accampo, *Blessed Motherhood, Bitter Fruit: Nelly Roussel and the Politics of Female Pain in Third Republic France* (Baltimore: Johns Hopkins University Press, 2006); Françis Ronsin, *La grève des ventres: propagande neo-malthusienne et baisse de natalité en France, 19e et 20e siècles* (Paris: Aubier Montaigne, 1980).
5. Martha Hanna, *The Mobilization of Intellect: French Scholars and Writers during the Great War* (Cambridge, MA: Harvard University Press, 1996).
6. Accampo, *Blessed Motherhood*, pp. 172, 177–8; Margaret Darrow, *French Women and the First World War: War Stories of the Home Front* (Oxford: Berg, 2000).
7. Laura Lee Downs, *Manufacturing Inequality: Gender Division in the French and British Metalworking Industries* (Ithaca: Cornell University Press, 1995); Laura Frader, *Breadwinners and Citizens: Gender in the Making of the French Social Model* (Durham, NC: Duke University Press, 2008). Although more women entered universities and the professions, they too faced a gender-based hierarchy beyond proverbial 'glass ceilings.' Robert Nye has argued that the etiquette of male honor codes governed masculine sociability (including smoking, drinking, and the use of profanity) in the professions, with medicine as a prime example, well into the twentieth century, shutting doors to the professional advancement of women. See Robert A. Nye, 'Honor Codes and Medical Ethics in Modern France,' *Bulletin of the History of Medicine*, 69 (1995): 91–111; 'Medicine and Science as Masculine "Fields of Honor,"' *Osiris*, 12 (1997): 60–79; 'Médecins, éthique médicale et État en France, 1789–1947,' *Mouvement social*, 214 (January–March 2006): 19–36.
8. Anne Cova, *Maternité et droits des femmes en France (XIXe–XXe)* (Paris: Anthropos Historiques, 1997), p.116.
9. See especially Frader, *Breadwinners and Citizens*.
10. Eksteins, *Rites of Spring*, pp. 254–61. See also Charles Rearick, *The French in Love and War: Popular Culture in the Era of the World Wars* (New Haven and London: Yale University Press, 1997).
11. Jeffrey H. Jackson, *Making Jazz French: Music and Modern Life in Interwar Paris* (Durham, NC: Duke University Press, 2003).
12. Judith Surkis, 'Enemies Within: Venereal Disease and the Defense of French Masculinity between the Wars,' in Christopher E. Forth and Bertrand Taithe (eds), *French Masculinities: History, Culture and Politics* (Basingstoke: Palgrave Macmillan, 2007), pp. 103–22.
13. Mary Louise Roberts, *Civilization without Sexes: Reconstructing Gender in Postwar France, 1917–1927* (Chicago: University of Chicago Press, 1994).
14. Mary Lynn Stewart, *For Health and Beauty: Physical Culture for Frenchwomen, 1880s–1930s* (Baltimore: Johns Hopkins University Press, 2001); Caroline Ward Comiskey, ' "I Will Kill Myself ... If I Have to Keep My Fat Calves!": Legs and Cosmetic Surgery in Paris in 1926,' in Christopher E. Forth and Ivan Crozier (eds), *Body Parts: Critical Explorations in Corporeality* (Lanham, MD: Lexington, 2005), pp. 247–63.
15. Accampo, *Blessed Motherhood*, pp. 218–20. In 1921 Eugène Humbert was sentenced to prison for five years – the maximum possible term under the Military

Code. Having dodged the draft, he was judged as having 'taken battalions from France' when he continued to wage a birth control campaign during the war from Barcelona.

16. See John Horne, 'Soldiers, Civilians and the Warfare of Attrition: Representations of Combat in France, 1914–1918,' and Leonard V. Smith, 'Masculinity, Memory, and the French First World War Novel,' in Frans Coetzee and Marilyn Shevin-Coetzee (eds), *Authority, Identity and the Social History of the Great War* (Providence and Oxford: Berghahn Books, 1995), pp. 223–49, 251–74.

17. Sophie Delaporte, *Gueules cassées de la Grande Guerre* (Paris: Agnès Vienot, 1996).

18. Michelle K. Rhoades, 'To Save Future Generations: Masculine Honor and Reproductive Duties, 1914–1918,' *Proceedings of the Western Society for French History*, 31 (2006): 230–42; Judith Surkis, *Sexing the Citizen: Morality and Masculinity in France, 1870–1920* (Ithaca: Cornell University Press, 2006).

19. Marie-Monique Huss, 'Pronatalism and the Popular Ideology of the Child in Wartime France: the Evidence of the Picture Postcard,' in Richard Wall and Jay Winter (eds), *The Upheaval of War: Family, Work and Welfare in Europe, 1914–1918* (Cambridge: Cambridge University Press, 2005), pp. 329–67.

20. Jackson, *Making Jazz French*, p. 102.

21. François Mauriac, *Le jeune homme* (1926), in *Œuvres complètes* (Paris: Fayard, 1950), IV, pp. 422–3.

22. Cheryl Koos, 'Gender, Anti-individualism, and Nationalism: the Alliance Nationale and the Pronatalist Backlash against the *Femme moderne*, 1933–40,' *French Historical Studies*, 19(3) (Spring 1996): 699–723. See also Koos, ' "On les aura!": the Gendered Politics of Abortion and the Alliance Nationale contre la dépopulation, 1938–44,' *Modern and Contemporary France*, 7(1) (February 1999): 21–33; Koos, 'Women: Gender, and the Extreme Right in France, 1919–45,' co-authored with Daniella Sarnoff, in Kevin Passmore (ed.), *Women, Gender, and the Extreme Right in Europe, 1919–1945* (Manchester: Manchester University Press, 2003).

23. Joan Tumblety, 'Revenge of the Fascist Knights: Masculine Identities in *Je suis partout*, 1940–1944,' *Modern and Contemporary France*, 7(1) (February 1999): 11–20; Miranda Pollard, *Reign of Virtue: Mobilizing Gender in Vichy France* (Chicago: University of Chicago Press, 1998); Francine Muel-Dreyfus, *Vichy and the Eternal Feminine: a Contribution to a Political Sociology of Gender*, trans. Kathleen A. Johnson (Durham, NC: Duke University Press, 2001); Alice Yaeger Kaplan, *Reproductions of Banality: Fascism, Literature and French Intellectual Life* (Minneapolis, MN: University of Minnesota Press, 1986); Melanie Hawthorne and Richard J. Golsan (eds), *Gender and Fascism in Modern France* (Hanover, NH: Dartmouth University Press, 1997).

Index